The Early History of Greed

The history of avarice as the deadliest vice in western Europe has been said to begin in earnest only with the rise of capitalism or, earlier, the rise of a money economy. In this first full-length study of the early history of greed, Richard Newhauser shows that *avaritia*, the sin of greed for possessions, has a much longer history, and is more important for an understanding of the Middle Ages, than has previously been allowed. His examination of theological and literary texts composed between the first century C.E. and the tenth century reveals new significance in the portrayal of various kinds of greed, to the extent that by the early Middle Ages avarice was available to head the list of vices for authors engaged in the task of converting others from pagan materialism to Christian spirituality.

RICHARD NEWHAUSER is Professor of English at Trinity University, San Antonio, Texas. He is author of *The Treatise on Vices and Virtues in Latin and the Vernacular* (1993) and *A Catalogue of Latin Texts with Material on the Vices and Virtues in Manuscripts in Hungary* (1996). He was recently awarded fellowships from the National Endowment for the Humanities, the Gladys Krieble Delmas Foundation/American Council of Learned Societies, the National Humanities Center (through the Lilly Endowment), and the John Simon Guggenheim Memorial Foundation to continue his work on the history of avarice.

CAMBRIDGE STUDIES IN MEDIEVAL LITERATURE

General editor
Alastair Minnis, *University of York*

Editorial board
Patrick Boyde, *University of Cambridge*
John Burrow, *University of Bristol*
Rita Copeland, *University of Pennsylvania*
Alan Deyermond, *University of London*
Peter Dronke, *University of Cambridge*
Simon Gaunt, *King's College, London*
Nigel Palmer, *University of Oxford*
Winthrop Wetherbee, *Cornell University*

This series of critical books seeks to cover the whole area of literature written in the major medieval languages – the main European vernaculars, and medieval Latin and Greek – during the period c. 1100–1500. Its chief aim is to publish and stimulate fresh scholarship and criticism on medieval literature, special emphasis being placed on understanding major works of poetry, prose, and drama in relation to the contemporary culture and learning which fostered them.

A complete list of titles in the series can be found at the end of the volume.

The Early History of Greed

The Sin of Avarice in Early Medieval Thought and Literature

RICHARD NEWHAUSER

Trinity University (San Antonio)

CAMBRIDGE
UNIVERSITY PRESS

PUBLISHED BY THE PRESS SYNDICATE OF THE UNIVERSITY OF CAMBRIDGE
The Pitt Building, Trumpington Street, Cambridge, United Kingdom

CAMBRIDGE UNIVERSITY PRESS
The Edinburgh Building, Cambridge CB2 2RU, UK   http://www.cup.cam.ac.uk
40 West 20th Street, New York, NY 10011–4211, USA   http://www.cup.org.
10 Stamford Road, Oakleigh, Melbourne 3166, Australia

First published 2000

Printed in the United Kingdom at the University Press, Cambridge

Typeset in Adobe Garamond 11.5/14pt [CE]

A catalogue record for this book is available from the British Library

Library of Congress cataloguing in publication data

Newhauser, Richard, 1947–
The early history of greed: the sin of avarice in early medieval thought
and literature / Richard Newhauser.
p.   cm. – (Cambridge studies in medieval literature)
Includes bibliographical references amd index.
ISBN 0 521 38522 9 (hardback)
1. Avarice – History.   2. Christian ethics – History – Middle Ages, 600–1500.
I. Title.   II. Series.
BJ1535.A8N48   2000
241'.3–dc21   99-25922 CIP

ISBN 0 521 38522 9 hardback

UXORI MEÆ ANDREÆ

SINE QUA NON

ET MEIS FILIIS DANIELI ET SIMONI

לאשתי חנה

שבלי עזותה לא היתה

העברדה מגיעה לסיום

ולבני דניאל ושמעון

Dixerunt in illam [i.e. avaritiam] multi et multa et magna et gravia et uera, et poetae et historici et oratores et philosophi, et omne litterarum et professionum genus multa dixerunt in avaritiam.

Augustine of Hippo, *Tractatus de Avaritia* (*Sermo* 177), 1

Infinita de scripturis exempla subpeditant, quae et auaritiam doceant esse fugiendam.

Jerome, *Epistula 22*, 32.5

Contents

List of abbreviations

ASE	*Anglo-Saxon England.*
CCL	Corpus Christianorum, Series Latina. Turnhout, Belgium.
CCM	Corpus Christianorum, Continuatio Medieualis. Turnhout, Belgium.
CPL	*Clavis patrum latinorum.* Ed. E. Dekkers and E. Gaar. *Sacris Erudiri* 3. Second ed. Bruges and The Hague, 1961.
CSEL	Corpus Scriptorum Ecclesiasticorum Latinorum. Vienna.
EETS os	Early English Text Society. Original Series. London.
GCS	Die griechischen christlichen Schriftsteller der ersten drei Jahrhunderte. Ed. Kirchenväterkommission der Preussischen Akademie. Berlin.
JbAC	*Jahrbuch für Antike und Christentum.*
MGH	Monumenta Germaniae Historica. Hanover and Berlin.
MGH Poet	Monumenta Germaniae Historica. Poetae latini medii aevi. Hanover and Berlin.
MSR	*Mélanges de Science Religieuse.*
NM	*Neuphilologische Mitteilungen.*
PG	J.-P. Migne. Patrologiae Cursus Completus. Series Graeca. 161 vols. Paris, 1857–.
PL	J.-P. Migne. Patrologiae Cursus Completus. Series Latina. 221 vols. Paris, 1844–.
PLS	A. Hamman. Patrologiae Cursus Completus. Series Latina, Supplementum. 5 vols. Paris, 1958–.
RAC	*Reallexikon für Antike und Christentum.* Ed. T. Klauser *et al.* Stuttgart.
RAM	*Revue d'Ascétique et de Mystique.*
RTAM	*Récherches de Théologie ancienne et médiévale.*
SC	Sources Chrétiennes. Paris.

List of abbreviations

SEC	Studies in Early Christianity: A Collection of Scholarly Essays. Ed. E. Ferguson *et al.* 18 vols. New York and London, 1993.
StP	*Studia Patristica.*
TU	Texte und Untersuchungen zur Geschichte der altchristlichen Literatur. Leipzig and Berlin.
VC	*Vigiliae Christianae.*

Preface

About the year 420 John Cassian completed his *Instituta* in a monastery he had established at Marseilles. The work was meant as a response to Castor, bishop of the nearby diocese of Apt, who had requested information about the rules and ethical precepts of the almost legendary monastic centers in the East. Cassian was particularly well-informed on these issues, having spent a number of years among the semi-anchoritic and cenobitic communities of the Egyptian desert before arriving in Marseilles. Book seven of the *Instituta* is concerned with the spirit of "*filargyria*, which we can call the love of money,"[1] which Cassian defines more precisely as follows:

> And hence, not only should the possession of money be avoided, but also the very desire for it should be completely expelled from the soul. For it is not so much that the result of *filargyria* should be avoided as that the predisposition for it should be cut out by the roots, because it will do no good not to have money if there is a desire in us for possessing it.[2]

Cassian thought of this evil in the first place as the desire for money, a meaning revealed in the term *filargyria*, the latinized transcription of a Greek word which had been made into a *terminus technicus* for Christian authors writing on greed. Etymologically, the term means nothing more than the "love of money," or more literally, the "love of silver." Nearly thirty years before this, Augustine had set about completing his treatise on free will at Hippo Regius. In *De libero arbitrio* he argues that evil is the result of humanity's free will and not, as the Manichaeans claimed, a substance pre-existent to the creation of the world. Among the details of immorality, Augustine comes to mention humanity's greed, for:

the root of all evils is *avaritia*, that is, wanting more than is enough. . . .
For avarice, which in Greek is called φιλαργυρία, a name which echoes
much better its derivation, should not be thought to consist in silver or
in coins alone (for, in former times coins were made of silver or, more
frequently, a silver alloy), but in all things which are desired immode-
rately, whenever someone wants absolutely more than is enough.[3]

Augustine's starting point is the same term which Cassian also used, but
he widens its meaning so that one can understand a desire to possess
anything which is not directed towards God, intangible qualities as well
as material objects, as a type of avarice. Although he has not been highly
valued by scholars as a Hellenist, Augustine's language skills cannot
account for the definition he gives; he is obviously well aware of the
Greek term's etymology,[4] and his use of *avaritia* accurately reflects this
word's derivation through *avarus* from *aveo* ("to crave"). Etymologically, *avaritia* stresses the forcefulness of yearning more than the object
of desire.

   The different understandings of avarice voiced by these authors mark
the borders of how greed was imagined throughout the Middle Ages.
Cassian's highly material understanding of *filargyria* draws on the
Capital Vice tradition which developed within the monastic communities he had come to know in Egypt, and it was tailored to their needs.
Augustine's thinking on the vice, part of his response to the demands of
a secular congregation, reflects aspects of an older patristic context
which numbered avarice among the Deadly Sins. From the narrowly
defined desire for money to a more inclusive sense of the overweening
desire merely to possess for oneself – these positions are the boundaries
of the definition of avarice as a vice into the fifteenth century, when one
begins to see a more open acknowledgment of what is positive in the
urge to acquire possessions. In Poggio Bracciolini's dialogue *On
Avarice*, for example, Antonio Loschi voices a utilitarian, even modern,
view of greed when he argues that avarice is the compelling reason for
business investment, the growth of cities, philanthropy, and wage-
earning, as well, for:

   It is obvious that avarice is not only natural, it is useful and necessary
   in human beings, for it teaches them to provide for themselves those
   things which are necessary for sustaining the frailty of human nature
   and for avoiding inconveniences.[5]

It was not Poggio's intention to justify the vice – he defines his work as a dialogue against avarice – but Loschi's articulation of a contemporary economic attitude makes it clear why studies on the growth of capitalism have often made special note of changes in the characteristics of acquisition at the end of the medieval period from what earlier would have been classified exclusively as greed.[6] Attitudes similar to this Renaissance transformation can be remarked only as precursory steps in the early Middle Ages, at a time when the ascetic ideal of a radical rejection of possessions and their acquisition remained the touchstone for all definitions of avarice, no matter how important the vice was seen to be. The history of avarice will reveal that the pressures of asceticism asserted a transformative power on the definition of the vice throughout the early Middle Ages.

Encouragement for the task of understanding avarice has never been wanting: already thirty years ago Siegfried Wenzel suggested that an investigation of this sin be a priority for medievalists.[7] Yet, since Huizinga's work in 1924 it has become a commonplace to speak of a rise in importance in avarice in the *later* medieval period. The "furious chorus of invectives"[8] which he heard in particular aimed against this vice has sounded clearly for other scholars as well. Morton Bloomfield observed that shifts in emphasis in the treatment of the seven Deadly Sins brought avarice and sloth to the foreground in the late Middle Ages as the two most important members of this arrangement of immorality.[9] Lester Little's important article on the topic and a chapter of a monograph by Alexander Murray have elucidated many of the facets of late medieval *avaritia*, beginning in earnest from the tenth century onward, as did the earlier work on venality satire by John Yunck.[10] In such studies the echo of Huizinga's chorus can still be heard; their authors refined considerably what he thought was the reason for an increase in attention to avarice in the central and late Middle Ages, but they followed him in assuming that moralists first concentrated their attention on curing the vice of greed during these periods. This assumption will not withstand a detailed look at avarice in the Christian literature of Late Antiquity and the early medieval period. Such an examination has been lacking up to now, for beside some suggestive comments by Heinrich Fichtenau and a few encyclopedia articles by Karl Suso Frank and others, the patristic period and the early Middle Ages (before the tenth century) have been relatively neglected in the study of avarice.[11]

The emphasis of the present work lies on the early history of a religious concept, from the waning of eschatological expectations in the first century to the pressures of an imminent apocalypse at the end of the tenth, and the majority of the sources examined are theological and literary texts. The major concern everywhere has been to elucidate the definition of the concept of avarice which occurs, explicitly or by inference through poetic imagery, in such works. The Appendix is designed to introduce the reader in schematic form to the most important of the poetic images used in discussions of the vice. The definition of avarice covered a broad range already in the patristic period. Those who have examined *avaritia* as a vice of money in the later Middle Ages have tended to overlook its frequent definition at this time as the desire for intangible objects (honor, knowledge, life itself), as well as for material goods. The source of this spiritualization of the vice is to be found in the theological concerns of the fourth and fifth centuries. It is, in fact, also at this time that one can observe the first concentration on the vice in western Christian literature as the source of all evil: the writings of a group of bishops in northern Italy associated with Ambrose of Milan give evidence of the way in which, at this time and place, avarice was considered to be the most important of the vices threatening Christian society. Avarice then remained available in the early Middle Ages to head the list of vices for all those authors who were engaged in the task of converting the newly European aristocracy from pagan materialism to Christian spirituality. In this light, it will be seen that Huizinga and those who have followed him heard indeed a sustained out-cry against avarice, but not one without precedence and foundation in the literature of the early Middle Ages.

This work was begun as my dissertation at the University of Pennsylvania and my greatest debt, and most lasting one, is to my thesis advisor, Siegfried Wenzel, who gave constructive criticism to support my research and writing every step of the way. Without Professor Wenzel's guidance as a scholar and advisor this work would never have taken the form it has today.

San Antonio, Texas;
November, 1997

Alms and ascetes, round stones and masons: avarice in the early church

THE DEADLY SIN TRADITION: AVARICE AND THE WANING OF ESCHATOLOGICAL EXPECTATIONS

The third vision in the *Shepherd of Hermas*, written in Rome for the young Christian community there during the early part of the second century, is an allegory of the ideal construction of the church, and it may serve as a guide in examining the responses to greed in early Christian literature. Hermas is shown angels erecting a tower of stones which fit together perfectly; these stones, he is later told by a woman who is herself another personified image of the church, are the ecclesiastical officials, martyrs, the righteous, and recent converts who form the solid core of the building. He also observes other stones found unsuitable for the masonry, though not rejected outright, and they include round, white rocks. To his ingenuous request for their allegoresis, Lady Church responds: they are the wealthy whose commerce interferes with their faith when persecution threatens. They will remain unfit for construction until they have been squared off, until their excess wealth has been hewn away. The situation presented by this allegory is in a number of ways an important point of departure for the history of avarice: first, it is decidedly not the possession of money in itself to which the lady objects, but to a spiritual danger, apostasy, which may be its result. Second, by describing the requirement to cut away needless riches, *Hermas* is not demanding that the church enforce poverty as a prerequisite for being numbered among the faithful; for the author of this allegory, only self-sufficiency can both counter greed and still leave the Christian with enough possessions to be able to aid the poor.[1]

The *Shepherd of Hermas* is typical of one type of Christian reception of the Jewish apocalypse in propagating moral instruction through the protagonist's visions, and as Lady Church patiently explains to Hermas, every evil desire, especially that greed which abandons eschatological goods for worldly profits, results in death and captivity. This may be an explicit reference to avarice's place among the Deadly Sins, a somewhat diffuse phenomenon the origins of which have been identified in Jewish and Christian traditions reaching back in written form at least to the rabbinical literature of the first century B.C.E. In this tradition, the sins are considered lethal because they lead to the death of the soul. Unlike the Capital Vices to be examined here later, the number and ordering of evils in the list of Deadly Sins was never fixed.[2] Avarice, however, was frequently included in lists of such evils in early Christian literature – both in descriptive catalogues and in those with a parenetic function[3] – or at least understood under the aegis of Deadly Sin. It is the first important intellectual context in which the sin is found in Christian culture.

The Deadly Sins are an expression of an authoritative and institutionalized morality; in early Christianity they were characteristically formulated on the basis of the commands and prohibitions handed down in the Decalogue, the distillation of the Law which was still retained and systematized by the early church. A foundation in the Ten Commandments is not made explicit in every discussion of avarice in this tradition, but it can be illustrated clearly among the writings of the "apostolic fathers" in the *Epistle of Barnabas* (first half of the second century). Part of this work, as part of the *Shepherd of Hermas* as well, is concerned directly with the most schematic representation of scriptural morality: the two-ways teaching, that is to say, the concept that there is a path of righteousness leading to heavenly bliss and another mode of behavior culminating in eternal torment. Among other criteria, *Barnabas* defines the Way of Light by adherence to the ethical principles of the Commandments: not to be desirous of more possessions (not to be *pleonektes* [πλεονέκτης]) is presented as a way of further specifying "Thou shalt not covet what is your neighbor's."[4]

The virulence of avarice for the author of the *Shepherd of Hermas* was due to its worldliness, for that was directly opposed to Christianity's eschatological concerns. This orientation had been announced by Jesus' call to store up riches where no moth and no rust destroy them (Matt. 6:19–21), words which also later served as the groundwork for Christianity's ethical rejection of worldly wealth as deceptive or false and in need of replacement by the true wealth of heaven. This relativizing of the value of material goods was an important step in reorienting Christian consciousness to an ideology dominated by otherworldly rewards; the process of this reorientation was reinforced homiletically by a consciousness of death's imminence. The rich man in the parable in Luke who decided to enlarge his grain silos is said to be foolish because God's judgment makes a permanent mockery of his futile attempt to guarantee his life with perishing wealth.[5] But even beyond this, avarice was one of the evils which themselves were made accountable for the approaching day of wrath. In a characteristic use of the Decalogue which combined the sixth and tenth Commandments interpreted on the basis of the injunction against idolatry, the Colossians are warned to put away the worldliness inherent in *pleonexia* (πλεονεξία – the desire to have more), because it ignites God's anger, and elsewhere the *philargyroi* (φιλάργυροι – the greedy) are depicted as representative of humankind's moral degeneration in the last age.[6] The depth of the vice's opposition to eschatological rewards is further demonstrated by its equation with idolatry, for in scriptural terms the servant of idols has renounced all hopes connected with the coming of the divinity.[7] The avaricious have given themselves up to another, a demonic, power and have thus cut themselves off completely from God and the spiritual ideals of His worshipers.

Hermas, too, must be warned not to give up the good things which are to come, for by the second century that expectation of an imminent eschatological moment which was held by the earliest Christian communities had begun to wane, and the attack on avarice came to be supplemented by a more philosophically founded ethic.[8] The influence of popular philosophy on the Christian concept of the vice can be detected most obviously in the varied uses of a gnome which in its circulation in Antiquity was attributed to an astonishing plethora of writers and which, as documented by the *Oracula Sibyllina*, had a firm place in Hellenistic thought as well.[9] Most important for the Christian understanding of the sin is the form of this proverbial wisdom in 1 Timothy 6:10: "For the root of all evils is *philargyria* (φιλαργυρία –

avarice)," and then in parallel statements by Polycarp, Tertullian, and Clement of Alexandria.[10] In its myriad forms, the gnome did inexhaustible service as the most common scriptural foundation for Christian authors' invectives against avarice; it neatly summed up the centrality of the vice in their view of immorality. The malleability of the proverb is clearly seen in the words of a fifth-century poet who, with encyclopedic fervor, warned his audience that:

> Because the minds of many have been tainted by this disease,
> Avarice is the root, the cause, the head, the fount, and the origin
> of evil.[11]

But the productivity of the gnome went even further: it served as a model for reflections on the nature of the sin itself and, eventually, on that of virtues opposed to the sin. Hence, one has *The Sentences of Sextus* (composed *c.* 180–210 C.E.): "A yearning to possess is the origin of greed" (*pleonexia*), and Lactantius' consideration that a desire for heaven which leads one to disdain others' earthbound longings is the mother of continence.[12] These inventive uses of proverbial wisdom can be observed again and again in commentaries on the vice of avarice throughout the Middle Ages.

In 1 Timothy 6:10, as in the *Shepherd of Hermas* as well, the sinfulness of avarice is opposed to a virtuous self-sufficiency, a satisfaction with fulfilling simple wishes.[13] Yet, in its connection with the vice in early Christian literature, this *autarkeia* is anything but a revolutionary concept: it is neither an all-encompassing end in itself, nor the motivation for rigorous asceticism it was to become. It has, rather, an essentially conservative character as an ideologically normative attribute to be cultivated by the individual so that he can ward off dangerous excesses of desire and be content with his present state.[14] Its ideal representative is not the Christian who is totally indigent, but the one who is content with modest prosperity.

AVARICE AS A SOCIAL PROBLEM IN EARLY CHRISTIANITY

Of course, in the early literature of the Christian era, the problem of avarice was not only defined in terms of the individual's spirituality. In the section of *Hermas* devoted to similitudes, the shepherd explains the parable of the elm and vine to the protagonist as an image of the harmony of social classes: a vine bears fruit by climbing up a tree which itself is without fruit, just as the wealthy (here not members of a nobility, but rather Christian freedmen, part of the "middle class" of Roman tradesmen) support society's indigent in a theocentric compromise. The rich give from their surplus to those who are in need, and the poor pray for their benefactors.[15] The image here is essentially a static one; what it depicts is, of course, not the institutionalized redistribution of wealth, but a functional class balance on the order of the estates theory of the Middle Ages: the organic universe of the parable remains productive only when each entity fulfills its preordained function, thereby retaining its distinctive essence. The wealthy and the indigent continue in harmonious symbiosis insofar as they keep their place as elms and vines. The *Shepherd of Hermas* is not alone in recognizing the sin of avarice as a threat to the existing social order, nor in prescribing alms as its cure. In these social dimensions, the desire for more was seen to express itself most destructively in the exploitation and deception of one's brethren, a point which had been made specifically in 1 Thessalonians 4:6 in an injunction against defrauding one's fellow human beings in legal or business affairs.[16] As will be seen, it was the social implications of the concept of avarice, more than any other factor, which account for the longevity of interest in the vice in intellectual history.

Among the lay groups which showed the practical consequences of avarice most clearly, merchants were singled out with particular frequency. Even bankers were exempt from such stern reproach, though one must also remember that the merchant in Late Antiquity was not the irreplaceable agent of trade he was to become, but frequently only a dealer in luxury goods.[17] The author of *Hermas* understood the problem of wealth primarily as an issue for the mercantile class. For Tertullian (*c.* 160–*c.* 220 C.E.), as well, greed seemed to be implicated in most acts of commerce. "Moreover," he noted, "if cupidity is done away with, what is the reason for acquiring? When the reason for acquiring is gone, there will be no necessity for doing business."[18] But along with this seeming radicalism, he also pointed out that there may be just businesses and that his arguments would not make all commerce impossible for Christians, though he does not refer to these justifications of trade at great length or with the clarity one might wish.[19] Merchants as an undifferentiated class, in any case, were to be linked firmly to the evil effects of the vice until the Carolingians heralded a decisive change in this attitude.

If it was important for the entire congregation of the saintly to be free of avarice,[20] this was all the more true for those among their number who had positions of authority. Some of the earliest references to an avarice of the perversion of authority are to teachers of the faith, or those passing themselves off as such, who in their covetousness exploited their followers.[21] Apparently, even Paul himself was not spared such accusations, at least not at the hands of the Corinthians, as he implies when he writes to them on the subject of his collection for the Jerusalem community.[22] Polycarp (110–156 C.E.), like the author of *Hermas*, focused on the importance of controlling one's desires in presenting this aspect of the vice. Of Valens, a fallen presbyter, Polycarp wrote: "For how can he who cannot control himself tell another to do so?"[23] It was essential, in other words, that those exercising spiritual leadership not be guilty of the base worldliness which the early church saw in avarice, for the purity of its social life on earth could only be guaranteed by that of its authorities. It is, thus, no surprise that the beginnings of conciliar legislation on the problem of cupidity, to be found later in the acts of the Council of Nicea (325), were directed at the clergy.

THE TERMINOLOGY OF GREED AND MALLEABILITY IN THE LIMITS TO POSSESSIONS

Although the first centuries of Christian thought are fundamental for the future development of the history of avarice, they do not as yet provide one with any systematic analyses of the vice. As will be seen, this lack was felt most keenly among the Cappadocians. It is apparent not only in the brevity of discussions of the sin, but also in the want of a firm *terminus technicus*. *Philargyria* and *pleonexia* (and their derivatives), though they are not the only designations one comes across, are the two most common.[24] They were, at times, used interchangeably as designations for the vice, but they are also indicative of the different tendencies inherent in the concept of avarice in early Christian

literature. *Philargyria* is, of course, the more narrowly defined, depicting a literal love of money as the most material of worldly goods.
Pleonexia, however, implies a broader sense of the vice. The "desire to
have more" which can be identified in its etymology is somewhat open-
ended, for while the majority of the word's uses is directed at the effort
expended for material possessions alone, other occurrences place it in
the context of fulfilling unclean desires of various kinds, including
sensual ones. Yet, whether for this reason *pleonexia* and its derivatives
can also be understood as referring to a sexual sin in 1 Thessalonians 4:6
and other passages, as later exegetes – most notably Jerome – have
argued, is questionable.[25] Such a reading is not supported by other,
non-Christian, texts in which avarice, whatever its designation, is found
in an environment similar to that of 1 Thessalonians and where it is
nevertheless clear that the object of avarice's desire is distinguished from
that of sexual longing.[26] As it appears, *"pleonexia"* was used by early
Christian authors to name a passion which was only similar to lust,
related to it in that both were seen as types of uncleanness and both
were used in a combination of the sixth and tenth Commandments
(forbidding, respectively, adulterous lust and covetousness) characteristic of early Christianity's use of the Decalogue. But without a
systematic discussion to guide them, later Christian interpreters were
able to take the word's textual proximity to terms for sexual excess as
part of the concept's essence.

If avarice was defined as the desire for more material wealth, the
question still remained at what point "more" began. There was no
authoritative answer to this problem. Jesus had called upon his
followers, or those among them who desired to be perfect, to give up
their possessions, and as long as the coming of God's kingdom was still
considered to be imminent, the thorough lack of care for possessions
implied in this injunction seems to have been taken literally at
Jerusalem and in Paul's mission.[27] When eschatological expectations
became less immediate, total indifference no longer always characterized the Christian attitude towards acquisitions. Jesus, too, had
described the heavenly kingdom in terms any person involved in
business could easily grasp: "A merchant looking out for fine pearls
found one of very special value; so he went and sold everything he had,
and bought it."[28]

Among the earlier literary contexts of avarice, as in the *Shepherd of Hermas*, "more" did not come to imply the mere fact of private ownership. The rejection of private property altogether by some Gnostics, voiced for example in the second century by Epiphanes as reported in Clement of Alexandria's *Stromata*, may highlight by contrast the common orthodox, Christian attitude. Epiphanes argues that the law of the divinity requires a justice which amounts to communal equality in material possessions (and, in fact, in all other things, and women, as well). To prove his point, he draws on a number of *topoi* which will be found later in the orthodox Christian use of the mythology of the Golden Age and its decline: natural elements, in this case sunshine in particular, are given equally to all; nourishment is provided for the entire animal kingdom, according to its species, in communal harmony; but humanity's law, the legislation which regulates property, has partially destroyed the communism demanded by the divinity.[29]

Orthodox theologians use many of these same commonplaces in their reflections on the Golden Age, but while they treat the *aurea saecula* as a lost era and find it necessary to come to terms with the post-lapsarian system of private ownership evinced in Late Antiquity and the Middle Ages, Epiphanes writes as if the conditions of the Golden Age were fundamentally still in force and could be reasserted merely by doing away with the law which governs individual property holdings. The *Sentences of Sextus*, too, is clearly more rigorous than other orthodox views, though it echoes 1 Timothy 6:8 in exhorting the Christian not to possess more than what is required for the needs of the body.[30] This injunction seems clear enough, but the vagueness which was later built into most appeals to mere propriety in ownership may be indicated in a gloss to the Latin translation of Irenaeus' *Adversus haereses*. Irenaeus (*c.* 130–*c.* 200 C.E.), Bishop of Lyons, was countering the pagan polemic which argued that several gods are mentioned in Christianity's spiritual literature. When Jesus referred to *Mammonas*, Irenaeus notes, he made use of a word which does not signify a deity, but only "the covetous man" (rendered here in Latin as *cupidus*). It is at this point that the Latin translator, in an attempt to clarify the meaning of Irenaeus' πλεονέκτης (*pleonektes*), adds his own definition of the *cupidus* as one "desiring to possess more than what is fitting."[31] Irenaeus himself had no illusions about the difficulty of avoiding the sin. Later in the same work he used the language of asceticism to note that Christians' possessions are the result of their avarice before conversion or the goods procured through injustice by parents, relatives, or friends and given them as gifts. And even after baptism Christians continue to acquire, for who sells and does not want to make a profit from the buyer? It was, in fact, impossible for them to reject commercial occupations altogether, and for Irenaeus this amounts to conceding that some degree of avarice will always be found among Christians, too, though this unavoidable evil can be offset by almsgiving.[32] In any case, the Latin gloss, which raises the question of propriety, also solves this question by necessarily introducing a subjective and supple element into the analysis of greed: what went beyond what is fitting for one person might be thoroughly appropriate for another. Much depended on one's social rank and the expectations which it legitimately allowed. Thus, the seeds for a future justification of wealth were contained already in the early condemnation of greed.

Nevertheless, criticism of the avarice of the rich remained frequent and severe, especially so in the Ebionitic tradition represented in apocalyptic literature (and perhaps also in the Epistle of James) which depicted in frightening detail the torments of the rich in hell.[33] Yet, as the shepherd's interpretation of the elm and vine shows, more room was allowed for the wealthy than what might appear at first sight. Tertullian asserted that God hates the rich, and yet he also had to admit that their wealth could be used to perform many deeds of justice.[34] Injunctions against avarice which understood it as the desire for more were not yet directed towards the very rich, but rather towards those, below them in social standing, who wished to become so. The rich were generally identified with that aspect of the sin which attempted to retain what it already had, which refused to share to whatever degree with others, in particular by withholding alms. Still, the urge to acquire was the expression of avarice which was potentially the most subversive to maintaining the institutions of society as they were and it remained in the foreground of earlier Christian invectives against the vice. Where miserliness is mentioned at all, it is generally condemned only in its relation to greedy acquisition, a phenomenon which once again points up the lack of a systematic distinction between these two aspects of avarice.[35]

CLEMENT OF ALEXANDRIA'S JUSTIFICATION OF THE RICH

By the third century, a spectrum of attitudes towards the rich and their possessions had developed within Christian thought, a variety which is reflected in the changing appearances of avarice. That members of the upper classes became a larger factor in the conception of the vice is hardly surprising, for there was an increasing number of them to be found in Christian communities. The later part of the second and early third century saw these congregations gradually incorporate all levels of society, including the senatorial class itself.[36] The situation in North Africa is typical for this period; four major writers who originated here will serve to illustrate the responses to greed and the rich at this point in the development of Christianity: from a moderate acceptance of the affluent in the community of the church to an ascetic rejection of them, from the pastoral emphasis on curing greed through alms to the beginnings of a "historical" analysis of the vice.

In particular at Alexandria, perhaps the wealthiest and most important city in the eastern Mediterranean, the rich were a vital force in the Christian social order. It is also here that one finds the first theologically argued moderation of the idea of avarice in the works of Clement of Alexandria, in his day the city's most famous Christian teacher and a member of its social elite. Clement's moderateness marks somewhat of a caesura in the history of the vice. This becomes all the clearer when his justification of private property found in *Quis dives salvetur?*, his apology for Alexandria's wealthy Christians, is compared to what Irenaeus had to say on the same topic. Though he knew of Irenaeus' work, Clement contends that a Christian's wealth is legitimate if he was born into a rich family or if he worked for his wealth before conversion and, through thrift, acquired a modest amount of possessions. Such thrifty earnings are precisely what Irenaeus had earlier qualified as the wages of avarice.[37]

Riches themselves are neutral, a tool only, as Clement noted further in *Quis dives salvetur?*[38] And in the same work he criticizes literal exegetes typical of the Ebionitic tradition who found in Jesus' words to the rich youth ("Sell your possessions . . .") a command to renounce everything that one owned. In keeping with his justification of the wealthy, Clement saw in this passage not primarily a call to action; he understood it figuratively (and Stoically, one might add) as a summons to free the soul from the passionate love of possessions.[39] But beyond this, for Clement the question of riches, and with them avarice, also revolved necessarily around the use of one's goods. In theological terms, his justification of possessions was based ultimately on their utilization for the offices of *caritas*. In the *Paedagogus* he termed the vice, in keeping with the gnomic wisdom of 1 Timothy 6:10, a "citadel (*akropolis*) of evil" and then identified this phrase not with wealth itself but wealth that is not governed well, which is to say, not put to the use of one's neighbor.[40]

Clement identified in avarice a pathological movement of the soul which rejected both support for the poor and, more importantly, moderation for itself. The Christian might cure this sinful condition by fully recognizing the distinction between real and false wealth. True riches are the spiritual values which alone must serve as his ultimate goal, and from this eschatological perspective the false wealth of this world should be seen as worth no more than excrement (cf. Phil. 3:8).[41] Nevertheless, despite this verbal radicalism, Clement is not advocating anything more socially revolutionary than the *Shepherd of Hermas*, for, as he further notes, the material response to the knowledge of false wealth was not to give away everything, but rather to give alms. All of creation had been made for the use of all humanity, but the individual could still legitimately possess things for himself alone, though only if he did so in moderation. Clement reserves his criticism for the extravagant excesses of vast wealth, where he echoes Haggai 1:6, likening the vain behavior of those who want more than what is sufficient for their needs to the foolish desire to store things in a bag with holes in it.[42]

If in Clement's analysis the affluent were not sinful merely because of their riches, then neither was poverty in itself a virtue. Were indigence praiseworthy in its own right, he noted, one would have to count every shabby beggar among the happiest and most Christian of human beings, and consider that simply because the poor possess nothing on earth, they deserve the bliss of heaven.[43] Like his exegesis of the words to the rich youth, Clement's interpretation of the beatitude of the poor (Matt. 5:3) underscores the legitimacy of the wealthy as members of the Christian community by remaining for the most part in the realm of figurative hermeneutics: for him Jesus' blessing refers only to those who are poor in the desire for wealth, and while Clement does not ignore poverty in material terms, he carefully points out that its moral value can only be measured by the motivation leading up to it.[44] To have no possessions is only worthwhile when this state is chosen for the sake of eternal life, for before Jesus many people gave up all their wealth and did so for what Clement considers morally repugnant reasons: to have time for philosophy or merely because of vainglory – people such as Anaxagoras, Democritus, and Crates. In other words, for Clement's implied audience, poverty would have been a matter of choice, not inheritance. The lower classes were not at the focal point of Clement's thought, and this becomes all the clearer in his observation in *Quis dives salvetur?* that humanity's ideal state is not poverty, regardless of its motivation, but rather that moderate prosperity envisioned by earlier Christian writers in which one possesses enough goods both to cover one's own needs and to help the poor. Indeed, if everyone rejected wealth completely, he asked, who would be left to give alms? Such sentiments had the effect of justifying the existing gulf between rich and poor, and of devaluing social change; ultimately, they amount not only to a theological idealization and legitimization of wealth in the church, but of poverty as well.[45]

Clement developed, in effect, a nascent psychology of the sin which reveals his debt to Stoic philosophy, for he saw in the morbid condition of avarice a state of unfulfilled passion which sets the sinner on fire with yearning and, even worse, destroys his rational understanding of the need for moderation. To treat this illness of the soul by removing from the sinner all the material goods which, at least potentially, might be useful to him is only to aggravate his condition. Without reason to guide him and in his state of physical need, the sinner has not rid himself of what is truly contemptible, that is, the *desire* for wealth; he has merely "ignited his inborn raw material of evil through the want of external goods."[46]

ORIGEN: ASCETICISM, PSYCHOLOGY, AND THE PROBLEM OF AVARICE IN THE CHURCH

The moderateness of Clement's thinking on the vice stands in contrast not only to the writers before him, but also to those who were his immediate successors. The next generation produced another famous teacher at Alexandria (though much of his career was spent in Caesarea), one who seems to have been taught only briefly by Clement himself, but whose rigorous asceticism was almost proverbial in his own day. Only an interest in the psychology of the sin connects Origen's thought with Clement's viewpoint, though even here one can describe Origen's stance as more radical than that of the earlier writer. For Origen, avarice was not merely a morbid condition of the soul, it was the soul's worst weakness or feebleness.[47] He is, furthermore, clear about the cause of avarice, for the germ of this debility is to be identified in the devil himself. Satan, of course, has no real interest in money or material goods. What he desires are *philargyroi*, people inclined to worldly things. He perverts a legitimate love, implanted in the soul by the Creator, using the same methods which had proven successful with Judas: after wounding the potential sinner with a fiery dart – at which point there is presumably an initial succumbing to temptation – either Satan or subordinate demons enter into him.[48] To guard against this encroachment was no easy matter. Origen's image for the task is drawn from Deuteronomy 7:1, where the Jews' battle against the seven nations for the possession of Israel is related.[49] As will be seen, with this demonology of avarice and the view of warfare against evil intruders into the soul, one is already in the intellectual environment which shaped early monastic thought on the vice.

Origen is uncompromising in demanding complete, material poverty as a prerequisite for avoiding the sin and achieving perfection, nor is he willing to make any metaphorical compromises in his hermeneutics on behalf of the wealthy. Such radicalism did little to help his standing among these classes, which would later find his writings theologically suspect. His understanding of scriptural passages was frequently enough allegorical, but in his exegesis of the words to the rich youth, Origen provides an example of the type of interpretation Clement had criticized earlier. "Sell your possessions . . ." could only have been meant literally, Origen argues, and those who give away their worldly property and store up treasure in heaven have taken a necessary step towards this perfection. One should never believe that the rich can be found in this group: "For who among the rich has given up the love of wealth, which I might also call the love of this world?"[50] Origen's examples of those who were virtuous enough to choose to live in poverty is instructive, for by including Crates here he again took a position which is diametrically opposed to Clement's viewpoint, and by referring to the apostolic community in the same light, he once more anticipates a favorite argument used later by the monastic communities of the Egyptian desert.[51]

With particular emphasis Origen points to the social disruption caused by the vice. During times of famine, he noted while commenting on Matthew 24:7–8, people are easily provoked to avarice and wars against those who do not have to suffer as great a lack as they do; and the sins of vainglory, greed, and avarice in corrupt leaders also frequently result in violent social upheaval.[52] In the community of the church Origen warned against hypocritical teachers who may instruct in Christian doctrine, but are only interested in the money they can earn from their students.[53] He also echoed earlier sentiments by complaining of deacons and bishops who misused the funds under their control and of presbyters who hung onto earthly goods.[54] But his most severe words of reproach are reserved for the affluent, in spite of his obvious dependence on wealthy patrons at the school in Alexandria and elsewhere. Clement had attempted to provide theological support for including the rich in the community of the faithful. Origen, on the other hand, argues that he who values money, admires wealth, believes that it is a good, who gives to the rich the rank of gods and scorns the poor for not having this divine character – this person makes a god of money and as such must be expelled from the church.[55]

COMPROMISE IN THE FACE OF PERSECUTION: CYPRIAN OF CARTHAGE ON PRECEPTS, COUNSELS, AND THE MISER

Clement's moderation and Origen's ascetic rejection mark the poles in the spectrum of attitudes towards the presence of the wealthy in the community. They do not, however, exhaust all the possibilities. In the western church, Cyprian, Bishop of Carthage, took a position on this issue based on the distinction between the precepts and counsels to be extrapolated from Jesus' words. To give alms was a command meant for every Christian; to give up everything was advice to those who desired to achieve spiritual perfection.[56] Cyprian, thus, insisted that the wealthy give at least some degree of help to the poor, but on the other hand by referring to the episode of the rich youth in its most conditional version, found in Matthew 19:21 ("*If* you would be perfect, go, sell your possessions . . ."), he suggested that if the wealthy were willing to follow Jesus' statement here, they could become like the apostles.[57] There is little doubt which course of action he preferred from his congregation: going beyond his Episcopal duty of hospitality for the poor, Cyprian himself is said to have given almost all his possessions to the needy and the church.[58] But he was prudent enough ultimately not to demand this degree of selflessness from everyone, a conciliatory attitude which may have been a result of his duties as bishop.

Almsgiving was a necessity for Cyprian because it solved at a stroke two pressing problems for the third-century church: the exhaustion of its treasury following the financial drain of persecution, apostasy by the rich, and the eroded economic situation of the community; and, second, the penitential requirements for those who had deserted the church during the waves of persecution but were now seeking re-entry to it. Cyprian emphasized again and again the duty of almsgiving for the Christian community, and it is in the context of this pastoral intent that he frequently made reference to avarice. The vice must be overcome because it is the evil which blocks someone from fulfilling the social precept of exercising justice by giving freely to the poor from those goods which God has seen fit to give him.[59] Cyprian, like Origen, saw the task of surmounting avarice as a battle, though not one of typological significance. He was a practical thinker, and his imagery situated the Christian soul in a real environment with which his community was all too familiar: in a stadium, as a gladiator or a runner in a race against evil.[60] Those who lose the contest – wanting to store up treasure on earth rather than in heaven, caring blindly for their inheritance here and not for their patrimony there – are led away in the leg-irons and chains of riches as slaves to their own money.[61] Obviously, some of the motivation for developing this imagery stemmed from the need to support the members of his own persecuted community: no matter how much the good Christians under his care are tormented by Roman officials, he implies, the sinner's lot is infinitely worse.

Cyprian found arguments everywhere to help humanity arm itself for the struggle against the vice. The plague of mortality is useful for this purpose, he noted, for it allows us to see if the rapacious will extinguish the insatiable ardor of their avarice at least through the fear of death.[62] Even the moneylender's occupation could be put to use. In a florilegium of eight quotations assembled from biblical sources, he referred to almsgiving (as had Clement before him) in terms taken from Proverbs 19:17.[63] Alms, in this view, are a way of lending to God on interest; repayment will come when He sits in judgment. For the rich, to give Jesus a share of their profits by aiding others in need (see Matt. 25:31–46) will result in a just exchange: in return they will receive a share in the heavenly kingdom. In their separate ways, both Cyprian and Clement orient themselves towards the needs of those with possessions: they emphasize almsgiving in particular not because it is a mechanism of social equity, but because it has redemptive value for the donor. Moreover, Cyprian's emphasis on financial support for the indigent also colored his view of Christianity's origins. For him, the apostolic community was not an example of virtuous poverty, but of liberality, where people sold their houses and fields and gave the proceeds to the apostles to distribute as alms.[64]

The anti-eleemosynary impulse seen in the vice culminated in one central expression of evil: the miser, found for the first time in detailed form in a Christian setting in Cyprian's work. The important figure of the miser, who threatened to upset the carefully worked-out ideological balance in Christian society between a moderate possession of wealth and moderate almsgiving, is described here through a series of external signs which all point up his fear and anxiety at the thought of giving up some of the immeasurable wealth which he thought would bring him security. The *avarus* quakes with dread lest a robber come, a murderer attack, or the envy of a yet richer person start lawsuits against him. He cannot eat or sleep in quiet, he sighs at the table and lies awake all night tossing and turning in his soft bed. Above all, he will not separate himself from the heaps of money he has piled up around him or buried in the earth, which for Cyprian is synonymous with a refusal to give alms.[65] These external signs were later to be supplemented by other observations of the miser's behavior, but also by a concentration on his internal life: roughly a century after Cyprian's work, Hilary of Poitiers drew the first meticulous portrait of the miser's emotional state in Latin

Christendom. After his soul is captured by avarice and made a slave to this mistress, Hilary commented:

> the *avarus* is afraid only of losing money, though he is on the brink of losing himself; he is full of busyness, sad, anxious, always held back restlessly by a fear of loss; he is unmindful of honesty, pays no attention to friendship, flees human kindness, does not acknowledge religion, hates goodness altogether.[66]

In this combination of external and internal indications of the vice one can make out the character sketch of the miser which was to be a commonplace throughout the Middle Ages.

The limited focus on the miser's own unsettled state is not an indication that Cyprian ignored the social component of the sin. His work also shows that the charge of acquisitiveness in avarice was now being leveled against those in the higher ranks of Roman society who, as landowners, are accused of adding field to field (see Isaiah 5:8), expelling the poor from their borders and stretching out their property endlessly, and of attempting to justify their incessant accumulation of wealth on the grounds of care for their children and provision for their inheritance.[67] Cyprian is drawing here on a corpus of activities already developed in classical Antiquity as indications of greed's uncontrollable urge to acquire. In a Christian context many of these activities were neatly catalogued about a generation after Cyprian by another African writer, Arnobius the Elder, in his depiction of the souls who might not have loved possessions while they were with God, but whose behavior on earth is a completely different matter. Here, their avarice is seen in a series of proto-capitalist ventures: the restless excavation of mountains, the mining of the earth's hidden treasures, long and dangerous journeys undertaken for the sake of merchandise, constant attention to price fluctuations, usurious money-lending practices, and innumerable litigations against friends and relatives alike for even the smallest material rewards.[68] To his own list of activities typical of avarice, Cyprian further observed that measured against the standards set by the apostolic community, the Christian society of his own day was too often characterized by its *ardor cupiditatis*. Such insatiable greediness among the rich may have been a response to the repeated Roman persecutions (to which Cyprian himself eventually fell victim) and worsening economic situation of the third-century empire. But Cyprian put the responsibility for these disasters at least partially on the shoulders of the congregation: when even bishops desire money in superfluity while the brethren go thirsty, no Christian need be surprised at the persecutions his religion is forced to suffer.[69]

LACTANTIUS: MYTHOLOGY AND THE BEGINNINGS OF SYSTEMATIC ANALYSIS

The social disruption caused by avarice was not only a contemporary problem, but – looked at from the vantage point of a Christianity which was developing into the dominant religion of the Roman empire and from an environment which allowed for leisurely and academic contemplation – the vice could also be seen as having a historical dimension. In the work of Lactantius, rhetorician and teacher of the emperor Constantine's son, cupidity was given a firm place in the Christian mythology of the Golden Age. Reflections on a former "utopian" state of humanity and the process of its degeneration had, of course, long been common in Antiquity. Avarice had frequently served in such considerations as an indicator of the progress of this deterioration, but in Lactantius' thought, in particular his reception of Seneca, the vice plays a much more active role in bringing the *aurea tempora* to an end.[70] Lactantius' remarks on this issue are, in essence, those of a theological apologist; they occur in the context of his attempt to convince the pagan reader of the moral inferiority of polytheism.[71] Historically prior to the Greco-Roman pantheon was an idyllic era characterized by the worship of the one, true God. In this age, the just gave of their reserves generously. No *avaritia* took for itself goods which had been bestowed on all by the divinity, no greed caused hunger and thirst to plague humankind. All things were in abundance for all equally, since the haves gave freely and copiously to the have-nots. Lactantius does not refer explicitly to this period in terms of the biblical account of Eden, but it is clear enough that he has this in mind, along with the Golden Age of the poets. He is, in fact, the first patristic author to unite these two conceptions.[72]

Monotheism made personal generosity, largess, and above all justice possible among human beings. With the transition to polytheism this situation changed radically, for social relations came gradually under the influence of avarice as humanity gave no more thought to God. Those who possessed something in surfeit not only kept it for themselves, but also seized things from others for their own treasure. What formerly each individual had put at the disposal of the community was now hoarded up in the homes of a few. This select group claimed the gifts of heaven for themselves, not out of philanthropy, but in order to collect all the instruments of greed and avarice so they could enslave the rest of humanity. For this purpose they also created unjust laws in the name of a perverted justice, put themselves in positions of authority over all others, and set about establishing the machinery of oppression to maintain their power. In Lactantius' mythical history of humanity, the tyranny of this overweening individualism, which he describes at one point as a *superba et tumida inaequalitas* and which might be defined in terms of the sin of pride itself, is seen as a direct result of avarice.[73] Personal egotism led in turn to an elitist injustice in society, but behind them both stands an initial act of "rabid and furious *avaritia*."[74]

The Golden Age was not destroyed once and for all by polytheism. With the resurgence of monotheism, by which Lactantius refers to the genesis of Christianity, at least a *species illius aurei temporis* returned to the earth.[75] This idea of a resurrection of the Golden Age would not have surprised his pagan audience; Virgil's fourth *Eclogue* and the *Oracula Sibyllina*, both of which Lactantius refers to directly elsewhere, had posited much the same.[76] But by insisting on the ethical function of Christianity as an image of the idyllic time to come, he goes a large step beyond his predecessors. This, of course, has everything to do with his apologetic intention of bringing his audience to an acceptance of the contemporary Christian community, with its inherited social disparity, as nevertheless a model, a type, for millenarian society. Thus, he argues that only through the *iustitia* of Christianity can the social injustice of avarice be undone. Were all of humanity to worship the one God, there would be no more wars, dissensions, treachery, frauds, and pillaging; rather, a "pious and religious assembly of those with possessions would support those without them."[77] For Lactantius, in other words, the defeat of avarice is necessarily a simple matter of conversion.

The clear distinction he made in his account of the decline of the

Golden Age between two major expressions of the vice – on the one hand a desire to retain goods for oneself alone, on the other a yearning to acquire from others – is part of what Lactantius had inherited from the analyses of the concept in Antiquity. The rudiments of his own methodical presentation of avarice are easily made out elsewhere. He was the first to begin developing an extended series of concretely defined evil actions stemming from the sin. In his epitome of the *Divine Institutions* he remarked that from the insatiable desire for wealth burst forth poisonings, deceptions, false wills, and all types of fraud, though in his major work itself this list includes only "frauds, robberies, and all types of evils."[78]

But above all, his reflections on the nature of avarice reveal that he represents the position of Christian Platonism in what was a continuing debate on the intrinsicality of greed in human beings. Lactantius considered the desire to possess in itself simply a part of human nature, given by God for a reasonable end, namely to help humanity maintain its life by gathering together what is necessary for that purpose.[79] Only through abuse can this morally acceptable function become sinful, when, going beyond their limits, human beings no longer yearn for heavenly matters ultimately, but for that which is earthbound. A Stoic might say that an act of will is necessary "to follow justice, God, eternal life, the perpetual light, and all those things God promises humanity," but, Lactantius notes, merely to want these things is too little.[80] With the first minor bodily discomfort, the will evaporates and the only thing which remains, if these virtuous qualities are truly to be achieved, is the *cupiditas* for them. *Ira* and *libido*, too, had been implanted in humanity by God for virtuous ends.[81] But as sins, they joined *avaritia* (at this point, Lactantius uses "cupidity" and "avarice" as interchangeable designations for the vice) in a triad of evil, perversions of the three parts of the soul, which must be resisted above all others and torn out so that the corresponding virtues may grow in their place. So deadly was the triumvirate of wrath, lust, and avarice that Lactantius credited it with being the source of all other sins and referred to these three as the Furies spoken of by the poets.[82] The natural and God-given impulses which lay behind them, however, could be neither eradicated, as the Stoics felt they should, nor tempered, as the Peripatetics argued. In Lactantius' view they could not be removed, since they had been bestowed on humanity by the Creator for a purpose; nor could they be tempered, for if they became vices, one had to avoid them altogether, and as virtues, one should encourage them completely.[83]

The early centuries of Christian literature provide nothing more systematic on avarice than what is seen in rudimentary form in Lactantius, nor do they show the more orthodox positions on greed and the affluent affirmed by all writers on these issues. The seeds of a radical "possessionlessness" propagated as a cure for the vice by the hermit communities of the fourth century can already be found in Origen's thought. Nevertheless, for the majority of church thinkers, riches and the impulses which amounted to avarice only by distortion were not rejected outright; rather, an attempt was made to find a place in the community for those who were already rich by describing the function they were to be encouraged to fulfill as almsgivers. As in the *Shepherd of Hermas*, the round stones symbolizing the wealthy were not thrown into the pit, but neither were the masons invested with police powers to force their reshaping. Yet, the further chapters here will reveal to what degree developments in the history of avarice are always to be measured against the Christian ideal of ascetic concepts of a limit to the desire for possessions in a life of purity.

2

Ascetic transformations I: monks and the laity in eastern Christendom

In Christian culture, Lactantius' rudimentary analysis of the vice preceded a number of other important discussions of avarice composed before the end of the fourth century, culminating in the fully articulated and systematic characterization of the sin in the work of Evagrius Ponticus. Most of the earliest of these discussions are to be localized in the eastern Mediterranean. The third and fourth centuries clearly witnessed the perception among some of the Orient's most important church thinkers of a greater need for precision when dealing with the vice, and this need only grew in proportion with the hastening deterioration of the Roman Empire. As the economic situation worsened in the third century, the discrepancy between the prerogatives of the rich and the suffering of the poor was seen to grow ever crasser throughout the empire. Corruption, too, was felt to be particularly rampant at this time.[1] Much of this perception of social disharmony is reflected in the more detailed examinations of avarice typical of Christian commentators everywhere in the Roman *imperium* during its last centuries, but it is voiced initially with the greatest clarity in the East, especially in Cappadocia where one finds evidence of intense intellectual activity aimed at coming to terms with the sin. The work of three major Cappadocian authors, the brothers Basil the Great and Gregory of Nyssa, and their friend Gregory Nazianzen, as well as the closely related thinking of John Chrysostom, gives a striking view of the issues which were moving church thinkers in their imagining of avarice.[2]

The two major tendencies already observed in Lactantius' treatment of the vice surface again in the work of the Cappadocians and John Chrysostom: a movement towards a more complete or systematic analysis of avarice and its combination with an emphasis on the social consequences of the sin understood in both historical and mythic terms. But these interests are set against a background which reflects both the practical, ascetic training of the Eastern writers and the learned, philosophical attitudes towards wealth which they inherited with their social station and then intellectualized during their formal education. All of them came from generally prosperous families, the Cappadocians perhaps even from the curial class, the rich urban elite.[3] After enjoying the benefits of legal and rhetorical training – Chrysostom was certainly under the tutelage of the orator Libanius in Antioch, perhaps Basil and Gregory of Nyssa were, as well – they became enthusiastic followers of cenobitic monasticism, or, in Gregory Nazianzen's case, of a milder form of asceticism.[4] And eventually they all moved, though more or less unwillingly, from ascesis to the episcopacy: at Caesarea, Nyssa, Sebaste, Nazianzus, Antioch, and Constantinople. Their views on avarice reveal the influence of this development: in their sermons and addresses as ecclesiastical officials, they combined rhetoric and ascesis, with varying degrees of emphasis, to produce an argument which would be effective in combating the vice but remain palatable for the laity. Their work demonstrates the power of Christian ascesis to transform the ideas of greed which Christianity had inherited from Judaism and classical Antiquity, even as their ascetic view of avarice was, in turn, being tempered by the realities which came with their episcopal duties in ministering to the spiritual needs of a developing lay Christian society.

ASCETICISM AND THE LAITY IN THE THOUGHT OF BASIL THE GREAT

The work of Basil the Great (330–379) is of particular importance, not only because he exerted a good deal of influence on the Eastern writers who were associated with him, but also because the authority of his thinking on avarice became prominent in the West. He approached the vice, whether dealing with ascetic, clerical, or lay audiences, from one and the same foundation, though his criticism of avarice among bishops or monks and his remedies for its cure in these contexts are much more rigorous than what he has to say to the laity. He is, for example, unmistakably disapproving of what was reported to him concerning certain provincial bishops who accepted fees from those they ordained and who then attempted to cover up their sin by taking the money only after the ordination. Such actions, wrote Basil, deserve the damnation with which Simon Magus was cursed (Acts 8:20), they are the results of *philargyria*, make of the clergy another Judas, and if the same actions occur in the future, their perpetrators will be punished by expulsion from office.[5] The same specificity and rigor can be noted in Basil's monastic works, which show the influence of what he knew of the organization of Pachomius' cenobitic communities in Egypt, where the ascetic ideal led monks to retain no individual property upon entrance to the monastery and no ties to the world beyond its walls. As Basil puts it, the ascete is to be "city-less" and without any possessions whatsoever; he is to live in his community, as Pachomius had pre-scribed, in absolute poverty.[6]

The ascetic rigor which Basil recommended for others was a model for his own behavior as well. The original impulse for his monastic outlook came from Eustathius of Sebasteia (*fl.* mid-fourth century) and his communities, but after visiting the monastic establishments of Egypt and Syria, Basil returned to Cappadocia, sold all of his posses-sions, gave the proceeds to the poor, and set up a monastery across the river from his sister's ascetic foundation. Later, as bishop, he established hostels for the poor at Caesarea.[7] Basil's work illustrates how easily this ascetic fervor could lead to a more radical criticism of the vice which at times appears to have distinguished only imprecisely between the rich and the avaricious. Yet Basil never condemned all Christians outside the cenobitic fraternities, nor did he categorically deny that the rich will enter heaven unless they give up all of their possessions, as did Eustathius' followers and members of other ascetically minded sects in Asia Minor, in particular the Messalians.[8] Nevertheless, Basil's outlook on avarice for the laity as well as for monks was inspired everywhere by the cenobitic ideal. Whatever his situation in life, Basil argued, no Christian could love his neighbor as himself if he possessed for his own use more than his neighbor. The monk took a first step towards avoiding this failure of love by his renunciation of material goods, the rich person a somewhat smaller step by his correct use of them. To be sure, the question of avarice was not always limited to the rich alone.

Basil was well aware that there were avaricious people among the poor, nor did he see a renunciation of the world by itself as a guarantee of the freedom from avarice. But whether intended for the rich or the poor, the limits which Basil recommended as sufficient for individual use were not at all left vague, but rather were specified with ascetic severity: ideally, the rich, too, needed only bread as food, only a simple tunic and coat as clothing.[9]

Ascesis served as the foundation for Basil's rejection of the vice, and his clearest and most concrete analysis of avarice can be found in his mature monastic thought, as well. In the *Regulae brevius tractatae*, a series of oral improvisations on ascetic issues, he responded to a question concerning the point at which one can begin to speak of a desire for wealth as being illicit by giving what amounts to a concise definition of the sin. *Pleonexia* occurs:

> whenever someone transgresses the limit of the law. Now in terms of the Old Testament this means that he gives more attention to himself than to his neighbor, for it has been written, "Love your neighbor as yourself" [Lev. 19:18]; but according to the Gospel, when he pays serious attention to something more for himself alone than what is necessary for the present day, just as he who heard, "Fool, this very night they will demand your soul – that which you have gathered together, to whom will it belong?" [Luke 12:20]. To this the Evangelist adds the more general, "Such is he who stores up treasures for himself and is not rich in the sight of God" [Luke 12:21].[10]

The two principles involved here, *caritas* towards one's neighbor and an absolute lack of care for one's own material needs, had at least been implied in Christian statements of the remedy for avarice before Basil the Great, but his precise formulation of them was occasioned by and designed for the exigencies of monasticism. In this context, the second element in his definition must be understood quite literally. Together, both principles also reveal his premises when attacking the vice in any setting, and they account for his view of avarice as an evil necessitating both social action and the spiritual reorientation of the sinner.

There was, however, some latitude in the stringency with which Basil made lay congregations accountable for a renunciation of their material cares. In an early ascetic work addressed to all Christians in general, he demanded that not only monks but also the laity purify themselves from avarice and the desire for excessive ornamentation. By concentrating their attention on God alone, they would avoid giving serious thought to a superfluous amount of life's necessities or possessions meant only for themselves. Yet the same chapter of the *Regulae morales* simply takes the presence of the rich in the community for granted when it reminds them of the necessity to care generously for the needs of their brethren.[11] Their duty here seems to be one of *caritas* alone, not the relinquishment of everything beyond what the present day requires. The leeway granted the rich is seen elsewhere as well. Avarice tempts them, Basil noted in a homily, just as Potiphar's wife tried to seduce Joseph. But again, the reality of dealing with the laity tempers Basil's demands on the rich. Their response to temptation need not be radical asceticism:

> Do not give everything to pleasure; give also something to your soul. And imagine that you have two daughters, temporal prosperity and life in heaven. If you cannot give everything to the better one, at least divide equally between the undisciplined and the temperate child.[12]

If Basil was not led by the ideology of monastic rigor to make radical demands on the laity, this ideology still guided him, as bishop, in advising his lay congregation on what he considered the preferred limits to possessions and the amount to be given in alms. In a homily delivered to a lay congregation, Basil moved the ascetic ideal as far as he felt was possible into his listeners' secular sphere. God had given some of them riches only so they could qualify for the rewards which come with its good governance. The legitimacy of their wealth carries the price of its public disposal, yet there are few who hold their acquisitive itch in check. These are commonplaces in the presentation of the vice, to be sure, but to them Basil adds a note of more rigorous social orientation by observing that the avaricious inability to be content with what is sufficient is the same thing as public theft.[13] Yet even here, the severity of his rhetoric connecting acquisition with theft must be put into perspective, for Basil only legislated a one-year exclusion from the sacraments for repentant thieves and two years if charges had to be brought against them. On the other hand, for the far less public crime of grave robbery, an offense of avarice against the self-presentation of well-to-do families and one to which all of the Eastern writers gave much attention, he demanded an exclusion from communion for a period of ten years.[14]

Ultimately, one must note, despite his personal preference for radical ascesis, Basil's preaching to the laity did not legislate a thorough redistribution of wealth, but rather, as was common with all orthodox theologians, it attempted to move those Christians with goods to share them with those without possessions. For this purpose he emphasized the praise in heaven for almsgivers and the pains of hell awaiting those who give nothing. The warning examples of the farmer who thought he could construct larger silos (Luke 12:16–21) and the rich youth (Matt. 19:16–22) provide the themes for two of his most important homilies treating the sin. In both, Basil points to the ease with which these figures could have changed their behavior. That they did not do so, but instead made themselves liable for infernal punishment, was due to the precarious nature of wealth: Basil understood in literal terms Jesus' proclamation that it was more difficult for the rich to enter heaven than for a camel to pass through the eye of a needle (Luke 18:25).[15] He brought this observation to bear on the *nouveaux riches* of his own community in a metaphor which compared them to someone climbing a ladder and, having achieved the goal of being at the highest rung, is then killed by a precipitous fall into the depths. Opposed to this suicidal behavior is the ease of giving up material goods in exchange for the security of one's soul. Here again, Basil's figurative language is geared to his audience: in the marketplace no one is made sad by spending money on personal needs. Alms, Basil argues, are thus a low price to pay for the precious reward of heavenly bliss.[16]

Basil rejected out of hand the excuses of the wealthy for not giving alms. Whoever gives only a portion of his superfluity in his last will, Basil told Caesarea's wealthy Christians, is unacceptable to heaven, for a reluctance to give even at the point of death is the consummation of avarice.[17] To say that all one's property is necessary for one's children – an explanation which Cyprian had refused to acknowledge and which all the Eastern writers criticize as well – is only a pretense of this vice. Even worse, who can guarantee that his children will use their inheritance correctly? If they do not, the *philargyros* (φιλάργυρος) is liable for double punishment: once for his own sin of denying alms and once for abetting others in sin. Basil does not demand from the layman to give everything to the poor to the point of disinheriting his own family; rather, a portion of the inheritance should be set aside in alms equal to what the first-born will get. The rest of the patrimony may be divided among the other children.[18] Those without offspring have even less excuse not to give to the poor. For them, Basil expressly forbids dispensing alms in the form of a last will and testament after a life of egotistic enjoyment, for whom should the poor thank in this case, death or the benefactor? As he further notes, a soldier who shows up for a battle after the war is already over cannot expect to be treated as a hero. Basil, as Chrysostom, is also well aware of the shady legal practices of his day, for the ultimate recipient of the inheritance may not be the poor at all.[19]

How desperate the situation of the poor can become is seen clearly in Basil's focus on the internal conflict of a father who must choose between starvation or selling one of his children into slavery, though the poignancy of this situation need not be considered an everyday occurrence. Here, the effects of the sin are measured in terms not only of the sinner's spiritual state, but of the misery his victims must suffer as well. Basil's control of rhetorical detail achieves a maximum amount of pity for the indigent father: can he forget nature? turn himself into a beast? how will he face the rest of his children after selling one of them? how can he eat the food bought at such a price? The only one unmoved by all of this is the avaricious person himself. His mind is fixed only on the profit to be made at the slave market, for he desires the unhappiness of others in order to make his money productive.[20]

The social disturbance of the *philargyros* was merely the most concrete evidence of the sin's disruption in what Basil accepted as an ideal and universal order. Here, too, within this larger dimension, which was based on the Christian understanding of the Golden Age, only an absolute minimum belonged to the individual for his exclusive use. Again, Basil's thought here shows the influence of both his ascetic and philosophical training, but – and this makes him typical of many other church thinkers of his day – it also demonstrates that it was possible for him to achieve the universal realization of his cherished ascetic ideal only within the realm of an essentially "imaginative" presentation. The monastic communities alone were able to put into practice what was mythically and historically presented as the ideal for all; for a more ordinary realm, the right of possession is never called into question. Thus, Basil adopted an image from the Stoics when he noted that like someone who takes a seat in the theater and drives all others away, so the person who possesses more for himself than what he needs has appropriated illicitly for himself what belongs to everyone, a metaphor which yet cannot be taken as calling into question this person's right to possess at all.[21] Elsewhere Basil wrote that the model for charity was to be found in God's initial dispensing of rain and sunshine to all equally. The person sinning by avarice rejects this Christian re-interpretation of the ideal of the Golden Age, as he also acts counter to the very workings of the earth, which brings forth its fruit for humankind's use, not for itself alone.[22] Basil's image of the workings of divine and natural law is in essence the paradigm not of evangelical poverty, but of charity as it should be practiced by the Christian. In the Jerusalem community, he argued, this paradigm served as the guiding principle for a Christian society.[23] All of creation has its limits, the sea knows its borders, the night-time does not violate its boundary; only the greedy person seeks to extend himself through desire beyond all measure, order, and time.[24] This imagery helps confirm that although Basil's vigorous attempt as bishop to bring the monastic ideal into the realm of his lay congregation was more rhetorically radical than what one will see from many of his contemporaries, his basic perception of the vice in a lay surrounding corresponds well to what was typical of the orthodox theologians of his period, for he saw in avarice the culmination of the egotism of possession, not the mere fact of possession itself.

PLATONIC ASCETICISM AND THE THREAT OF HERESY IN THE THOUGHT OF GREGORY OF NYSSA

The need for a systematic analysis of avarice was apparently felt with some urgency in Cappadocia not only because of the perception, throughout the fourth century, of an epidemic greediness among the wealthy in this area and a concurrent state of misery among the have-nots, but even more because of the realization that the vice had worked its way into the church hierarchy itself. The latter topic is specifically what motivated Gregory of Nyssa (335–394) to issue "canons" on the question of avarice in his letter to Letoius, Bishop of Melitene. Gregory was obviously unaware of the ground Lactantius had covered in analyzing greed, for he shows some surprise at the vacuum left by earlier Christian thinkers in treating the vice. In fact, he makes their negligence indirectly responsible for the spread of avarice among the clergy:

> I do not know how, untreated, that species of idolatry – for thus does the holy Apostle term the desire for more – has been overlooked by our fathers. . . . For the holy Apostle proclaimed it to be not only idolatry, but also the root of all evils, and nevertheless such an illness – unexamined and uncared for – has indeed been overlooked. And for this reason there is more than enough of this infirmity in the church, and no one diligently examines those who are being taken into the clergy, lest perhaps they have been defiled by this species of idolatry.[25]

In order to fill the gap in knowledge of the vice, Gregory then specifies its precise position in the soul and the concrete activities to which it leads. In his psychological analysis of avarice, based on the Platonic conception of the soul, the virulence of the sin is apparent in its ability to empassion all three parts established by Plato's model. *Pleonexia* leads reason astray into maintaining that virtue consists in earthly matter alone, desire is brought to give itself only to inferior things, and the irascible portion of the soul also finds opportunities for evil in the vice. Although avarice exercises its control over the entire soul, it arises in the *epithymetikon*. As is true for all the vices, the occasion for greed's origin is provided by the senses, in this case their ability to draw desire away from what is truly virtuous. This process results in sins opposed to love or, in the same terms Origen had used to describe it, perversions of this virtue. Thus, when desire is transferred to wealth, vainglory, or the mere surface embellishments of the body, the result is above all the love of money or fame or pleasure, a triad which is also important in the early moral exegesis of Jesus' temptations in the desert.[26] With the same care, Gregory remarks that on the authority of earlier writers, all should know that theft, grave robbery, and sacrilege must be considered under the rubric of avarice, and he adds that Scripture just as clearly proscribes as types of greed usury, charging interest, and any other form of taking another's possessions for oneself, even if this occurs under the pretext of business.[27] His classification of the vice's sub-divisions is something more than an academic exercise, for it forms part of a practical guide for dealing with penitents who seek forgiveness for having sinned in these ways, and it further specifies under what conditions those sinning by theft, grave robbery, and sacrilege can be accepted back in the church. His view of theft committed without endangering the victim's life is of particular interest. Along with confessing his crime to a priest, the moneyed thief must give liberally of his goods to the poor to be considered free of avarice. If he possesses nothing, however, the thief must perform manual labor to heal his infirmity (see Eph. 4:28). Yet, however socially responsible this may all appear to be, nowhere does Gregory mention the necessity of restitution.

The influence of asceticism on Gregory's thought becomes clear when he deals with the connections among the *pathe* (πάθη), the passions of the soul. Avarice's most important relationship for Gregory is with licentiousness or riotous living (*akolasia*). Both are imagined as savage and frenzied masters (*despotai*) ruling over the sinner who is enslaved to them, the licentious passion scourging the mind with pleasures, *pleonexia* granting the sinner no respite but driving him on with greater cupidity the more he tries to satisfy his greed.[28] Avarice is the more fundamental of the two; it has a preparatory function in this regard, for it provides the other passion with the raw material of desires which licentiousness then turns into superfluous vestments, silver vases, gold, and jewels. At one point Gregory draws on more graphic medical language to express the anterior role of avarice: *philargyria* in this sense is like a tumor which, when it bursts, releases a discharge of licentiousness that eats its way further into the skin.[29] All of the passions can exercise a tyranny over humankind when they are not countered by ascetic exercise and the sacraments, but Gregory stresses that avarice's reign is harsher even than that of wrath, envy, hatred, or pride. His metaphor of the insatiability of greed alone develops further an image which Plato had used to describe the totality of the passions: a many-headed beast. For Gregory, this monster, now the beast of avarice alone, requires its myriad mouths to supply nourishment for its unquenchable appetite to possess.[30]

Gregory's oration against usurers, as much of his thought on avarice, contains many echoes of Basil's words on the same subject, but it is above all the corruption of love evident in the merciless interest charged by the usurer which attracted Gregory's attention. The decisive contrast at work in his oration is that between the needs of a voluntary philanthropy and the selfish cares of *philargyria*. His portrait of the usurer, in this way, has many elements in common with the satiric description of the miser. The usurer resembles this figure in his painstaking and tireless efforts to keep track of his debtors' movements, but also in the excessive frugality with which he makes his own life unbearable, and that of his family as well. Gregory illustrates this similarity between the miser and the usurer by the example of a moneylender from a city he leaves unnamed:

> Constrained by the passion of avarice, he was also miserly with his own expenditures (for the *philargyroi* are like this), not setting the table with enough, never changing his clothes except out of necessity, not granting his children the bare minimum for carrying on life . . .[31]

Gregory's words here reveal something more than the work of a disinterested psychologist, for whether the usurer's loans were used for commercial activity or for consumption alone, his clientele are represented in the *Oratio contra usurarios* as coming from, or closely related to, Gregory's own high social station. Just under the surface of Gregory's disdain for the usurer is the knowledge that the lowly retailing mentality (*tropos kapelikos*) which Gregory so disdained in those who took interest also spelled the slow ruin of the well-born class to which he was heir. The threat of the slavery of his class to the whims of the usurer surely added to the sharpness of his satire.[32]

His feelings for the oppressed and his full depiction of their misery surface elsewhere, in the two sermons known commonly as *De pauperibus amandis*. Written perhaps as early as 379, these works mirror the unstable conditions following the Gothic wars, the first focusing specifically on the plight of uprooted war refugees who made their way to Nyssa and wandered the streets there.[33] Gregory pleads with his congregation to use their fasting – the sermon was probably delivered during Lent – not just to deprive their bodies of food, but to dampen their hunger for profit, to starve to death the avarice of Mammon. At one point he states that the wealth of one household could relieve multitudes of the poor, though unfortunately he is not concrete enough to describe exactly how many households would suffice to provide for all of Nyssa's poor. Nevertheless, the mere possibility of such a solution remained an attractive rhetorical argument; later, John Chrysostom also repeated similar sentiments. But almsgiving was not limited to the rich alone. Gregory specifically mentions the duty of the poor themselves to aid these strangers in the city as far as their means allow them. He suggests that all give the needy what amounts to a brother's share of their patrimony, but at least a third or a fifth of it.[34]

Almsgiving for Gregory is indicative of a healthy detachment from the world, though he, too, can further recommend as the ideal remedy for avarice a more complete monastic renunciation: to desire nothing but what is absolutely necessary for life is an existence only one step below that of the angels.[35] To be sure, this cosmological position taken by ascetic poverty in Gregory's thought makes it all the more ethereal and, thus, somewhat less a part of the common life of the laity. With similar emphasis Gregory also refers to the efficacy of the sacraments in countering vice. In particular, he stresses the power of baptism, though he also asserts that this sacrament must be strengthened by penance if the Christian continues in his avarice after undergoing baptism.[36] His insistence on the need for all to give alms and on the role of baptism in curing sin may perhaps best be understood in the framework of a refutation of Messalian ideas. This heretical sect, which was widespread in the East, held baptism to be ineffective and prayer the only activity which could guarantee salvation. The sect considered itself so perfect that its members abrogated to themselves the exclusive right to be continual recipients of alms, but never its donors. The vagrant way of life espoused by this group represents one of the most radical forms of asceticism witnessed in the later fourth and fifth centuries.[37] Gregory specifically attacked Messalian monks in his *De virginitate*, accusing them of laziness in not working for themselves but merely depending on others, and elsewhere he corrected the Messalian character of Macarius/Symeon's *Epistola Magna* in an attempt to lead this author's followers back to orthodoxy.[38] It is these same anti-Messalian concerns which appear to have influenced his thought on avarice, as well. In Gregory's work, as in that of Basil before him, one can identify an attempt to integrate ascetic ideals and lay needs, and it should come as no surprise to see both authors distancing themselves in their understanding of avarice from a sectarian group which claimed moral and spiritual purity for itself alone, making compromise with the secular church and the Christian laity impossible. Gregory's orthodox cure for avarice, formulated perhaps partially to counteract Messalian ideas, could hold out the distant possibility of monastic perfection, but for the same reason it did not represent ascesis as the only legitimate remedy for the sin, nor did it suggest that those who chose this path deserved complete and unending financial support from the community at large.

THE PHILOSOPHICAL ASCETICISM OF GREGORY NAZIANZEN

The intellectualized refinement which could be achieved by a combination of philosophical attitudes to greed adopted from Classical models and ascetic Christian views of the sin may be illustrated best in Gregory Nazianzen's (329/30–390) depiction of avarice's historical development, especially in his *Oratio 14*. Like the earlier work by Lactantius, Gregory's view of the history of the vice unites the mythological tradition of the Golden Age with Christian thinking on the Fall. Gregory's emphasis, however, lies as much on the Christian component as on the conception of the Golden Age in Antiquity. The basis for his depreciation of the worth of money is not to be found in eschatological considerations, but rather in the ontology of man's first state: in paradise, riches, being inedible, simply had no value.[39] For his description of the pristine origins of human society, Gregory drew on the same traditional *topos* Basil had used: the unhindered use of natural elements by all people. Before the Fall, natural law reflected the egalitarian intentions of the divinity. Humanity's freedom and wealth consisted only in following God's commandments; in transgressing them lay its real poverty and servitude. Gregory's analysis echoes certain Platonic themes. With original sin, the envy, contention, and deceptions brought about by the devil stole their way into the community, inciting the stronger against the weaker and dissolving the family of humankind into a diversity of names. This process of disintegration into the present state of society was brought to completion by avarice. As Lactantius before him, Gregory identifies the final counterpoint to humanity's original equality in a perverted legal system under the sway of the vice:

Avarice tore apart the nobility of nature, in addition taking hold of the law as well, the helper of political domination.[40]

In Gregory's rhetoric, then, the excesses of private property are a direct result of the Fall, a conception which much later in the Middle Ages was also to be argued vigorously by some Franciscans. To rectify these ills, Gregory recommends a behavior inspired directly by the divinity: each act of plentiful almsgiving, in this view, recapitulates God's first liberality.[41] Thus, the initial step towards the resurrection of humanity's pre-lapsarian condition amounts to a simple act of aiding the poor.

For the rest, Gregory's depiction of the difference between the *philochrysos* and *philochristos*, as he put it once,[42] follows the general lines of criticism of the vice seen already in Cappadocia. He censures the avarice of the clergy with particular severity; among the laity, his attention is focused on the excesses of the rich.[43] But Gregory's initial friendship with the philosopher Maximus the Cynic, his interest in the thinking of other Cynics, and his familiarity with a popular philosophy which was heavily influenced by Cynic-Stoic ideas and imagery also added to the refinement of his attack on the vice. The importance of these schools of thought is especially noticeable in his poetic work. He drew attention in particular to the culmination of the yearning for more to be seen in the figure of Midas and his insane greed to turn everything into gold. Nor did Gregory's references to the Phrygian king remain only on the level of myth. The "descendants" of Midas were an all too common nuisance in fourth-century Cappadocia, he maintained, though he did not look for them in contemporary royal circles, but rather in common grave-robbers. The frequency of attacks on the avarice of those who stole from tombs may indicate how widespread the phenomenon had become, but in any case it certainly demonstrates that a good amount of property was being interred with the corpses of those from the upper levels of society. Epigram 34 brings together neatly the mythic example of avarice and its contemporary equivalent:

> In Phrygia lived that Midas who demanded
> All things turn to gold. They did; but he
> Succumbed to hunger: rich by wish, yet he
> Still died. You'll suffer now the same, graves' thief,
> So that all men may learn to honor graves.[44]

Such cupidity was only the most extreme appearance of what Gregory, borrowing from Cynic-Stoic diatribe, characterized as the essential foolishness of the vice. He gave much attention to this diseased state of the avaricious sinner. The pathography he developed reveals his first-hand knowledge of contemporary medical science, as well as a sensitivity to illnesses occasioned by his own frail physical condition.[45] His description of the vice as a disease is, in fact, a collection of numerous symptoms and illnesses. They are seen in most concentrated fashion in his poem *Adversus opum amantes* (PG 37:856–84). There is, first of all, the insanity of one who loves money. He considers he is flying without wings, ploughing without oxen, is healthy when actually he is sick. This final misconception only aggravates his condition, for thinking he is not ill, he refuses to turn to a doctor for help (verses 6–20). Gregory also makes a number of observations on the imagined or real actions of the *philargyros* which give evidence of his thinking in rudimentary iconographical terms. At one point he mentions the greedy man vomiting up his wealth (a detail found already in the Book of Job) and when speaking of usury, Gregory notes that the business of interest-taking is always enacted on the fingers.[46] The movement of the hands, counting, grasping, touching money, subsequently became a common part of the iconography of avarice.

The proper attitude towards the goods of this world was for Gregory one of truly philosophic rejection. That is to say, he found a model for his own ascesis in the behavior of those pagan philosophers, and especially the Cynics, who had renounced wealth for a simple and leisurely life of contemplation. In his farewell address to the ecclesiastical authorities at Constantinople, he spoke of his contempt for their worldly ambitions in terms which made of himself a Christian Democritus, whose "temperance caused him to be accused of insanity, since he laughed at everything, perceiving that the things which were given serious attention by the majority were worthy of laughter."[47] But the philosophers' model was not one Gregory could accept without some revision: philosophy could at best be merely a forerunner of Christian ascesis for him.

How Gregory's synthesis worked becomes clear in his view of Crates the Cynic, who had been rejected by Clement of Alexandria for his vainglory, but had been approved by Origen for his renunciation of wealth. Gregory, in fact, harmonizes both of these views. He, too, saw in Crates a man of real stature, for while on a ship caught in a storm at sea, Crates had not hesitated a moment to prove his freedom from physical attachments by throwing all his riches off the overloaded vessel into the deep.[48] This latter anecdote was to catch the imagination of the monastic communities in particular, and was in fact to become a common and central metaphor of their own renunciation of wealth. Yet, for Gregory, Crates had also paraded his liberation from worldly cares ostentatiously by proclaiming it to all who would listen, and this clearly marked him as a lover more of fame than of wisdom. It was precisely here that in Gregory's thinking Christian asceticism provided a corrective to philosophy, and it is also here that Gregory's ethical imagination most influenced developing anchorites such as Evagrius Ponticus. Gregory illustrated Christianity's vision of the philosophers by referring to Crates in the midst of an accolade for one of his own intimate friends, Basil the Great:

> [Basil's] wealth was to possess nothing and he considered the cross with which he lived alone more precious than a great amount of riches. . . . He had no need of a dais and a vain glory nor of that public proclamation: "Crates liberates Crates the Theban," for he gave his effort to be morally best, not to seem to be. . . . He was poor and unkempt, but also not ambitious; and after cheerfully throwing overboard everything he ever owned, he sailed lightly over the sea of life.[49]

In his retirement, Gregory also described his own renunciation of worldly cares, including the preparation of speeches, as an act of throwing all his gold into the deep.[50] Yet, at this point one has clearly arrived at the limits of rhetoric, for however much Gregory inveighed against the avarice of the rich and is reported to have led a simple life himself, this did not mean to him that he had to relinquish all the prerogatives of the wealthy.[51] He did not demand complete poverty from the rich: they were free to chose between giving everything to Jesus (that is, the poor) or sharing with the indigent by giving alms. But even more, he did not feel called upon to demand from himself a renunciation of all possessions. Like many other ecclesiastical officials of the fourth and fifth centuries, Gregory retained as bishop the estate he had inherited, using it finally as the place of his retirement.

Ultimately, he willed all his property to the church of Nazianzus for the poor. Yet, Basil's earlier words on such testamentary almsgiving show that this hardly represented what his contemporaries considered ideal behavior.[52] Gregory's monastic practice and his views on the sin amount, in effect, to a gentleman's ascesis. His pronouncements on avarice, as influential as they were, must be seen in the light of his intellectual pursuits rather than the practical demands of cenobitic perfection.

JOHN CHRYSOSTOM'S RHETORIC OF AVARICE

This situation is quite different with John Chrysostom (344/54–407), who only left the *coenobium* because his ascetic zeal had severely deteriorated the state of his health. His monastic preferences sharpened his attack on the vice, and the rich altogether, something which did little to lengthen his tenure as bishop in Constantinople. Everywhere one can feel the cutting edge of his rhetoric, blending together Christian principles with philosophical commonplaces acquired through his formal education to create an admonition against the sin which focuses on both its social disruption in Christian society and the internal disturbance of the *philargyros* himself. So convinced was Chrysostom of the centrality of the vice that he used every possible occasion to demand its correction. In fact, no matter what he chose as the main topic of a homily, he was able to bring avarice into the moral exhortations with which he concluded his speech.[53]

The social dimension of Chrysostom's thinking is apparent first of all in the pastoral intent with which he approaches the vice in his myriad homilies and treatises. Almsgiving is raised to a new level of immediacy and importance here, becoming the primary means for counteracting social injustice. In Chrysostom's works one can see in especially sharp outline what was developing into the common pastoral method for dealing with the sin. It is essentially the same double-edged weapon Basil had used: on the positive side, intimating the joys of heaven attendant on avarice's defeat through almsgiving; on the negative side, pointing to the gloom which awaits those who persist in the vice. It is typical of Chrysostom's ascetic leanings that he frequently emphasized the latter element. An echo of the Ebionitic tradition is unmistakable in his stress on the pains of hell as the just deserts for those who persevere in their avarice. Indeed, he presented the yearning of the avaricious sinner as a type of hell already: death will only bring about a change in the location of the punishment he undergoes.[54]

In keeping with his view of almsgiving, Chrysostom perceives wealth in itself as a neutral entity, an *adiaphoron*; its moral value depends finally on its use.[55] It comes as no surprise to see him express this balanced and considered opinion, generally accepted by Christian thinkers since Clement of Alexandria. Nevertheless, Chrysostom's ties to cenobitic monasticism also made him capable of throwing the negative possibilities of wealth into the greatest relief. Yet, as with the Cappadocians, Chrysostom was frequently not preaching to monks but to lay audiences composed of the rich and the poor alike, and his monastic fervor was held in check by these contexts. Here, his point of view is that both those with and those without possessions have a legitimate function in the social order, though the just exchange involved in this system is somewhat different from the socio-economic vision of *Hermas*. For Chrysostom, God endures the existence of the rich so that they might care for the indigent. Poverty has its place because it strengthens the poor in virtue, but at the same time it is an occasion for the rich, as well, to gain heaven through almsgiving. The balance in Chrysostom's view is more completely moral; that is to say, both sides must overcome temptations which grow out of penury or wealth. The poor, too, may be avaricious by desiring only a small amount of money.[56] But it is just as obvious that the focal point remains for Chrysostom what it had been for *Hermas*. The rich are at the center of attention here, as well:

> Do you not see how God allowed us all things in common? For if He permitted there to be poor people in the midst of prosperity, this, too, was for the encouragement of those who are rich, so that by giving alms to the indigent, the wealthy might be able to strip their sins from themselves.[57]

So completely is Chrysostom's attention focused on almsgiving that he is willing to make allowances for the possession of wealth, if only it be put to good use. His justification of the patriarchs' property demonstrates clearly one way in which this principle works. Job and Abraham, to whom he refers most frequently, were not damned by their wealth because they received it from God Himself and used it to aid the poor. They also opened their homes to all travelers.[58] Of course, Chrysostom's presentation of the patriarchs makes of them obviously idealized studies, but he is even willing to accept, though with great reservation, the less pastoral world of fourth-century commerce as a potentially justifiable source of income.[59] If someone has not acquired with greed and gives to the poor, Chrysostom tells a fictive interlocutor in one work, then such a person is not evil.[60] There are, in fact, relatively few means of acquisition which he rejects *a priori* as the result of avarice, and they are all commonplaces: usury; tax-collecting; the artificial raising of prices, especially during famines; and hunting for an inheritance (which Libanius had also found distasteful).[61] In practical terms, riches from most other sources do not fall under Chrysostom's concept of the sin, as long as they are used for alms.

But of course in absolute – and mythic – terms, they all do. Any division of property based on the distinction "mine–yours" can only be a result of the deterioration of humankind's original equality. It is this lesson from humanity's mythic history which Chrysostom has in mind when he tells a fictitious rich man that his inheritance is ultimately illicit:

> Now could you, going back through many generations, show that your acquisition is just? You could not maintain this. It must be that its origin and its root are located in someone's injustice. Why? Because from the beginning God did not make one person rich and the other poor; nor, directing the one, did God show him many treasures of gold, but cheat the other of the search; rather, He left the same earth to all.[62]

Private property's historical foundation in avarice provides Chrysostom with an explanation for the inequalities of contemporary society which amounted to robbery. But it is obvious to him that reverting to the original commonwealth is not a realistic blueprint for society's cure. For the majority of humankind, the return to an ideal state can merely be an eschatological projection: the cold expression "mine–yours" does not exist in heaven, he notes.[63] On the earth, meanwhile, it is only the monks who have succeeded in resurrecting the pristine selflessness of the Jerusalem community. Where Chrysostom describes to the congregation at Constantinople how easily they could do away with private property and poverty, where he comes closest to formulating a practical way of achieving the ideal, his suggestions (and he repeatedly points out they are no more than this) amount, in effect, to changing the city into a *coenobium*.[64] Yet the bishop does not seriously demand monasticism from all humanity, though his refusal to accept any lesser standard for measuring complete perfection was uncomfortable enough for the rich among his congregation. In Chrysostom's work, then, the mythic background of avarice becomes one more homiletic device in the service of almsgiving. As he pointed out to the rich man whose inheritance he had just disallowed, the wealthy can indeed be good, but only by giving to others.

When the vice is allowed to fester in society, the results are catastrophic. In fact, Chrysostom radicalizes avarice's hegemony in gnomic wisdom by making it the beginning, middle, and end of all evils.[65] The egotism lying behind the vice is the cause of wars, robbery, and the strife which divides humans from each other in hatred,[66] and Chrysostom emphasizes the insatiable ferocity of the *philargyroi* by describing their destructiveness in three historical phases which mark out the corruption of human society. Avarice turned the original equality of human beings into the pettiness of private possessions. Then, through the actions of Judas, it brought treachery and betrayal into the very midst of the assembly of apostles.[67] And the end of its virulence can only be described in apocalyptic terms. The avaricious sinner is a monster:

> attacking all like hell, swallowing up everything, going about as the common enemy of the human race. For he actually desires that no one else should exist, so that he might be in possession of every-thing.[68]

To make avarice's hold on the individual sinner more rhetorically palpable, Chrysostom reverts to a technique fully developed in the diatribe literature of Antiquity, namely personification. It was common enough in this genre for the author to address directly the concepts he was dealing with, though Seneca and Persius seem to have been the first to apply this literary device to avarice.[69] Chrysostom uses a personified *philargyria* to characterize the demonic sexuality and cruelty of the vice:

> For to me poverty seems to resemble a maiden, well-behaved and beautiful and comely; but avarice a woman shaped like a beast, a Scylla and Hydra and other such monsters imagined by the fabulists.[70]

Avarice's final opponent for the control of humanity's heart and mind was the ethical nucleus of Christianity itself. The precepts of mercy and charity were countered point by point in the commands issued by the sin in the form of Mammon. Chrysostom, the trained rhetor, does not envisage this as a pitched battle between warring abstractions, but rather as a type of rancorous debate. Jesus' orders of almsgiving and love for the poor and Mammon's counter-commands of selfishness and robbery echo through the soul of humankind, where "Have mercy on the poor!" vies with an opposed "Strip away even the things they have!" The adjectives Chrysostom chose for Mammon's orders also describe the quality of the vice's reactions to humanity, for Avarice is a cruel tyrant. Chrysostom frequently applied this term of opprobrium to the personified sin; on one occasion he strengthens it by referring to the vice as an inhuman mistress (*despoina*) and savage barbarian, as well.[71] The avaricious, on the other hand, are at best oblivious to their immanent downfall, are in fact normally willing accomplices to it. They are ignorant of a wisdom so patently clear to all that Chrysostom notes it is proverbial, namely that whoever yearns for even a small profit must suffer great losses. They follow Avarice's commands at all moments in a blind obedience which Chrysostom describes as more depraved than the worship of idols. For idolaters:

> sacrifice cattle and sheep to their graven images, but *philargyria* says, "Sacrifice your own soul to me," and it has its way.[72]

The final stage of the service offered by the greedy to their master is one of slavery or forced labor. The devotion to wealth had, of course, long been understood as a form of bondage; Chrysostom's own instructor in rhetoric had included in his oration *Peri Douleias* a detailed description of the avaricious, and above all Midas, as slaves to their love of money.[73] But to this image Chrysostom adds a view of the *philargyroi* as prisoners sentenced to hard labor in the mines. Here again, their behavior is marked by an acquiescence in self-destruction and aggressiveness against all who would free them from their self-imposed torture. In this context, Avarice takes the form of their jailor, forcing them to undergo the utmost hardships, though they find her a mild and gentle mistress. They are condemned to the darkness of prison – and willingly lay chains on themselves that cannot be broken. Chrysostom's portrayal of the sinner's attributes amounts to a collage description which unites aspects of the miser with traits of his acquisitive counterpart.

This satirical burlesque is completed by the physical description of the avaricious sinner as someone with fire shooting from his eyes, snakes instead of arms, swords in the place of his teeth, winged feet, and a face half dog, half wolf.[74] At this point, of course, the sinner has clearly abandoned humanity and been joined to the vice in the all-too-real realm of demons. It was easy enough for Chrysostom to visualize this transformation because he also classified the sin as one of the desires (*epithymiai*) which is neither necessary for, nor natural to, humankind. These two criteria relate the yearning for food, drink, and sleep (natural and necessary) to lust of the flesh (natural but unnecessary) and avarice. The greed for gold and silver differs from the others because it is not an inborn part of humanity, and the proof of its alien character is supplied by the length of time this subversion was unknown to society.[75] Chrysostom refers to avarice's unnatural state very frequently. The parallels between his understanding of this matter and the inner-monastic pronouncements on the same topic in the later work by John Cassian are unmistakable.

Chrysostom, however, unlike Cassian, is generally not systematic in relating avarice to other sins and the *philargyros* to other sinners, though his works offer many scattered views of these connections. Nowhere does he establish a definitive list of vices, but those which play the greatest role in regard to avarice are the excesses of carnal desire mentioned already (i.e., gluttony, drunkenness, and lust), and, above all, envy and vainglory. The authoritative foundation for finding similarities between gluttony or drunkenness and avarice was established in the related statements of Matthew 6:24 ("You cannot serve God and Mammon") and Philippians 3:10 (Many are headed for destruction, for "their belly is their god . . ."). The glutton or drunkard is the slave of his belly, the avaricious person that of his idolized gold;

both suffer from a type of intoxication. Yet the *philargyros* is worse than the glutton, for whereas the latter may recover after a night's sleep, greed always stays with the avaricious sinner, if he can sleep at all.[76] Lust, too, is an overwhelming urge, though for Chrysostom it is born of an imbalance in the humors, while avarice stems from a mental laziness and stupor.[77] The lecherous sinner also differs from his avaricious counterpart in that he can satisfy his passionate desire, however fleetingly; the *philargyros* on the other hand, is reduced to constant yearning. Chrysostom uses a striking image of infertile sexuality drawn from ben Sirach to clarify at once the futility of the greedy sinner's empty desire and the relationship of avarice to lust. In these terms, the avaricious sinner who attempts to gain satisfaction from money is like a eunuch trying to seduce a maiden.[78]

The relationship of avarice to envy and vainglory is more complex than its connection to the carnal sins.[79] Above all, Chrysostom's attitude towards their relative seriousness is not without some ambiguity. When he compares avarice to one or the other of these vices, his varying responses to the question of which is the deadliest must be approached from the context of the homily in which each occurs and not from a hierarchical theory of hamartiology. Thus, when he insists that each Christian see himself as a member of the body of the church, he can also assert that nothing divides people from each other so much as envy. In this way, it is even worse than the root of all evils, for the greedy person is only pleased when he himself gets something, but the envious person only when someone else does not.[80] On the other hand, when Chrysostom's emphasis lies on the evil of the love of money, he can maintain that by removing wrath and envy, a sinner will more easily be able to correct his avarice.[81] Here, envy appears to be only a product of the root vice, a view which is supported elsewhere by Chrysostom's remark that the avaricious person himself, as a type of *nouveau riche*, stimulates envy of his successes even in those who are above him in social standing and see him as a threat to their authority.[82] The relationship of avarice to vainglory is similar to its relationship with envy. In a homily dealing with those who make a show of fasting (Matt. 6:16), Chrysostom argues that the question of avarice comes up at a later point in Matthew's text (see 6:19) because vainglory is of greater causal importance: nothing conditions people to love money more than the love of human glory.[83] Yet elsewhere, vainglory joins avarice in providing the occasion for all other evils, and this position of fundamental importance is also extended to pride, which Chrysostom did not altogether distinguish from vainglory.[84] The intertwined nature of avarice and vainglory's relationship is also indicated by the number of themes they have in common. Both presuppose the inherent value of possessing material objects rather than spiritual qualities. And central to the remedy for both vices is the rejection of wealth. As it appears, in Chrysostom's thought the struggle against one of these sins necessitates coming to terms with the other as well because here, too, as in Basil's work, avarice is perceived as the egotism of possession. Voluntary poverty and almsgiving are effective against the sin, but they must be accompanied by the correct motivation: Chrysostom draws on the commonplace figure of Crates and other pagan philosophers as examples of a renunciation of wealth undertaken for vainglory and warns frequently of the same faulty impulse in Christians who give alms to make a show of their wealth.[85] It is, in any case, clear that the interplay between greed and an unadulterated egotism, such as that identified in pride and vainglory, which was later to account for much reshuffling in the list of vices, is already at work in the preaching of the Cappadocians and John Chrysostom.

The bishop addresses himself to the twin problem of avarice and vainglory more frequently than to any other complex of vices, and with greater intensity than many theologians who came after him. His focus on these two sins reflects his sensitivity to the perception of a widening gap between the rich and the poor in the East at this period. Yet his homiletic concerns also left him little time to dwell systematically on either vice; his interests, in a way similar to what will be seen in the work of many Western moralists, were more pastoral than analytic. Within the framework of his solicitude to identify and cure the sinner, he did much to detail the consequences of avarice in both society and the individual soul, and his work, like that of the Cappadocians, provides us with an important view of the deepening relations between the ascetic approach to this sin and the needs of the laity. In Chrysostom's view, the monks in the hills above Antioch had succeeded in principle in overcoming avarice; their model was there for all to follow. But the practical demands of dealing with avarice's threat were not met by legislating this radical approach for the laity. Without losing sight of his ideal, Chrysostom is willing to accept a more gradual cure: for Christian society outside the *coenobium*, his compromise took the form of a daily insistence on expelling avarice through almsgiving.

3

Ascetic transformations II: soaring eagles or safety in the herd – from anchoritic to cenobitic monasticism

THE CAPITAL VICE TRADITION: EVAGRIUS PONTICUS AND THE EVIL THOUGHT OF GREED

The absolute rejection of an individual's possession of wealth, an attitude which remained an influential component in the Christian imagining of avarice, found its most analytic and organized expression initially among the ascetes who retired to the Egyptian desert in the fourth and fifth centuries to perfect their spiritual life. Their rise to prominence, and with them the power of their ascetic ideal and their poverty, signaled vast changes to come in Roman society on its way to the Christian Middle Ages.[1] The conception of material goods and greed developed by Evagrius Ponticus and John Cassian, the most important hamartiological theorists to emerge from this monastic movement, was influenced by the earlier ideas of their instructors in spiritual matters among the Cappadocians and by the thinking of John Chrysostom: Evagrius was ordained a *lector* by Basil the Great and made a deacon by Gregory Nazianzen, and Cassian was under the tutelage of John Chrysostom. Yet their imagining of avarice progressed, in effect, in the opposite direction from that of their predecessors, for whereas each of the church thinkers examined in Chapter 2 went from ascesis to the episcopacy in the course of his career, Evagrius and Cassian moved from positions within the ecclesiastical administration to life in an ascetic community by the end of their careers. It was also exclusively for these monastic groups that they composed their treatises. One finds, thus, little compromise with the realities of a lay community in their conception of avarice. Their work on the vice is not the projection of a broadly pastoral concern, but an expression of the monastic concentration on the spiritual progress of the individual and the community – the earliest, complete, analytic description and examination of avarice to be found in Christian culture. To be sure, there are important distinctions between their views of avarice which were occasioned by the differences in the specific organization and location of their audiences: Evagrius was writing for anchorites in Egypt; Cassian became acquainted with the leading personalities of the ascetic institutions in Egypt during his stay there, but he is important as a major figure in the movement of cenobitic monasticism from the East into the Latin West, though in general his role here is more that of a transmitter and adapter of received knowledge than that of an original thinker.

Evagrius Ponticus (*c.* 345–399) is the source of much of Cassian's thinking on avarice, and indeed on all the evil spirits.[2] The communities with which Evagrius was associated in Egypt, at Nitria, Scete, and the Desert of Cells, were rigorous in their approach to the Christian life and the spiritual perfection of the monk. The men living in such communities led a semi-anchoritic life: they spent most of their time in prayer, contemplation of the Scriptures, or manual labor, alone in separate cells out of sight or hearing of anyone else's dwelling, and only came together for a communal meal in the church on Saturday evening and worship on Sunday. When he entered one of these communities, the monk was expected to withdraw from the world entirely, which in spiritual terms meant that he was to sever himself from all worldly thoughts and in material terms that he was to give away all his former possessions. He maintained himself after that generally by making simple objects, such as baskets, or tending a garden near his cell and then offering the products of his labor for sale at a low price in the marketplace. From the proceeds he was to buy a small quantity of food and to give the rest of the money as alms to the poor. The need for each monk to perform his own labor was often emphasized. The Pauline dictum, that "he who will not work shall not eat" (2Thess. 3:10), was taken quite literally. Through his handiwork, the anchorite was able to avoid what was considered the disgrace of having to beg, and at the same time he was in a position to give charity to others. It is in this environment that one must understand Evagrius' description of the temptation of avarice (*philargyria*) seen in the *Practicus*, his textbook of monastic discipline for novices:

> Avarice suggests [to the monk] a long old age and the incapacity of
> the hands for work, famines which will occur and sicknesses which
> will come about, and the bitter pangs of poverty, and how shameful it
> is to receive from others what one needs.[3]

This was the evil thought (*logismos* [λογισμός]), or demon, or spirit,
as it was also called, which in the final stage of its sinful operation
persuaded the unwary monk to give up his faith in God's provision for
him and to put it instead both in his own actions to gain material
possessions and in those goods themselves, especially money.[4]

The identification of this thought with a dependence on earthly
matter and a persistence in the monk's habit of thinking in worldly
terms – in short, the identification of avarice with a type of intransigent
worldliness itself – is seen frequently in Evagrius' writings. This
attribute was especially noxious for the Egyptian communities because
it was a denial of one of their major prerequisites for spiritual
perfection: *anachoresis* (ἀναχώρησις), or the withdrawal from worldly
society. It is characteristic of Evagrius' thinking that in one of his works
he called the evil which prophesies to a monk an approaching old age
and the illnesses that come with it and which brings him to "divide his
hope with riches," not the thought of avarice, but simply the thought of
earthly matter (*hyle*).[5] Evagrius not only encouraged a renunciation of
the world, but even more an attitude of active scorn towards it. The
monk who has purged himself of avarice, he noted, derides what is here
and now, and in this way is raised up to the company of those who are
in heaven.[6] Such worldliness, when unchecked, could express itself in
three different reactions on the part of the monk towards possessions
and monetary wealth. For, the thought of avarice:

> lingers in us and upsets our contemplating, either through the
> memory of the personal estate we have given away, or through the
> eagerness with which we busy ourselves to get things that were not
> there up to now, or through the care and caution for things we
> already possess.[7]

All three of the categories established by Evagrius were tailored to the
demands of Egyptian monasticism, but this is especially true of the first.
It represents an extension by the ideology of rigorous asceticism of what
had been presented in earlier analyses as only two types of avarice,
acquisition and retention.

The remembrance of what had been given away amounted to an imperfect *anachoresis* and hence was a stumbling-block at the initial stage of the movement towards perfection. It was, perhaps, to be expected that this issue would emerge in Evagrius' writing, because the semi-anchoritic life in Egypt was one of extreme abstinence. The monks who lived in these communities denied themselves nearly all worldly possessions so that their contemplation of God would remain unimpeded by worldly matter, and it meant anything but progress in the spiritual life for a monk who had given away his house and all his former personal property to remember the comforts he had enjoyed earlier.[8] But Evagrius also has something else in mind when he speaks of the memory of what was given. Twice he uses this category in connection with almsgiving, and here he refers to the sense of regret a monk might feel after he has distributed his money to the needy.[9] It was just such regret which could lead him to give less alms, or none at all, the next time, and instead to retain for himself what he had earned in the marketplace.

In anchoritic terms, the retention of possessions was not primarily a sign of anti-social behavior, but rather another way in which the monk remained bound to the world, not liberated in the contemplation of the divinity, for no matter how insignificant he might try to make his goods appear, they had to be cared for and preserved in some manner. Every moment he spent in giving attention to such details was one less moment in which his thoughts were with God. The vexations and torments which he incurred along these lines were frequently contrasted to the freedom seen in the monk who neither retained anything more than he absolutely needed nor wished to do so:

> A monk with many possessions is a burdened vessel, and one which sinks easily in the beating of the waves, for just as an overloaded ship is racked by every wave, so is someone who has many possessions flooded over with cares. A monk without possessions is a well-equipped traveler, one who finds lodging everywhere. A monk without possessions is a soaring eagle who only flies down for provisions when need presses him. . . . Death comes and [the monk without possessions] passes away calmly, for he did not bind his soul with earthly fetters. But he who has many possessions is shackled with cares and bound with a chain like a dog. . . . And if death should

come, he gives up his possessions in a state of wretchedness: he gives over his soul in death and he does not take his eyes from material things. He is dragged away against his will like a runaway slave.[10]

For the category of acquisition, as well, Evagrius and his companions were responding to a specific monastic need rather than simply countering a general longing to have more, for "more" in this case followed the ascetic guidelines set up in 1 Timothy 6:8 (". . . if we have food and clothing, let us be content with these").[11] Among the anchorites at Scete in particular, acquisition was felt to be a highly dangerous temptation, for they were actually not without all possessions: they were permitted to own tools and materials needed for their work, a habit, and enough food for one meal a day of some bread, or a few beans, and water. As will be seen, cenobitic monasticism in Egypt clearly addressed the problem posed by even these few belongings. For anchorites to desire the possession of more clothing than was allowed, or money with which their needs could be more comfortably satisfied, was considered the result of φιλαργυρία. Once the monk was seized by this desire, there was no end to his longing for more, nor the amount of effort he would expend to acquire ever more possessions. In an echo of earlier Christian concerns, avarice was, thus, described as "the enchantress of the love of work, the adviser for insomnia . . . an insatiable mania, an iniquity obsessed by many cares,"[12] and this desire seemed to feed on itself, to have a life of its own.

The ascetic rigors which Evagrius recommended for members of the Egyptian communities could not sustain such a disruption as that caused by avarice. These rigors had as their goal the true knowledge of the divinity, but this was a level of perfection which could only be reached after the passions (*pathe*) of the soul had been brought under firm control and the monk, no longer subject to the turmoils the passions produced, was able to engage in the contemplation of God and the substances He had created. Hence, Evagrius established the initial stage of monastic discipline for anchorites as a spiritual method for purifying the impassioned part of the soul in order to achieve the condition of *apatheia* (ἀπάθεια).[13] Demons attempted to keep the monk from this state of peace by attacking that part of the soul in which the passions resided; against anchorites their normal weapon in this onslaught was one of the evil thoughts. Because all further progress in the spiritual life depended on the monk's combat against the *logismoi*, a major portion of Evagrius' written works is devoted to their analysis, and within this corpus one can identify the origins of the treatise on vices and virtues as a medieval genre.[14] One of the monk's essential duties established by these writings was the expulsion of the evil thoughts before they had a chance to linger in the soul and stir up the passions. To help the ascete accomplish this task, Evagrius suggested certain remedies. For each of the eight evil thoughts he recommended a series of biblical passages which could serve as meditative armament in driving out the enemy. Specific virtuous habits were also to be cultivated. In the combat against avarice, the chief means to be used by the monk were charity (*agape*) and an almost complete poverty, or state of "possessionlessness" (*aktemosyne* [ἀκτημοσύνη]), which is to say, a state in which the monk owned only what was necessary for his productive labor and a minimum of food and clothing. Charity was the virtue that could not only destroy the monk's desire for money and keep him from storing up stockpiles of food, but even more eliminate his connection to and dependence on the transitory world itself.[15] By exercising this virtue carefully, Evagrius taught, the monk would achieve a condition of poverty in which he desired only the acquisition of wisdom and not that of wealth or fine clothing.

That the monk was faced here with an enormously difficult task was all the more reason for him to be vigorous and watchful when driving out this thought. The particular obstacles to be overcome lay in the nature of the enemy he was opposed to. Avarice, as all Christian authors knew from 1 Timothy 6:10, was the root of all evils. For Evagrius, this meant it played a special role in nourishing the passions, and therefore it was essential that the monk rid himself of it completely:

> Whoever wants to cut down the passions must chop out the root, for – if *philargyria* remains – it is absolutely of no use to prune the branches, since even if they are cut off altogether they will flourish again in no time.[16]

The very tenacity of worldly thinking, of the bonds which tied human beings to earthly matter, created a problem for the monk's spiritual progress and made avarice appear to him ubiquitous as the source of all actions counter to God. This tenacity is what Evagrius had in mind when he wrote that greed kept the thoughts of an avaricious person on possessions in the same way as a hungry person's desire for food kept his thoughts constantly on bread and a thirsting person's need to drink kept his on water.[17]

The perseverance of avarice was one of the major obstacles the monk was up against; its deceitfulness was the other. All of the demons resorted to ruses to fight against ascetes, but *philargyria* was especially cunning and inventive in this. The demon of avarice could bring a monk to profess love openly for his brothers and to perform good deeds for them, and yet all the while his eye was really on the acquisition of money.[18] Even charity, the chief weapon for the expulsion of this thought, was liable to perversion. Almsgiving was a necessary activity for the monk; however, the desire to have money to give to the poor was not a virtue, but rather the deceit of evil.[19] Most particularly, avarice could bring the monk to nullify his renunciation of the world and accept instead the position of an administrator who took pains to ease the plight of the needy. The deeds he performed in their service were all good, but they did nothing to sever his ties to earthly matter, and they led him imperceptibly to care more for his reputation in society than for meditation on the divinity. Such a person:

> inspects the city's prisons and, but of course!, he redeems those who are sold as slaves. He cleaves to rich women and he points out those who are worthy of help and, again, he admonishes others who are abundantly wealthy to renounce the world. And so in this way, having gradually deceived his soul, he subjects it to thoughts of avarice and delivers it to the demon of vainglory.[20]

As can be seen from this quotation, in Evagrius' thinking *philargyria* was related very specifically to the other *logismoi*. The most important context in which this connection is found, significant because of its influence on Cassian and, thus, its implications for the further history of avarice throughout the Middle Ages, is that of the eight evil thoughts. This conception of eight chief categories of sinfulness, which later became known as the eight Capital Vices (the precursors of the Seven Deadly Sins), had its beginnings in the monastic environment of fourth-century Egypt. Whether Evagrius was an innovator in creating the octad of evil thoughts or simply handed on what had become the common oral teaching of his predecessors in the monastic life is impossible to know. This issue must remain for us where it stood for the historian Gennadius of Marseilles in the fifth century. Evagrius, he remarked, was either the first to give attention to the eight chief thoughts or learned of them from those who were the first.[21] Using an acronym taken from the initial letters of the Latin names for the Capital Vices, one can describe the usual Evagrian order of *logismoi* as GLATIAVS (gluttony, lust, avarice, sadness, wrath, sloth, vainglory, pride).[22] However, Evagrius pointed out in chapter ten of the *Practicus* that sadness could be understood to follow from the frustration of the desire to possess, but it could also result from the action of wrath. In only one work, *De octo spiritibus malitiae*, did he vary the order of thoughts so that sadness was placed after wrath, but it was this resultant GLAITAVS sequence which was used by Cassian and was the one familiar to medieval writers who drew upon the Latin author's works. The composition and sequence of evils making up the *logismoi* (or Capital Vices) was to change significantly in the course of the Middle Ages, but it is important to note that even at the very earliest stage of the octad's history, the order of these categories of immorality was liable to alteration.

Avarice is always found in the third position within Evagrius' octad. Its placement in this system was more than a matter of numerical nicety. The evil thoughts were ordered, as Irenée Hausherr first suggested, in a way which roughly reflects the monk's spiritual progress.[23] At the beginning of his monastic career (and at the head of the list of *logismoi*), the monk was faced with the task of controlling the coarse desires of the body; as he made progress in the anchoritic life he had to confront more spiritualized temptations, and these culminated in vainglory and pride, which became especially dangerous when all the previous demons had been defeated. Avarice had very firm links in both of these directions. It was connected to gluttony and lust in that it, too, was an overweening desire for what one might call creature comforts. Like the first two thoughts, *philargyria* could be identified as one of humanity's more dangerous desires, and, as has already been seen, Evagrius likened its tenacity to the unending need of the body for food and drink. But avarice also looked towards the more spiritualized evils which followed it. Since expelling this thought meant severing one's spiritual ties once and for all to the world outside the monastic cell, it stood, in effect, on the threshold of those temptations which arose more directly from the difficulties of the meditative life itself. Most immediately, the failure to come to grips with *philargyria* was seen to lead to anger and depression, for these partially had their origin in the frustrations caused by a greedy desire which, by its very nature, could never be satisfied fully. Evagrius gave voice to this connection in a typically metaphorical gnome:

> The houses of the avaricious will be filled with the beasts of wrath, and the birds of sadness will nest in them.[24]

The particular importance of avarice in Evagrius' thinking can be seen all the more clearly by taking note of the other context in which he placed it. The archetypal pattern for any spiritual trial of a Christian, and especially for one involved in the struggles of anchoritic monasticism, had been supplied by the gospel accounts of Jesus' temptations in the desert (Matt. 4:1–11, Luke 6:1–13, see also Mark 1:12). Evagrius provided an exegetical interpretation of these three attempts at seduction by referring to three of the evil thoughts. When the devil challenged Jesus to turn stones into bread, he used gluttony to tempt Jesus to sin; his next offer of the kingdoms of the world and their glory in return for Jesus' homage was a temptation through avarice; and his final attempt, to make Jesus throw himself from the parapet of the temple, was a provocation through the evil thought of vainglory.[25] This triad responded to the single most important model of resisting temptation which the Christian had at his disposal and, in a certain sense, gluttony, avarice, and vainglory provided the leadership for the rest of the evil thoughts as well. These three were the captains, the front line of battle, in the demons' fight to keep the monk from *apatheia*. Before the anchorite could move on to the higher stages of monastic discipline, Evagrius taught, he had to be successful in particular in expelling the same evils Jesus had had to contend with, for once he was wounded by one of these three, he would quickly fall into the hands of the battalions which followed them.

Within the terms of this triad, *philargyria* was raised to a position of primary importance in the monastic tradition long before Pride's hegemony in this role, a fact which must be kept in mind when investigating the further history of avarice. It can also be noted that, as opposed to the uncertainty surrounding the origins of the octad of evil thoughts, Evagrius' interpretation of the scriptural passage seen here has a very definite and identifiable background. Many earlier writers had mentioned one or the other of the evil qualities in their exegesis of the temptations of Jesus, and their work provides an initial point of departure from which one can identify the tradition in which Evagrius' interpretation stands. By virtue of the scriptural narration alone, the first temptation was liable to be seen as gluttony, and such an understanding of the matter is at least implied in patristic commentary as early as the work of Tertullian.[26] Clement of Alexandria may have been alluding to the second temptation when he noted that Jesus was rich because he disdained the earth and the gold which is found in and under it and which had been offered to him, along with all the glory possible, by the devil. This suggestive relationship between the devil's action and a temptation of monetary wealth was made explicit as early as the *Pseudo-Clementines homily 8.*[27] Finally, the last temptation was examined in the light of the devil's self-exaltation, and its destruction by Jesus' humility, in the work of Irenaeus.[28]

Somewhat closer to Evagrius' triad is the exegesis by Origen, who used all three of the *termini* his spiritual disciple was to employ later. However, Origen neither mentioned all three together in one work, nor, with the exception of gluttony, did he use the technical terms as a means for interpreting specific temptations. Avarice and vainglory, for example, are mentioned together with lust and other unnamed *pathe* in the course of his commentary on the temptation of the kingdoms, but only as a description of the devil's method of control over the empires of human beings.[29] Origen may have influenced the development of the triad, but only indirectly. Much more to the point is the interpretation by Gregory Nazianzen. Gregory, whom Evagrius regarded as his spiritual father, had encouraged the Christian to use Jesus' example when fighting the temptations of the devil. When Satan attacked through a feeling of want (*chreia*), as he had done when he urged Jesus to turn rocks into bread, the Christian was to think of the spiritual bread sent him from heaven. If he laid snares of vainglory (*kenodoxia*), which he had used on the parapet of the temple, the Christian was to be mindful of controlling his self-elation. And when he wrestled against him using greediness (*aplestia* [ἀπληστία]), the Christian was to refuse this temptation as Jesus had rejected the offer of the kingdoms.[30] The differences between Evagrius' triad and Gregory's exegesis are obvious: Gregory used the order of temptations found in Matthew's account, did not specify here that the devil's weapons were evil thoughts, and also employed two terms which are not to be seen in Evagrius' interpretation. Nevertheless, the evidence of Gregory's work is highly suggestive, for it contains in embryo the essence of what Evagrius, too, found in the gospel account.[31]

The triad, as well as the concept of eight evil thoughts, remained a familiar construction in moral theology. This is especially true in the East where, like the octad, Evagrius' moral exegesis of the temptation narrative was passed on directly from his works with very little alteration.[32] The Latin West frequently gave more attention to a different grouping of three evil qualities which is found first in Augustine's writings, but Evagrius' exegesis of the temptations in the desert, though it was not the only one which authors drew upon, still formed the basis for one of the most common understandings of Jesus' temptations well into the late medieval period.[33] There were also, as one might expect, numerous attempts to harmonize all of the existing triads into one parallel system of threes.[34] In all of this, it should be reiterated, avarice, the evil thought which was comprehended as the love of money and possessions, retained the same position of basic importance which it had occupied for a monastic environment in the work of Evagrius Ponticus.

EARLY MONASTIC LITERATURE AND THE TEMPTATION OF GREED

The positioning of avarice within the Capital Vice tradition may be said to begin, then, in the later fourth century in Nitria, Scete, and the Desert of Cells. The conception of the evil thought developed here found its most systematic statement in Evagrius' many treatises, but it remains to be seen how much it was in accordance with the understanding of *philargyria* among other eastern ascetic communities. Here, too, the specificity provided by a monastic context is clearly in the foreground of considerations of the evil thought, and in a number of different genres.

Athanasius' early saint's life documenting the career of Anthony (*c.* 251–356) had already demonstrated how dangerous avarice and the memory of one's former possessions were to beginning anchorites. Both are described as part of the arsenal of evil thoughts which the devil, envious of Anthony's resolve to be an ascete, whispers to him in an attempt to make him abandon his plan. Among those qualities which Athanasius specifically mentions the demons fear in conscientious monks is their lack of avarice (τὸ ἀφιλάργυρον).[35] Furthermore, a later example of the developing *tractatus de vitiis* genre transmitted under the name of the fifth-century abbot Nilus depicts the careless monk's failure to come to terms with *philargyria* precisely as a disregard for ascetic priorities. The avaricious monk makes the physical labor needed to earn money his primary occupation; prayer and other spiritual exercises only play a secondary role for him. Worse still, he justifies his behavior by a deliberate misinterpretation of 2 Thessalonians 3:10 ("he who will not work shall not eat"), the authoritative text used in its common ascetic understanding to insist on each monk's doing an *appropriate* amount of work with his hands.[36]

But the ramifications of monastic φιλαργυρία are seen most vividly in the genre of short anecdotes composed as reports of the deeds and sayings of some of the desert monks. These "apophthegms" are a product of the fourth- and fifth-century ascetic communities. A few of the narratives in the *Historia Lausiaca*, assembled about 420 by Palladius, a disciple of Evagrius and later Bishop of Helenopolis, emphasize the interrelationship between defeating avarice and success-fully withdrawing from worldly society. In one of these, Palladius speaks autobiographically of a certain brother who has been with him from his youth. He has defeated the passion for wealth, and he leaves it to God to provide for his daily sustenance, but he still must always pray that he press no one, especially not rich people and sinners, to give him something for his needs.[37] The *Apophthegmata Patrum*, another collection of stories dealing with the lives of the desert monks, was put into written form somewhat later in the fifth century, though it reflects monastic developments of a much earlier period.[38] As in Evagrius' work, the subject of numerous apophthegms in this assemblage is the necessity of a complete renunciation of possessions at the outset of the ascetic life and the dangers inherent in ignoring this dictum. In one frequently transmitted narrative, a brother who distributed his property to the poor but retained a few things for his own use is told by Anthony to buy some fresh meat in town and attach it to his body before returning. He is mauled by hungry dogs and birds of prey on his way back. In the same way, Anthony tells him, demons torment those who wish to keep money for themselves.[39] Elsewhere, the monks were admonished to retain only the means necessary for a bare subsistence. Money was, of course, to be avoided altogether,[40] but an indication of the essentially oral ideal of anchoritic life is that books were also represented as being suspect. The ascetic communities' literal understanding of Matthew 19:21 is well illustrated by the anecdote of the monk who possessed only a copy of the gospels. He disposed of it eventually, saying, "I have sold the word which said, 'Sell everything you have and give it to the poor.'"[41]

Of course, the anchorites whose literary bequest has been the subject of investigation up to now were not alone in the desert. In the earlier fourth century Pachomius established a system of walled monasteries in Egypt which one can identify as the origin of cenobitic monasticism as it was also to appear in the West. The influence of Pachomius' thought and of his ascetic foundations reached eventually from Basil the Great in Cappadocia to Cassian in Gaul. There is even some evidence to suggest that Evagrius may have borrowed from him as well.[42] These Pachomian monasteries aimed for a uniform communal life in which the cenobites lived and worked together in poverty, but they also necessitated more obedience from the individual monk than did the looser-knit communities of anchorites. The smooth functioning of the *coenobium* made binding legislation unavoidable. The inchoate monastic rules which Pachomius and his disciples developed to ensure the success of their institutions also show the importance of avarice in this new monastic environment.

Pachomius stressed the exclusive control of possessions by the corporate unit of the monastery and, thus, he legislated the total poverty of the individual ascete within that unit. The precepts he established in his rule expressly forbid the monk to have any personal property in his cell whatsoever, especially not money.[43] Specific admonitions against avarice in cenobitic legislation were then intensified by Orsiesius, who succeeded Petronius to the abbacy of the Pachomian monasteries (and was soon himself to be succeeded by

Theodore) after the death of their founder. The wall around the monastery made it easier to ensure that a monk's separation from his former life was complete, but it was obviously not foolproof; the *Liber Orsiesii* warns against the avaricious temptation to retain ownership of some property upon entrance to the monastic community:

> lest someone deceived by a foolish thought – nay, even ensnared by the devil's traps – say in his heart, "When I die, I will give what I have to the brethren."[44]

As the Pachomian ideal spread, so did avarice in the context of cenobitic texts. Basil the Great asserted in his *Regulae brevius tractatae* that total renunciation is the keynote of monastic life: when Jesus said that no one could be his disciple without giving up all he possessed, he taught that it is impossible for someone to please God among all the things which distract the soul.[45] The works of the unknown author who is referred to now under the double name of Macarius/Symeon, writing at the end of the fourth and beginning of the fifth centuries and closely associated with the Cappadocian monks, contain frequent admonitions against *philargyria* as the "stronghold of evil" and repeated appeals to defeat this monastic enemy in one's thoughts:

> For it happens that [a monk] is externally poor and without wealth and internally he rejoices in wealth and is a friend of the rich; and if it happens that someone bequeaths him his wealth, he turns away [from ascesis]. Thus, I demand a way of life which is *aphilargyros*, so that should he happen across riches, he experiences distaste for them, he hates them, he avoids them like fire.[46]

These saints' lives, treatises on the vices, apophthegms, rules for cenobites, and homilies all make it clear how central the defeat of avarice was considered to be for initiates into the monastic life. But while they assert the specificity of the evil thought in its ascetic context, their presentation of it is never as analytically precise as what Evagrius offered. Evagrius is the first author to systematize the monastic conceptions of *philargyria*, to make the Greek noun into a *terminus technicus* in his analysis (undoubtedly on the basis of its use in 1Tim. 6:10), and to depict the temptation in full detail. With Evagrius Ponticus, the theory of avarice as a stumbling block to monastic perfection achieved its most fully realized statement. Yet Evagrius is also the theoretician of anchoritic monasticism. For him, avarice remained primarily a threat to the individual's progress towards a spiritual union with God; it did not yet take the form of a disturbance in the network of monastic society.

JOHN CASSIAN'S TRANSFORMATION OF *PHILARGYRIA* FOR WESTERN MONASTICISM

Evagrius' thinking did not, on the whole, reach moralists in the West without intermediaries. His major interpreter in this direction was John Cassian (*c.* 360–433/35). As will be seen, Cassian did not act as a slavish disciple, but rather as an adapter and reviser of Evagrius' asceticism for the cenobitic requirements of Roman Gaul. His transmission of eastern concepts of monasticism to the West was in itself only the continuation of a general tendency which can be observed as early as Athanasius' exiles in Europe and the work of Jerome or Rufinus.[47] However, the octad of evil thoughts, which he learned about among the Egyptian monks and made an essential element of his own teaching, was an innovation which he introduced into western moral theology. Cassian had become acquainted with the cenobitic life at a monastery near the Cave of the Nativity in Bethlehem, had moved on to the communities of Egypt, including the anchoritic colonies of Nitria and Scete, and then arrived in Gaul around 415 to establish monasteries after having been a disciple of John Chrysostom in the church hierarchy in Constantinople.[48] The history of the octad in the West, and of avarice in its context, can be said to begin in earnest with Cassian's literary activity for his monastic communities in Marseilles.

His concept of *filargyria* is, in its outlines, largely dependent on Evagrius, and the wider contexts in which he placed it, though they already afford a glimpse of his more eclectic spirit, in the main show the influence of the earlier writer.[49] In both the *Instituta*, his major description of cenobitic monasticism, and the *Conlationes*, which he modeled on the conferences of the desert monks, Cassian used the octad in its GLAITAVS order.[50] Furthermore, he also drew upon Evagrius' exegesis of the temptation narrative. However, he referred to both detailed gospel accounts of this episode and offered a different list of correspondences for each, without feeling compelled to harmonize their disparate triads: gluttony, vainglory, and pride for the order of temptations given by Matthew; and the more closely Evagrian gluttony, avarice, and pride for Luke's version.[51] From Evagrius he also borrowed a number of other methods for dividing the eight categories of evil into smaller units, though here again the specifics of his discussion cannot, finally, be said to result from one source alone.[52] Each of these subdivisions is based on a different principle and Cassian's scheme which presents all of them together in the *Conlationes* is more a collection of ideas on the interrelation of the concepts rather than an attempt to integrate them into a new system. But in any case, they reflect on avarice's connection with the other members of the octad.

The eight concepts are distinguished first of all by their kinds, which is to say that some, such as gluttony, are natural to humanity, whereas others – and avarice is the exclusive example taken from the octad – are not part of human instinct, are outside human nature.[53] In *Conlationes*, 5.8, Cassian looked back to related statements by earlier Christian writers, among others Gregory Nazianzen and above all John Chrysostom, to explain in more particular detail what he meant by this distinction.[54] Avarice's object, he argued, is not an essential element for the human soul, body, or the maintenance of biological life. The instinctive needs of human nature are met by food alone; possessions are merely foreign to it, and a greed for material objects can only be the result of its corruption.[55] Avarice is, thus, not inevitable in human society, and Cassian proves this point by citing two familiar *topoi*, one historical (humankind's Golden Age, during which the temptation was unknown), the other anthropological (the existence of a tribal communism among certain primitive peoples which allows them to be thoroughly free of avarice).[56] The "inhuman" quality of *filargyria* had a positive side, too, since precisely because it lay outside humanity's nature, the prospects for avoiding it were good. A monk would always feel the pangs of hunger, so that gluttony would remain a constant threat. But through a correct renunciation of worldly possessions and submission to monastic obedience, the monk could at a stroke extinguish all the desire of avarice within the soul.

Cassian again relied on Evagrius in distinguishing four groups within the octad in terms of their mode of performance: gluttony and lechery can only take place through bodily activity, pride and vainglory do not require physical action at all, the temptations of avarice and wrath often come about through an external impulse, sloth and sadness arise from an inner provocation.[57] For the third group here, Cassian seems to have meant only that some material object, a coin in the case of avarice, frequently served as the catalyst leading to evil action. It was for this reason that he emphasized the necessity of a total renunciation of property, teaching that a monk must live "according to the cenobitic discipline, so that from the goods he has given away he does not allow even a single penny to remain in his possession."[58] The special relationship Cassian asserted between *filargyria* and wrath has its place in Evagrius' work, as has already been seen; but here, too, other sources may have influenced him as well.[59]

Avarice's genetic connection with both lust and wrath is part of Cassian's reflection on the concatenation of the first six members in the octad. These are related in such a way that an excess of the preceding evil becomes the breeding ground for the one following. An over-abundance of lust leads to avarice and avarice, then, spills over into wrath. The eradication of these six follows the same pattern, moving from gluttony to sloth. Of *filargyria* and its immediate relatives, Cassian notes that "in order to extinguish wrath, we must stamp out avarice; in order to uproot avarice, we must prune off lust."[60] Vainglory and pride are distinguished from the previous six because they flourish precisely when these others have successfully been removed. Though a structured relationship of this type may have been implied at least by the very ordering which Evagrius gave to the eight evil thoughts, its full genetic characteristics were made an explicit and enduring part of the presentation of the octad first by Cassian.[61]

His analysis of avarice itself again reveals the forming hand of Evagrius. Cassian used the same three internal divisions of the concept as are found in the *Antirrheticus* and presented its origins and motivation in much the same way as had the earlier writer.[62] Yet, if the outlines of Cassian's view of avarice are familiar from Evagrius' work, his detailed analysis of the subject is not. Cassian was too eclectic a writer to remain bound to a solitary model or to add nothing of his own. In effect, his examination of the concept shows evidence of change in two different areas: organization and exemplary images. Some of what is new here amounts only to the reworking of material he had become acquainted with in Evagrius' teachings, some alterations are the result of new influences on his thinking, and others represent his own real innovations in the tradition. Whatever their origin, these changes illustrate his orientation of the idea of avarice along new monastic lines, ones which were to be of major importance for the further history of the topic.

One must remember that Cassian wrote in Gaul for a monasticism that was becoming increasingly cenobitic, more likely to emphasize the orderly spiritual progress of the monk within his community than the outstanding achievements of individual anchorites, and which needed for its adherents a practical and methodical guide to the daily exercise of communal asceticism such as is seen in the *Instituta*.[63] Cassian's organizational talents were well suited for this task. The various methods for subdividing the eight categories of the octad – he now referred to them as *vitia* or *spiritus* – which Evagrius had dealt with in separate works, Cassian brought together in one and presented in a more tightly organized form. More importantly, he developed a list of progeny for each of these Capital Vices, collecting in a brief and easily memorized series phenomena that had come to be related to each major heading of evil. The individual faults born from avarice are given as: lying, fraudulence, thefts, perjury, desire for filthy lucre, false testimony, violence, savageness, and rapaciousness.[64] Though earlier writers were obviously acquainted with the notion that certain evils follow in subordinate fashion from other more serious failings, no writer before Cassian had generated the particular groupings he did, and certainly not with his thoroughness. After his work, the production of such series became a habit of moral theologians.

There are various precedents, scriptural and patristic, for viewing some of the sins which Cassian included among *filargyria*'s entourage as part of the phenomenon of greed, but the final form of the list is his own creation. Theft and false testimony are mentioned together in a biblical passage which Cassian cited as the authoritative injunction against material possessions in the monastery, namely Jesus' words to the rich youth in Matthew 19:16–22. Mark's account of this incident adds the avoidance of fraud to the commandments which must be completed by total poverty.[65] Titus 1:7 gives the desire for filthy lucre among the criteria proving a man's unsuitability to be made bishop, and

Paul enjoins the Corinthians to have nothing to do with a Christian who is, among other things, avaricious and rapacious.[66] The remaining progeny make explicit appearances in patristic discussions of greed's qualities or its subordinate followers. Tertullian had already written of *mendacium* and *periurium* as servants of cupidity, and the author of the *Vita S. Syncleticae* included perjury with fraud in a series of vices which follow φιλαργυρία.[67] More suggestively, Basil the Great had asked:

> Who is the father of lying? Who is the maker of forgeries? Who brings forth perjury? Is it not wealth? Not the zeal for wealth?[68]

Inhumanitas and *violentia*, too, had their firm place in analyses of the sin's characteristics before Cassian, especially in the works of the Cappadocian fathers and above all John Chrysostom.[69] These last two descendants of avarice show how traditional were Cassian's sources in creating his list of progeny, for earlier authors had used them as attributes of the worldliest of human beings.

Cassian used a wide range of images and examples to impress this material on his monastic audience. The organic relationship among the vices was the subject of two metaphors which he seems to have been the first to develop: he turned contaminated water running from a spring into an image of the sins flowing from their source and, more important for the development of myriad *arbores vitiorum* later in the Middle Ages, he found a symbol of the octad in a too-shady tree which had to be cut out at the roots.[70] For each of *filargyria's* three subdivisions he pointed to a biblical figure who not only typified that variety of the vice, but had also been fittingly punished for it. The monk's desire for possessions he had never owned in his secular state was prefigured by Gehazi, Elisha's servant who was cursed with leprosy by his master for taking silver and clothing from Naaman (2Kgs. 5:20ff). In Ananias and Sapphira, struck dead for withholding money from the apostles (Acts 5:1–10), Cassian found a parallel to the avaricious monk's desire to retain some possessions out of a fear of poverty and the lack of faith. And with Judas Iscariot and his death Cassian provided his readers with a biblical warning against the desire to return to the property they had given up at their entrance to the monastic life.[71] All of these figures had been related to the negative effects of avarice before Cassian's work, though it was his innovation to place them in the scheme of the vice's internal divisions. The writer who supplied him with a model for using all three of the personages was his bishop in Constantinople, John Chrysostom.

Before Chrysostom brought them together in one work, the biblical figures had appeared separately in admonitions against avarice almost exclusively in the East. Gehazi in particular belonged to the stock repertoire of the anchoritic monks. He is the only one of the three used by Cassian's mentor in Egypt, though Evagrius identified him with the evil thought in all its varieties.[72] Palladius referred to Gehazi when reporting the words of Macarius to his avaricious disciple John; and Jerome, too, gave him a place in the hermit Hilarion's rebuff to Orion, one of the richest citizens of Eilat, who had attempted to give him gifts.[73] The episode of Ananias and Sapphira is far less frequently cited in analyses of avarice before Cassian. Its use in Chrysostom's homily may, of course, be his own creation, but Jerome's reference to it in letters to Demetrias and Heliodorus may also point to its wider circulation in the teachings of the oriental monks on *filargyria*.[74] That Judas' treason was motivated by avarice is an assertion which appears often in the Christian literature of the East, though surprisingly it is not found in explicit terms before Origen.[75] Yet, Origen's sensitive analysis of the fallen apostle, emphasizing the remnants of his goodness as well as his sin, was hardly echoed by other commentators. Didymus the Blind is representative of the larger tradition which pointed only in revulsion to his serfdom to *philargyria* and the humiliating nature of his death.[76] A text attributed to Basil the Great, furthermore, linked Judas' crime to a failure in the ascetic life by noting that a monk with possessions becomes, in fact, another Judas.[77]

As instructive as these examples are, they are isolated uses of the figures. Only Chrysostom employed them all in a concerted attack on the vice for which we have, if not his own text, then at least the notes of secretaries who listened to his homily.[78] The wild beast of avarice, he remarks here, is what "made a leper of Gehazi instead of a disciple of the prophet, brought about the death of Ananias and his people, created Judas the traitor."[79] Though it has always been notoriously difficult to find verbal echoes of Chrysostom's texts in Cassian's work, we can identify in this homily at least a model for Cassian's own.[80]

The importance of Judas in the *Instituta* went beyond his use as a mere pedagogic device, for his betrayal had not only been aimed at Jesus, but had struck at the central ideals of the apostolic community of which he had been a member.[81] For Cassian, the most valid attempt to ensure the continuity of that earliest Christian communal life was through the *coenobium*. It was for this type of asceticism that he was writing in the work he had undertaken in Marseilles at Castor's request. Its social goals were articulated first in the literature of the Pachomian tradition which Cassian praised highly in *Instituta* 4. Orsiesius, for example, paying tribute to an essentially social conception of the evil thought, had pointed out that avarice lay behind conflicts within the *coenobium* itself, when the individual monk only looked out for his own good and not for that of his neighbor.[82] Such a conception of greed colored Cassian's thinking on *filargyria* and brought to it two new impulses which accompanied the monastic concept of the vice throughout the Middle Ages. First of all, the monk's presence in a society of ascetes allowed for his own total poverty. Through the complete renunciation of all possessions, he not only separated himself from earthly matter but, as Cassian mentioned specifically, recapitulated a preliminary step towards perfection taken by the first congregation of Christians.[83] The monastic understanding of Acts 4:32 projected a community in which there had been no private ownership and all things were held in common. This rejection of personal property was actually more radical in the *coenobium* than it had been for anchorites. As has already been seen, it was impossible for pre-cenobitic monks to live without some possessions, as minimal as these might be. On the other hand, where the monastery as a whole retained the sole right of ownership, the individual monk could be absolutely free of property and, thus, apostolically poor.[84] Nor did the cenobite have to face the dangers of selling the products of his labor in the marketplace; the task of handling such matters for the community as a whole became a function of a monastic office. Here, too, the institution relieved the individual of economic responsibility. Of course, such an organization of poverty was not without its own dangers, for the wealth of monastic communities had increased rapidly – and had become a point of contention – almost from their inception, because of the threat that economic expansion would lead to the secularization of the monastic ideal.[85] Rich monasteries would continue to provide the source for a long line of accusations of avarice in the very midst of professed possessionlessness.

The other renunciation Cassian established as a prerequisite for ascetic discipline was that of the self.[86] The organization of communal life had necessitated this new impulse, for the *coenobium* needed a fairly strict regimentation of lines of authority which were based, finally, on the obedience and humility of its members. The welfare of monastic society depended to a large degree on the willingness of each monk to do the work required of him, and the social threat of avarice was felt most keenly when it led someone to refuse to labor for others and to elevate his own well-being above that of the community.[87] But Cassian took this line of thought one step further. If the individual was necessary for the group, the group was an even more important safeguard of the individual's progress towards perfection. The anchoritic authorities had achieved much in the desert, he noted, but this was only possible for very few; the majority of monks needed the protection of communal discipline.[88] The monastic reorientation of Cassian's thinking on avarice appears nowhere more clearly than in the social implications of the sin's destructiveness. Evagrius had described the non-avaricious monk as an eagle soaring alone far above earthly matter; for Cassian's readers, such isolation was at the core of the vice's danger. Using animal imagery as had his mentor in Egypt, Cassian maintained that *filargyria* separated the avaricious cenobite:

> like some wild beast from the company of his herd, making him through the lack of companions an animal fit for prey and causing him to be devoured easily through the separation from his comrades . . .[89]

Cassian's contribution to the history of avarice is chiefly a function of this monastic realignment. The lucidity and conciseness with which he revised Evagrius' concept of the evil thought were necessitated by the *coenobium*'s demand for precise instruction in the exercise of a communal spirituality. The egotism of the *avarus*, the threat posed to the society of monks by the self-centered drive for money, moved to the foreground of Cassian's deliberations on the vice. He introduced avarice in the framework of the Capital Vices to western monasticism, but he did so by drawing into this cenobitic discussion social considerations which had engaged authors in the Christian community at large.

The danger of an individual's unbridled possession of what were public resources would remain an impulse for reflections on the vice throughout the Middle Ages, but for the monastery, Cassian's solution to the problem was the accepted ideal: only the absolute possessionless-ness of each individual could guarantee the eradication of the vice in the community.

4

Ascetic transformations III: The Latin West in the fourth and fifth centuries

The process of ascetic transformation which Cassian engaged in was also carried on by others in the West, though in a much different form and with different intentions. Here, too, ascesis remains the touchstone against which definitions of avarice can be measured, but outside the cenobium in the fourth and fifth centuries one finds more differentiated responses to the problem of greed, ranging from the secularization of ascetic ideas to their artistic analysis and to the "spiritualization" of the concept of avarice. The process involved here can be seen particularly well in the works of Ambrose, Bishop of Milan, whose familiarity with Basil's homilies dealing with avarice and the rich shaped much of his own concept of the vice. In Ambrose's hands the monastic rigor with which Basil attacked *philargyria* becomes altered fully in the service of the lay church and its clergy. As Basil before him, Ambrose can be quite detailed in specifying what the clergy is to do to rid itself of avarice; with the laity he is a good deal less demanding. But Ambrose also allowed his clergy the possession of property and was content to describe to them how to put it to best use.[1] The *fuga saeculi* he had in mind was a moral one, not a physical withdrawal from the world.[2]

Ambrose was sharply critical of private property, or at least its historical origins, for he makes avarice responsible for the destruction of the human commonwealth in regulating and allowing the growth of individual ownership at all. But unlike Gregory Nazianzen's view, Ambrose's theory of the genesis of private property is based more completely on a concept of natural law and is articulated in terms of his criticism of Cicero.[3] For the Roman author as well as for the bishop, private ownership runs counter to nature, though nature for Ambrose is of course not an independent entity but the concrete appearance of God's will. Ambrose, moreover, can find only one explanation for the rejection of this aspect of divine volition, and it is a moral one: *Natura igitur jus commune generavit, usurpatio jus fecit privatum*. A good deal of scholarly discussion was focused at one time on the question of whether *usurpatio* only reflects Cicero's more objective stance, but from the context and Ambrose's normal use of the word elsewhere it seems clear enough what he is asserting here: the right of private ownership came about only through unjust acquisition.[4]

The pejoration implicated for Ambrose in the very beginnings of the process leading to private property becomes all the clearer when one takes note of avarice's role in it. The bishop's thought here, too, shows his critical use of the earlier *De officiis*, in particular Cicero's statement that striving to increase one's goods is legitimate and avarice only a perversion of this justifiable desire.[5] For Ambrose, on the other hand, the sin has an elementary force; he sees it acting in much the same way as had Lactantius and Seneca, as the cause of the moral decline of the commonwealth and the appearance of private property.[6] And diametrically opposed to his Ciceronian model, Ambrose finds the repercussions of this original sin at work in the very activity the Roman author had justified, for as long as human beings desire to increase their wealth, he says, they have cast off the form of justice and lost the sense of benefiting all. Avarice, in Ambrose's reflection of the Golden Age mythology, is not a perversion of the desire to increase one's possessions; it is the desire itself.

In spite of his view of the sin's long history as a seducer of mankind, Ambrose is convinced that avarice is unnatural. In his treatment of Naboth, a figure suggested to him by Basil's homily to the rich, Ambrose expands on Achab's greed by accusing the affluent citizens of Milan of laying claim not only to the earth as their exclusive property, but to the heavens themselves, the air, the sea.[7] In effect, the vice turns upside-down the common *topos* which Christian writers had inherited from descriptions of the Golden Age and had employed in depicting divine liberality. The products of nature are no longer the common goods of all humankind; through avarice, the very elements themselves are treated as private property.[8]

Unlike the monastic anthropology of Evagrius and Cassian, the bishop sets this aspect of avarice which is "outside nature" fully in a social framework with nature as its model. Of all creatures on earth which live a communal life, only humankind, seduced by avarice, excludes its own species from sharing what is there for all to use.[9] For Ambrose, then, helping others to the utmost of one's ability is not simply a desirable and virtuous action, it is rather a *lex naturae*, which is to say, it is the mode of behavior God established as proper to all beings. It is also this selflessness which Ambrose has in mind when he speaks of *iustitia*, or the specific form of the virtue witnessed among humankind, *humanitas*.[10] The injustice of contemporary society brought about when avarice parceled out the laws of possessions can only be counteracted by the *caritas* (or free almsgiving) which is justice.[11]

Thus, Ambrose's comments here, as most of his practical thought on avarice and wealth, simply assume the perpetuation of a system of individual property holdings. With all of the rigor he evinces in rejecting the historical underpinnings of private property and with his insistence on self-denial as the way of justice demanded by God, he nevertheless accepts the reality of private ownership among his congregation as a matter of fact. Nor does he, in all cases, even reject the theoretical necessity of such a system in this post-lapsarian world. His resistance to Justina's attempt to install an Arian bishop in Milan's Basilica Portiana, her challenge to the Catholic church's right to its property, revolved partially around the inviolate nature of private ownership: if the emperor could not legally desecrate the home of an individual, he argued, even less could he seize the house of God. And in the sermon Ambrose preached in the basilica, perhaps on Palm Sunday in 386, while Justina's soldiers threatened a massacre outside, he compared himself to Naboth who had not given up his rightful ownership of a vineyard to suit the whim of an avaricious king.[12] In Ambrose's thought, as in that of the Cappadocians and John Chrysostom, one can observe a distinction between the absolute nature of avarice, as it was imagined to have affected the origins of social injustice in private property, and the practical appearance of the sin in the contemporary life of the community after the Fall.

If anything, one must say that Ambrose's argument against the vice entails even more understanding for the possession of material goods than what has been observed so far. He goes beyond the line of criticism of avarice begun by Clement of Alexandria, which at the same time was an apology for the rich, by drawing the virtue of thrift into his consideration of the sin in a way which ran counter to the thinking of some of his contemporaries. At one point in the eulogy for his dead brother, Ambrose pauses to commemorate the *parsimonia* of Satyrus' business transactions, his "chastity in possessing," which he put to good use, for example, when recovering the family's property that had been seized by a certain Prosper:

> He does not seek another's goods who takes care of his own, nor is he inflamed by excess who is content with what is his. Thus, [Satyrus] did not want to get back anything other than what was his own, more in order not to be cheated than to grow rich. For those who seek others' goods he rightly called "hawks of money" – for if "the root of all evils is avarice," then he certainly has rid himself of vices who does not go after money. . .[13]

What is presented here as all important for overcoming the sin is not the fact of possessing, but the attitude of the possessor. Ambrose states explicitly that his brother, who administered both the episcopal household and the family estates, was not poor in means but nevertheless was poor in spirit because he was indifferent to his prosperity, neither rejoicing in his wealth nor considering it only a trifle. Even more decisive for this secularization of an ascetic ideal, Ambrose presents his brother's care in maintaining the extent of his possessions, which must have been considerable, not as a necessity forced on him, but as a virtue strictly contrary to the sin of avarice.

THE RISE OF AVARICE – IN NORTHERN ITALY IN THE LATE FOURTH AND EARLY FIFTH CENTURIES

When Ambrose writes of the vice, he most frequently has the immoderate desire for more acquisitions in mind and only secondarily the yearning to retain what one already has. In the Latin West the accumulation of ever more wealth in ever fewer hands had reached much vaster proportions than in the East, and the immediacy of such unbridled greed provided the wider context for Ambrose's focus on this aspect of the sin.[14] He stands at the head of a group of urban bishops who, though sometimes using methods not recommended by Ambrose, were nevertheless also laboring to consolidate the church's position in northern Italy in the face of adverse conditions which ranged from economic stagnation and population loss to the barbarian invasions of the fourth and early fifth centuries – men such as Zeno, Bishop of Verona (362–371/72); Gaudentius of Brescia (*d.* after 406); Chromatius, Bishop of Aquileia (387–407); Peter Chrysologus, Bishop of Ravenna (before 431); and Maximus of Turin (*d.* before 423). Though the fact has not been recognized until now, it is actually among the writings of these bishops that one finds the first concentrated and sustained emphasis on *avaritia* in western Christian literature. Each of the bishops was responding to the exigencies of his particular local situation, of course, but most of them were moved to deliver at least one sermon or homily which not only dwells at length on the sin, but even more makes it the central issue, the organizing principle, of the work, something which is reflected in the titles given to these pulpit addresses in manuscript or by early cataloguers such as Gennadius.[15] It is, furthermore, remarkable that no other vice was seen to be important enough to qualify as the major topic of discussion in these writers' works. For the mere statistical evaluation of occurrences of *avaritia* in the Middle Ages, these northern Italian bishops are also not without importance. Those who have discerned an increase in references to the sin in the eleventh century and have related this phenomenon to the social changes accompanying the rise of a money economy in western Europe[16] must see that in fact here, long before the introduction of a new economic technology, there is a quite dramatic concentration on the vice.

What lies behind this early stress on avarice as the central focus of homiletic interest? Certainly the lack of an established scheme of sins with *superbia* at its head, as it was to develop following Gregory the Great, made 1 Timothy 6:10 more accessible to moralists as their leading authority and avarice as the dominant vice in their preaching.[17] Yet, obviously, this path had been available for quite some time. There are, I would suggest, two factors which must be considered here, both of them reflecting on the social situation of Christianity at this moment in history: the barbarian invasions, which aggravated to the breaking point crises that had long been underway, and at the same time the religious confrontation between Christianity and paganism, with the resultant emphasis within the church on conversion, in particular of the notables, as one of the main elements in the process of strengthening its position in northern Italian society. *Avaritia*, more than any other vice, summed up perfectly for the bishops the common elements of sinful behavior precipitated by these extreme conditions which were impeding its progress.

As Ambrose, these writers exhibit little patience for fitting avarice schematically into a system of vices, but rather apply themselves to identifying and correcting the concrete appearances of the sin. And as in Ambrose's works, avarice is understood here principally in terms of acquisitiveness, not retention. The bishops, of course, complain about the habit of protecting oneself from impending disaster by hoarding up coins or jewels (indeed, buried caches of wealth from this period have been unearthed frequently in the Po valley), but the relative importance of the two major aspects in the sin's definition comes out clearly in Zeno's description of *Avaritia*'s violence:

> It seethes at all times, unable to rest, rages furiously, contends with others, plunders, rakes in money, holds on tenaciously to its own goods, desires what belongs to another; and is not content with its own goods, nor with what belongs to another, nor even with the whole globe itself.[18]

Such aggressive concupiscence is not only characteristic of the bishops' depiction of the sin, it is also an indication of the ruthless behavior to which they were witnesses. The social and economic crises of the period, though debilitating enough in themselves, were eventually overshadowed by the pressures of the Visigothic presence south of the Alps.[19] And it was in the Germanic armies that the bishops came to see one of the catalysts for the avaricious behavior found everywhere around them. Thus, Maximus castigates some of the citizens of Turin whom he depicts as wolves of avarice though they act within the bounds of imperial legislation by buying from the invaders the booty (including slaves) which the barbarians had plundered from their neighbors.[20]

It is not only the number of references to avarice and the vivid detail that accompanies them which testify to the extreme conditions of the period.[21] The very alacrity which these writers show in drawing on images and examples of brutal behavior when chastising the vice points as well to the urgency of the problem as they saw it. Zeno already referred to *avaritia* as the cause of wounds felling all nations, of piracy bringing more terror at sea than storms, of streets being barred by swords and glistening with blood, of poisonings, of the murder of unborn children. To this Gaudentius was to add his horror in the face of an excessive greed which looks on while human beings starve to death. Maximus, perhaps the most eloquent adversary of his contemporaries' avarice, speaks of Christian slave traders who drag away from the feet of priests their own brethren seeking refuge there.[22] And in his sermon "On Avarice and Ananias," he condemns the *avarus* who enjoys profits from another's misery, illustrating this with events he says he witnessed recently:

> Behold, an old father weeps for his captured son, and you are already rejoicing over him as a slave boy; an innocent peasant bewails his lost bullock, and you are arranging to work your fields with it and imagining you can take possession of the fruits of another's sighs; behold, a righteous widow grieves for her home plundered of all its household goods, and you are joyful that your home has been adorned with these same goods. Tell me, Christian, will you feel no remorse, will you not be restrained when you see another's tears in your guest chamber?[23]

It is obvious that some of the examples these bishops use are not without precedent in the work of earlier writers against avarice.[24] But there is little doubt that their emphasis on the brutality of avaricious behavior corresponds to the violent situations they had to face.

Nor is it surprising to see them emphasize the social context of avarice at a time when the fabric of Roman society was being strained to the utmost. The ubiquity of the sin in its urban setting was measured best by enumerating the variety of members of the community already corrupted by it. Zeno gives a cross-section of the specific actions and social groups traditionally associated with the vice: those of moderate means indulge their avarice through fraud, the rich by their want of self-restraint, judges by favoring one side over the other, orators through a mercenary and two-faced rhetoric, kings by their pride, merchants by their underhandedness, the poor by desiring wealth they cannot have, the clergy by feigning hatred of the sin itself.[25] Of course, in all this the richer members of society bear the brunt of criticism from the pulpit. The justification of wealth which appealed to the riches of the patriarchs was not yet discarded altogether, but Peter Chrysologus relegates it finally to the realm of the ideal. No one can take comfort in the possessions of an Abraham, a Job, or a David, he argues, for these were God-given riches. A figure more applicable to the situation of his audience is to be found in Matthew, a tax-collector so wounded by avarice that his only possible remedy was the apostleship. Jesus had not chosen him to justify his wealth, but to cure his greed.[26] Yet the use of this figure by Chrysologus also emphasizes the possibilities left open for the upper levels of society which the bishops were trying to win for the church, for these notables, too, could maintain their social position after conversion by performing deeds of Christian charity with their wealth. The distance between the bishops' contemporary society with its lack of almsgiving and the purity of the Jerusalem community was also an indication to them of the desperation of their own times.[27] Thus, in its connection with arguments against avarice, the apostolic community was not the exclusive property of cenobitic authors at this point, and neither did the northern Italian writers find in the first Christian congregation the same model of a monastic life organized strictly without possessions which Cassian had posited there. The bishops were looking back, rather, to the emphasis first seen in Cyprian's work on the social concord in which the apostles had lived, and which they felt was most lacking in their own surroundings. Avarice made the imitation of this pristine life impossible, as Chromatius complained:

> But, I fear, that harmoniousness and *caritas* of believers which existed under the apostles is nothing but our condemnation: by our careful attention to avarice, we preserve neither harmony, nor peace, nor *caritas*. They regarded their own possessions as at the disposal of the community; we want to make others' goods our own.[28]

Nevertheless, Maximus found it important to account for the one exception to this ideal. His identification of Ananias' failure as an unforgivable sin is all the more pointed when it is placed in the context of the incomplete Christianization of northern Italy at this time and the persistence of paganism there.[29] All the bishops must have found it necessary to deal with cases of moral backsliding, for their urban congregations, which included landowners, members of the military, tax-collectors, civil servants, judges, household servants, and the poor, also contained many people in these positions who were recently converted pagans or neophytes who had deep-seated allegiances to traditional Roman religion and for whom the boundary between Christianity and the old religion was still extremely fluid.[30] At the same time, though the Germanic tribes who crossed into the Roman provinces in the fourth and fifth centuries were converted within a generation of their entrance into the empire, inculcating them fully with the spiritual values of the new belief and instilling in them the necessity to abandon their old customs was a continuing process.[31] The background of the conflict between paganism and Christianity also throws the equation of avarice with idolatry into a new light. Far from being merely a theological commonplace, it belongs to the bishops' repertoire of arguments to make the sin appear more abhorrent by identifying it with cult practices they were also doing their best to stamp out. Gaudentius asked explicitly:

> Do you really think God is loved by a lukewarm and negligent Christian who permits the worship of idols on his estates, who allows a demon's temple and devil's altar to stand as an insult to God, who does not cease committing adultery and ravishment, who daily snatches what belongs to another, daily covets, longing by whatever means to kill his neighbor, against whom he can most presumptuously carry out his lust or greed, though he cannot fully satisfy it?[32]

In *avaritia*, then, the bishops found another indicator of the irrevocable gap between Christianity and all aspects of the old religion. For them, the perception of avarice was directly related to the rhetoric of conversion, and arguments against the vice would remain an important element in missionary activity throughout the early Middle Ages. As with Ambrose, the bishops' remedy for the sin is frequently enough the concrete form of justice which amounts to an altruistic sharing of one's goods with the have-nots, for in this way the power structure of northern Italian society could be maintained. And they, too, emphasize the fundamental antagonism between faith itself and the vice which should underlie such selflessness.[33] Zeno, Peter Chrysologus, and Maximus all state explicitly that avarice breaks the faith, that whoever seeks money loses the spiritual rewards of belief.[34] The defeat of avarice, that is to say, had become by this point an intrinsic part of the conversion from a materially oriented way of thinking altogether, and it required from those now entering the new religion a basic transformation in their attitude towards the world. On the one hand there was the base worldliness of avarice, and on the other, the reality of spiritual values leading to eternal life. The gulf between them and the choice faced by the neophyte are clearly represented in Chromatius' examination of Matthew 6:24. As Christians, he says,

> we are forbidden to serve a former master, that is to say, the devil who has ruled over us like a tyrant, or even more, avarice and cupidity which Jesus terms "Mammon" and which for some time even used to capture the minds of believers. Thus, we must flee and avoid the greed for money, the avarice of the world, lest we subject ourselves to its intolerable slavery, or to the devil who is the author of avarice.[35]

But of course the urbanity of their congregations and the high social status of those they were seeking to convert also left these bishops no choice but to describe the spiritual advantages of Christianity in the worldliest of metaphors, using the familiar distinction between the true value of belief and the illusory worth of material goods. Peter Chrysologus pointed to Matthew himself for this purpose. His transformation to an apostle, argues the Bishop of Ravenna, actually brought him a greater customs office than the one he had left behind, and here he collected, not the thirtieth, fortieth, fiftieth penny in tax, but the thirtieth, sixtieth, hundredth joy of heaven. The high administrative officials who came to church every Sunday might not have been swayed by any lesser arguments.[36]

THE ALLEGORY OF GREED: PRUDENTIUS' *PSYCHOMACHIA*

The position of overwhelming importance which avarice held for the bishops of northern Italy is exceptional for this period, but only in the consistency with which they emphasized it as the primary vice. Elsewhere in the West one also finds continuing accord on the view of avarice as a major evil, but there was little consensus on the precise nature of its causal relationship with other vices. References to 1 Timothy 6:10, especially in exegetical works, were often nothing more than a way of underlining the seriousness of the offense of greed, without actually asserting it as the source of evil.[37] But regardless of where Latin authors placed the vice in a hierarchy of immorality, their image of it was generally shaped at this point by the same emphasis on violent behavior which characterized the sermons of the northern Italian bishops. Here, too, the social situation of the collapsing empire and the barbarian invasions left an indelible imprint on the conception of avarice. The external violence described by these authors is echoed in the depiction of avarice's destructive effects within the human soul. Their relationship is demonstrated most clearly by Prudentius, in his *Psychomachia* (*c.* 405), the first work in which the ascetic view of avarice is subsumed fully in an artistic context which is representative of the new and emphatically orthodox piety typical of Spanish Christianity in this period. In an important sense, of course, all the vices and virtues which appear in this work reveal the correspondence between their outward and interior appearances: the *Psychomachia* is essentially a typological poem, and its allegory of vices and virtues serves as only one part of what might be called a figural epic. This is to say that the moral battle within the human heart which is depicted in such influential detail has, in turn, been envisioned by its author within the context (both a literary and a real one) of *Heilsgeschichte*. The historicity of the archetype of this battle is implicit for Prudentius; it is a combat which reveals its historical presence daily.[38] The battles between vices and virtues also contain sufficient markers to show that Prudentius is not only concerned with encounters within the individual, but that contemporary society is also implied in them as well. Chastity, for example, refers to Judith's victory over Holofernes as one which "prefigures our days" (verse 67), and, as will be seen, *Avaritia*'s defeat occurs in a familiar social surrounding.

Avarice's battle with her opponent, Beneficence, is the penultimate conflict between a series of personifications which was, and remained, peculiar to Prudentius. None of the sources which scholars have proposed so far for his list is completely satisfactory; at best these earlier presentations of vices and virtues as combatants may have stirred the poet's imagination, but led him ultimately to create his own grouping.[39] The rationale for the order of most of the vices here is also unclear, for while there is a steady rise in the intensity of violence involved in their defeat, the vices are not generally bound together by a systematic linkage. It is fitting that *Fides* and her opponents begin and end the combat, but not compelling that *Libido* follow *Cultura Veterum Deorum*.[40] The only clear narrative link occurs in the movement from *Luxuria* (Riotous Living) to *Avaritia*: when the latter first appears, she is gathering up the baubles left behind by the hasty flight of the preceding vice and her entourage. It should come as no surprise to see this close connection between the two vices. As has already been observed, greed and a life of over-indulgence were frequently identified as related phenomena. But even beyond this, one may detect in Prudentius' unique linkage an allegorization of the same understanding of the more immediate genesis of greed as is found in Ambrose's thought. The ostentatious lifestyle of the privileged stimulated *avaritia* by using up the riches necessary for feasts and endless entertainment. "When someone has drained his wealth by being dissolute," Ambrose observed, "he then goes after greedy profits."[41] For Prudentius, too, the dissipation of wealth, more than anything else, brings on the avaricious yearning for wealth.[42] In this instance, then, Prudentius went out of his way to express the causal connection between vices through allegorical action.

In the descriptive and narrative allegory of *Avaritia*, many of the elements common to the discursive examination of avarice appear again, but in a new guise. The iconographic detail is resolved into a lasting portrait of the vice as a woman wearing a flowing robe, the ample pockets of which she has crammed with gold, and who hides behind the folds on her left side yet more pouches and money bags stuffed with the goods her right hand is engaged in scraping together (verses 454–63). The precise nature of the objects of her greed is only revealed after her demise: they are the same worm-eaten and corroded treasures which had traditionally been used to characterize the wealth of this world (verses 598–603; cf. esp. Matt. 6:19). Gnilka has drawn attention to the important detail of *Avaritia*'s gaping mouth (verse 457), a commonplace element in the portrayal of the vice which Prudentius echoed again in his description of *Avaritia*'s death, suitably brought about in part *obliso gutture* (verse 590).[43] But perhaps even more important for the depiction of Avarice in illustrated manuscripts of the *Psychomachia* as well as for the later iconographic history of the vice is the poet's focus on *Avaritia*'s rapacious right hand, curved like a hook (verses 455–56) and tipped with brass nails (verse 463). The matter was significant enough for him to employ it elsewhere, too, as the sole characteristic of the avaricious sinner:

> But here the *avarus* pulls back
> his crooked hands, and balling up
> his fist, with his hook-like nails,
> he cannot relax his sinews.[44]

The widespread use of hand movements as a manifestation of greedy behavior has already been indicated with the example of Gregory Nazianzen. In Latin, too, usurers are commonly depicted as reckoning up the interest owed them on their fingers, and the *avari* were characterized as holding back their hands instead of giving alms.[45] Moreover, when the vices later came to be understood as acting on particular senses, avarice was associated with that of touch.[46] In the *Psychomachia*, it is her right hand which *Avaritia* brings to bear most often, whether through her own aggressive actions against the clergy (verse 497) or in the deceit of Judas (verse 532). And it is, then, fitting that Beneficence defeats the vice by the muscular power of her arms, strangling her opponent *duris ulnarum nodis* (verses 589–90) and closing her greedy maw *conpressis vinclis lacertorum* (verses 591–92).

The correspondence between the external and internal effects of avarice emerges in clear fashion when Prudentius catalogues the attendants on the vice (verses 464–66). These hardly comprise an arbitrary list, for they fall neatly into those which define the attributes of the *avarus* (*cura, famis, metus, anxietas, pallor, insomnia*) and those which describe the actions of this figure in society (*periuria, corruptela, dolus, commenta*).[47] That the *Psychomachia* is concerned with more than an individual moral conflict is further manifest in the use of human figures to describe both a part of *Avaritia*'s opponents in battle (verses 482–93) and a portion of her own front line (verses 467–76).[48] These latter, semi-demonic mortals behave in no way differently from the personifications which quarrel alongside them (verses 477–79). The mixture of the personified and the human allows the allegorical level in the poem to find its fulfillment on the societal plane, for the human types and their inhuman actions are nothing other than the results of the interior battle lost.[49] The mortal objects of the vice's attack point in the same direction. *Avaritia* employs methods here which echo allegorically qualities that had long been attributed to the *avarus*, blinding one victim, burning others in the same fire which consumes gold (verses 482–93). That the clergy become the most recognizable group to suffer, and with the protection of *Ratio* to repel, *Avaritia*'s onslaught is likewise not without precedent, as has already been seen. But what might have amounted to severe clerical critique elsewhere remains relatively harmless in the *Psychomachia* where Avarice is able to injure merely a few priests, and then only with slight flesh wounds (verses 497–508).

The vice is defeated in her appearance as the greed for more; only after she camouflages herself as Thrift does she meet, temporarily, with a degree of success (verses 551–72). A disguise as what Prudentius expressly terms the virtue which takes pleasure in living frugally and maintaining what is its own allows Avarice to parade her immorality in a type of behavior moralists had long identified as a mere excuse for miserliness:

> What amounts to plundering and thieving
> and greedily concealing acquisitions
> She would flaunt under the tender name of
> care for one's children.[50]

Only through this metamorphosis does the poet finally reveal the entire range of evil involved in avarice, a spectrum marked by the traditional extremes of the desire for more possessions and the hoarding of things already acquired. Only the allegorical action can complete the reader's understanding of the personification; it is not enough, as Jauss has implied, merely to have learned its name.[51] In Prudentius' treatment of *Avaritia*, in other words, full meaning is only achieved through a variety of allegorical forms.

Avarice's change to the appearance of *Frugi* has attracted a good deal of critical comment.[52] Her metamorphosis echoes verbally Allecto's transformation in *Aeneid*, 7.415–20, but while Prudentius' use of this passage in the service of Christian morality may be novel, other evidence shows that his contemporaries also well understood the threat of vices masquerading as their opposites. In the East, Chrysostom took to task the practice of hiding sin under the name of virtuousness; and in a much closer context, Augustine wrote at length in a letter to Jerome on the subject of those vices which are contrary to virtues and nevertheless resemble them by a deceitful pretense. His consideration of frugality and miserliness is of particular interest here:

> It is quite obvious that extravagance is opposed to frugality, but that which one generally calls miserliness is, of course, a vice, though it appears to be similar to frugality, not by its nature but by a fallacious appearance.[53]

No doubt, as C. S. Lewis would have it, Prudentius and Augustine prove themselves to be adept psychologists by their observation of the tight-fisted reality beneath the surface of a conventional virtue, but more to the point historically, they show how the church was grappling with the definition of one type of avarice. It was difficult enough to be precise about the amount of possessions a Christian could acquire legitimately; here one can note as well that the limits of retention posed similar difficulties, of the same type as those implied in Ambrose's defense of his brother. It is precisely the still fluid border between what was considered thrift and what was defined as avariciously guarding one's possessions which accounts for the vice's momentary success in the *Psychomachia* over the virtues' battle line.[54]

Clarity on this issue is brought by the decisive action of Beneficence, whose appearance in the allegory demonstrates the efficacy of understanding Jesus' words to the rich youth in their most literal terms (verses 573–83). Her defeat of *Avaritia* is a triumph of the paradoxical nature of spiritual strength: stripped of all protective covering, she is now invincible in battle; having emptied her pockets by giving all her former wealth to the needy, she can count up the interest accruing on her eternal riches. *Operatio*, thus, represents far more than active charity alone. Her victory speech exhorts all Christians to the same life of renunciation which Basil the Great also recommended, and with equal specificity. Not content with the guidelines to the limits of possessions contained in the open-ended formula of wanting no more than what need calls for, *Operatio* stipulates how little this necessity should be:

> The greatest peace is to want no more than what due need
> requires: that plain food and one garment
> cover and refresh, in moderation, our weary limbs
> and not go beyond the fulfillment of nature's mean.[55]

If thrift and almsgiving are important virtuous habits in Prudentius' morality, they are also insufficient in themselves to meet the challenge of avarice. The successful completion of this part of Abraham's archetypal battle, perhaps all the more decisive because it occurs in the realm of literature, can only be guaranteed for Prudentius by the ascetic ideal of detachment from worldly cares which Beneficence depicts.

JEROME AS A SOCIAL CRITIC OF AVARICE

Implicit in Prudentius' emphatic call for ascesis is the criticism of what was seen to be the increasingly burdensome materialism of contemporary Christianity. Such a verdict is only hinted at in the *Psychomachia*, but elsewhere it was pronounced in unmistakable terms as part of the denigration of avarice and the presentation of ascesis as its proper remedy. The critique of the times is, thus, another important element in the imagining of avarice. In the work *Ad ecclesiam* (*c.* 440), a treatise which Gennadius and generations of scholars after him referred to with the title *Adversus avaritiam*, Salvian, presbyter of Marseilles, noted that only the number of Christians had increased in his age, not the amount of faith itself, and he illustrates this moral deterioration in great detail with the example of Christians' avaricious attachment to material wealth in its most personal form, patrimonies. Elsewhere, Salvian drew on the common *topos* of praising virtuous pagans (in this case the Fabii, Fabricii and Cincinnati) for their life of poverty and the ascetic endurance of affliction instead of a career avariciously hunting for gold.[56] Here, he contrasts the selflessness of the Jerusalem community to the state of contemporary church society.[57] For Salvian, too, as for the northern Italian bishops, the apostolic community did not amount to Cassian's archetype of the *coenobium*, but represented rather the model of an altruistic ideal applicable to the whole of Christendom. The attitudes towards inheritance which the vice fosters are merely a reaffirmation of humanity's old bonds to the world, are in fact an attempt to prolong these ties even after death. Salvian's perspective is, finally, an eschatological one: earth and hell are the ultimate rewards for avarice and cupidity, he notes; heaven and eternal goods the repayment for generosity.[58]

The ideal response to possessions which Salvian envisaged for the entire community of the faithful combines deeply-felt repentance for sin with the donation of all one's goods to the poor during one's lifetime. As a final remedy the Christian might will his property to the church, though Salvian defends his utilitarian attitude by insisting on the donor's belief, as well: it is not money which recommends the faith, but faith which makes money acceptable.[59] In practice, however, one can see that Salvian, too, demands more from the religious than from the *saeculares*, though without the cenobitic outlook of a John Cassian. In the first book of *Ad ecclesiam*, addressed to the laity, he notes that riches may legitimately be sought for, possessed, and increased if they are bequeathed ultimately to the church for the use of the poor. The Christian who leaves all his goods to his family, or other acquaintances, is rejected as proof of the statement in Ecclesiasticus 10:9 that nothing is more wicked than the *avarus*.[60] Yet for the religious, whom Salvian dealt with in book two, it is clear that wealth is at best a stumbling block to perfection, that salvation cannot be achieved without divesting oneself of all possessions.[61]

The criticism of cupidity by the religious contained in *Ad ecclesiam* is directed explicitly towards those who only profess the name of religion but still retain wealth for their own personal use.[62] Jerome's analysis of *avaritia* also frequently identified it as a form of rampant materialism infecting the religious of his day, and his examination was highly regarded by his contemporaries. Though Jerome never seems to have composed the tractate on the vice which he announced to Eustochium he would like to write, Sulpicius Severus, for one, found his fervent criticism of the avarice committed by monks worthy of special notice. A Gallic friend, Sulpicius reports in the *Dialogi*, once told him he had read a text by Jerome which took certain monks to task, omitting "absolutely nothing which he could find fault with, scourge, and expose: above all it attacked their avarice, and no less their vanity."[63]

Jerome repudiated the avarice underlying religious pretensions in contemporary Christianity wherever it made itself felt, and it is this insistence on looking beyond material concerns which partially accounts for his reputation as a famous ascete at a time when the organized renunciation of the world was still new to Roman society. Among the laity he satirized Rome's most prominent matron, who made a great show of dispensing one penny to each beggar in St. Peter's basilica, but who then beat an old woman attempting to get two. The love of money exhibited by such Christians, complained Jerome, is a mockery of Peter's words in Acts 3:6 and Paul's definition of sufficiency: by their behavior alone, these *avari* say, "I do not have faith and mercy; and what I have, gold and silver, I am not giving to you. Thus, we who possess food and clothing are content."[64] Elsewhere, Jerome remarked how shameful it was that the greed of the clergy and monks made it necessary for Valentinian to exclude them legally from inheriting property: even worse, in spite of the law, monks still want to accept inheritances, and priests continue to amass fortunes.[65] From those who sought perfection through ascesis, Jerome, too, demanded the prerequisite of a complete renunciation of goods, at least after he had come to embrace this way of life himself. In an echo of his teacher, Gregory Nazianzen, Jerome could also find words of qualified praise for Crates and Antistenes, pointing out to Lucinus, a wealthy Spaniard who wished to come to Bethlehem, that the philosophers' admirable rejection of gold was a necessary first step towards perfection which must be completed by a Christian's offer of his very self to God.[66]

This is not to suggest, however, that Jerome, any more than Gregory Nazianzen, insisted that the rich must give up all their possessions before they could call themselves good Christians. Near the end of his life he was asked to write a letter of spiritual guidance to Demetrias, a young aristocrat who had fled with her wealthy parents to North Africa after the fall of Rome in 410. His response, which he explicitly says is directed *ad uirginem diuitem et uirginem nobilem*, shows a careful consideration for the future ability of this young woman of rank to donate money in support of monastic communities, perhaps including Jerome's own ascetic establishments, which were suffering financially at the time. For Demetrias, in any case, Jerome described the vice in terms similar to those Augustine used, as a temptation which could be overcome merely by one's internal distance to wealth. "I deem it superfluous to warn you against avarice," he wrote to her at one point, "since it is the nature of your family both to possess riches and to despise them."[67] Those who chose to do so would follow Jesus' words to the rich youth, but Demetrias had been entrusted with a careful governance of wealth. For her, Jerome suggests, the criterion of use applies. His moderation in defining avarice here should be contrasted to what one of Pelagius' avid followers had to say on the vice, for

Pelagius was another of Demetrias' spiritual counselors. As will be seen, some Pelagians, if not their mentor himself, were taking radically ascetic positions in the West which make of them second cousins in this regard to the Messalians in the East and their absolute rejection of the rich. Just as ascetic writers in Cappadocia distinguished themselves from uncomfortably revolutionary views on wealth held by the Messalians, so those in the West had to differentiate themselves from Pelagian thinking on the rich.[68]

AUGUSTINIAN ORTHODOXY VS. PELAGIAN RADICALISM

Augustine, it has already been shown, understood the temptation of avarice in its widest sense, though the basis for his analysis always remained the material definition of the sin. In this analysis avarice was not seen in isolation. Augustine was of course concerned with the effects of the material aspect of avarice on the sinner, but his investigation also came to place *avaritia* in a social context. One of its most immediate and deadliest consequences was that it destroyed justice in human beings' relationships with each other.[69] *Justitia* allotted to each member of society (insofar as it approached a perfect social order) that which was due to each and was sufficient for each, but the *avarus* sought more than that, and thus the greedy person attempted to take for himself what was justly the property of another.

What, however, did Augustine have in mind precisely when he wrote of wanting more materially than what was sufficient? It is somewhat difficult to say, for he is no more specific on this point than most other writers who were transforming an ascetic ideal to suit the laity. In effect, he, too, was guided by the theological distinction between the precept of using wealth to aid the poor and the counsel of renouncing all possessions in order to achieve perfection. On the one hand, when speaking to the laity he implied, in a way clearly related to what the monastic writers had insisted on explicitly, that food and shelter were enough for life; but on the other hand, when he wrote to the rich and aristocratic Proba, grandmother of the Demetrias whom Jerome advised, he did not encourage her to reject the superfluously luxurious surroundings in which she lived, and he furthermore suggested to her that one could legitimately seek worldly power if one performed good deeds through it.[70] It can, then, only be said that in Augustine's analysis outside a specifically ascetic context, "enough" in material terms was roughly equivalent to the limits of an individual's social and economic circumstances. When someone desired through avarice more than what these boundaries allowed legitimately, he or she strained one of the important bonds that held the social order together. Roman law supplied Augustine with an image of how society reasserted the primacy of its justice by punishing the *avarus*. The civil code had established that whoever attempted to get more from a debtor than what was really owed had to forfeit altogether the amount owed. In moral terms, Augustine notes, this meant that by wanting more than enough, the avaricious person made himself liable to lose what he possessed already.[71]

The threat which the vice posed to society showed itself most clearly in the disruption of the relationship between rich and poor. The worldly wisdom of the vice argued that individuals were what they possessed: its proverbial truth read *quantum habebis, tantus eris*.[72] This is not to say, of course, that wealth by itself was a sign of avarice. Augustine follows the main line of patristic thought in maintaining that riches could be inherited legitimately or earned through honest labor without bringing with them the slightest hint of sin.[73] He defined the vice materially as an inappropriate desire (or love) for wealth, but this could be seen as well in those without possessions as in those with them. Augustine was well aware that ascetics can become avaricious, and beyond this he was also more direct and severe than most writers examined so far in warning the poor against being needy in wealth and yet burning with greed.[74]

His articulation of this position must be seen in the light of his controversy with the Pelagians. He had received from Sicily in 414 a letter written by a certain Hilarius asking for help in combating a recent work in circulation on the island which maintained, so Hilarius argued, that the rich could not enter heaven unless they divested themselves of all their property. A copy of this text was sent to Hippo as well, and Augustine agreed with his correspondent's summary of it. The work in question is the *Tractatus de divitiis*, probably not by Pelagius himself but rather by one of his followers and a fellow countryman who has since come to be known as the "Sicilian Briton."[75] He addressed his work to the highest ranks of society in Sicily, perhaps also in North

Africa and at Rome, and demanded of them an extreme asceticism which is, however, not quite as radical as its opponents represented it as being. Nevertheless, it gives ample evidence of how far some Pelagians could take their mentor's doctrine of the perfectibility of humankind, of humanity's potential to rid itself completely of sin.[76] For the Sicilian Briton argues that wealth is a state which can, indeed must, be cured in society at large. The renunciation of material goods which he prescribed for the wealthy so they could qualify for entry to heaven did not amount to total possessionlessness – here is where Augustine and Hilarius must be credited with rhetorical exaggeration of their own. The Sicilian Briton, too, that is to say, valued a quite traditionally stated concept of sufficiency.[77] But Augustine must have found his *Tractatus de divitiis* threatening because it blurred the distinction between merely possessing wealth and being avaricious, and because it advocated ridding society of avarice by doing away with the rich.

The vice has an important place in the Sicilian Briton's scheme of morality. It is not only part of a basic triad of sins (along with *gula* and *libido*); it is, due to its insatiability, the most dangerous member of this group. Augustine's care in differentiating between those sinning by avarice, on the one hand, and the rich, on the other, has no place in the *Tractatus de divitiis* – the two are very nearly identical here.[78] What stands behind wealth, for this revolutionary author, is always avarice. This implacable observation is all the more potentially explosive when one sees that the Sicilian Briton is not referring to the dimly remembered history of wealth's origin when he asks whether there can be riches without injustice. As he says explicitly, he is inferring a past lack of justice from what he sees in the present. Nor is he content to prescribe a remedy for the ills of society which only follows the Ambrosian and Augustinian emphasis on a change in religious attitudes. His retort is clear enough to those whom he characterizes as *saeculi amatores* and who repeat the same "renowned argument" Clement of Alexandria had used centuries earlier, namely that if everyone gave his wealth away, no one could give alms. Such people:

> do not understand that some are needy because others possess a superfluity. Get rid of the rich person and you will not find a poor one. Let no one possess more than is necessary and all will have as much as is necessary.[79]

If Augustine, on the other hand, gave somewhat more attention to the rich person's avarice than to that of the pauper, it was because the wealthy had more opportunities and greater means to feed their greedy desires – and to do so more ostentatiously. When he turned to remedies for the vice, the rich were once again his central concern. And his suggestions to them are based on the metaphorical transformation of worldly wealth to something unreal, on a view which rises above material reality to a point of theocentricity. What he said had to be achieved, as Ambrose, too, had insisted on, was a reorientation of the will: temporal matters were to be used for life's necessities, the divinity to be enjoyed for its own sake. The distinction here, between use and enjoyment, *uti* and *frui*, is a basic one for Augustine and runs through all of his ethical thought.[80] Specifically in terms of avarice, he emphasized that the world should be treated only as a resting place for travelers, not as an estate for possessors. Real riches were the fruit of justice, faith, piety, and charity; they led to God. The desire for material wealth was a yearning for false riches, for what was only perishing.[81] The correct attitude towards having possessions was summed up for Augustine in the figure of Job:

> For he was not really senseless (although, externally, he seemed to have nothing) who said, "The Lord gave and the Lord took away; as it pleased the Lord, so was it done. Blessed be the name of the Lord." Such fullness is laudable, it is remarkable wealth; he is empty of gold, and filled with God; empty of all transitory goods, he is filled with the will of his Lord.[82]

AVARITIA GENERALIS: THE SPIRITUALIZATION OF GREED

With such a view of the non-*avarus*, one has already arrived at the borders of the vice understood in material terms alone. This material aspect, that is to say, was only one expression of a broader complex of ideas which made up the sin, ideas which fourth- and early fifth-century authors analyzed with more consistency than any writers before them and which fully transformed the mere material and ascetically based definition of the vice. Three views will illustrate the emergence of a "spiritualized" avarice in this period.

With his insistence on approaching, and solving, the problem of the sin primarily as a religious issue, with his clear distinction between the zeal for Christian values, on the one hand, and the yearning for material riches, on the other, Ambrose prepared the way for a more thorough-going spiritualization of avarice which would identify the sin in an overweening desire for falsely oriented intangible qualities as well as for wealth. Ambrose himself did not go quite this far, but he spoke of the positive counterpart to a spiritualized *avaritia*. The mother of Zebedee's sons had asked Jesus to allow them to sit at his left- and right-hand side in the coming kingdom (Matt. 20:21). It was an error to have asked this, Ambrose says, but an error of piety, for mothers are always impatient for their children's well-being: "And though she was eager for her desire, yet it was a pardonable greed, which was not avid for money, but for grace."[83]

Jerome, too, gives evidence of the same wider understanding of *avaritia* in his philological work. As the examination of Lactantius showed, it was possible for Latin authors to use *cupiditas* and *avaritia* as interchangeable designations for the vice, though to the former belonged many of the same broad connotations which surrounded *pleonexia* as a *terminus technicus*, and to the latter some of the restricted-ness of *philargyria*. Jerome's efforts on the Vulgate text went a good way towards making the Latin terms more nearly equivalent for future generations of moralists by reversing this tendency. In almost every instance where the original Greek corpus has *pleonexia* or a derivative, and in most of those where the Hebrew text was rendered by the same class of words in the Septuagint, the Vulgate translation has *avaritia*, *avarus*, etc. For *philargyria*, however, Jerome almost invariably accepted *cupiditas*, in particular for his revision of the text of 1 Timothy 6:10.[84] This usage had the further effect of bringing *avaritia*, that is to say the most characteristic term for the vice in Latin as well as the conception of the vice for which it stood, into a larger context described more by "the desire to have," regardless of its object, than something only as specific as "the love of money."

What these wider boundaries included for Jerome is revealed clearly in some of his exegetical treatises. His commentary on Ephesians 4:19 makes of *avaritia* a sin of sexual excess, in effect synonymous with adultery.[85] As was argued earlier, his understanding of Paul's words is historically inaccurate, but it gives evidence of his willingness to move the concept beyond the borders of a desire for wealth alone. Once freed of its material foundation, the concept was able to take on more spiritualized qualities, but also to be re-evaluated in a startling fashion. In his commentary on Habacuc 2:9 ("Woe to you who gather evil avarice for your house," according to the Vulgate text), Jerome explained the seemingly superfluous qualification of *avaritia* on grounds which probably reflect his own personal desire for disciples:

> Now "evil avarice" is said to distinguish it from the good variety, as there is a good avarice in the ecclesiastical teacher who is never satisfied by a crowd of followers, and the more disciples he has, the more he is motivated in the study of doctrine.[86]

The avarice of money alone was moved out of the center of examination in this spiritualizing tendency, for the uncontrollable desire which defined the vice was observed to make itself felt in many other areas as well.[87] Essentially, then, the relationship between an avarice which amounted to the love of money or possessions and an avarice defined in wider terms was one of species to genus. In one of his earlier treatises against the Manichaeans, for example, Augustine argued that the wisdom which maintained that the beginning of sin is pride (Sir. 10:15) did not stand in contradiction to Paul's words in 1 Timothy 6:10, as the followers of Mani maintained. The passages are in harmony, as long as:

> we understand here a general avarice through which someone eagerly desires more than is fitting, out of his own grandeur and out of a certain love for his own affairs. . . . There is also an avarice in the specific sense, which is very commonly called "the love of money" (*amor pecuniae*). By using the word as he did when he said that "the root of all evils is *avaritia*," Paul meant the genus (that is, the broad sense of *avaritia*) to be understood for the species.[88]

The "general" avarice to which Augustine referred amounts to nothing less than self-aggrandizement interpreted in its widest sense. Its direct source was pride, as he went on to note in the work just quoted, though in effect *avaritia generalis* was almost equivalent to the idea of pride which Augustine derived from Neoplatonist metaphysics. One should, in any case, note that the most common monastic conception of morality in the early Middle Ages, which was to make pride the root sin, and to conceive of avarice (and all other vices) in its relationship to pride, has its clear foundation in Augustine's thought.

What differentiated the two vices for him was the idea of possession always implicated in avarice. If the sinner overemphasized the self through *superbia* as well as *avaritia*, then in the latter case this occurred through the desire to possess for oneself. The full extent of this desire was revealed in the fall of humanity. Adam and Eve's yearning to have more power and knowledge than what they had received was itself a re-enactment of the devil's avarice. Though there were also a number of other vices involved in both falls, Augustine gave special attention to the role of *avaritia* in bringing about humankind's loss of paradise. The first human beings had possessed God himself, and it was their inability to be content with this gift which he identified as the basis of their sin.[89]

The avaricious desire for a no longer only materially understood "more" took on many forms. Augustine spoke at one point of an *avaritia vanitatis* and clarified this phrase by noting elsewhere that the vice led a sinner to ignore God, who was everywhere present for the sinner, and instead to love gold or honor, even when both were unattainable.[90] But the conception of the vice was wider yet, for Augustine also wrote of an *avaritia vitae*. What were to happen, he asked, if someone demanded you either give false testimony for him in court or lose your life? If you choose to live by perjury, is this not avarice as well, for what else makes you want to live longer than the period of time God has established for you?

> Do not have a greed for living and you will not have eternal death. Do you see that everywhere this avarice makes us sin, since we want more than is necessary? Let us beware of all avarice if we want to enjoy eternal wisdom.[91]

The wider implications of the vice, as its material bases likewise, were measured along a scale of sufficiency. Humankind needed spiritually neither honors on earth nor a longer life than was its due; all that was sufficient for humanity was God alone. A desire on the part of human beings to possess anything which did not lead to God was, thus, for Augustine the final extension of general avarice.[92]

In this widest sense of the vice, one already sees the contours of what will be recommended as its remedy. If the sinner wanted to free himself from avarice, he had to yearn to have, and the more eagerly the better, what was spiritually sufficient for him. The cure for *avaritia generalis*, that is to say, was to be avaricious – but only for God: "For if we are greedy, we ought to be greedy for eternal life."[93] By redefining avarice in this way, Augustine could relativize the harmfulness implied in the term and at the same time legitimize the desire for possession in an area far removed from the social and material plane. Indeed, the very arguments avarice used to control the sinner could be turned to the sinner's benefit if only they were directed towards God. Avarice told the sinful person to think of the future and to want limitless possessions. Just so, remarked Augustine, for to desire eternal life with God was to care for the future, and to store up goods in heaven was to have a treasure without end. This, in other words, was the desire that amounted to one part of the *caritas* which he defined, in a conscious reversal of 1 Timothy 6:10, as the *radix omnium bonorum*.[94]

There is, at this point in its history, no better representative of the Deadly Sin tradition and the possibilities it offered in the interpretation of *avaritia* than Augustine of Hippo. Like the work on *filargyria* by John Cassian, his counterpart in the tradition of Capital Vices, Augustine's broadly based consideration of the topic is an outgrowth of the importance avarice held in Christian moral thought in Late Antiquity.[95] This era of transition was soon to be followed by an epoch in which in a monastic environment pride fully replaced every other sin as the source of all evil, but the fourth and early fifth centuries remain the period of initial emphasis on *avaritia* in the examination of immorality. No era was more decisive for the development of the concept of avarice in the West in the early Middle Ages. Not until the late eleventh century was the vice again to demand the same amount of attention from moralists as it had received at this time. The broad contours of avarice's definition, which were to continue more or less intact throughout the course of its medieval history, are, thus, clearly products of late antique culture. It is in their adaptation to new contexts that they were to live on in the early Middle Ages.

5

Secularizing avarice and cupidity

The various systematic contexts that included avarice which have been examined so far were to be supplemented by a plethora of others throughout the early stages of the medieval period, and the burgeoning of these new systems demonstrates that in the West paradigms of immorality were still very much in a formative stage. The continuing transformation of Europe's social structure from Late Antiquity to the early Middle Ages is reflected as well in the state of flux in which one finds the responses moralists were developing to avarice and the rest of the sins. Even where an authoritative work on the Capital Vices, such as that by John Cassian, was well known to authors of the fifth and sixth centuries, it was not universally accepted as the context most suited for formulating a response to avarice. Caesarius, for example, who was a monk at Lérins (a monastic foundation which did much to promote and transmit Cassian's writings in Gaul) and who later became Bishop of Arles (c. 470–542), preached frequently against avarice without once referring to the octad, though he drew readily enough on other material from Cassian.[1] Caesarius used any number of groupings of vices in his homiletic works; in one sermon borrowed in large part from Augustine he also fitted *avaritia* into an elaborate analysis of the parallels between violations of the Decalogue and the plagues inflicted on the Egyptians before the exodus. The sin here is implicated both in offenses against the seventh commandment ("You shall not steal"), which parallels the plague of hail, that is to say, the just loss which comes with all unjust gain, and in offenses against the tenth commandment ("You shall not covet . . . anything that is your neighbor's"), which is comparable to the death of the first-born, i.e., the death of faith itself.[2] The later Middle Ages were to witness a far more thoroughgoing application of individual vices to transgressions against specific injunctions among the Ten Commandments, but the inchoate form of such a scheme was only one of many attempts at locating an intellectual context for avarice to be observed in Caesarius' sermons. His experimentation with the contextual environment of avarice is typical of the treatment of the vice in the earliest centuries of the Middle Ages – at a time, that is to say, when the context of authority itself was being redefined throughout European society.

Further indicative of the developing comprehension of avarice and its placement in new systematic contexts are innovations in the virtues which were considered to oppose the vice. Justice and largess, the two most common remedies seen so far outside the Capital Vice tradition, are still well represented in the works of late fifth- and sixth-century authors.[3] The virtues which come to supplement these traditional adversaries against *avaritia* give evidence of the growing use of the sin's spiritualized definition as well as the search for new contextual arrangements of moral entities. Thus, Cassiodorus (*c.* 485–*c.* 580), whose exposition of the Psalms draws heavily on Augustine, typifies the monastic reception of *avaritia generalis* by making humility the virtue opposing greed. And Martin (*d.* 579), abbot and bishop in Dumium, later metropolitan at Braga in what is today Portugal, reworked a lost treatise by Seneca on the four cardinal virtues, a moral systematization which Martin adapted to present avaricious tenacity and prodigality as the contrary and sinful extremes restrained by the virtue of continence.[4] Martin's work documents the fact that the geographical area in the West in which one finds the first important literary evidence of the reception of Evagrius' and Cassian's octad of vices, and the monastic understanding of avarice which it transmitted, is the Iberian peninsula. Furthermore, the capacity for variation in the octad which was already seen to be at work in Evagrius' tractates continues here, as well. Martin, for example, drew directly on Cassian in the first section of his *Pro repellenda iactantia* in order to illustrate the vices committed by all and recognized as such by all. However, his brief mention of avarice and the concrete actions to which it leads uses the fully Latinate designation for the sin (not *filargyria*, but *avaritia*), drops *turpis lucri adpetitus* from the list of its progeny, and changes the order of these subdivisions.[5]

REGULATING THE SIN: EARLY MONASTIC LEGISLATION

On the whole, the octad remained almost the exclusive possession of monastic communities at this stage of its history. Nevertheless, though early monastic legislation reflects the same material definition of avarice as is to be found in Cassian's work, it rarely cites him directly. There are two major contexts in which the sin is mentioned in such legislation. The earliest is simply a parenetic catalogue of vices and sinful behavior to be corrected by the monks, such as that contained in the *Monita* drawn up by Porcarius, Abbot of Lérins *c.* 485–90 and teacher of the young Caesarius of Arles.[6] More complex than this are the warnings against avarice included in the descriptions of various monastic offices. *Avaritia* here in its narrowest sense refers only to an over-zealously tightfisted use of the monastery's property, the opposite of wastefully squandering it. This is the operative definition seen in the admonition in the *Regula orientalis* (composed perhaps *c.* 515 in the monastery of Condat, France), and in the parallel statement in Benedict's *Rule*, that the cellarer must avoid the extremes of both miserliness and prodigality when dispensing communal goods to the brothers.[7] On the other hand, those who sold the products of the monks' labor outside the monastery also had to be put on their guard against the temptation of avarice, understood for this monastic function in terms of the acquisitive form of the sin as a desire to achieve monetary profit through commerce in the marketplace. Both Benedict and the Magister recommend restraint in such an enticing situation by always selling at a lower price than the going retail rate. Here again, one can measure the difference between the hermits of the Egyptian desert and the cenobites in Europe, for in anchoritic contexts the same recommendation to sell below market value had been utilized as a way, not to combat avarice, but rather to impress the monk with the necessity of returning to meditation in his cell with all possible speed. For Benedictine monasticism, however, this injunction to sell at a lower price is also firmly anchored in the necessities of monastic economy. Benedict goes on in the same chapter in which he speaks of the cellarer to mention the related danger of defrauding the *coenobium* when offering its craftsmen's wares for sale, and he holds up the threatening example of Ananias and Sapphira to warn against such behavior.[8]

The advice to monks filling these cenobitic offices amounts to instruction in the correct use of property, but the ultimate path leading away from avarice which was valid for all monks, whatever their duties within the community, remained a complete detachment from worldly goods. The traditionally monastic view of the sin in its most inclusive material definition implied by such a remedy is illustrated well in Ps.-Basil's *Admonitio ad filium spiritualem*, strictly speaking not a legislative work, but one which nevertheless has been considered a direct influence on Benedict's *Rule*. It contains a chapter advising the novice in the spiritual life on matters dealing with avarice, and in language already quite familiar:

> Let us avoid the riches of this world, for our possession is the kingdom of heaven. . . . Be content with your daily sustenance; whatever is superfluous thrust from you as an impediment to your purpose. . . . Estrange yourself, son, from this vice and willingly take up a life of voluntary poverty.[9]

And the *Admonitio*, too, uses warning examples drawn from biblical texts to support its view that avarice leads to death. Yet surprisingly not the punishment of Ananias and Sapphira, but rather the demise of Achan, Saul, Achab, and Judas serve to illustrate this principle here.

SEEKING THE BOUNDARIES: PRIDE AND AVARICE

At the same time, the spiritualized sense of avarice hardly went unmentioned in the West, and its use gives evidence of further development in the relationship between it and the sin of pride. The early reception of Augustine's *avaritia generalis* shows, in fact, that initially there was some hesitation in fixing the hierarchical connection between the two vices. The Benedictine order of morality, in which pride became the foundation of all sinfulness, only developed as the West's dominant harmartiology in a lengthy historical process. Thus, Julianus Pomerius, native of North Africa, rhetorician at Arles, and for a few years at the end of the fifth century Caesarius' teacher there, drew the conclusion from Augustine's harmonizing of Ecclesiasticus 10:15 and 1 Timothy 6:10 that greed and pride must actually be the same vice:

> To be sure, *cupiditas* and *superbia* are one evil insofar as one cannot find a proud person without cupidity, nor a greedy one without pride. Indeed, the devil, too, in whom pride holds the mastery, was greedy for his own power and for humankind's fall; and humanity itself demonstrated the passion of morbid greed by a desire for the forbidden tree and by striving to be similar to the divinity.[10]

Later, his student in Arles repeated the same idea, while preaching on the subjects of humility and pride, in order to explain why his sermon also included both cupidity, the root of all evils, and *caritas*, the foundation of all good qualities.[11] Yet Caesarius is unsure how far to take this matter: he reaffirms the interdependence of the two vices, only to turn then to the position represented by the thought of the northern Italian bishops and assert that avarice is the mother of pride and must be eradicated first before one can be freed of its daughter. Cassiodorus, too, discussed avarice in his commentary on Psalm 118:36 in terms which made it equivalent to the vanity of self-exaltation. Like Pomerius, he looked back to Augustine when arguing that avarice was the sin involved in Adam's fall and the source of the devil's misinterpretation of Job's love for God. It is important to note, in any case, that in none of the writers just mentioned is the relationship between pride and avarice a fixed and invariable one.

GREGORY THE GREAT'S SYNTHESIS OF CASSIAN AND AUGUSTINE

The example of Cassiodorus or that of Caesarius of Arles also shows clearly that it was possible for many fifth- and sixth-century moralists writing on the vice to draw on Augustine as well as Cassian, and the separate views of avarice which they represented, without the least attempt to integrate their standpoints into a new conception of the sin. Cassiodorus himself was more of an encyclopedist than an original thinker. But one does not have to wait long for the development of a context in which both of the early authorities fit comfortably: the first author whose work can, in effect, be understood as providing a type of synthesis of the monastic and Augustinian positions on the vice is

Gregory the Great (*c.* 540–604). Gregory was a descendant of the Roman senatorial aristocracy, but after his conversion and the death of his father, he used the family estates to found seven monasteries. His devotion to the *coenobium* remained with him to his death, but he was also forced to play a decisive role in the politics of the Christian community at large when he was eventually (though, it is said, very much against his will) elected pope in 590. Gregory proved to be an able administrator of ecclesiastical resources at a time when the economic and social foundations of Italy were being devastated by the Lombards and outbreaks of the plague. As will be seen, his consideration of avarice, too, reflects the breadth of his activity, from the theoretician of spirituality to the practical church official.[12]

Gregory presents numerous groupings of vices to which he refers frequently in his works, but the complete statement of a system of seven *principalia vitia* occurs only once, in book 31 of the *Moralia in Iob*.[13] The detailed interpretation of the Book of Job which he offers here was originally designed to serve the instruction of monks exclusively, but even in his own lifetime the work was being read aloud in public at vigils.[14] Regardless of the author's original intention, the solitary description of a sin heptad contained in the *Moralia in Iob* came to be used in moral theology beyond the walls of the monastery throughout the Middle Ages.[15] There is, in fact, much in Gregory's thinking on the vices and virtues which recommended itself to a more general audience. Gregory was aware of the authority of Cassian's work on the vices, but his revision of Cassian's list of eight evils, in effect, met the needs of a broader reading public, partially because, like Martin of Braga's work on vanity, it replaced certain technical, monastic designations for the vices which were of Greek origin with their Latin equivalents: avarice appears here, too, as *avaritia*, not *filargyria*.[16] This alteration is symptomatic of more important differences between Cassian's and Gregory's orientation: for Cassian, temporal matters altogether were unfortunate necessities, and his language is directed to the elite corps of those who would use his technical guides for spiritual instruction; for Gregory, public responsibility was something to be kept in balance with spiritual contemplation.[17] As a revision of Cassian's list of vices, Gregory's heptad marks a new departure in moral theology, for there are no extant precedents for truncating and adding to the scheme of Capital Vices before Gregory, alterations which account for his VIITAGL scheme, with pride considered the root and queen of all seven evils.[18] His heptad no longer follows the anchoritic steps to perfection which posited a monk's initial battles against bodily temptations before he was qualified to grapple with those of a more spiritualized nature. Instead, the five vices which Gregory explicitly characterizes as *spiritalia* and which amount to outgrowths of the ego, come at the beginning of the series and call for the cenobite's most immediate attention. Not a growing liberation of the individual from the material constraints to meditation is depicted in the VIITAGL sequence, but rather the absolute necessity for the monk to diminish that very individualism which lies behind all sin, for him to internalize a disposition of humility towards both God and his abbot. An early medieval audience outside the monastery must have found it immediately easier to comprehend the need for obedience to authority, secular as well as divine, which Gregory assumes, than to grasp the importance of suppressing natural appetites legislated by Cassian.[19]

Avarice's place in the heptad, as it was in the octad, comes at the interface between *vitia spiritalia* and *vitia carnalia*, but for Gregory the vice belongs only to the former group. In his statement of the concatenation among the seven vices, a linkage which had been somewhat mechanical for Cassian but which Gregory sees in more profoundly psychological terms, the movement from *tristitia* to *avaritia* marks the point at which the diseased mind begins to turn outside itself. Yet just as Cassian had separated the last two categories of the octad from the concatenation of the rest, so does Gregory as well. Avarice, in this way, does not lead to gluttony; it is simply the last of the vices which act upon the sinner internally, not upon his flesh:

> Sadness also leads to avarice, since when the disturbed heart has lost the benefit of joy within itself, it seeks to find consolation without; and it desires to get possession of external goods the more it has no happiness to which it might return internally. But after these there remain two carnal vices . . .[20]

A further indication of Gregory's critical reception of Cassian can be found in his thinking on the subdivisions of the vice, the army which follows its captain, *avaritia*, into battle.[21] Two of these (*periuria* and *violentiae*) are direct verbal echoes of the sub-sins born from Cassian's *filargyria*; Gregory's *fraus* also closely parallels the *fraudationes* in his predecessor's list. Two others, *proditio* and *fallacia*, correspond some-what less directly to Cassian's *mendacium* and *falsa testimonia*. But for *inquietudo* and *contra misericordiam obdurationes cordis* there are no equivalents in the earlier writer's description, nor did Gregory draw here on such specific designations for concrete actions as Cassian's *furta* or *turpis lucri adpetitus*. In defining avarice through its progeny, in other words, Gregory lays more stress on the internal, psychological state of the *avarus*, and less on his sinful deeds, than was seen in the Capital Vice tradition before him.

His descriptions of *avaritia* throughout the corpus of his writings emphasize further the spiritual nature of his understanding of the vice. Behind much of his thinking here one can detect the influence of Augustine. In his first homily on the gospels, for instance, Gregory expands on Augustine's observation that *avaritia* was involved in Adam's fall. Gregory uses the triad of gluttony, vainglory, and avarice – which Evagrius had developed in his exposition of the devil's unsuc-cessful temptations of Jesus and which Gregory now employs for the same purpose – to describe the three stages of humanity's initial descent into sin. The devil successfully lured Adam:

> with the advancement of avarice when he said "Knowing good and evil." For avarice is not only a matter of money, but of high standing as well. For it is correctly called avarice when someone strives for loftiness beyond measure.[22]

Without losing sight of avarice's material foundation, Gregory effec-tively expanded the concept here along lines which had been indicated to him by Augustine, making avarice explicitly more than simply a matter of material greed. The possession of tangible or intangible goods for oneself alone becomes the most distinguishing characteristic of the vice for Gregory.

How avarice affects the sinner, its psychological mechanism, is depicted in far greater detail in Gregory's work than in that of any writer before him. Previous authors had commonly referred to the *avarus* as insane; Gregory describes in concrete terms the development of this condition. Once the *avarus* has passed through suggestion, delectation, and consent, he confirms himself in his vice by actively desiring the property of another. He turns time upside-down generating a plan to fulfill his wishes: his days are spent in unproductive idleness, his nights are taken up with frenzied thought, and when he finally devises a subtle scheme to acquire the property he wants, he exults as if he were already in possession of it. The fact that, in reality, it does not yet belong to him can no longer hold back his fancy: he imagines ways to improve it and, since its greater value will make it more attractive to others, he goes on to formulate already the arguments he will need later to defend his right of possession in a court of law.[23] The precise nature of the self-delusion to which *avaritia* incites its victim does not appear for the first time in Gregory's work. One of his older contemporaries, Gregory of Tours, had already described in similar terms King Charibert's avaricious attempt to claim as his own certain property which belonged to the Basilica of St. Martin. Charibert, too, imagined he owned what he did not possess, a notion which he paid for with his life.[24] But the exacting, step-by-step evolution of this mania is detailed by no other writer before Gregory the Great.

The practical duties attendant on the central figure of the church did not allow Gregory to leave the matter there. Not only the psychological analysis of the vice and its effect on the psyche of the sinner claimed his attention, but also the pragmatic task of correcting avaricious behavior and the attitudes which lay behind it. These guidelines for the spiritual treatment of *avaritia* are contained in the *Regula pastoralis*, which he wrote at the commencement of his tenure as pope and which presents his ideal of the pastor of souls. The self-reflection called on from this figure demanded an ability to distinguish in himself what is actually a virtue and what only masquerades as such. The examples Gregory uses to illustrate the ease with which evil takes on the outward form of virtue are a direct echo of Augustine's earlier words on this matter:

> For often miserliness cloaks itself under the name of frugality and on the other hand extravagance hides itself under the title of largess. . . . Hence it is necessary that the tutor of souls differentiates virtues and vices with a watchful care, lest either miserliness take possession of his heart while he rejoices in appearing frugal in his expenditures, or he boast of his largess as if it were compassion when things are wasted extravagantly. . .[25]

When he came to describe the pedagogic supervision which the pastor was to exercise over his congregation, Gregory again included advice on therapy for the avaricious. If he had emphasized almost exclusively the internal aspects of avarice in the *Moralia in Iob*, his focus in the *Regula pastoralis* is on the more concrete appearances of the sin. The remedies he recommends for activities brought on by avarice include admonishing the sinners with specific scriptural passages which should enlighten them concerning the spiritual danger of their present behavior. Those, for example, who are bent on seizing others' goods should take to heart Habacuc 2:6 (in Gregory's text: "Woe to him who heaps up what is not his own; to what end does he add to the weight of thick mud upon him?"), though he notes one can also frequently effect a change in the conduct of such people by teaching them how suddenly death brought to an untimely end the avarice of people they themselves would be moved to condemn.[26] His cures for avarice are altogether far removed from the radical demands of some earlier thinkers, and they demonstrate the relatively high social station of the parishioners he has in mind: it is typical of the conciliatory approach he had to take when directing his thought to secular Christendom that at a time when the violent usurpation of property was disrupting the social stability he held as an ideal, he could appeal to a "reasonable" retention of possessions, to an exacting observance of the law of ownership, as a way to counteract greed:

> Thus, those who give of what they own but do not cease taking what belongs to others should first be admonished to learn to retain what is their own in a reasonable way and then afterwards not to go out after others' goods. For if the root of the fault is not destroyed when it is sprouting luxuriantly, the thorn of avarice which flourishes among the branches will never be dried up. Hence, the occasion for seizing from others is removed if the law of ownership is first put in right order.[27]

To be sure, Gregory is as convinced as his predecessors that the products of the earth were created for all in common and that giving to the poor is an act of justice, not mercy; but for him this does not, even in theory, undermine the right of private property. The shift in emphasis is important, for it presages another more thorough step in the justification of wealth to be found later during the Carolingian period. Gregory's *jus possidendi*, in effect, is the legitimation of much of what Ambrose's understanding of *jus privatum* had attributed to avarice.

As complete as is Gregory's list of scriptural authorities for combating avarice, it does not contain 1 Timothy 6:10, nor does he cite this passage at all frequently in his works.[28] Within something more than a century of the sermons and homilies which the bishops of northern Italy had dedicated to avarice, the development of the Gregorian heptad already provided a model for moral thought which would largely, though certainly not exclusively, replace *avaritia* with *superbia* as the chief vice for much of the early Middle Ages. That Gregory identified pride as the root sin clearly shows his commitment to the same ideals of monasticism as those being institutionalized by the Benedictine *Rule* which saw obedience and humility as the central virtues for monks. The frequent acceptance of this Gregorian classification by early medieval authors has been variously ascribed to the feudal and hierarchic thought of the age (Huizinga); to the relative lack of absolute wealth in fluid form in an agrarian society which held order and discipline as its major ideals (Bloomfield); or to the clergy's confrontation with Germanic tribes for whom riches could not be translated into a "bürgerliche Sicherung," but for whom power over people meant everything (Fichtenau). Far more to the point is Lester Little's observation that with great frequency the authors who adopted Gregory's view were also monks and members of the nobility, whose complaints against pride amount to the self-criticism of the powerful and a check to the potential abuse of the weak by the mighty.[29] Nevertheless, it should be emphasized again that one cannot speak of an exclusive superiority of pride over avarice in the early medieval period, for, as will be seen, works which emphasize *avaritia* over all other vices are not altogether missing from these centuries, in particular not in environments where, as was observed in the works of the northern Italian bishops, converting others to the spiritualized ideals of Christianity was the moralist's goal. But in any case, one can note that after Gregory the Great, writers on avarice had three traditions at their disposal from which they could draw arguments against the vice: the Deadly Sins; the octad of Capital Vices; and the Gregorian heptad, in effect a synthesis of both.

EARLY MEDIEVAL SYSTEMS OF THE VICES: ISIDORE OF SEVILLE

In its modified forms, the Gregorian heptad later came to provide the most important systematic contexts in which the examination of avarice was to occur, but one of the earliest influential alterations in the list made of it an octad again. This is seen first in Isidore of Seville's (*c.* 560–636) presentation of eight *perfecta vel principalia vitia* in his early *De differentiis rerum*.[30] He adopted here the Gregorian vices and, with one exception, their Gregorian designations as well, but maintained an approximately Cassianic order to yield a GLAITIVS sequence of vices.[31] Isidore's handling of the systematic contexts in which avarice appears throughout his works is typical of numerous early medieval authors, for it is characterized more by an experimental and encyclopedic approach than by an attempt to reconcile the differences between these diverse systems. Thus, though he spoke of them as seven evils, Isidore used Cassian's GLAITAVS list, with its subdivisions, in his exposition of Deuteronomy; and elsewhere he placed avarice in the second position in a series of seven *spiritus vitiorum* which occupy the mind of a relapsed penitent.[32] He also drew on the same understanding of the Furies which Lactantius had used, noting in the *Etymologiae* that the three loves which disrupt human beings' thoughts are *ira*, *libido*, and the *cupiditas* "which desires wealth."[33] In the same way, Isidore did not find it necessary to clarify the exact relationship between pride and avarice. He was able to echo Gregory the Great's position on this issue in one work by referring to pride as the "queen and mother of the vices," and then only a few chapters later quote I Timothy 6:10 as the scriptural authority for asserting that avarice and the love of money are worse than any sin, that greed (*cupiditas*) is the mother of all misdeeds.[34] Isidore also carried further the tendency to oppose the vice by a number of different virtues, and these virtues reflect the needs of the various audiences to which his works were directed. Thus, in his monastic rule, he described the virtue of humility as the chief incentive leading the monk away from the desire for money.[35] For a more general reading public, however, he asserted that *fortitudo* was the quality which "finds money worthless, flees avarice," though elsewhere in the same work he also noted that "alms overcome avarice," an idea which he supported in yet a different treatise by describing *liberalitas* as the virtue which should fight against *avaritia*.[36] The pairing of liberality and greed as its opposed vice occurs in the context of a battle between vices and virtues, an Isidorian variant of the *Psychomachia* which was to attain some degree of popularity in the seventh and eighth centuries.[37]

Isidore's more detailed analysis of the vice, while containing many ideas which merely show the breadth of his reading and his reception of earlier thought on the topic, also provided later moralists with elements which were to become commonplaces in the examination of avarice. Like most writers before him, Isidore saw an essential part of the vice's danger in its insatiability, but he also explained this characteristic of avarice on etymological grounds. He emphasized here the avaricious sinner's intense desire to possess, as well as the object of that desire:

> *Avidus* is so called from *avendo*, for *avere* is "to desire." Hence also *avarus*. For what is it to be an *avarus*? It is to go beyond what is sufficient. For that reason someone is called an *avarus* because he is *avidus auri* and can never be satisfied by wealth; and the more he has, the more he desires . . .[38]

But, in fact, *avaritia* and *avarus* are not Isidore's exclusive designations for the sin of avarice or for someone sinning by greed. *Avaritia* is the term he uses most often in lists of the vices, though *philargyria* appears as well wherever he is thinking in specifically monastic terms – when citing Cassian's octad and in his own *Regula monachorum*.[39] But besides these *termini*, his vocabulary for the vice also contains *cupiditas*. Though this word frequently signifies desire in general for Isidore without positive or negative moral connotations, as it had for numerous earlier writers, it also occurs as a synonym for the vice conceived in the most narrowly material terms, for example, for the evil which drove Judas to betrayal. "Many have even renounced the faith itself because of worldly greed," he notes, "for *cupiditas* sold Jesus."[40] In the Isidorian vocabulary, *avarus* and *cupidus* also have more specific meanings, as designations for the sinners affected by one of the two major divisions of the vice as these were examined outside the Capital Vice tradition. The "twin punishments" of avarice, as Isidore refers to them, those of acquisition and retention, receive their lasting *termini technici* for the first time in his *De differentiis verborum*:

> The [difference] between *avarus* and *cupidus*: the *avarus* is one who does not put his own goods to use, the *cupidus* one who desires what is another's.[41]

Isidore frequently repeated Cassian's list of the vice's subdivisions, which included *violentiae*, but he also took pains to specify what form this aggressiveness assumes in the sinner by noting that the avaricious do not hesitate to commit murder. He may have been inspired in this by Ps.-Basil's *Admonitio ad filium spiritualem*, not generally recognized as one of Isidore's sources, though a comparison of the two texts will show where they are at least parallel:

Admonitio, 9 (ed. Lehmann, p. 45)	Isidore, *Sent.*, 2.41.3–5 (PL 83:645–46)
Cupidus etiam animam suam venalem habet (Sir. 10:10). Si invenerit tempus, pro nihilo perpetrat homicidium, et	hic enim animam suam venalem facit. . . . Nam et plerisque tantum in rebus alienis est desiderium, ut etiam homicidium perpetrare
sicut	non vereantur, sicut
qui effundit aquam in terram, ita est si effundere sanguinem proximi sui.	Achab, qui appetitum cupiditatis suae sanguinis explevit effusione.[42]

Besides the reference to Judas noted already, Achab is the only other figure Isidore uses to illustrate the effect of the vice on humanity. He identified greed frequently as a form of the violent oppression of the poor by the mighty, but this could be seen as much in the corruption of the legal system as in Achab's open bloodshed: as Michel Mollat has written, the problem for the Merovingian pauper was one of basic survival.[43] Isidore's view here varies the use of the Golden Age myth by earlier authors for whom a legal system was the result of primeval greed altogether, but in spite of his reception of Gregorian thought, Isidore's sense of the ubiquitous presence of avarice is no less urgent than what has already been observed among earlier moralists:

> Avarice has spread, the law has perished with the love of cupidity, legal rights have no validity, bribes and gifts have weakened the laws. Everywhere money conquers, everywhere there is a purchasable judgment . . .[44]

Nor is this situation relieved essentially by the ability riches gave those who possessed them to aid the poor. Achieving the possession of wealth, for Isidore, is not a test of the willingness of the rich to share with the indigent, but merely a sign of the impending punishment those *avari* may suffer in hell.[45]

CHANGING RELATIONSHIPS BETWEEN THE VICE AND ITS PROGENY: AVARICE AND *CUPIDITAS*

The need to atone for and correct avarice was, of course, implicated in Isidore's doctrine of penitence, though detailed canons to regulate this practice were still in the process of being formulated in the penitentials which were developing within the Irish and, later, the Anglo-Saxon and Frankish churches. These works depend to a large extent on Cassian's and Isidore's analyses of avarice and the rest of the vices. However, one of the innovative tendencies to be observed, in particular in Anglo-Saxon penitential handbooks, is the growing independence of some of what Cassian had presented as subdivisions of avarice to a status equal with the vice itself. These works, intended as functional guides to the examination of the conscience, often combine Deadly Sins and Capital Vices indiscriminately into one series of misdeeds. Psychological reflections on the basis and development of evil, which had played a central role in Cassian's examination of the octad, form no part of the penitential discipline of these texts, now given over to more practical ends, and thus they emphasize concrete acts of greed.[46] Here, the generic requirements of the penitentials allowed for a growing juridical independence of what had earlier been considered subordinate examples of avaricious behavior. The changing relationship between avarice and its subdivisions can also be observed in other genres, as well, for example in the biblical exegesis composed by another Anglo-Saxon writer, the Venerable Bede (*c.* 673–735). Bede was probably aware of the Cassianic octad, though he does not seem to have used it anywhere as a systematic way of organizing aspects of immorality. Nevertheless, references to *filargiria* are not missing from his works, not even where he draws on Augustine by employing 1 John 2:16 to construct a paradigm of moral failings.[47] He draws a distinction here, mentioned explicitly by Gregory the Great, between corporeal evils and spiritual ones, but his understanding of these categories gives certain traditional subdivisions of avarice (and other vices) a life of their own. In his exposition of Luke 11:40, Bede notes that this scriptural passage also implicates all those:

> who detest, as if they were the most serious matters, the corporeal sins such as fornication, uncleanness, *libido*, *furtum*, *rapina*, and other such, but the spiritual ones (which the Apostle denounces no less), that is, bitterness, wrath, indignation, clamor, blasphemy, pride, and *avaritia* which is idolatry, those they condemn as if they were not severe.[48]

In statements of both the octad and the heptad, theft and rapine would have been found among the progeny of avarice before Bede. In any case, the importance of the vice for Bede made only a mild censure of it incomprehensible, for he considered *avaritia* and *luxoria* (*sic*) the most dangerous allurements by which the devil persuades humankind to sin.[49] Bede conceives of the vice in material terms, but with a general disregard for the schematic filiations of either Cassian or Gregory the Great, and this testifies to the continuing vigor of the Deadly Sin tradition and avarice's presence in it.

Other insular writers on moral issues were more receptive to Cassian's scheme of the vices, though not without making changes of their own. The designation they used to name the sin, for example, even in those cases where Cassian was their major source of inspiration, is frequently *cupiditas*. It has already been shown that Isidore employed this term as a synonym for *avaritia* or *philargyria*, and this tendency becomes more prevalent through the seventh and eighth centuries. The view of *avaritia* and *cupiditas* as equivalent designations for the sin was supported by the growing dominance of the Vulgate text of the Bible, for many of the writers who use these terms as synonyms refer to the Vulgate version of 1 Timothy 6:10 (*radix enim omnium malorum est cupiditas*) as a major authority for condemning the vice.[50] There was also evidently some uneasiness with the strange appearance of the term *philargyria*, even in its more Latinate spelling. In fact, Aldhelm, abbot at Malmesbury and Bishop of Sherborne (*c.* 639–709), felt it necessary to gloss the Greek designation. In that portion of his *De virginitate* which presents the GLAITAVS sequence in the form of a psychomachia, he introduces the vice with the words:

> Then *Philargiria* goes into battle as the third,
> A powerful vice, which is translated as *cupido*.[51]

The soldiers which this personification musters for attack are generally drawn from Cassian's list of the vice's subdivisions, but one can also find a similar mixture of human figures (*fures, falsi testes*) and abstractions among avarice's battalion as was observed in Prudentius' poem. Nor does Aldhelm follow Cassian strictly in his choice of figures to exemplify the vice. His work has Judas in common with Cassian's analysis, but his use of Achab, Jezebel, and Achan shows that he understood the sin almost exclusively as a form of greedy acquisition. Cassian's three species of the vice can also be found in the Irish *Prebiarum de multorium exemplaribus*, written before the middle of the eighth century, perhaps by an associate of Virgilius, Abbot of St. Peter's monastery and Bishop of Salzburg. The anonymous author of this collection, however, abandons the Greek designation altogether, referring to the vice only as *cupiditas*.[52]

The same designation is also regularly employed by Boniface (*c.* 675–754) to refer to the vice. His full description of avarice can be found in the *Aenigmata* among those evils which he describes as the poisoned fruit hanging from the tree of death which brought about Adam's fall.[53] The image of greed presented here continues many of the lines of thought seen already in Late Antiquity outside the Capital Vice tradition. Thus, the monstrous beast *Cupiditas* speaks of herself as ruling to the ends of the globe, as the cause of hatred and murder, as dominating people in slavery who mistakenly think they are controlling her. But in place of the merchants or judges used in late antique works to typify such people, Boniface's *Cupiditas* identifies herself as a contemporary of the author's audience in early medieval society by mentioning the aristocracy as the primary group she has debased, for their sins cannot be described exclusively as the result of pride:

> I have taught kings and noblemen to violate through oppression
> Their treaties, their native lands, and their own relatives,
> So that, in no way different from these things, peoples of
> lesser station will lose their rights.[54]

Boniface also broaches the question of whether greed is within or outside nature in *Cupiditas'* description of her "birth." Her procreation came about, she claims, not as an act of God in accordance with the laws of creation, but rather she descended from the bowels of the serpent in paradise after humanity's fall (verses 50–53). She boasts frequently of this demonic affiliation and of the vast numbers of people she has sent to hell by the bite of her fangs. These serpent teeth are an unusual iconographic detail which Boniface's text shares with the chapter on avarice in the *Liber scintillarum*, written *c.* 700 by Defensor, a monk of Ligugé (France).[55] Finally, in a last intimation of her identity to the audience of this riddle, Boniface's *Cupiditas* threatens to punish Paul with her fangs for having spoken of her as the root and cause of all evils.

PLACE FOR THE PRIMACY OF GREED IN THE EARLY MIDDLE AGES

Cupiditas' reference to 1 Timothy 6:10 has little structural significance for Boniface's conception of evil: in his collection of riddles intended for a literate audience, avarice does not take the dominant position in a hierarchy of vices. Elsewhere, however, the passage was used to support just such a view of the sin. In the *Scarapsus* of Pirminius (*d.* 753), founder of the monastery at Reichenau and the spiritual guide of the Alemanni, *cupiditas* stands at the head of an octad of vices which, however, represents Cassian's list in all other ways. This is surely a small, but nevertheless a significant, change in the traditional order of the eight chief sins. The work was intended for the Christian laity among the Alemanni, though obviously a laity only recently introduced to Christianity and not yet fully versed in the elements of catechesis and morals, whose heathen practices had still not yet been eliminated completely. It was a Germanic laity with many of the same needs for instruction in full conversion which had elicited the sermons and homilies on *avaritia* from the bishops of northern Italy centuries earlier. As Pirminius notes when introducing the subject of the octad:

> For he should not boast of being a Christian who has this title but not
> its deeds. . . . Thus, brethren, we who have been baptized and have
> vowed to do God's commandments must keep them as the Holy
> Ghost admonishes us to do through the Holy Scriptures, that is: to
> turn away from evil and to do good. What is it to turn away from evil

if not to abandon the devil with all his deeds? These evils, thus, are the eight chief vices which submerge people in ruin and destruction: *cupiditas, gula, fornicatio, ira, tristitia, accidia, vana gloria, superbia.*[56]

Pirminius maintains the vice's position at the beginning of the octad throughout this part of the *Scarapsus*, in the chapter listing biblical authorities which elucidate these evils, and in his description of the virtuous actions which sinners must perform in the face of the coming end. This latter section shows the influence of Isidore, for Pirminius clearly distinguishes here two types of avaricious sinners, the *cupidi* and the *avari*, and recommends largess in alms both for having taken what is another's and for having retained one's own possessions unjustly.[57]

That a place for the primacy of greed over the other vices had been developed as a particularly important lesson for the laity is made even clearer in the work of Ambrosius Autpertus (*d.* 784), presbyter, monk, and briefly (777–78) Abbot of St. Vincent's monastery on the Volturno, north of Naples. Ambrosius, in fact, gives evidence of how medieval moralists could fill the position of chief vice with either pride or avarice, depending on the specific needs of their audience. His *Libellus de conflictu vitiorum atque virtutum*, a debate between virtues and twenty-five vices, or pairs of vices, commencing with *superbia*, was intended for monastic readers – its author found it suitable to send to Landfrid, first abbot of Benediktbeuern, for use there. The work credits pride alone with being the source of all sin.[58] Gregory's heptad and its subdivisions account for most of the vices named here, and the Gregorian influence is just as apparent in Ambrosius' *Oratio contra septem vitia.*[59] The position of avarice in these works is for the most part, though not altogether, a subordinate one. This situation is quite different in Ambrosius' sermon on *cupiditas*, the very title of which announces its special usefulness for the laity. Here, greed functions as the origin of a series of vices which unites elements of Cassian's octad with its revision by Gregory:

> For although the vice of gluttony is one thing, that of lust another, envy another, sadness another, vainglory another, and pride another, and although they bring forth from themselves a great and innumerable brood, nevertheless . . . they grow from the one root of cupidity, as the Apostle testifies who says, "The root of all evils is *cupiditas.*"[60]

And elsewhere, as well, Ambrosius refers to the *cupiditas* of 1 Timothy

6:10 to prove that it is the foolishness of human beings seeking profits from earthly goods which produces all the sins.[61] The different positions of the vice in his organizations of morality cannot be accounted for by differences in terminology, for *cupiditas* and *avaritia* are almost wholly synonymous in Ambrosius' vocabulary. Both are designations for the narrowest sense of the sin, the love of money and property, as well as for the vice in its widest contours, the Augustinian *avaritia generalis*.[62] The most significant factor to account for the varying importance of avarice in his works is the immediate audience he has in mind: for him, combating greed could become more of an urgent necessity for those in a secular state than for the religious. In Ambrosius Autpertus, thus, one finds another early medieval thinker for whom pride does not go before avarice when conversion from a materialist habit of thought is the issue at hand. Indeed, he may remind one again of the claims of avarice's ubiquity which had been voiced by numerous authors in Late Antiquity, and would be proclaimed again in the late eleventh and twelfth centuries, when he observes to the laity with genuine conviction that greed "now in our times is seen to have taken over almost everything already."[63]

The ultimate opponent of the vice for Ambrosius is Contempt of the World – it is this virtue which argues against *Cupiditas* in the *Conflictus*, as well – and the ascetic perspective underlying this analysis is evident everywhere in his writings. To monks who may suggest that the religious should possess more goods because they are more conscientious in giving alms than the laity, he points out that this is a consideration for prelates, but not for those who have left the world, who should be deterred from such temptations by the example of Lot's wife.[64] Yet the connection between avarice and worldliness itself also guides him in judging those most intimately connected with the world among those particularly endangered by this sin. The momentary elevation of greed to a position of dominance in his sermon intended for the laity is only one part of the relationship he sees between the secular estate and avarice: in its material form, the vice is most frequently defined for him by lay behavior. Even in a treatise meant specifically for a monastic audience, such as the *Conflictus*, in which greed is shown to be dangerous for monks, too, *Mundi contemptus* begins its rebuttal of Cupidity's justification for the desire to possess by pointing out how precarious such thinking is for those in the secular estate. In the *Oratio*, as well, where Contempt of the World again appears as the virtue opposing *avaritia*, the vice takes the form, not of hoarding things up in one's monastic cell, but of desiring "precious metals, gleaming and shining gems, servants and maids, farms and estates."[65]

The way to perfection is open to those who have renounced the aspiration for precisely these things, Ambrosius explains to the audience of the *Sermo de cupiditate*, but it is also meant for the laity, "in proportion to the limited measure of your estate, and according to the capacities of your station."[66] He applies this moral lesson, as Boniface had as well, to the acme of society, its princes and administrators of justice. To their corruption and deceit he directs many of his exhortations to reform throughout the sermon. He is not unaware that *avari* may be found among the poor, but their possibilities for obtaining the object of their desire are limited, and so "the effect of cupidity is rendered minor in them."[67] In the rich, on the other hand, he notes that the fire of avarice burns hotter, first resulting in envy, but more importantly in the oppression of the poor.[68] Greed, in its most virulent form, is a vice of social corruption for Ambrosius and is found most typically among those who wield power in society. As with the bishops of northern Italy, his emphasis on the vice as the most serious of lay faults has nothing to do with the question of a money economy. The examples of wealth which he uses are generally concerned with landed property. Pride is, of course, a dangerous vice for him as well, but it is not defined by the abuse of power in society. That is the realm reserved for *avaritia* and *cupiditas*.

CAROLINGIAN REFORM AND MODERATION IN POSSESSING

The focus on the laity observed in Pirminius' handbook and the sermon on greed by Ambrosius Autpertus is only a preview of the most important development in works dealing with the vices and virtues during the Carolingian period. The program of reforms instituted by Charlemagne and his court circle was intended to affect not only the organization of the government, *scriptoria*, and centers of education, but also the very moral life of the empire itself, from monks to *saeculares*. The promoters of a "renaissance" in Carolingian culture attempted to spread to the nobility their (essentially still clerical) vision of a moral and doctrinal renewal, to win over the upper levels of society for the purposes and goals of a renewed code of conduct within the framework of clerical culture. Though the laity was often the center of the Carolingian clergy's attention, and real attempts were made to reach all segments of lay society, the evidence suggests that, in effect, only the highest strata of society – its rulers and aristocrats – were in any way directly involved in this ethical renewal.[69] Carolingian legislation dealing with the monastic life re-emphasized the importance of complete possessionlessness and a renunciation of all goods when becoming a monk, admonishing, for example, against the widespread habit of reserving a portion of one's property for oneself upon entry into the *coenobium*.[70] The official interest in combating avarice and the other sins in a more inclusive context, and the employment of lists of vices and virtues for the program of Carolingian morality, enjoyed the greatest contemporary authority, that of the head of the empire himself. In the *Libri Carolini*, completed in 793 by Theodulf of Orléans in Charlemagne's name, the Christian's moral adversaries are defined as the chief vices in a GLIIATVS list of vices which amounts to a combination of the Evagrian/Cassianic and Gregorian systems. With the help of scriptural testimony, it is noted here, avarice can be defeated by alms and the hope of eternal recompense.[71] This political and theological document within the Frankish church took a position on the iconoclastic controversy by arguing that the primary source for instruction in the faith must be found in Scriptures, not images. The work did not have the force of law; indeed, as Ann Freeman has shown, the publication of the text as a refutation of the Second Nicene Council's words on images was quickly abandoned on political grounds. But the vices are mentioned in the *Libri Carolini* for the first time in what was originally designed as a governmental policy statement on ethics.[72] Charlemagne's instructions to priests to educate their charges in all the major and minor vices was more binding in the *Capitula ecclesiastica* (810–813), and it found immediate support in other texts and in the councils convened at Arles, Châlon-sur-Saône, Mainz, Rheims, and Tours in 813, which adopted Charlemagne's guidelines in legislating the use of the octad (or heptad) for instruction in the act of confession.[73]

That this program of education was thoroughly concerned with the upper levels of the laity is seen in the number of works written specifically for a secular audience of the nobility, or chiefly with its needs in mind. Yet the image of avarice which emerges in these tractates on lay piety, mirrors for princes, and treatises on the vices and virtues must still be seen against the background of the monastic analysis of the vice. The presence of ascetic morality can be noted clearly in the chapter devoted to the avoidance of greed in the *Liber exhortationis*, written before 799 by Paulinus of Aquileia for the Margrave Eric of Friuli. Like much of this work, the section in question here was taken almost word for word from Ps.-Basil's *Admonitio ad filium spiritualem*. The only indication of Paulinus' secular orientation in his borrowings from Ps.-Basil's chapter on avarice is his specification of what leads the *cupidus vir* to homicide, for while his source passed over such matters in silence, Paulinus notes that the avaricious man becomes murderous due to very secular motives: the desire to possess gold or silver or fine clothes or someone else's beautiful wife.[74]

Far more important is Alcuin's *Liber de virtutibus et vitiis*, written *c.* 800 for Wido, Margrave of the Marca Britanniae. This treatise on vices and virtues, in fact, shows one of the paths of development being taken by that genre, for it offers instruction on spiritual perfection in the form of a guide to the everyday moral conflicts confronting the laity, in this case a soldier and judge. Its chapter on avarice was repeated nearly verbatim by Alcuin's pupil, Hrabanus, and much of it was taken over in Jonas of Orléans' *De institutione laicali* (before 828), an ethical handbook for the laity addressed to Count Mathfredus of Orléans. Alcuin's material on the vice was, thus, influential enough to be quoted here in its entirety:

> Avarice is the excessive greed for acquiring, possessing, or retaining wealth and is an insatiable plague. Just like the dropsical person, who, the more he drinks, the more incessant his thirst grows, so it is with avarice: the more it has, the more it desires. And as long as it exhibits no moderation in possessing, it will not show itself otherwise in desiring. Its progeny are acts of envy, thefts, robberies, murders, lies, perjury, acts of rapine, acts of violence, restlessness, unjust judgments, contempt for the truth, forgetfulness of future bliss, and hardheartedness. It exists contrary to mercy and alms for the poor and all pity for

those who suffer. It is defeated by the fear of God and by brotherly
love and by deeds of mercy and by alms for the poor and by the hope
of future bliss, since indeed the false riches of this world are defeated
by the true riches of future bliss.[75]

Alcuin's description owes to the monastic analysis of the vice the names
of the progeny he used which had originally been transmitted in
Cassian's list (*furta*, *mendacia*), as well as his enumeration of three
major species of the vice. Yet Alcuin's attempt to adapt Cassian's
threefold division of avarice to a non-monastic environment was not
much more satisfactory than many others which were to follow it,
because the distinction between possessing wealth and retaining it (i.e.,
in its original sense, retaining what should have been given up on entry
into the monastery) remained somewhat artificial in a secular context.
Hrabanus, in any case, dropped this distinction from his extensive use
of Alcuin's treatise and defined avarice only as the "excessive greed for
acquiring or retaining wealth."[76]

Further subdivisions in Alcuin's list can be accounted for by
Gregory's influence or a combination of Gregory and Cassian (*periuria*,
uiolentiae, *inquietudo*, *obduratio cordis*); others may reflect the influence
of Paulinus of Aquileia, Isidore, or penitential literature (*latrocinia*,
homicidia, *rapinae*). Alcuin's use of *inuidiae* as the initial offspring of
avarice is especially interesting and finds an earlier parallel in Ambrosius
Autpertus' *Sermo de cupiditate*, which also presents envy as the "first
twig" growing from cupidity.[77] The legal context of avarice was widespread, of course, but the presence of *iniusta iudicia* among the vice's
progeny may also have been noted with particular attention by
someone with the title of judge such as Wido. *Contemptus ueritatis* and
futurae beatitudinis obliuio are new in enumerations of avarice's descendants, but the latter also suggests parallels between Alcuin's *Liber de
virtutibus et vitiis* and the *Libri Carolini*, as do the opponents to the vice
in Alcuin's analysis. In effect, his cures for avarice represent a combination of the remedies for *invidia* and those for *avaritia* as they are
specified in the *Libri Carolini*.[78]

As lengthy as is the list of avarice's progeny found in this part of
Alcuin's treatise, he also counted *falsum testimonium* among their
number, as can be seen in chapter 19 of this same work, based in part on
Caesarius of Arles' *Sermo* 222.[79] The subject of this chapter is the

avoidance of deceit, but *fraus* and *avaritia* are spoken of here in a way which inextricably unites them. Deceit was an essential element of the vice already in Evagrius' analysis and was closely connected with *Avaritia* in Prudentius' *Psychomachia*, but Alcuin's virtual identification of them is only equaled in the work of another of Charlemagne's advisors, Theodulf of Orléans, who brings them together verbally by including *fraus avaritiae* among the Capital Vices in his poem on this topic.[80] Alcuin appears to have had three aspects of deceitful avarice in mind in his treatise. Along with fraud carried out in the interest of gaining wealth, which he illustrates by references to the avaricious person's willingness to give false testimony and to commit perjury, he also emphasizes the self-deceit of the *avarus*.[81] What connects both of these aspects is the deceitful nature of material wealth itself. Alcuin draws here on a common distinction in Late Antiquity and its Christian reception (seen as early as the work of Clement of Alexandria and included in Alcuin's long description of the vice in chapter 30), namely that between true riches, which amount to spiritual values, and the false wealth of this world.

Nowhere, however, does he recommend that the laity combat the deceptiveness of greed by possessing only what is sufficient, no matter how loosely defined. And in clear distinction to the monastic analysis of the vice, Alcuin speaks consistently of the legitimacy of having a moderate amount of wealth. It may be seen, in fact, that there is even room in his moral universe for a quite legitimate desire for profit. But "avarice disregards moderation": it is this lesson which the similes uniting the vice with dropsy in chapter 30, and with hell in chapter 19, express in his analysis. The usefulness of desire itself for the development of humankind is explained elsewhere, in his *Liber de animae ratione*, a handbook of morality and psychology which is based on the Platonic conception of the tripartite soul. In this context, he explains that the concupiscible portion of the soul "has been given to humanity to desire those things which are useful, and those things which are conducive to eternal salvation."[82] Only through its corruption does desire give birth to what had been enumerated as the first three Cassianic vices: *gastrimargia, fornicatio*, and *philargyria*. But as a further contrast to strictly monastic views of the sin, the list of *utilia* in Alcuin's analysis includes the necessary flow of trade within the empire.

Nowhere in his works is commercial activity *per se* an indication of avarice. Indeed, in a letter to Offa, King of Mercia, he wrote in Charlemagne's name of the importance of protecting merchants transacting their lawful business, and in a poem of patriotic intent perhaps directed to the clergy of York, Alcuin praised the city precisely for its ability to attract settlers with the motivation of achieving mercantile success there:

> From diverse peoples and from kingdoms, everywhere they come
> In hope of gain, those seeking wealth out of the wealthy land,
> A dwelling for themselves and profit and a household.[83]

Gregory the Great, among other early medieval authors, had written a justification of possessing wealth, but in Alcuin's work, and in other Carolingian texts, as well, the laity's desire for profit has also taken a step on the way to moral acceptance – subject, of course, to its governance by the rule of moderation. Beyond that, one can also say that legitimate merchant activity in the marketplace has begun a process of amelioration in the eyes of moralists from what had been its virtual equation with avaricious behavior seen frequently in patristic literature. The path leading to the full justification of commercial activity in the moral tradition was not without obstructions – the rapid economic changes in late eleventh-century Europe witnessed an outpouring of opprobrium for the greediness of the merchant's occupation before mercantile activity was finally justified in moral terms in the early thirteenth century – but Alcuin's work is already moving in that direction.

LITERARY FOUNDATIONS FOR THE SECOND RISE OF AVARICE

The observation that "avarice disregards moderation" also forms the nucleus of the advice on avoiding the sin in the *Via regia* which Smaragdus of St. Mihiel wrote early in the ninth century, perhaps for Charlemagne, though the addressee has also been identified as Louis the Pious while he was still King of Aquitaine.[84] The danger of the vice as it is presented here is twofold. First, it imperils the spiritual health of the king, as it would any Christian, and Smaragdus advises him to love mercy and shun avarice so that he may have an eternal inheritance with

Jesus. But greed is also, in terms more specific to counsel for a prince, a liability in governing. "You should not throw your house into disorder as an *avarus*," Smaragdus exclaims, "but build it up as one who gives freely."[85] The internal corruption of the chief of state will be mirrored in the external decay of society itself, or using Smaragdus' more metaphorical language, the fire of avarice which devastates the mind finds its equivalent in the monstrous vice which insatiably eats away at everything with its "beastly teeth." Furthermore, the public evils which Smaragdus attributes to *avaritia* are not limited to the oppression of the poor by the aristocracy; they are on all levels of society, from forgers in the court circle to bandits in the city and sorcerers among the people.[86]

The task of correcting avarice and the other chief vices was not only important for those advising the nobility, of course, but continued to be part of the instructional and pastoral work of the clergy dealing with the laity as a whole. Both of the capitularies by Theodulf of Orléans place *avaritia* in a GLAAVIIS sequence which was to be used by the confessor in his questioning of the Christian seeking absolution.[87] Theodulf's emphasis is on the need to correct avarice through alms, not cenobitic possessionlessness. The same pastoral concerns observed in Theodulf's capitularies can be noted again in Hrabanus' work. His *De institutione clericorum*, written in 819 and dedicated to Haistulf, Archbishop of Mainz, uses the Gregorian sin list in its final section devoted to a theory of Christian preaching and takes the form of a psychomachia where not only the commanders of the armies oppose each other in single combat, but the individual soldiers are paired against each other as well. The battalion of *Avaritia* is composed of the Gregorian subdivisions of the vice.[88] The opposing virtues, as Hrabanus conceives of them in this chapter, do not form an independent system of their own, but are modeled on the sense and order of the Gregorian vices. Later, in his *De ecclesiastica disciplina*, written between 842 and 847 as an aid to Bishop Reginbald's missionary activities in Thuringia, Hrabanus described the successful fight against the eight *principalia vitia* as dependent on the Christian's acquisition of the four cardinal virtues.[89] In the section on avarice, Alcuin's influence stands out, observable not only in the material quoted directly from the *Liber de virtutibus et vitiis*, but in the emphasis on deceit as an integral part of avarice's effect on humankind. This deceptive aspect of *avaritia* assumes the tangible form here of the treachery of Judas, a central act of evil which, Hrabanus explains, all too infrequently serves as a daily reminder today: "Although many detest Judas' crime, there are still only a few who are anxious to avoid it."[90]

Of course, Hrabanus' focus on the laity when examining avarice was not limited to his works of pastoral intent but can also be illustrated in his exegesis, and in most complete form in his commentary on Ecclesiasticus. He discussed the vice here in its political context while explaining the significance of the order of the verses in chapter 10 of ben Sirach's text:

> After he has spoken of the transference of rule, he fittingly adds something on avarice, since the virtue of correct governance is chiefly neglected because of avarice. For when someone lays claim to worldly goods for himself through cupidity beyond moderation, becomes puffed up with pride, then he strives enviously to repel others from his borders.[91]

Hrabanus looks back to the analysis of the sin in Late Antiquity which identified it with an aggressive egotism. A similar political view of avarice can be found in the third book of Ps.-Hrabanus' *Quadripartitus* (second half of the ninth century, written at Reims).[92] The chapter on the vexation of the vice here offers an encyclopedic catalogue of the motivations and desires of the *avari*. Some of these sinners are driven to want public acclaim, others the highest office, still others the possession of superfluities. But all, or nearly all, are tortured by the vice, for they believe these goals can be achieved by money alone. The author returns to Hrabanus' concern with lay avarice and provides perhaps the most complete depiction of the rich *avarus*' anti-social behavior to be found in Carolingian literature:

> With his own possessions spread out far and wide, he does not allow someone else to possess things in his vicinity – while he joins one land-holding to the next, stretches out his own borders, curses the poor person, oppresses the one with a small bit of property, drives away his neighbor and scatters everyone round about by disturbing and pursuing them, he who does not acquire without someone weeping, does not make a profit without someone else groaning: for him alone is that thing beneficial which is a public evil.[93]

All of this gives evidence of the continuing importance of the vice in the moral past and the political present of humankind as it was examined by ninth-century theologians. But in more practical terms, the urgently felt ubiquity of avarice also demanded a response from these writers. Hrabanus counseled Reginbald not to be silent on the subject of the vice because it is the evil which above all others captures humanity. And Wettin brought back this same lesson to his brethren from his visionary journey to hell in Walahfrid's rendering of it:

> The ardor of avarice does not know how to give up anything,
> But it tortures all and sends all to hell.[94]

The sensitivity to the practical consequences of the vice which Alexander Murray has illustrated using a sermon written *c.* 925 by Odo of Cluny, and which he has described as a precursor of the concern with contemporary *avaritia* by eleventh-century moralists, is not missing altogether in the ninth century. In other words, the Carolingians and their immediate successors laid the literary groundwork for the topics which were to play such a large role in the preoccupation with the vice in the centuries to come. Indeed, there is already a magnified sense that avarice is on the rise, that it is on the way to becoming the dominant vice it had been for the northern Italian bishops and would be again in the late tenth and eleventh centuries in response to the development of a money economy in Europe. Alcuin, in any case, saw in the attacks of the Norsemen in England in 793 a sure sign of God's punishment of the English for their sexual sins, but above all for their *avaritia*:

> What should I say about avarice, acts of rapine, and judicial violence when it is clear as day how much these crimes have sprung up everywhere, and a plundered people is witness to it? He who reads the Holy Scriptures and considers ancient histories and reflects on the development of the world will find that for sins of this kind kings have lost their kingdoms and peoples their homeland. And when the powerful have unjustly seized others' goods, they have justly lost their own.[95]

Future perspectives

TOWARDS AVARICE IN THE MONEY ECONOMY

Continuity in the history of avarice following the inheritance of the Carolingians can be observed first of all in the relative stability of modes of analyzing the vice. The accepted norm of representing greed as either sinful acquisition or immoral retention can be observed in all major writers on the vice, as can the common equivalence of its typical designations in Latin: *avaritia, cupiditas*, or *philargyria* (*filargyria*).[1] The combination of Evagrian/Cassianic and Gregorian analyses of lists of the vices and their sub-sins marked the most productive path for systematic presentations of avarice, but the foregrounding of the vice by Pirminius also remained available for homilists intent on converting their congregations from a material ideology to Christian spiritual aims.[2] The exemplification of avarice remained stable in the period following the Carolingians, as well, with moralists drawing most often on the internal life of the clergy in attacks on the vice, their secular targets including – as earlier – the rich and merchants. Nevertheless, Alcuin's praise for commercial activity did not remain without successors; in England Ælfric (Abbot of Eynsham *c.* 995–*c.* 1012) had much to say about the essential role of merchants in his depiction of the social strata of Anglo-Saxon England.[3] Yet, as often as Carolingian texts and those composed during the immediately succeeding generations speak of payments in money to merchants, it is safest to assume that prices were most often still measured in equivalents of goods, not in standards of currency. Gold in particular remained at this time what it had always been: something to hoard, not to circulate as capital.[4] The Carolingians lay the foundations for the formal analysis of greed in the period following their work on the sin, but the application of these modes of imagining avarice to the reality of a world beginning to change economically in the tenth and eleventh centuries shows evidence of discontinuity in many important ways.

As a number of historical studies have demonstrated, beginning with the late Carolingian period Jews were a frequent presence in the area north of the Alps as traveling merchants bringing with themselves that burgeoning of trade which went along with liquid capital exchange, and they increasingly came under attack as exemplifications of avaricious behavior. In spite of Carolingian thinkers' ambivalence towards trade noticed already, the rulers encouraged Jewish merchants to settle in their territories.[5] Certainly, Jews were not the only ones to carry out such an occupation at this time, but they so dominated the field in the imagination of Christian observers that from the tenth century on, the historical sources contain phrases which virtually equate Jews with business activity by describing those engaged in commerce as "merchants, that is to say, Jews and other merchants," and similar phrases.[6] In the midst of the theoretical justification of commerce as a necessary and useful activity, the distrust of merchants as agents of avarice, inherited from Late Antiquity, could not be wholly suppressed. In other words, those who were in a position to reap the benefits of the growing use of currency in what has been called the "commercial revolution" or the incipient "money economy" were still marked as marginal to the mainstream culture of northern Europe. Nevertheless, the alterations which were then occurring in the economic situation of this region, as Lester Little has pointed out, were slowly replacing gift exchange as the cement of social relations with the commodification of liquid capital exchange: the system of feudal obedience, in which loyalty was given freely to those in positions of power, was giving way gradually to demands for a salary.[7]

By the late tenth and into the eleventh century, moralists began to register this change to a profit economy, in which social relationships were becoming commercialized, as a disturbance in the ethical continuum by which avarice was often perceived as the dominant vice and, because the use of cash as an agent of exchange allowed more people to manifest the signs of wealth and to desire to be wealthy than the limited number of the aristocracy which had had access to the immovable wealth in land in the early Middle Ages, the complaints of moralists from the late tenth century onwards contain descriptions which once again emphasized the trope of the entire world falling prey to greed. From the vantage point of the monastic chronicler Rodulfus Glaber (*c.* 980–*c.* 1046), the vice had decimated all of society, and he refers to *filargiria* as an insatiable vice, a queen dominating the entire world.[8] The image of avarice came to reflect the growing consciousness of money and its influence by returning to the Cassianic literal etymology of the vice so that by the eleventh century avarice was virtually equated with the desire for coin. Peter Damiani (1007–1072) noted that when Paul calls avarice idolatry (Col. 3:5), "he teaches in a clearer light that the *avarus* is a servant not of God, but of coins."[9] The critique of avarice encompassed eventually an array of venal behavior all focused on the acquisition of coins.[10] The *Fecunda ratis*, for example, composed by Egbert of Liège around 1025 as a collection of school exercises, echoes the satires of Horace in criticizing a situation in which "not art, but the goddess Money" is found more excellent than any honor.[11] The interests in an ecclesiastical reform which occurred together with the Investiture Contest generated legions of satires which censured the avaricious behavior of the clergy as illustrations of the power of money. In particular, the greed of Rome and of the papacy itself was expressed in the proverbial wisdom that "Roma" was an acronym for *radix omnium malorum avaritia* (the root of all evils is avarice).[12] The very iconography of the vice and the sinner afflicted by avarice developed in the visual arts to show a marked tendency to represent greed by the presence of coins or a money bag, generally slung around the neck of the avaricious sinner.[13]

The striking example of Gerhoh of Reichersberg's (1093–1169) *On the Fourth Night-Watch* may be used to illustrate the results of changes brought about by a profit economy and the way in which they replaced an older, feudal order. In these reflections on the history of the church and the stage of its turmoil in the twelfth century which he composed in 1167, Gerhoh drew on the language of the apocalypse to describe the conflict between imperial rule and the power of the *ecclesia*, characterizing the final, apocalyptic stage of church history in which he himself lived as one dominated by greedy behavior. The previous watch had been presided over by the popes, from Gregory the Great to Gregory VII, but after that:

more dangerous times began, it seems, because from that point on a new avarice arose in the city of Rome. For previously, the Roman people had the habit of voluntarily pledging feudal loyalty to their pastor with due obedience, but after the contention arose between the priesthood and the kingdom, the citizens of Rome who were followers of the Pope did not want to struggle in such a war for nothing, but demanded a great deal of money as if it were a kind of salary owed for their military service. . . . Thus, in this fourth watch an avarice enlarged with the greediness for gain rules the whole body of the church from head to foot. . . . Now, however, you would be pouring out a sermon [against this sin] in vain where there is no hearing, in the sight of men who think that gain is a form of piety . . .[14]

That Gerhoh resorted to the language of the apocalypse to express the demise of an older social order will come as no surprise, nor is it unusual that of all the vices, avarice was seen as decisive in bringing about these cataclysmic changes, for it had fulfilled this function earlier in the Middle Ages, since the growth of apocalyptic expectations with the approach of the year 1000.

AVARICE IN THE GROWTH OF ESCHATOLOGICAL EXPECTATIONS

If the waning of eschatological expectations in the first century had forced the young Christian community to take a stance on the acquisition and retention of material goods that helped establish the definition of avarice at the beginning of its history in Western culture, the approaching millennium exerted pressures of its own on the concept of avarice at what appeared to be the end of that history. The perception of a rapid spread of vice fueled anticipation of the coming end. "Now barely any tender shoots of *caritas* bloom," one poet termed it; "good qualities sink down, bad ones are on the rise, the vices are repeated. Thus does the devil's trickery make sport of the appearance of God."[15] Before the year 1000 the time of the Antichrist was understood to be a period, as Adso (Abbot of Montier-en-Der, *d.* 933) wrote, during which the wicked would be exalted and the apocalyptic perverter of divinity would teach the "vices which are opposed to the virtues." Adso, in fact, refers to the figure of the Antichrist himself as the "man of sin" (cf. Acts

13:10).[16] Albuin (*d.* 1031 as abbot in Tegernsee), who used Adso's material freely, combined his own tract on the Antichrist with a dossier on hamartiology in two of his works.[17] The *Liber Albuini*, addressed to an unknown woman, is given over solely to material on the vices and virtues – but even here, Albuin explains his purpose in collecting material from the moral tradition in apocalyptic terms:

> If, therefore, you can carry out all the things which you will find written here, I know for certain that you will come safely on doomsday before the seat of judgment of Jesus Christ, and safe-guarded from all enemies, you will possess a perpetual crown in heaven . . .[18]

The coming of the end of days might have been presaged by the rampant spread of avarice and other vices, but as Albuin shows, and as Johannes Fried has emphasized, the ideal reaction to the knowledge of sin spreading in the world in anticipation of the apocalypse was not to be petrified with fear, nor to lose one's self in the perception of social disruptions evoked by millenarian *Angst*, but to redouble one's efforts, internally and individually, to achieve a life of virtue.[19] What this meant in practical terms was often a vigilant study of avarice and the other vices,[20] which turned signs of the world's end into a matter of contemplative meditation and moderate action, modulating between the hysterical reaction to repent because the end is just around the corner, on the one hand, or, on the other, to repent in order to keep the end from turning that corner.

There was reason for a particularly marked focus on avarice and the end of the world in the view of those who saw simony as the destruction of the church, since moral theologians frequently ranked simony as a progeny of avarice. Eschatological vision in general highlights defects of the present moment; the glaring fault of a rampant materialism in the church drew all the more alarmed comment as the tenth century anticipated the apocalypse. In the area of the old Carolingian empire, as Maisonneuve has noted, the movement of reform which was underway left its mark in acts of the councils of the time in suggested remedies for Christian society among the clergy, monks, and laity. Simony among the clergy is apparently not mentioned often in the councils (though it was specifically condemned in 916 at the council of Hohenaltheim), but they contain various warnings against receiving or demanding payment for giving penance or baptism. In the eleventh century, the reforming attempts of the preceding period were taken up with great vigor, and from the council of Pavia (1023) and the efforts of Leo IX onward, the repression of simony became more severe.[21] Among those who were attuned to signs of the apocalypse, combating simony and re-establishing order in the church were firmly linked to the question of when the world would end. Among other errors which Abbo of Fleury (945–1004) complains about to Kings Hugo and Robert in his famous *Apologeticus*, one finds a great deal of attention to the simony which amounts to buying and selling bishoprics:

> See, most equitable princes, to where cupidity is leading us while *caritas* grows cold; from the gifts of omnipotent God, which are received freely, we are made into merchants, and we attempt to sell what we in fact do not own.[22]

He continues with little pause to complain of the error which had filled almost the whole world (at least according to some Lotharingians): that exactly when the feast of the Annunciation coincided with Good Friday the world would end. Clerical greed is here part of the errors afflicting the church, like the attempt to be too exact in reckoning the moment of the apocalypse, but while the problem of simony, being specific only to the clergy, may provide supporting evidence for the significance of avarice, it does not account completely for the particular relationship of greed and the end of the world.[23]

That humanity will become avaricious in the last days, and that this fact has a special value in the system of eschatology, belongs to the tropes of the signs of deterioration leading to the apocalypse, and such rhetorical forms were notoriously conservative in medieval texts. Even a literary form such as the ecclesiastical charter reveals the view that unbridled avarice is intimately connected with the end of the world. In one charter from Saint-Hilaire in Poitiers written between 997 and the turn of the millennium, for example, Geoffrey, treasurer of the chapter there, complained of the dissipation of ecclesiastical goods, which "we see are plundered in our time, in which greed is on the rise and the end of the world is imminent, and since a briefer life distresses people, a harsher greediness vexes them."[24] This decisive function of avarice as a sign of the hastening end of the world was prepared for in the early

Christian use of the myth of the Golden Age and its demise. For Lactantius himself, not always an original writer, but generally a reliable gauge of themes which resonated for the entire Patristic period and beyond, the correspondence of the vice and the destruction of the world was apparently evident enough to be reflected in his apocalypticism. His description of the end of the world drew on the same language he used to describe the end of the Golden Age, encouraging the comparison between the present time and the Golden one, both having succumbed, or now succumbing, to the sin of avarice:

> Therefore, as the end of the world approaches, the situation of human affairs must change and sink into worse decay while evil prevails, so that our own times, in which iniquity and ill-will have grown to the highest degree, can nevertheless be judged as a happy and almost golden time in comparison to the incurable evil of that one. For justice will become so rare, impiety and avarice and covetousness and lust will increase to such a degree, that even if by chance good people should exist, they will be plunder for the wicked . . .[25]

The vice of avarice, the sin of worldliness *par excellence*, was uniquely placed to be one of the leading signs of the approaching end of the world in the tenth century perhaps because it had already served that purpose and was transmitted as such in Patristic thought and earlier in the Middle Ages. The precise contours of avarice changed in eschatology as the demands on apocalyptic thought were altered, from a tool in the Christian transformation of Late Antique society to a meditative and social-critical step in the renewal of the church in the tenth century to what would then become the critique of a burgeoning mercantilism in the twelfth century and beyond. In all of these cases, greed had a pre-eminent place among the signs of decay because it served as a determining factor in the understanding of humanity's deterioration from its pristine beginnings. Avarice had a role in the end of human history, that is to say, because it had a similar one near the beginning of that history.

Imagery surrounding avarice

The following is intended as a guide to the use of imagery in connection with the vice of avarice in the literature of Late Antiquity and the early Middle Ages. Only concrete images and not abstractions (e.g., avarice as insatiability, the source of all evil, idolatry, or the like) have been included in the Appendix. In part I, the images are given in alphabetical order and the documentation for their use is listed in chronological order for each image. These citations are meant to be representative, not exhaustive, of the range of works in which the images occur in the literature treated in this study. Part II is arranged alphabetically according to the name of the authors or the title of the works found in Part I. The numbers following the names or titles in Part II refer to the entries in Part I and can serve as an index to the range of imagery for avarice used in the individual texts or employed by separate authors examined in this study.

I IMAGES

1 ACHAB (1Kings 21): **Chrysostom**, *Hom. 11 in Ep. 1 ad Cor.*, 5 (PG 61:94); *Hom. 23 in Ep. 2 ad Cor.*, 6 (PG 61:562); **Ambrose**, *Nab.*, 3.11 (CSEL 32,2:474); *Exameron*, 5.10.27–28 (CSEL 32,1:161); **Ps.-Basil**, *Admon. ad fil. spirit.*, cap. 9 (ed. Lehmann, pp. 45–46); **Isidore**, *Sent.*, 2.41.3–5 (PL 83:645–46); *Sent.*, 2.41.10 (PL 83:647); **Sedulius Scotus**, *In Ep. 1 ad Tim.*, 6 (PL 103:237); **Hrabanus Maurus**, *Comm. in Reg.*, 3.22 (PL 109:220); **Hincmar**, *De cav. vit.*, 2 (PL 125:881).

2 ACHAN, ACHAR (Josh. 7): **Chrysostom**, *Hom. 11 in Ep. 1 ad Cor.*, 5 (PG 61:94); **Ambrose**, *De off. min.*, 2.26.129–31 (PL 16:137–38); **Ps.-Basil**, *Admon. ad fil. spirit.*, cap. 9 (ed. Lehmann, pp. 45–46); **Jonas of Orléans**, *De inst. reg.*, 10 (ed. Reviron, p. 163).

3 ADAM AND EVE (Gen. 3): **Jerome**, *Enarr. in Ps. 118, serm. 11*, 6 (CCL 40:1699); **Augustine**, *De mor. eccl. cath.*, 19.35 (PL 32:1326); *Serm.*, 177.9 (ed. Lambot, p. 71 – PL 38:959); **Odo of Cluny**, *De vit.*, 2.4 (PL 133:551).

Appendix

4   ANANIAS AND SAPPHIRA (Acts 5:1–10): **Chrysostom**, *Hom. 65 in Ioan.*, 3 (PG 59:363); *Hom. 11 in Ep. 1 ad Cor.*, 5 (PG 61:94); **Jerome**, *Ep.*, 130.14 (CSEL 56:194) and *Ep.*, 14.5.3 (CSEL 54:51); **Cassian**, *Inst.*, 7.14, 30 (CSEL 17:137–38, 148); **Maximus of Turin**, *Serm.*, 18.1 (CCL 23:67); **Peter Chrysologus**, *Serm.*, 29.2 (CCL 24:169); *Reg. Mag.*, 87.24 (SC 106:358); **Benedict of Nursia**, *Reg. Ben.*, 57.4–8 (SC 182:624); **Ambrosius Autpertus**, *Expos. in Apoc.*, 2.2.6 (CCM 27:107); **Ps.-Hrabanus**, *De vit.*, 3.51 (PL112:1375); **Odo of Cluny**, *De vit.*, 3.22 (PL 133:606).

5   ANT: **Plutarch**, *De cup. div.*, 5 (*Moralia* 525E) (ed. Bernardakis, vol. 3, p. 361); **Libanius**, *Orat.*, 25.23 (ed. Schouler, p. 187): The avaricious always talk of the ants of India; **Augustine**, *De Gen. ad Litt.*, 7.10 (CSEL 28,1:209).

6   ANTISTENES: **Jerome**, *Ep.*, 71.3.3 (CSEL 55:4).

7   ARISTIPPUS as non-*avarus*: **Cicero**, *De inv.*, 2.58.176 (ed. Stroebel, p. 155); **Diogenes Laertius**, *Vitae Philos.*, 2.77 (ed. Long, vol. 1, p. 89).

8   ASS: **Plutarch**, *De cup. div.*, 5 (*Moralia* 525E) (ed. Bernardakis, vol. 3, p. 361).

9   BAD SEED: **Cassian**, *Inst.*, 7.21 (CSEL 17:146–47).

10 BAG: **Clement of Alexandria**, *Paed.*, 2.3.39.1 (GCS 12:180): The behavior of those who want more than what is sufficient is like the desire to store things in a bag with holes in it (cf. Hag. 1:6).

11 BALAAM (Num. 22): **Ambrose**, *De off. min.*, 2.26.129–31 (PL 16:137–38); **Peter Damiani**, *Contra phil.*, 4 (PL 145:534).

12 BEARS: **Plutarch**, *De cup. div*, 6 (*Moralia* 526A) (ed. Bernardakis, vol. 3, pp. 361–62); **Chrysostom**, *Hom. 9 in Ep. 1 ad Cor.*, 4 (PG 61:80).

13 BEAST: **Chrysostom**, *Hom. 65 in Ioan.*, 3 (PG 59:363); **Augustine**, *Serm.*, 367.1 (PL 39:1651): The sin of avarice is like wild beasts, but they rob only to still their momentary hunger while avarice knows no measure; **Cassian**, *Inst.*, 7.10 (CSEL 17:135–36); **Maximus of Turin**, *Serm.*, 18.3 (CCL 23:68–69); **Caesarius of Arles**, *Serm.*, 100A.13 (CCL 103:415): the wild beast of avarice; *The Old-Irish Penitential*, 3.1a (ed. Binchy, p. 265); *Aenigm. Bonif.*, *De vit.*, 3.61 (CCL 133:323); *De caritate et avaritia*, 2, 6 (MGH Poet 2:255).

14 BEASTLY TEETH: **Defensor**, *Lib. scint.*, 25.12 (CCL 117:108); **Smaragdus**, *Via regia*, 26 (PL 102:965).

15 BIRD OF PREY: **Plutarch**, *De cup. div.*, 5 (*Moralia* 525E) (ed. Bernardakis, vol. 3, p. 361); **Barnabas**, *Ep.*, 10.4 (SC 172:150): The birds of Lev. 11:13–15, Deut. 14:12–18.

16 BIRDLIME: **Ambrose**, *De bono mortis*, 5.16 (CSEL 32,1:718); **Augustine**, *Serm.*, 107.8 (PL 38:631); **Gregory the Great**, *Regulae pastoralis liber*, 3.20 (PL 77:86).

17 BLINDNESS: **Cicero**, *In M. Antonium Orat. Philippica 2*, 38.97 (ed. A. C. Clark); **Seneca**, *Ep. mor.*, 15.9 (ed. Reynolds, vol. 1, p. 40); *Phaedra*, 528 (ed. Giardina, vol. 1, p. 271); **Cyprian**, *De lapsis*, 11 (CCL 3:226); *De op. et eleem.*, 13 (CCL 3A:63); *Ad Donatum*, 13 (CCL 3A:11); **Basil**, *Hom. in div.*, 1 (PG 31:280); **Chrysostom**, *Hom. 11 in Ep. 1 ad Cor.*, 4 (PG 61:92–93); **Prudentius**, *Psychomachia*, verses 482 ff.

18 CAMEL: **Maximus of Turin**, *Serm.*, 32.1 and 48.2 (CCL 23:125 and 187–88); **Gaudentius of Brescia**, *Tract.*, 18.13 (CSEL 68:156) (cf. Luke 18:25).

19 CHILDREN: **Plutarch**, *De E Delphico*, 21 (*Moralia* 393E) (ed. Flacelière, p. 34): To spend money on defensive walls instead of alms is like being a child; **Basil**, *Hom. in illud*, 5 (PG 31:269): The man sinning by avarice is worse than a child; *Hom. in div.*, 4 (PG 31:289): See Plutarch (above); **Zeno**, *Tract.*, I 5 (I 9).1.3 (CCL 22:38): Avarice is the cause of the murder of unborn children; **Prudentius**, *Psychomachia*, verses 562–63 (CCL 126:169): Care for one's children.

20 COW: **Peter Chrysologus**, *Serm.*, 29.2 (CCL 24:168): Gold captured the Jews and turned them into cattle (who honored the golden calf).

21 CRAB: **Ambrose**, *Exameron*, 5.8.23 (CSEL 32,1:157–58): Crabs rob oysters just as humans defraud each other.

22 CRATES as non-*avarus*: **Gregory Nazianzen**, *Orat.*, 4.72 (PG 35:596); *De virt.*, verses 236ff. (PG 37:697); **Gregory Presbyter**, *Vita s. pat. nostri Gregorii theologi* (PG 35:256); **Jerome**, *Ep.*, 71.3.3 (CSEL 55:4); *Comm. in Matt.*, 3.19 (CCL 77:172).

23 CROESUS: **Gregory Nazianzen**, *De virt.*, verses 299ff. (PG 37:701–02); **Jerome**, *Comm. in Hiez.*, 8.prol (CCL 75:333); *Ep.*, 53.11.2–5 (CSEL 54:464–65).

24 DARKNESS: **Chrysostom**, *Hom. 11 in Ep. 1 ad Cor.*, 4 (PG 61:92–93).

25 DAUGHTER OF DEVIL: **Bede**, *In Prov. Sal.*, 3.30.15–16 (CCL 119B:143–44).

26 DELILAH (Judg. 16:5–31): **Ambrose**, *De off. min.*, 2.26.129–31 (PL 16:137–38): Delilah's avarice deceived Samson.

27 DEMOCRITUS as non-*avarus*: **Horace**, *Ep.*, 1.12.12–13 (ed. Klingner, p. 260).

28 DIOGENES as non-*avarus*: **Gregory Presbyter**, *Vita s. patris nostri Gregorii theologi* (PG 35:256).

29 DOG: **Aesop**, *Fabulae*, 136 (ed. Hausrath, second ed., vol. 1,1, pp. 161–62); **Isa.** 56:11; **Chrysostom**, *Hom. 20 in Matt.*, 3 (PG 57:288); *Hom. 2 in Ep. ad Phil.*, 4 (PG 62:203): The avaricious person is like a dog chained to a tomb; *Hom. 81 in Matt.*, 3 (PG 58:733); *Hom. 13 in Ep. ad Rom.*, 11 (PG 60:522); **Evagrius Ponticus**, *De octo sp.* (PG 79:1152C).

30 DRAGON: **Jerome**, *Ep.*, 125.3–4 (CSEL 56:122).

31 DROPSY: **Gregory Nazianzen**, *De virt.*, verse 446 (PG 37:712); *Adversus opum amantes*, verses 151–58; **Chrysostom**, *Hom. 14 in Ep. 1 ad Cor.*, 5 (PG 61:120–21); **Gregory the Great**, *Mor.*, 14.12.14 (CCL 143A:705–06); **Alcuin**, *Liber de animae ratione*, 4 (PL 101:640).

32 EAGLE: **Ambrose**, *Exameron*, 5.14.47 (CSEL 32,1:176).

33 ELEPHANTIASIS: **Palladius**, *Historia Lausiaca*, 17 (ed. Butler, vol. 2, pp. 43–47).

34 ELIJAH as non-*avarus* (1Kings 19:19–21): **Evagrius Ponticus**, *Antirr.*, 3.13 and 21 (ed. Frankenberg, p. 494).

35 ENCHANTRESS: **Evagrius Ponticus**, *De vit. quae opp.*, 3 (PG 79:1141).

36 EPHAH (Zech. 5:5–11): **Gregory the Great**, *Mor.*, 14.53.64–65 (CCL 143A:737–39); **Hincmar**, *De cav. vit.*, 2 (PL 125:881D-882B).

37 FEVER: **Chrysostom**, *Hom. 11 in Ep. 1 ad Cor.*, 4 (PG 61:92–93).

38 FIGURE OF RIDICULE: **Chrysostom**, *Hom. 83 in Matt.*, 3 (PG 58:749).

39 FINGERS: **Lucian**, *Orat.*, 25.13 (ed. Macleod, vol. 1, p. 315); **Seneca**, *Ep. mor.*, 88.10 (ed. Reynolds, vol. 1, pp. 314–15); **Gregory Nazianzen**, *Adv. op. am.*, verse 117 (PG 37:865); **Ambrose**, *De Tobia*, 7.25 (ed. Giacchero, p. 103); **Zeno**, *Tract.*, I 5 (I 9).4.12 (CCL 22:40).

40 FIRE: **Clement of Alexandria**, *Quis dives*, 15.3 (GCS 17:169); **Macarius/ Symeon**, *Hom.*, 10.2.4 (SC 275:158); **Basil**, *Hom. in div.*, 5 (PG 31:292); **Gregory Nazianzen**, *Adversus opum amantes*, verse 28; **Chrysostom**, *Quod nemo laedatur*, 6 (PG 52:467); *Hom. 18 in Ep. 1 ad Tim.*, 6, 3 (PG 62:595); **Cassian**, *Inst.*, 7.23–24 (CSEL 17:147–48); **Prudentius**, *Psychomachia*, verses 482 ff.; **Gregory the Great**, *Mor.*, 7.28.34 (CCL 143:357), 12.53.61 (CCL 143A:666), 12.54.62 (CCL 143A:667), 12.54.63 (CCL 143A:667), 14.23.28 (CCL 143A:766), 15.19.23 (CCL 143A:763), 26.28.53 (PL 76:381); *Reg. past.*, 1.11 (PL 77:26); *Hom. in ev.*, 2.25.10 (PL 76:1196); **Defensor**, *Lib. scint.*, 25.12 (CCL 117:108); **Smaragdus**, *Via regia*, 26 (PL 102:965); **Ambrosius Autpertus**, *Serm. de cup.*, 6 (CCM 27B:967); **Odo of Cluny**, *De vit.*, 2.3 (PL 133:550).

41 FIREPLACE: **Peter Damiani**, *Ep.*, 1.15 (PL 144:253).

42 FISH: **Horace**, *Serm.*, 2.5.25 (ed. Klingner, p. 224); **Lucian**, *Dial. mort.*, 6.4. (ed. Jacobitz, vol. 1, p. 144); *Orat.*, 25.22 (ed. Macleod, vol. 1, p. 319); **Origen**, *Comm. on Matt.*, 13.12 (GCS 40:211–12); **Basil**, *Hom. 7 in Hexaem.*, 3 (SC 26:402–04); **Ambrose**, *Exameron*, 5.5.12–14 (CSEL 32,1:148–50): The biggest fish eats the smaller ones; **Zeno of Verona**, *Tract.*, I 5 (I 9).4.12 (CCL 22:40): Money as a fish hook.

43 FIVE FOOLISH VIRGINS (Matt. 25:1–13): **Chrysostom**, *Hom. 81 in Matt.*, 4 (PG 58:736).

44 FORTRESS: **Clement of Alexandria**, *Paedagogus*, 2.3.39.3 (GCS 12:181); cf. **Macarius/Symeon**, *Hom.*, 10.2.4 (SC 275:158).

45 FOUL ODOR: **Gregory the Great**, *Mor.*, 14.53.65 (CCL 143A:738–39); **Caesarius of Arles**, *Serm.*, 29.2 (CCL 103:127).

46 FOX: **Clement of Alexandria**, *Stromata*, 4.6.31.2 (GCS 52 [15]:261–62): Lovers of possessions are like foxes hiding in their holes.

47 GAPING MOUTH: **Prudentius**, *Psychomachia*, verse 457.

48 GEHAZI (2Kings 5:20–27): **Origen**, *Comment. on 1Cor* (ed. Jenkins, p. 364); **Palladius**, *Historia Lausiaca*, 17 (ed. Butler, vol. 2, pp. 43–47); **Chrysostom**, *Hom. 80 in Matt.*, 3 (PG 58:728); *Hom. 65 in Ioan.*, 3 (PG 59:363); *Hom. 11 in Ep. 1 ad Cor.*, 5 (PG 61:94); *Hom. 23 in Ep. 2 ad Cor.*, 6 (PG 61:562); **Evagrius Ponticus**, *Antirr.*, 3.15 (ed. Frankenberg, p. 496); **Jerome**, *Vita S. Hilarionis Eremitae*, 18 (PL 23:36–37); **Ambrose**, *Expos. Evang. sec. Luc.*, 4.54 (CCL 14:125); **Cassian**, *Inst.*, 7.14, 30 (CSEL 17:137–38, 148); **Hrabanus Maurus**, *Comm. in lib. 4 Reg.*, 3.22 (PL 109:221); **Ps.-Hrabanus**, *De vit.*, 3.51 (PL 112:1375); **Peter Damiani**, *Ep.* 6, 32 (PL 144:426); *Contra phil.*, 4 (PL 145:535).

49 GRIFFIN: **Jerome**, *Ep.*, 125.3–4 (CSEL 56:122).

50 HAND: **Sir.** 4:36; **Jerome**, *Comm. in Esaiam*, 1.1.23 (CCL 73:22–23); **Laurentius of Novae**, *Hom.*, 1 (PL 66:96); **Quodvultdeus**, *De accedentibus ad gratiam*, 1.5.1 (CCL 60:444); **Maximus of Turin**, *Serm.*, 43.4 (CCL 23:176).

51 HAWK: **Plautus**, *Persa*, 409 (ed. Lindsay, vol. 2, p. 163); **Ambrose**, *Exameron*, 5.14.47 (CSEL 32,1:176); *De excessu fratris*, 1.55 (CSEL 73:238–39).

52 HELL: **Basil**, *Hom. in div.*, 5 (PG 31:293): The φιλάργυρος is like hell; neither of them can say, "Enough" (see Prov. 27:20, 30:16); **Chrysostom**, *Hom. 28 in Matt.*, 5 (PG 57:356); *Hom. 63 in Matt.*, 4 (PG 58:607); *Hom. 41 in Matt.*, 4 (57:450–51); **Ps.-Basil**, *Admon. ad fil. spirit.*, cap. 9 (ed. Lehmann, pp. 45–46); **Aldhelm**, *De virg.*, 2.2620–24 (MGH Auct. ant. 15:459); **Theodulf**, *Capitulare*, 10.59 (ed. de Clercq, p. 343); *De eo quod avarus adglomeratis diversis opibus satiari nequit*, verses 1–4 (MGH Poet 1,2:460); **Alcuin**, *Liber de animae ratione*, 4 (PL 101:640).

53 HOOK-LIKE HAND: **Prudentius**, *Psychomachia*, verses 455–56; *Peristefanon*, 2.241–44 (CCL 126:265).

54 HORSE: **Cassian**, *Inst.*, 7.8 (CSEL 17:134): The *avarus* is like an ill-tempered horse.

55 HUNGER: **Evagrius Ponticus**, *De div. mal. cog.*, 23 (PG 79:1225).

56 IMPETIGO: **Gregory the Great**, *Reg. past.*, 1.11 (PL 77:26).

57 INFERTILITY: **Chrysostom**, *Hom. 83 in Matt.*, 3 (PG 58:749). See **Sir.** 20:4, 30:20.

58 INHUMAN MISTRESS: **Chrysostom**, *Quod nemo laedatur*, 6 (PG 52:467).

59 INSANITY: **Basil**, *Hom. in illud*, 4–5 (PG 31:269); *Hom. in div.*, 3 (PG 31:285); **Gregory Nazianzen**, *Adversus opum amantes*, verses 6–20 (PG 37:856–84); **Chrysostom**, *Adversus oppugnatores vitae monasticae*, 2.3 (PG 47:335); *Hom. 51 in Matt.*, 6 (PG 58:518).

60 INSOMNIA: **Claudianus**, *In Rufinum libri*, 1.37–38 (ed. Koch, p. 12); **Plutarch**, *De cup. div.*, 3 (*Moralia* 524B) (ed. Bernardakis, p. 357); **Ecclus**. 31:1; **Tatian**, *Orat. ad Graecos*, 11.2 (ed. Whittaker, p. 22); **Evagrius Ponticus**, *De vit. quae opp.*, 3 (PG 79:1141).

61 JAILER: **Chrysostom**, *Hom. 14 in Matt.*, 4 (PG 57:222).

62 JEWS: **Luke** 16:14: Pharisees are avaricious; **Tertullian**, *De baptismo*, 20.4 (CCL 1:294–95): Connected the temptations of the Israelites in the desert with those of Jesus; **Origen**, *Comm. ser.* 145 (GCS 38:299): Pharisees are avaricious; **Chrysostom**, *Hom. 4 in Ep. ad Col.*, *cap. 1*, 4 (PG 62:331): The Israelites were avaricious during the exodus; *Orationes contra Judaeos*, 1.7 (PG 48:853): Anti-Jewish polemic; **Ambrose**, *Expos. Evang. sec. Luc.*, 7.247–48 (CCL 14:297–98); **Jerome**, *Comm. in Esaiam*, 1.2.7 (CCL 73:32): No nations are more avaricious than the Romans and Jews; **Ps.-Basil**, *Admon. ad fil. spirit.*, *cap. 9* (ed. Lehmann, pp. 45–46).

63 JOB as non-*avarus*: **Ambrose**, *De off. min.*, 1.39.194 (PL 16:87); *Nab.*, 13.57 (CSEL 32,2:501–02); **Augustine**, *Serm.*, 177.4 (ed. Lambot, p. 67 – PL 38:955); *Serm.*, 107.10 (PL 38:632); 261.5 (ed. Lambot, pp. 91–92 – PL 38:1205); *Enarr. in Ps. 118, serm. 11*, 6 (CCL 40:1699).

64 JOSEPH (Gen. 47:11–19) as non-*avarus*: **Basil**, *Hom. in illud*, 2 (PG 31:265); **Ambrose**, *Nab.*, 7.33 (CSEL 32,2:485–86).

65 JUDAS (Matt. 26:14–16): ***Acta Thomae***, 84 (ed. Bonnet, pp. 199–200); **Origen**, *Contra Celsum*, 2.11 and 20 (GCS 2:139 and 151); *Comment. on Matt.*, 11.9 and 16.8 (GCS 40:49–50 and 489); *Comm. ser.*, 75, 78, and 117 (GCS 38:176, 186–87 and 244); *Comment. on John*, 20.22.180 and 32.19.241, 244 (GCS 10:354 and 458); *Philocalia*, 23.13 (SC 226:174); **Didymus the Blind**, *Comment. on Job*, 4.5–9 (ed. Henrichs, pp. 32–34); *Expos. in Ps. 9* (PG 39:1200, 1204–05); **Basil** (?), *Constitutiones asceticae*, 34 (PG 31:1424–48); **Basil**, *Ep. 53* (ed. Courtonne, vol. 1, pp. 137–39); **Gregory of Nyssa**, *De beneficentia (De pauperibus amandis, 1)* (ed. Van Heck, p. 94); **Chrysostom**, *Hom. 65 in Ioan.*, 3 (PG 59:363); *Hom. 23 in Ep. 2 ad Cor.*, 6 (PG 61:562); *Hom. 1 in prodit. Judae*, 3 (PG 49:376); *Hom. 2 in prodit. Judae*, 3 (PG 49:386); *Hom. 28 in Matt.*, 4 (PG 57:356); *Hom. 81 in Matt.*, 3 (PG 58:733); *Hom. 83 in Matt.*, 2 (PG 58:747–48); *Hom. 85 in Matt.*, 2 (PG 58:760); *Hom. 6 in Ep. ad Phil.*, 5

(PG 62:225); **Bohairic Life of Pachomius**, 186 (trans. Veilleux, p. 226);
Cassian, *Inst.*, 7.14, 30 (CSEL 17:137–38, 148); **Gaudentius**, *Tract.*, 13.13
(CSEL 68:118); **Isidore**, *Sent.*, 2.41.5 (PL 83:646); **Ps.-Basil**, *Admon. ad
fil. spirit.*, cap. 9 (ed. Lehmann, pp. 45–46); **Paulinus of Aquileia**, *Lib.
exhor.*, 30 (PL 99:227); **Hrabanus Maurus**, *Comm. in Matt.*, 8.27.3 (PL
107:1151); *Hom.*, 62 (PL 110:119); **Ps.-Hrabanus**, *De vit.*, 3.51 (PL
112:1375); **Hincmar**, *Opusculum 55 capitulorum adversus Hincmarum
Laudunensem*, 51 (PL 126:489); **Rather of Verona**, *Serm. in Cena Dom.*, 3
(CCL 46:99).

66 LEAD WEIGHT: **Gregory the Great**, *Mor.*, 14.53.63 (CCL 143A:736–37);
cf. **Julianus Pomerius**, *De vita contemp.*, 2.15 (PL 59:458).

67 LION: **Plutarch**, *De cup. div*, 6 (*Moralia* 526A) (ed. Bernardakis, vol. 3,
pp. 361–62); **Testament of Dan**, 5.7 (ed. de Jonge, p. 108); **Gregory
Nazianzen**, *Adv. op. am.*, verse 51 (PG 37:860); **Chrysostom**, *Hom. 9 in
Ep. 1 ad Cor.*, 4 (PG 61:80); **The Old-Irish Penitential**, 3.1a (ed. Binchy,
p. 265).

68 LOT'S WIFE (Gen. 19:26): **Ambrosius Autpertus**, *Conflictus*, 16 (CCM
27B:921–22).

69 MANIA: **Evagrius Ponticus**, *De vit. quae opp.*, 3 (PG 79:1141).

70 MANY-HEADED BEAST (HYDRA): **Plato**, *Respublica*, 9 (590B) (ed.
Burnet); **Gregory of Nyssa**, *Orat. 5 de beat.* 5 (PG 44:1257–60);
Chrysostom, *Hom. 90 in Matt.*, 4 (PG 58:791).

71 MATTHEW as non-*avarus* (Matt. 9:9): **Peter Chrysologus**, *Serm.*,
28.3–5 (CCL 24:163–65); *Serm.*, 29.3 (CCL 24:170).

72 MEGARIANS (*aedificant quasi semper uicturi, uiuunt quasi altera die
morituri*): **Jerome**, *Ep.*, 123.14.6 (CSEL 56:91); *Ep.*, 128.5.1 (CSEL
56:161).

73 MIDAS: **Gregory Nazianzen**, *Epigram 34* (PG 38:101–02); *De virt.*,
verses 407–11 (PG 37:709–10); *Adversus opum amantes*, verses 148–50
(PG 37:867); *Ad suam animam*, verses 13–17 (PG 37:1435–36); **Chrysostom**, *Orat.*, 25.22–25 (ed. Schouler, pp. 187–89).

74 MIS-SHAPEN WOMAN: **Chrysostom**, *Expos. in Ps. 9*, 1 (PG 55:122).

75 MONSTER: **Jerome**, *Ep.*, 125.3–4 (CSEL 56:122): In India mountains of
gold and gems are guarded by monsters, the watchmen of Avarice;
Chrysostom, *Hom. 28 in Matt.*, 5 (PG 57:356).

76 MOTHER OF ZEBEDEE'S SONS (Matt. 20:21): **Ambrose**, *De fide*, 5.5.57
(CSEL 78:239).

77 NABOTH (1Kings 21): **Ambrose**, *Ep.*, 10.76 (see esp. sect. 19) (CSEL
82,3:118–19); *Serm. contra Auxentium de basilicis tradendis*, see sect. 17
(PL 16:1055).

78 PHARISEES: **Ps.-Basil**, *Admon. ad fil. spirit.*, cap. 9 (ed. Lehmann, pp. 45–46).

79 PIG: **Chrysostom**, *Hom. 23 in Ep. 1 ad Cor.*, 5 (PG 61:196).

80 PLAGUE: **Gregory Nazianzen**, *Adversus opum amantes*, verse 28.

81 POTIPHAR'S WIFE (Gen. 39:7–20): **Basil**, *Hom. dicta temp. famis et sicc.*, 8 (PG 31:325): Avarice tempts the rich, as Potiphar's wife tried to seduce Joseph.

82 RAVEN (or CROW): **Clement of Alexandria**, *Strom.*, 5.8.52.1–2. (GCS 52 [15]:361).

83 RICH YOUTH (Luke 18:18–27): **Ps.-Basil**, *Admon. ad fil. spirit.*, cap. 9 (ed. Lehmann, pp. 45–46).

84 RIVER: **Plutarch**, *De amicorum multitudine*, 2 (*Moralia* 93F) (ed. Bernardakis, vol. 1, p. 227); **Basil**, *Hom. in div.*, 5 (PG 31:293); **Gregory Nazianzen**, *De virt.*, verse 28.

85 ROOMY POCKETS: **Juvenal**, *Saturae*, 1.87–88 (ed. Housman, p. 4); **Prudentius**, *Psychomachia*, verses 458–59.

86 SAILORS: **Basil**, *Quod rebus*, 7 (PG 31:552): Christians should throw their excess goods overboard (as alms).

87 SARDANAPALUS: **Gregory Nazianzen**, *De virt.*, verses 612ff. (PG 37:724–25).

88 SATAN: **Ps.-Hrabanus**, *De vit.*, 3.34 (PL 112:1364): Satan's fall from heaven was due partially to his avarice.

89 SAUL (1Sam. 15:9–30): **Ps.-Basil**, *Admon. ad fil. spirit.*, cap. 9 (ed. Lehmann, pp. 45–46); **Paulinus of Aquileia**, *Lib. exhor.*, 30 (PL 99:226).

90 SELEUKES: **Basil**, *Hom. in div.*, 5 (PG 31:293): This bird was created insatiable by God to free humankind from insatiability.

91 SERPENT: **Chrysostom**, *Expos. in Ps. 48*, 1 (PG 55:501); *Hom. 18 in Ep. 1 ad Tim.*, 6.2 (PG 62:600); **Paulinus of Nola**, *Ep.*, 34.1 (CSEL 29:303); **Maximus of Turin**, *Serm.*, 37.5 (CCL 23:147) (see Luke 10:19); **Laurentius of Novae**, *Hom.*, 1 (PL 66:96); *The Old-Irish Penitential*, 3.1a (ed. Binchy, p. 265); **Peter Damiani**, *Contra phil.*, 3 (PL 145:534): Avarice is like a two-headed snake.

92 SERPENT FANGS: **Aenigm. Bonif.**, *De vit.*, 3.22–24 (CCL 133:319); **Defensor**, *Liber scintillarum*, 25.12 (CCL 117:108).

93 SERVANT (Matt. 25:14–30): **Chrysostom**, *Hom. 81 in Matt.*, 4 (PG 58:736): Who does not give to his fellow servants; *Hom. 81 in Matt.*, 4 (PG 58:736): Who buried the talent.

94 SHACKLES: **Caesarius of Arles**, *Serm.*, 48.7 (CCL 103:220).

95 SHIPWRECK: **Evagrius Ponticus**, *De octo sp.*, 7 (PG 79:1152).

96 SICKNESS: **Basil**, *Hom. in div.*, 4 (PG 31:288).

97 SIMON MAGUS (Acts 8:18–24): **Gregory the Great**, *Hom. in ev.*, 1.4.4 (PL 76:1091–92); **Peter Damiani**, *Contra phil.*, 4 (PL 145:535); **Othlo of St. Emmeram**, *Dial. de trib. quaest.*, 15 (PL 146:79).

98 SLAVES: **Chrysostom**, *Hom. 21 in Matt.*, 1 (PG 57:294); *Hom. 44 in Matt.*, 4 (PG 57:470); *Hom. 45 in Matt.*, 3 (PG 58:475); *Hom. 4 in Ep. ad Col., cap. 1*, 4 (PG 62:331): The Israelites were lovers of money during the exodus; *Hom. 7 in Ep. 1 ad Tim., cap. 2*, 3 (PG 62:538); *Hom. 12 in Ep. ad Rom.*, 7 (PG 60:504): Lecherous and avaricious sinners are similar in being slaves to their desire, in a state of anxiety, etc.; **Evagrius Ponticus**, *De octo sp.*, 7 (PG 79:1152): When the monk with many possessions dies, he is dragged away against his will like a runaway slave; **Chromatius**, *Tract.*, 31.3.3 (CCL 9A:347): Avarice is slavery to Mammon; **Prudentius**, *Amartigenia*, 432–36 (CCL 126:131): The *avarus* as a person greedily increasing his estates and fettered by a thousand chains though he does not even realize he is a slave.

99 SNARE: **Cassian**, *Inst.*, 7.23–24 (CSEL 17:147–48).

100 SONS OF SAMUEL (1Sam. 8:1–4): **Gregory the Great**, *In Lib. Reg.*, 4.42–45 (CCL 144:316–18); **Peter Damiani**, *Contra phil.*, 1 (PL 145:531).

101 SPIDER: **Ambrose**, *De off. min.*, 1.49.242–44 (PL 16:102): Why, *avarus*, do you spin a web which is fruitless?

102 THEATER: **Basil**, *Hom. in illud*, 7 (PG 31:276): Like someone who takes a seat in the theater and drives all others away, the person who possesses more for himself than what he needs has appropriated illicitly for himself what belongs to everyone.

103 THIRST: **Chrysostom**, *Hom. 11 in Ep. 1 ad Cor.*, 4 (PG 61:92–93): The avaricious person is like a patient with fever and the insatiable thirst caused by high fever; **Evagrius Ponticus**, *De div. mal. cog.*, 23 (PG 79:1225): Greed keeps the thoughts of an avaricious person on possessions in the same way as a thirsting person's need to drink keeps his on water.

104 THORN: **Gregory the Great**, *Reg. past.*, 3.21 (PL 77:88).

105 TUMOR: **Gregory of Nyssa**, *Orat. 4 in Ecclesiasten* (ed. McDonough and Alexander, pp. 346–47).

106 TYRANNY: **Gregory Nazianzen**, *Adversus opum amantes*, verse 48 (PG 37:860).

107 TYRANT: **Chrysostom**, *Expos. in Ps. 48*, 1 (PG 55:499); *Hom. 13 in Ep. ad Rom.*, 11 (PG 60:523); *tyrannis* in *Hom. 21 in Matt.*, 1 (PG 57:294); *Hom. 85 in Matt.*, 2 (PG 58:760); *Hom. 65 in Ioan.*, 3 (PG 59:363); *Hom. 6 in Ep. ad Rom.*, 2 (PG 60:434); *Hom. 6 in Ep. ad Phil., cap. 2*, 5 (PG 62:225).

108 VOMIT: **Gregory Nazianzen**, *Adversus opum amantes*, verse 141 (PG 37:867 – see Job 20:15).

109 WAR: **Pachomius**, *Catechism Concerning a Vengeful Monk* (Corpus Scriptorum Christianorum Orientalium 160:22): Avarice conducts a war against ascetes.

110 WEAKNESS OF SOUL: **Origen**, *In Num. hom.*, 26.12 (GCS 30:272).

111 WHORE: **Chrysostom**, *Quod nemo laedatur*, 6 (PG 52:467).

112 WOLF: **Ezek**. 22:27; **Chrysostom**, *Hom. 69 in Matt.*, 4 (PG 58:654): Caring for superfluous things, we act like wolves and leopards; *Expos. in Ps. 48*, 1 (PG 55:500); *Hom. 17 in Ep. 1 ad Tim.*, 6.3 (PG 62:594–95): The avaricious should be exiled from the world like wolves; *Hom. 18 in Ep. 1 ad Tim.*, 6.2 (PG 62:600): Avarice orders the avaricious to surpass the wolf in rapaciousness; **Prudentius**, *Psychomachia*, verses 467ff. (CCL 126:166): The descendants of Avarice are crimes which leap like ravenous wolves; **Maximus of Turin**, *Serm.*, 18.3 (CCL 23:68–69); **Boethius**, *De cons. phil.*, 4.3.17 (CCL 94:72); **Caesarius of Arles**, *Serm.*, 152.3 (CCL 104:624); **Hrabanus Maurus**, *Comm. in Ecclus.*, 3.8 (PL 109:853); *The Blickling Homilies*, 17 (EETS os 58,63,73:211).

113 WOMAN HIDING MONEY BAGS: **Prudentius**, *Psychomachia*, verses 454–63.

114 WORMS: **Peter Damiani**, *Serm.*, 6 (PL 144:540): Avarice produces worms (see Isa. 66:24).

115 WOUND: **Zeno**, *Tract.*, I 5 (I 9).1.3 (CCL 22:38): Avarice is the cause of wounds felling nations.

116 ZACCHAEUS as non-*avarus* (Luke 19:8–10): **Ambrose**, *Exp. Luc.*, 8.84–86 (CCL 14:330); **Gregory the Great**, *Hom. in ev.*, 2.25.10 (PL 76:1196).

II AUTHORS (NUMBERS REFER TO THE ENTRIES ABOVE)

Acta Thomae: 65
Aesop: 29
Alcuin: 31, 52
Aldhelm: 52
Ambrose: 1, 2, 11, 16, 21, 26, 32, 39, 42, 48, 51, 62–64, 76, 77, 101, 116
Ambrosius Autpertus: 4, 40, 68
Augustine: 3, 5, 13, 16, 63
Barnabas: 15
Basil the Great: 17, 19, 40, 42, 52, 59, 64, 65, 81, 84, 86, 90, 96, 102
Ps.-Basil: 1, 2, 52, 62, 65, 78, 83, 89
Bede: 25

Benedict of Nursia: 4
The Blickling Homilies: 112
Boethius: 112
Bohairic Life of Pachomius: 65
Boniface: 13, 92
Caesarius of Arles: 13, 45, 94, 112
De caritate et avaritia: 13
Cassian: 4, 9, 13, 40, 48, 54, 65, 99
Chromatius: 98
Cicero: 7, 17
Claudianus: 60
Clement of Alexandria: 10, 40, 44, 46, 82

Notes

1 *De institutis coenobiorum et de octo principalium vitiorum remediis libri 12*, 7.1 (ed. M. Petschenig, CSEL 17 [Vienna, 1888], p. 130). See also *Conlationes 24*, 5.2 (ed. M. Petschenig, CSEL 13 [Vienna, 1886], p. 121). On the backgrounds of the *Instituta* see Owen Chadwick, *John Cassian*, second ed. (Cambridge, 1968), esp. pp. 37–50.

2 *Inst.*, 7.21 (CSEL 17:144).

3 *De libero arbitrio*, 3.17.48.165–66 (ed. W. M. Green, CCL 29 [Turnhout, 1970], pp. 303–04).

4 For Augustine's knowledge of Greek, see Walter Berschin, *Griechisch-lateinisches Mittelalter* (Bern and Munich, 1980), pp. 69–73 and n. 40; Peter Brown, *Augustine of Hippo: A Biography* (Berkeley and Los Angeles, 1967), p. 271 and n. 2.

5 *Poggii Florentini historia convivalis disceptative de avaritia*, in *Opera omnia* (Basel, 1538), p. 17; repr. in Poggius Bracciolini, *Opera omnia*, ed. R. Fubini, vol. 1 (Turin, 1964), p. 17.

6 On the intention and reception of Poggio's dialogue, see Richard Newhauser, "Patristic Poggio? The Evidence of Győr, Egyházmegyei Könyvtár MS. I.4," *Rinascimento* 26 (1986), 231–39. On the theories of Max Weber and R. H. Tawney, see Winthrop S. Hudson, "The Weber Thesis Reexamined," *Church History* 30 (1961), 88–99; repr. *Church History* 57 (suppl.) (1988), 56–67.

7 "The Seven Deadly Sins: Some Problems of Research," *Speculum* 43 (1968), 1–22.

8 *The Waning of the Middle Ages*, trans. F. Hopman (London, 1924; repr. New York, 1954), p. 28.

9 *The Seven Deadly Sins* ([East Lansing, Mich.], 1952; repr. 1967), p. 95.

10 Lester K. Little, "Pride Goes before Avarice: Social Change and the Vices in Latin Christendom," *The American Historical Review* 76 (1971), 16–49; Alexander Murray, *Reason and Society in the Middle Ages* (Oxford, 1978), ch. 3; John A. Yunck, *The Lineage of Lady Meed: The Development of Mediaeval Venality Satire*, The University of Notre Dame, Publications in Mediaeval Studies 17 (Notre Dame, IN, 1963).

11 Heinrich Fichtenau, *Askese und Laster in der Anschauung des Mittelalters, II: Lasterkampf und Lasterlehre*, rev. and repr. in his *Beiträge zur Mediävistik*

(Stuttgart, 1975), vol. 1, pp. 64–107; Karl Suso Frank, "Habsucht," *RAC*, vol. 13 (1984), cols. 226–47. Dr. Brian S. Rosner is currently completing a theological monograph on greed as idolatry.

1 ALMS AND ASCETES, ROUND STONES AND MASONS: AVARICE IN THE EARLY CHURCH

1 For self-sufficiency, or *autarkeia* (αὐτάρκεια), in this work, see *Sim.*, 1.6 (ed. M. Whittaker in *Die apostolischen Väter, I: Der Hirt des Hermas*, GCS 48 [Berlin, 1956], p. 47). The image of the tower is found in *Vis.*, 3.6.5–6 (p. 13) and *Sim.*, 9.30.3–5 (p. 98). See Hans-Ulrich Perels, "Besitzethik in den apokryphen Apostelgeschichten und in der zeitgenössischen christlichen Literatur" (Dissertation, University of Heidelberg, 1976), pp. 109–11; W.-D. Hauschild, "Christentum und Eigentum. Zum Problem eines altkirchlichen 'Sozialismus'," *Zeitschrift für Evangelische Ethik* 16 (1972), 35–36; Jacques Liébaert, *Les enseignements moraux des pères apostoliques*, Recherches et Synthèses, Section de morale 4 (Gembloux, 1970), pp. 166–67, 170–71, 186. In *Sim.*, 9.20.1–4 (pp. 92–93), the rich appear again in the allegory of the twelve mountains which are arranged from most sinful to most blessed. The mountain of the wealthy is covered with thorns and prickly plants which are symbolic of the rich themselves (see Matt. 13:22) and those who give their attention only to business. The wealthy are not considered to be as bad as apostates (for whom penance is impossible), but they are only two steps above them.

2 Morton Bloomfield, *The Seven Deadly Sins: An Introduction to the History of a Religious Concept* ([East Lansing, Mich.], 1952; repr. 1967), p. 44; *Hermas, Vis.*, 1.1.8 (p. 2).

3 For the place of avarice in the first type of list, see 1Cor. 6:9–10; in the second, 1Cor. 5:10. The distinction between the two is based on Ehrhard Kamlah, *Die Form der katalogischen Paränese im Neuen Testament*, Wissenschaftliche Untersuchungen zum Neuen Testament 7 (Tübingen, 1964). Cf. also S. Wibbing, *Die Tugend- und Lasterkataloge im Neuen Testament*, Beihefte zur Zeitschrift für die Neutestamentliche Wissenschaft 25 (Berlin, 1959); A. Vögtle, *Die Tugend- und Lasterkataloge im Neuen Testament, exegetisch, religions- und formgeschichtlich untersucht*, Neutestamentliche Abhandlungen 16, 4/5 (Münster, 1936).

4 *Epistle of Barnabas*, 19.6 (ed. and trans. P. Prigent and R. Kraft, SC 172 [Paris, 1971], p. 202). On cupidity's relationship to the Decalogue here, see Liébaert, *Les enseignements*, pp. 146–47. See also *Didaché*, 2.6 (ed. and trans. W. Rordorf and A. Tuilier, SC 248 [Paris, 1978], p. 150). On the use of the Ten Commandments in early Christianity, see Robert M. Grant, "The Decalogue in Early Christianity," *Harvard Theological Review* 40,1 (1947), 1–17 (repr. in E. Ferguson, ed., *Christian Life: Ethics, Morality, and Discipline in the Early Church*, SEC 16:1–17).

5 Luke 12:15–21. On the special position of Luke see Halvor Moxnes, *The Economy of the Kingdom: Social Conflict and Economic Relations in Luke's Gospel* (Philadelphia, 1988); H.-J. Degenhardt, *Lukas – Evangelist der Armen. Besitz und Besitzverzicht in den Lukanischen Schriften* (Stuttgart, 1965); Robert Koch, "Die

Wertung des Besitzes im Lukasevangelium," *Biblica* 38 (1957), 151–69. As Wayne Meeks notes in *The Origins of Christian Morality* (New Haven and London, 1993), p. 129, Luke may "idealize the moral economy of the peasant, but he knows well that the spread of Christianity was dependent from the beginning upon the protection and support of people with greater wealth and higher status than any peasant."

6 Col. 3:5, 2Tim. 3:2, see also Jas. 5:1–6. On the characteristic early Christian combination of the sixth and tenth Commandments of the Decalogue, see Grant, "The Decalogue," p. 6, and below, p. 7.

7 Col. 3:5; Eph. 5:5; also emphasized by Polycarp, *Epistula 2 ad Philippenses*, 11.2 (ed. T. Camelot, fourth ed., SC 10 [Paris, 1969], p. 190).

8 Robert M. Grant, *Early Christianity and Society* (New York, 1977), pp. 122–23; Pier Cesare Bori, *La chiesa primitiva*, Dipartimento di scienze religiose 2 (Brescia, 1977), pp. 38–41.

9 The proverbial expression of avarice as the *metropolis pases kakias* (μητρόπολις πάσης κακίας) was attributed to Bias, Bion the Sophist, Demetrius, Democritus, and Diogenes, and in variant forms to a host of others, as well. See Jan F. Kindstrand, *Bion of Borysthenes: A Collection of the Fragments with Introduction and Commentary*, Acta Universitatis Upsaliensis, Studia Graeca Upsaliensia 11 (Uppsala, 1976), p. 243; Hans Herter, "Zur ersten Satire des Horaz," *Rheinisches Museum* N.F. 94 (1951), 19; Leo Sternbach, "De Gnomologio Vaticano inedito, III," *Wiener Studien* 10 (1888), 231–32. See *Oracula Sibyllina*, 2.3., 3.641–42, 8.17 (ed. J. Geffcken, GCS 8 [Leipzig, 1902], pp. 32, 81, 143). For further gnomic wisdom on avarice, see Karl Suso Frank, "Habsucht," *RAC*, vol. 13 (1984), col. 228.

10 1Tim. 6:10. See also Polycarp, *Ep. 2 ad Phil.*, 4.1 (SC 10:180); Tertullian, *De patientia*, 7.5 (ed. J. G. Ph. Borleffs, CCL 1 [Turnhout, 1954], p. 307). Clement of Alexandria, *Paedagogus*, 2.3.39.3 (ed. O. Stählin, third ed., ed. U. Treu, GCS 12 [Clemens 1] [Berlin, 1972], p. 181), speaks of avarice as the *akropolis* (ἀκρόπολις) of evil. Cf. Martin Hengel, *Eigentum und Reichtum in der frühen Kirche* (Stuttgart, 1973), p. 18.

11 Orientius, *Commonitorium*, 1.489–90 (ed. R. Ellis, CSEL 16 [Vienna, 1888], p. 223). On Orientius, see *CPL* 1465.

12 *The Sentences of Sextus*, 137 (ed. H. Chadwick [Cambridge, 1959], p. 28); Lactantius, *Divinae institutiones.*, 6.17.11 (ed. S. Brandt, CSEL 19 [Vienna, 1890], p. 543).

13 Rüdiger Vischer, *Das einfache Leben*, Studienhefte zur Altertumswissenschaft 11 (Göttingen, 1965), esp. pp. 60–83.

14 Hengel, *Eigentum*, pp. 65–68. The contrast between a life led for riches and contentment with one's present state is made explicit in Heb. 13:5.

15 *Hermas, Sim.*, 1.6ff., 2.5ff. (GCS 48:47–50). Cf. Hengel, *Eigentum*, p. 64; Liébaert, *Les enseignements*, pp. 170–71, 217–20; Ansgar Baumeister, *Die Ethik des Pastor Hermae*, Freiburger Theologische Studien 9 (Freiburg/Br., 1912), pp. 43–45. The arguments for seeing freedmen as the object of *Hermas'* criticism have been presented by Carolyn Osiek, "Wealth and Poverty in the *Shepherd of*

Hermas," in E. A. Livingstone, ed., *StP* 17,2 (Oxford, 1982), pp. 725–30. Note the parallel in early rabbinic thought: in *Talmud Bavli, Baba batra* 10a (ed. I. Epstein, trans. M. Simon *et al.*, Hebrew–English Edition of the Babylonian Talmud 18 [London, 1990]), the second-century Rabbi Akiva is asked by Tineius Rufus, Roman governor of Judea, why God does not support the poor; Akiva responds that they are the opportunity for others to give alms and be saved from hell. Peter Brown has called attention to the spiritual dimension of almsgiving as repentance in Judaism and Christianity in *The Rise of Western Christendom: Triumph and Diversity AD 200–1000* (Cambridge, MA and Oxford, 1996), pp. 30–31.

16 The precise meaning of *pragma* (πρᾶγμα) used in this verse is a matter of contention. See Gerhard Delling, "Πλεονέκτης, πλεονεκτέω, πλεονεξία," *Theologisches Wörterbuch zum Neuen Testament*, vol. 6 (1949), col. 271; Robert Beauvery, "Πλεονεκτεῖν in I Thess 4,6a," *Verbum Domini* 33 (1955), esp. 84–85.

17 Early Christian authors almost never condemn bankers, though usurers are a different matter. See Raymond Bogaert, "Changeurs et banquiers chez les pères de l'église," *Ancient Society* 4 (1973), 239–70. On the disapproval of merchants, see John W. Baldwin, *The Medieval Theories of the Just Price: Romanists, Canonists, and Theologians in the Twelfth and Thirteenth Centuries*, Transactions of the American Philosophical Society, n. s. 49,4 (Philadelphia, 1959), pp. 12–15.

18 *De idololatria*, 11.1 (ed. A. Reifferscheid and G. Wissowa, CCL 2 [Turnhout, 1954], p. 1110).

19 *De idol.*, 11.2 (CCL 2:1110–11). Cf. Claude Rambaux, *Tertullien face aux morales des trois premiers siècles* (Paris, 1979), esp. pp. 156–57; compare Perels, "Besitzethik," pp. 128–30. Tertullian eventually accepted trade, as did most Christian communities since Paul's conversion of Lydia, a dealer in purple fabric (Acts 16:14). On merchant activity in Tertullian's community, see his *Apologeticum*, 42.1–9 (ed. E. Dekkers, CCL 1 [Turnhout, 1954], pp. 156–58); Hans-Joachim Drexhage, "Wirtschaft und Handel in den frühchristlichen Gemeinden (1.-3. Jh. n. Chr.)," *Römische Quartalschrift* 76 (1981), esp. 44–49.

20 See Eph. 5:3. In 1Cor. 5:11 Christians are advised to avoid members of the community who are avaricious. Tertullian could not deny that there were *avari* among his congregation, though he asserted there were not many of them. See *Ad nationes*, 1.5.1 (ed. J. G. Ph. Borleffs, CCL 1 [Turnhout, 1954], p. 16).

21 2Pet. 2:3; *Didaché*, 11.6 and 11.12 (SC 248:184, 186–88). Compare L. Wm. Countryman, *The Rich Christian in the Church of the Early Empire: Contradictions and Accommodations*, Texts and Studies in Religion 7 (New York and Toronto, 1980), p. 73, arguing that "early Christian attacks on avarice were directed more often at the clergy than at the rich layman." Both groups are important. The critique of the clergy should be compared to complaints against the "priests of the seventh week" seen in Jewish apocalyptic literature, as in the *Testament of Levi*, 17.11 (ed. M. de Jonge in *The Testaments of the Twelve Patriarchs*, Pseudepigrapha Veteris Testamenti Graece 1,2 [Leiden, 1978], p. 45); see Christopher Rowland, "Apocalyptic, God and the World. Appearance and Reality: Early Christianity's Debt to the Jewish Apocalyptic Tradition," in

J. Barclay and J. Sweet, eds., *Early Christian Thought in Its Jewish Context* (Cambridge, 1996), pp. 238–49. The antiquity of expecting above all one's leaders to be free of avarice is indicated in Exod. 18.21, where Jethro advises Moses to choose for the people judges who are men of truth and haters of "unjust gain" (בצע). On this Hebrew *terminus technicus*, see D. Kellermann, "בצע," *Theologisches Wörterbuch zum Alten Testament*, vol. 1 (1973), cols. 731–36.

22 See 2Cor. 9:5, 7:2, and 12:17–18. Similar sentiments are expressed in 1Thess. 2:5. Cf. Delling, "Πλεονέκτης," p. 273. On Paul's collection for Jerusalem, see Dieter Georgi, *Remembering the Poor* (Nashville, 1992). As Reinhart Staats, "Deposita pietatis – Die Alte Kirche und ihr Geld," *Zeitschrift für Theologie und Kirche* 76 (1979), 1–29, has pointed out, the fact that the church possessed vast wealth was generally not problematic for early Christian thinkers.

23 *Ep. 2 ad Phil.*, 11.2 (SC 10:190). Cf. Liébaert, *Les enseignements*, pp. 78–79. See also 1Tim. 3:3 and 3:8; Tit. 1:7; *Didaché*, 15.1 (SC 248:192). For other texts which describe avarice as a vice of the clergy in particular, see John J. Machielsen, "Le problème du mal selon les pères apostoliques," *Eglise et Théologie* 12 (1981), 209 n. 87. In *Didascalia*, 3.[1]-[4] (ed. and trans. A. Vööbus in *The Didascalia Apostolorum in Syriac, I: Chapters I–X*, Corpus Scriptorum Christianorum Orientalium 401–02, Scriptores Syri 175–76 [Louvain, 1979], pp. 27–29 of trans.), freedom from avarice is listed as a necessary prerequisite for election to the offices of bishop, deacon, and presbyter.

24 Among other *termini* used to refer to the sin in early Christian literature, the most frequently seen are αἰσχροκέρδεια, ἀπληστία, φιλοκέρδεια, φιλοπλουτία, φιλοχρηματία, φιλοχρημοσύνη and in some cases ἀνελευθερία. Πλεονεξία and φιλαργυρία were in some cases used as not clearly distinguished, complementary terms to provide a more complete designation of the sin – see Polycarp, *Ep. 2 ad Phil.*, 2.2 (SC 10:178); Origen, *Commentarium in Canticum Canticorum*, prol. and 3 (ed. W. A. Baehrens, GCS 33 [Origines 8] [Leipzig, 1925], pp. 72 and 195), where the terms *ad amorem pecuniae . . . et avaritiae studium* (p. 72) and *cupiditatis et avaritiae* (p. 195) represent Origen's attempts to distinguish the different senses of avarice.

25 Other passages along these lines include Mark 7:21–22; Rom. 1:29; Eph. 4:19, 5:3–5; Col. 3:5; 2Pet. 2:14. For the arguments of Jerome and other early Christian exegetes, see below, ch. 4, p. 92 and n. 85. The interpretation of *pleonexia* as a sexual offense, or even more specifically adultery, has been rejected by Delling, "Πλεονέκτης," p. 271; Beauvery, "Πλεονεκτεῖν," pp. 78–85; and P. Rossano, "De conceptu πλεονεξία in Novo Testamento," *Verbum Domini* 32 (1954), 257–65. Scholars who have attempted to support such an understanding find it necessary to qualify their position: Marco Adinolfi, "Le frodi di 1 Tess. 4,6a e l'epiclerato," *Bibbia e Oriente* 18 (1976), 29–38, would not rule out some combination of sexual and economic offenses; Erich Klaar, "Πλεονεξία, -έκτης, -εκτεῖν," *Theologische Zeitschrift der Theologischen Fakultät der Universität Basel* 10 (1954), 395–97, admits that there are no non-Christian texts which back up this reading. For the combination of the sixth and tenth Commandments from the Decalogue seen in the linkage of lust and avarice, see above, n. 6.

26 See, for example, Exod. 20:17 and the *Testament of Judah*, esp. 16.1, 17.1, 18.2 (ed.
M. de Jonge in *The Testaments of the Twelve Patriarchs*, pp. 69–71) along with
the texts referred to by Delling, "Πλεονέκτης," pp. 267, 269, 271; and Rossano,
"De conceptu πλεονεξία," pp. 257–58. Early Christian literature may also be
cited here. Tertullian distinguished lust from avarice when he spoke of them as
the vices which chiefly draw humanity away from divine teachings, the former
per lasciuiendi uoluptatem, the latter *per adquirendi cupiditatem* – see *Ad uxorem*,
1.5.4 (ed. E. Kroymann, CCL I [Turnhout, 1954], p. 379). In *Epistula 2 Clementis
ad Corinthios*, 4.3 (ed. F. X. Funk in *Patres Apostolici*, second ed. [Tübingen,
1901], vol. I, p. 188), Christians are called upon to show their belief in Jesus in
their actions, including not being adulterous and avaricious. The verb used for
the latter is *philargyrein*, which precludes any identification between an act of
avarice and one of adultery.

27 The members of the Jerusalem community did not give up the right of private
property (Mark's mother owned a house, Barnabas sold a field he owned and
brought the money to the apostles), but rather put their possessions at the
disposal of all. This is the attitude which Paul preaches as well. Cf. O. Schilling,
Der kirchliche Eigentumsbegriff, second ed. (Freiburg/Br., 1930), pp. 18–20.
Compare, on the other hand, Karl Bornhäuser, *Der Christ und seine Habe nach
dem Neuen Testament*, Beiträge zur Förderung christlicher Theologie 38,3
(Gütersloh, 1936), pp. 32–38, for whom Jesus' words to the rich youth are to be
interpreted as meaning only, "Sell what you can afford to . . ." I have consistently
referred to the incident related in Mark 10:17–31, Matt. 19:16–30, and Luke
18:18–30 as "Jesus' words to the rich youth," following Matthew's version which
was used most often in the patristic period and the Middle Ages, frequently being
employed to clarify the difference between precepts and counsels to be found in
Jesus' words. Cf. G. E. M. de Ste. Croix, "Early Christian Attitudes to Property
and Slavery," in D. Baker, ed., *Church Society and Politics*, Studies in Church
History 12 (Oxford, 1975), pp. 25–26, repeated again in the author's *The Class
Struggle in the Ancient Greek World* (London, 1981), p. 431. On the differences
between the Gospel accounts of this incident, which reveal various conceptions
of the value of poverty in the earliest stages of Christianity, see Balázs Barsi, "La
péricope du jeune homme riche dans la littérature paléochrétienne," Dissertation, Strasbourg, 1982, vol. I, pp. 1–129; S. Légasse, *L'appel du riche (Marc
10,17–31 et parallèls)* (Paris, 1956).

28 Matt. 13:46. See also Matt. 13:44. Cf. Cecil J. Cadoux, *The Early Church and the
World* (Edinburgh, 1925), pp. 61–66; Alfred Winterstein, *Die christliche Lehre
vom Erdengut nach den Evangelien und apostolischen Schriften* (Mainz, 1898),
pp. 26–30. The "typical" member of the community, particularly among the
Pauline Christians, was a free artisan or small trader, in some cases fairly well off.
See Wayne A. Meeks, *The First Urban Christians* (New Haven and London,
1983), esp. pp. 51–73.

29 *Stromata*, 3.2.5.1–8.1 (ed. O. Stählin, fourth ed., ed. L. Früchtel, GCS 52 [15]
[Clemens 2] [Berlin, 1985], pp. 197–99); trans. in Werner Foerster, *Gnosis*, trans.
R. McL. Wilson (Oxford, 1972), vol. I, pp. 38–40. For Epiphanes' place in the

Gnostic rejection of wealth, see Kurt Rudolph, *Die Gnosis*, second ed. (Göttingen, 1980), pp. 288–91; and cf. Grant, *Early Christianity*, pp. 105–07; de Ste. Croix, "Attitudes," p. 32; Hauschild, "Christentum und Eigentum," p. 40; Wilhelm Capitaine, *Die Moral des Clemens von Alexandrien* (Paderborn, 1903), pp. 349–51. Compare also the undifferentiated use of passages with these *topoi* cited from Clement, Cyprian and others by Lujo Brentano, "Die wirtschaftlichen Lehren des christlichen Altertums," printed in the author's *Der wirtschaftende Mensch in der Geschichte* (Leipzig, 1923), pp. 87–101. For Cyprian's and Basil's use of some of these *topoi*, see below, ch. 2, nn. 22–23.

30 *The Sentences of Sextus*, 115 (ed. Chadwick, p. 26).

31 *Adversus haereses*, 3.8.1 (ed. A. Rousseau and L. Doutreleau, SC 211 [Paris, 1974], pp. 90–91). Cf. the editors' comments on this passage in SC 210:260. The Latin translation was finished perhaps in the third century.

32 *Adv. haer.*, 4.30.1 (ed. A. Rousseau *et al.*, SC 100/2 [Paris, 1965], pp. 772–73). See Perels, "Besitzethik," p. 147. De Ste. Croix, "Attitudes," p. 28 (and *Class Struggle*, p. 438), has argued that "the concept of a 'sufficiency' of property, whenever it was introduced, was always left vague . . ." This is generally true; however, the *Sentences of Sextus* are not the only exception to the rule. As will be seen, ascetic and monastic authors are very precise in defining sufficiency.

33 Cf. Hengel, *Eigentum*, pp. 54–56.

34 *Adversus Marcionem*, 4.15.8 (ed. E. Kroymann, CCL 1 [Turnhout, 1954], pp. 578–79). Cf. Georg Schöllgen, *Ecclesia Sordida? Zur Frage der sozialen Schichtung frühchristlicher Gemeinden am Beispiel Karthagos zur Zeit Tertullians*, *JbAC* Ergänzungsband 12 (Münster, 1984), pp. 286–94; Michel Spanneut, *Tertullien et les premiers moralistes africains* (Paris, 1969), p. 41.

35 Tertullian notes that not suffering the loss of property with patience amounts to the same evil as yearning for what is another's: *De pat.*, 7.5–6 (CCL 1:307). As W. H. C. Frend, *Saints and Sinners in the Early Church* (London, 1985), p. 31, has pointed out, the Pauline tradition in Christianity did not advocate a revolutionary change of the Roman Empire's institutions.

36 W. Eck, "Das Eindringen des Christentums in den Senatorenstand bis zu Konstantin d. Gr.," *Chiron* 1 (1971), 381–406, has surveyed the historical evidence for Christianity's slow movement into this class.

37 Clement of Alexandria, *Quis dives salvetur?*, 26.3 (ed. O. Stählin, GCS 17 [Clemens 3] [Leipzig, 1909], p. 177). For Irenaeus, see above, p. 8. See Grant, *Early Christianity*, p. 109. Clement himself "must have had considerable private means" (Richard Tollinton, *Clement of Alexandria: A Study in Christian Liberalism* [London, 1914], vol. 1, p. 305).

38 *Quis dives*, 14.1–6 (GCS 17:168–69). The moral indifference of wealth, both in itself and to the value of the human being who possesses it, is an aspect of Stoic thought emphasized by Heinrich Greeven, *Das Hauptproblem der Sozialethik in der neueren Stoa und im Urchristentum*, Neutestamentliche Forschungen 3,4 (Gütersloh, 1935), esp. pp. 62–65. For Clement's debt to the Stoics in his apology for wealth, see Max Pohlenz, *Die Stoa*, fourth ed. (Göttingen, 1970), vol. 1, p. 421; Michel Spanneut, *Le stoïcisme des pères de l'église*, Patristica Sorbonensia 1

(Paris, 1957), p. 244; Johannes Stelzenberger, *Die Beziehungen der frühchristlichen Sittenlehre zur Ethik der Stoa* (Munich, 1933), p. 136. Paul Christophe, *L'usage chrétien du droit de propriété dans l'Ecriture et la tradition patristique*, Théologie, Pastorale et Spiritualité, Recherches et Synthèses 14 (Paris, 1964), p. 83, and Stanislas Giet, "La doctrine de l'appropriation des biens chez quelques-uns des pères," *Recherches de Science religieuse* 35 (1948), 60, see a distinction in Clement's works between *ktemata* [κτήματα], wealth which one can legitimately acquire for oneself, and *chremata* [χρήματα], wealth which is to be shared with the poor. According to Flavius Josephus, *The Jewish War*, 2.8.3.122 (ed. and trans. H. St. J. Thackeray [Cambridge, MA, 1927; repr. 1967], p. 368), the Essene sect of Judaism despised riches; see Todd Beall, *Josephus' Description of the Essenes Illustrated by the Dead Sea Scrolls*, Society for New Testament Studies, Monograph series 58 (Cambridge, 1988), p. 43. In early rabbinic thought, on the other hand, the value of wealth is never called into question, though poverty can be praised in some contexts; see Jacob Neusner, *The Economics of the Mishnah* (Chicago, 1990), p. 92.

39 *Quis dives*, 11.2–12.1 (GCS 17:166–67); *Strom.*, 4.6.26.4–31.5 (GCS 52[15]:259–62). Cf. Barsi, "La péricope," vol. 1, pp. 205–06. For Clement's use of Stoic terminology when speaking of wealth as neither good nor evil but rather an *adiaphoron* [ἀδιάφορον], see Christian Gnilka, "Usus Iustus. Ein Grundbegriff der Kirchenväter im Umgang mit der antiken Kultur," *Archiv für Begriffsgeschichte* 24 (1980), 57–59; Johannes Stelzenberger, "Adiaphora," *RAC*, vol. 1 (1950), cols. 83–87.

40 *Paed.*, 2.3.38.5–39.3 (GCS 12:180–81). A. M. Ritter, "Christentum und Eigentum bei Klemens von Alexandrien auf dem Hintergrund der frühchristlichen 'Armenfrömmigkeit' und der Ethik der kaiserzeitlichen Stoa," *Zeitschrift für Kirchengeschichte* 86 (1975), 1–25, has emphasized Clement's theological stance on private property as located between the Ebionitic rejection of the wealthy and the Stoic approach which is "rein *individual* ethischer Natur" (p. 15). For Clement's criterion of the use of wealth, not its mere possession, see Henry Chadwick, *Early Christian Thought and the Classical Tradition* (Oxford, 1966), p. 61.

41 *Paed.*, 2.3.39.2 (GCS 12:181). For the distinction between true and false wealth, see *Quis dives*, 16.1–19.1 (GCS 17:169–71.). Cf. Ignaz Seipel, *Die wirtschaftsethischen Lehren der Kirchenväter*, Leo-Gesellschaft, Theologische Studien 18 (Vienna, 1907; repr. Graz, 1972), pp. 62–70. In *Quis dives*, 15.6 (GCS 17:169), Clement includes avarice among the "languors and passions of the soul."

42 *Paed.*, 2.3.39.1 (GCS 12:180); see also, for the idea that friends possess all goods in common, *Protrepticus*, 12.122.3 (ed. O. Stählin, third ed., ed. U. Treu, GCS 12 [Clemens 1] [Berlin, 1972], p. 86). For the difficulty in defining what Clement meant by sufficiency, compare *Paed.*, 2.12.120.3–6 (GCS 12:229) with *Quis dives*, 16.3 (GCS 17:170). The former asserts that "it is unnatural for one to live sumptuously while many are in need." Thus, it is more reasonable to use one's wealth for others than for gems, more useful to have virtuous friends than jewels. In the latter he remarks that whoever possesses wealth as gifts of God, and who can "bear their loss with a balanced disposition just as he does their over-

abundance," is praised by the Lord and called poor in spirit. In both cases the rich are to place their goods at the disposal of all; but how far they can go in a placid acceptance of superfluity before they begin to be perceived as living in luxury, is not stated explicitly anywhere. Compare Ritter, "Christentum," p. 16 n. 87.

43 *Quis dives*, 11.3 (GCS 17:166–67). This, in effect, anticipates (and rejects) an argument current in the late Middle Ages which was used at times by the spiritual Franciscans.

44 *Strom.*, 4.6.25.1–26.4 (GCS 52[15]:259–60).

45 For Clement on almsgiving, see *Quis dives*, 13.1–7 (GCS 17:167–68). For the development of Clement's thought on the motives for almsgiving, see Countryman, *The Rich Christian*, pp. 54–60. Clement's words on Anaxagoras *et al.* can be found in *Quis dives*, 11.4 (GCS 17:167). Clement is critical not only of the philosophical schools of Antiquity, but of Philo of Alexandria, as well. Compare Philo, *De vita contemplativa*, 14–15 (ed. L. Cohn and S. Reiter in *Philonis Alexandrini opera quae supersunt*, 6 [Berlin, 1915], pp. 49–50), who also criticized Anaxagoras and Democritus, not because they freed themselves from wealth for the sake of philosophy, but because they acted impractically by giving their money away for sheep pasture instead of using it to help friends or family in need. See David Mealand, "Philo of Alexandria's Attitude to Riches," *Zeitschrift für die neutestamentliche Wissenschaft* 69 (1978), 258–64; cf. Ronald Williamson, *Jews in the Hellenistic World: Philo*, Cambridge Commentaries on Writings of the Jewish and Christian World 200 BC to AD 200, 1, part 2 (Cambridge, 1989), pp. 241–42. On the theological justification of poverty in early Christianity, see Carter Lindberg, "Through a Glass Darkly: A History of the Church's Vision of the Poor and Poverty," *The Ecumenical Review* 33,1 (1981), esp. 41.

46 *Quis dives*, 15.3 (GCS 17:169). For Clement's debt to the Stoic teaching on the passions, see Olivier Prunet, *La morale de Clément d'Alexandrie et le Nouveau Testament*, Etudes d'histoire et de philosophie religieuses 61 (Paris, 1966), pp. 71–77.

47 *In Numeros homiliae*, 26.12 (ed. W. A. Baehrens, GCS 30 [Origenes 7] [Leipzig, 1921], p. 272). For Clement and Origen on the psychology of avarice, see Richard Newhauser, "The Love of Money as Deadly Sin and Deadly Disease," in J. O. Fichte *et al.*, eds., *Zusammenhänge, Einflüsse, Wirkungen*, Kongressakten zum ersten Symposium des Mediävistenverbandes in Tübingen, 1984 (Berlin and New York, 1986), p. 318. On Origen's relationship to the thought of Clement of Alexandria, cf. Joseph Wilson Trigg, *Origen* (Atlanta, 1983), pp. 65–66. For consideration of a possible connection between the Middle Platonists, Philo of Alexandria, and Origen, see John Dillon, "Plotinus, Philo and Origen on the Grades of Virtue," in H.-D. Blume and F. Mann, eds., *Platonismus und Christentum: Festschrift für Heinrich Dörrie*, JbAC Ergänzungsband 10 (Münster, 1983), pp. 92–105.

48 *Commentary on John*, 20.22.180 (ed. E. Preuschen, GCS 10 [Origenes 4] [Leipzig, 1903], p. 354). For Origen's understanding of the temptation of Judas, see below, ch. 3, p. 66 and n. 75. That the demons use the same method with other sinners is

Origen's view in *Comm. in Cant. Cant.*, 3 (GCS 33:195). For the exemplary function of Judas' temptation, see Raymundo Trevijano, *En lucha contra las Potestades* (Rome, 1967), p. 215.

49 See *In librum Jesu nave homiliae*, 12.3 and 15.4 (ed. W. A. Baehrens, GCS 30 [Origenes 7] [Leipzig, 1921], pp. 370, 387).

50 *Commentary on Matthew*, 15.8 (ed. E. Klostermann, GCS 40 [Origenes 10] [Leipzig, 1935], p. 402). See also Origen's commentary on Ps. 118:72 (ed. R. Cadiou in *Commentaires inédits des psaumes* [Paris, 1936], p. 111). On Origen's refusal to desert the literal sense of this passage in Matthew, see R. P. C. Hanson, *Allegory and Event* (London, 1959), p. 238. Cf. also de Ste. Croix, "Attitudes," p. 29.

51 *Comment. on Matt.*, 15.15 (GCS 40:391–92). For Cassian's references to the Jerusalem community, see below, ch. 3, p. 67 and n. 83.

52 See *Commentariorum series*, 36 (ed. E. Klostermann, GCS 38 [Origenes 11] [Leipzig, 1933], p. 69). Cf. Jas. 4:1–2 for the backgrounds of Origen's comments.

53 *Com. ser.*, 14 (GCS 38:27).

54 See *Comment. on Matt.*, 11.15, 16.22 (GCS 40:59, 549–54); *In Genesim homiliae*, 16.5 (ed. W. A. Baehrens, GCS 29 [Origenes 6] [Leipzig, 1920], pp. 142–43). See also *Com. ser.*, 12 (GCS 38:22–24). Cf. Georg Teichtweier, *Die Sündenlehre des Origenes*, Studien zur Geschichte der katholischen Moraltheologie 7 (Regensburg, 1958), p. 255. In *Com. ser.*, 61 (GCS 38:141), Origen admitted that according to 1Cor. 9:14 church officials could expect to be supported by their communities, but this included only simple food and necessary clothing and should not amount to more than what the poor received. See Adolf von Harnack, *Die Mission und Ausbreitung des Christentums in den ersten drei Jahrhunderten*, fourth ed. (Leipzig, 1924), vol. 1, p. 182; Cadoux, *The Early Church*, p. 447.

55 *Homiliae in Jeremiam*, 7.3 (ed. P. Nautin, trans. P. Husson and P. Nautin, SC 232 [Paris, 1976], p. 348). On the implications of expulsion from the church for Origen, see Hermann Josef Vogt, *Das Kirchenverständnis des Origenes*, Bonner Beiträge zur Kirchengeschichte 4 (Cologne and Vienna, 1974), pp. 129ff.

56 *De opere et eleemosynis*, 7 (ed. M. Simonetti, CCL 3A [Turnhout, 1976], pp. 59–60). On this distinction in Cyprian's thought, see José Capmany-Casamitjana, *"Miles Christi" en la Espiritualidad de San Cipriano*, Seminario Conciliar de Barcelona, Colectanea San Paciano, Serie Teológia 1 (Barcelona, 1956), pp. 162–66.

57 *De lapsis*, 11 (ed. M. Bévenot, CCL 3 [Turnhout, 1976], pp. 226–27); *De dominica oratione*, 20 (ed. C. Moreschini, CCL 3A [Turnhout, 1976], pp. 102–03). On the different versions of the parable of the rich youth, see above, n. 27.

58 See the *Vita Caecilii Cypriani*, 2 (ed. W. Hartel, CSEL 3,3 [Vienna, 1871], p. xcii). See Barsi, "La péricope," vol. 1, pp. 237–38; Hengel, *Eigentum*, p. 83. On bishops' responsibility for hospitality, see Henry Chadwick, "The Role of the Christian Bishop in Ancient Society," *The Center for Hermeneutical Studies in Hellenistic and Modern Culture, Protocol of Colloquy* 35 (Berkeley, 1980), pp. 5–6 (repr. in Henry Chadwick, *Heresy and Orthodoxy in the Early Church*, Variorum Collected Studies, CS 342 [London, 1991]).

59 *De op. et eleem.*, 25 (CCL 3A:71–72). For the dual function of almsgiving for Cyprian, see Countryman, *The Rich Christian*, pp. 190–95; compare Justo González, *Faith and Wealth* (San Francisco, 1990), p. 127. On the readmission of the rich in 252, see Robin Lane Fox, *Pagans and Christians* (New York, 1987), p. 557.

60 *De mortalitate*, 4 (ed. M. Simonetti, CCL 3A [Turnhout, 1976], pp. 18–19); *De zelo et livore*, 16 (ed. M. Simonetti, CCL 3A [Turnhout, 1976], pp. 84–85); *De op. et eleem.*, 26 (CCL 3A:72).

61 *De lapsis*, 11 (CCL 3:226); *De op. et eleem.*, 13 (CCL 3A:63); *Ad Donatum*, 13 (ed. M. Simonetti, CCL 3A [Turnhout, 1976], p. 11). By speaking of the avaricious as blind, Cyprian uses a *topos* common in Antiquity; see Simone Déleani, *Christum sequi. Etude d'un thème dans l'œuvre de saint Cyprien* (Paris, 1979), p. 127 n. 577, and the Appendix.

62 *De mort.*, 16 (CCL 3A:25). Cyprian's own response to the plague of 252 in Carthage was to organize relief in the city for Christians and non-Christians alike – cf. Peter Hinchliff, *Cyprian of Carthage and the Unity of the Christian Church* (London, 1974), pp. 79–80.

63 The florilegium is found in *Ad Quirinum*, 3.61 (ed. R. Weber, CCL 3 [Turnhout, 1972], pp. 151–52). For Cyprian's use of the investment metaphor, see *De lapsis*, 35 (CCL 3:241); *De op. et eleem.*, 13 (CCL 3A:63); *De habitu virginum*, 11 (ed. W. Hartel, CSEL 3,1 [Vienna, 1868], p. 195). The redemptive value of alms for Cyprian and Clement has been emphasized by Rebecca H. Weaver, "Wealth and Poverty in the Early Church," *Interpretation: A Journal of Bible and Theology* 41,4 (1987), 369–74.

64 *De lapsis*, 6 (CCL 3:223); *De ecclesiae catholicae unitate*, 26 (ed. M. Bévenot, CCL 3 [Turnhout, 1976], p. 267).

65 *Ad Don.*, 12 (CCL 3A:10–11). Envy can also lead to avarice when someone who is not content with what is his sees someone who is richer than he is – see *De zelo*, 2 (CCL 3A:84–85). The *avarus'* insomnia was a common *topos* in Antiquity. The Stoics, too, had emphasized the cares and fears necessarily involved in the possession of wealth; see Greeven, *Das Hauptproblem*, pp. 66–67, and the Appendix.

66 *Tractatus in psalmum 125*, 5 (ed. A. Zingerle, CSEL 22 [Milan, 1891], p. 608).

67 *Ad Don.*, 12 (CCL 3A:10–11); *De op. et eleem.*, 10, 11 and 16 (CCL 3A:61–62, 65). See also *De lapsis*, 11 (CCL 3:226). Cf. Spanneut, *Tertullien*, pp. 103–04; Christophe, *L'usage*, p. 106.

68 *Aduersus nationes libri VII*, 2.40 (ed. A. Reifferscheid, CSEL 4 [Vienna, 1875], pp. 80–81). This digest of *topoi* serves as the background for criticism of the "capitalist" as it was to emerge in the late Middle Ages.

69 *De lapsis*, 6 (CCL 3:223). See also *Epistulae*, 11.1 (ed. W. Hartel, CSEL 3,2 [Vienna, 1871], p. 496). Tertullian, Cyprian's mentor, had also spoken of avarice by noting that during religious persecution the attempt to buy one's way out of oppression is a form of serving Mammon – see *De fuga in persecutione*, 12.6 (ed. J. J. Thierry, CCL 2 [Turnhout, 1954], pp. 1151–52). Cf. Capmany-Casamitjana, "*Miles Christi*," p. 156, for Cyprian's words on avarice as the cause of laxity before

the persecutions of Decius, numerous apostasies after it, and the actions of Fortunatus.

70 *Div. Inst.*, 5.5.8–6.6 (ed. P. Monat in SC 204 [Paris, 1973], pp. 152–56). See Seneca, *Epistulae morales*, 90.3 and 38 (ed. L. D. Reynolds in *L. Annaei Senecae ad Lucilium epistulae morales* [Oxford, 1965] vol. 2, pp. 332, 342–43). On the backgrounds of Seneca's thought, see Manfred Wacht, "Gütergemeinschaft," *RAC*, vol. 13 (1984), col. 9. Alois Kehl and Henri-Irénée Marrou, "Geschichts-philosophie," *RAC*, vol. 10 (1978), col. 750, argue that Greeks and Romans generally attributed the historical decline from an ideal state to the appearance of avarice. Yet, authors other than Seneca use avarice to characterize society's deterioration, not to account for that decline: in *Catilinae coniuratio*, 2.1 (ed. A. Kurfess, third ed. [Leipzig, 1968], p. 3), Sallust merely states that the Golden Age was *sine cupiditate*, a period during which *sua quoique satis placebant* (but see 10.1–3 [p. 10], where Sallust analyzes the specific case of Rome's moral fall and attributes it to *fortuna* first of all and then to the greed for money and power); in Virgil's *Aeneidos*, 8.327 (ed. R. A. B. Mynors in Virgil, *Opera* [Oxford, 1969; repr. with corrections 1972], p. 292), King Euandrus describes the end of the Golden Age as a transition from a period of peace to one characterized by the madness of war and the love of possessing; in *Cynicus*, 15 (ed. K. Jacobitz in *Luciani Samosatensis opera*, vol. 3 [Leipzig, 1881], pp. 399–400), Lucian's Cynic maintains that public discord, wars, conspiracies, and slaughters grow from the desire for gold and silver, but this is not part of a historical argument about the decline from the Golden Age.

71 See Vinzenz Buchheit, "Goldene Zeit und Paradies auf Erden (Laktanz, inst. 5,5–8)," *Würzburger Jahrbücher für die Altertumswissenschaft* N.F. 4 (1978), 161–85; 5 (1979), 219–35, here esp. 163–64; and Louis J. Swift, "Lactantius and the Golden Age," *American Journal of Philology* 89 (1968), 144–56.

72 Buchheit, "Goldene Zeit," 4, pp. 162–63; Bodo Gatz, *Weltalter, goldene Zeit und sinnverwandte Vorstellungen*, Spudasmata 16 (Hildesheim, 1967), p. 178. Cf. Hesiod, *Works and Days*, 106–201 (ed. M. L. West [Oxford, 1978], pp. 100–04); Ovid, *Metamorphoses*, 1.89–162 (ed. W. S. Anderson, second ed. [Leipzig, 1982], pp. 4–7); Virgil, *Georgicon*, 1.125–59 (ed. R. A. B. Mynors in *P. Vergili Maronis opera* [Oxford, 1969; repr. with corrections, 1972], pp. 33–34). There is a biblical reflection of the myth in Dan. 2:31–45. On the Golden Age in classical thought, see Wacht, "Gütergemeinschaft," 4–11; Hans Schwabl, "Weltalter," *Paulys Realencyclopädie der classischen Altertumswissenschaft*, Supplementband 15 (1978), cols. 783–850, esp. 821–50; Arthur O. Lovejoy and George Boas, *Primitivism and Related Ideas in Antiquity* (n.p., 1935; repr. New York, 1965).

73 *Div. Inst.*, 5.6.4 (SC 204:156). Greed for Lactantius is the negation of the all-important virtue of *iustitia*, which leads to *aequitas*, the love of one's neighbor founded on the equality of all human beings. For justice in Lactantius' thought, see Vinzenz Buchheit, "Die Definition der Gerechtigkeit bei Laktanz und seinen Vorgängern," *VC* 33 (1979), cols. 356–74; Albrecht Dihle, "Gerechtigkeit," *RAC*, vol. 10 (1978), cols. 335–36; and P. Monat's introduction to his edition, SC 204:20–33.

74 *Div. Inst.*, 5.5.6 (SC 204:152); cf. also Konrad Farner, *Christentum und Eigentum bis Thomas von Aquin*, Mensch und Gesellschaft 12 (Bern, 1947), p. 61. Lactantius considered that the delight in images made of gold, gems, and ivory had led pagans astray so they could not conceive of religion without these precious materials. They were not even serving the gods, but only avarice and cupidity – see *Div. Inst.*, 2.6.2–3 (CSEL 19:121–22).

75 *Div. Inst.*, 5.7.1–2 (SC 204:160).

76 See Samuel Brandt's notes to his edition of *Div. Inst.*, 7.24.6ff. (CSEL 19:659ff.) for the passages in question. In *Div. Inst.*, 5.7.1–2, there are also numerous Virgilian echoes – see Buchheit, "Goldene Zeit," 5, pp. 219–22; Hans Larmann, *Christliche Wirtschaftsethik in der spätrömischen Antike*, Furche-Studien 13 (Berlin, 1935), p. 84. That Lactantius quoted from the Sibylline Oracles is typical of his reading; see R. M. Ogilvie, *The Library of Lactantius* (Oxford, 1978), pp. 28–33.

77 *Div. Inst.*, 5.8.7 (SC 204:166). Compare the list of evils to be corrected to that which Arnobius, Lactantius' teacher, found to be typical of the evil souls of this world in *Adu. nat.*, 2.43 (CSEL 4:83).

78 *Epitome divinarum institutionum*, 56(61).5(19) (ed. S. Brandt, CSEL 19 [Vienna, 1890], p. 739); *Div. Inst.*, 6.19.10 (CSEL 19:555).

79 *Epit. div. inst.*, 56(61).5(19) (CSEL 19:739).

80 *Div. Inst.*, 6.17.10ff. (CSEL 19:543–44). Lactantius continues his discussion of ethical concepts by noting that neither parsimony nor frugality can be virtues (the former because it looks only towards earthly goods, the latter because it descends from the love for possessing), and by distinguishing prodigality from the virtue of liberality (one guilty of the former pours out goods to those who are undeserving, when it is unnecessary, and without regard for his family; one practicing the latter gives freely to those who are deserving, when it is fitting, and as much as is enough). All four concepts are seen in their relation to *cupiditas/ avaritia*.

81 *Epit. div. inst.*, 56(61).3(17) (CSEL 19:739).

82 *Div. Inst.*, 6.19.4 (CSEL 19:553–54); *Epit. div. inst.*, 56(61).1(15) (CSEL 19:738). *Ira, cupiditas/avaritia, libido* form a relatively fixed triad in Lactantius' thought – see Spanneut, *Tertullien*, p. 156.

83 *Epit. div. inst.*, 56(61).2(16) (CSEL 19:738). For Lactantius' knowledge of the arguments between Peripatetics and Stoics concerning the "affects," see Pohlenz, *Die Stoa*, vol. 1, p. 444.

2 ASCETIC TRANSFORMATIONS I: MONKS AND THE LAITY IN EASTERN CHRISTENDOM

1 The economic situation of the East was actually stronger and healthier than that of the West, but the signs of decay were clear here as well. See A. H. M. Jones, *The Later Roman Empire, 284–602* (Oxford, 1964; repr. 1973), vol. 2, pp. 1064–68; and on corruption at this time, *ibid.*, pp. 1053–58.

2 How much the volume against the sin composed by Antiochus of Ptolomais

would have added to this picture is impossible to say. Unfortunately, the long work he is reported to have written on the topic by Gennadius of Marseilles, *De viris inlustribus*, 20 (ed. E. C. Richardson, TU 14 [Leipzig, 1896], p. 69) has been lost.

3 The case for the curial origins of the Cappadocians has been argued by Thomas A. Kopecek, "The Social Class of the Cappadocian Fathers," *Church History* 42,4 (1973), 453–66. On the duties and responsibilities of this class in Cappadocia, see Kopecek's "Social/Historical Studies in the Cappadocian Fathers," Dissertation, Brown University, 1972, pp. 95–113.

4 Gregory Nazianzen seems to have desired to become a monk early in life, but never to have realized this wish. On the lives of these church thinkers, with bibliography, see Berthold Altaner and Alfred Stuiber, *Patrologie*, ninth rev. ed. (Freiburg, 1980).

5 *Epistolae*, 53 (ed. and trans. Y. Courtonne in Saint Basile, *Lettres* [Paris, 1957], vol. 1, pp. 137–39).

6 See the *Regulae fusius tractatae*, 8.3 (PG 31:940–41), as well as works attributed to Basil: *Praevia institutio ascetica*, 2 (PG 31:621); *Sermo de ascetica disciplina*, 1 (PG 31:648). For Basil's thought on monastic renunciation, see David Amand, *L'ascèse monastique de Saint Basile* (Maredsous, 1949), pp. 129–34 and 167ff. On Pachomius, see below, ch. 3, pp. 59–61.

7 See his description of his retreat in *Ep.*, 14 (ed. Courtonne, vol. 1, pp. 42ff.) and his motivation for establishing a hostel for the poor in *Ep.*, 94 (ed. Courtonne, vol. 1, pp. 204ff.). Basil's establishments should be seen in the context of similar charitable foundations in this area beginning in the middle of the fourth century; see Rudolf Brändle, *Matth. 25, 31–46 im Werk des Johannes Chrysostomos*, Beiträge zur Geschichte der biblischen Exegese 22 (Tübingen, 1979), pp. 105–06.

8 On Eustathius, see J. Gribomont in *Dictionnaire d'Histoire et de Géographie ecclésiastiques*, vol. 16 (1967), cols. 26–33. For the Messalians, see below, n. 37. The followers of Eustathius were condemned at the Council of Gangra (*c.* 355), among other reasons for maintaining that the rich must give up everything to qualify for entrance to heaven. See J. M. Mansi, ed., *Sacrorum conciliorum . . . collectio*, vol. 2 (Venice, 1759), col. 1099; Timothy D. Barnes, "The Date of the Council of Gangra," *Journal of Theological Studies* n.s. 40 (1989), 121–24 (and Barnes, *Athanasius and Constantius* [Cambridge, MA and London, 1993], pp. 285–86 n. 23). For the question of property ownership, see also G. E. M. de Ste. Croix, "Early Christian Attitudes to Property and Slavery," in D. Baker, ed., *Church Society and Politics*, Studies in Church History 12 (Oxford, 1975), p. 33; Ignaz Seipel, *Die wirtschaftsethischen Lehren der Kirchenväter*, Leo-Gesellschaft, Theologische Studien 18 (Vienna, 1907; repr. Graz, 1972), pp. 68–70. Basil's monastic works were addressed to Eustathius' followers, as well, as an attempt to bring these ascetes back into the orthodox church.

9 Basil's ascetic guidelines for the rich are in *Homilia in divites*, 1–2 (PG 31:281–84) where he notes that it is the devil's trick to make the rich consider as necessary what is actually superfluous. Fritz Tillmann, "Besitz und Eigentum bei Basilius dem Großen," in M. Meinertz and A. Donders, eds., *Aus Ethik und Leben: Festschrift für Joseph Mausbach* (Münster, 1931), esp. p. 36, maintained that

according to Basil "jeder hat ein Recht auf den standesgemäßen Unterhalt," though he provides no evidence for this assertion. Basil's ascesis is, in fact, an exception to the common early Christian view of possessions which left the notion of "sufficiency" or "superfluity" vague and made room for class differences in the amount the individual could own. In *Ep.*, 150.3 (ed. Courtonne, vol. 2, p. 75) Basil noted that one must distinguish a poor person who begs because of need from one who begs out of cupidity. In the *Regulae brevius tractatae*, 181 (PG 31:1204) he pointed out, on the basis of two monastic communities, one rich and one poor, that the indigent monks must simply endure their poverty regardless of what they knew their neighbors possessed. Again, in *Ep.*, 22.2 (ed. Courtonne, vol. 1, p. 57) he warned monks against being too involved in their work and thus being led astray into desiring more than what was necessary for themselves.

10 Interrogatio 48, resp. (PG 31:1116).

11 *Regulae morales*, 48.3–5 (PG 31:769–72). The work was composed *c.* 360. On the text and its audience, see J. Gribomont, "Le renoncement au monde dans l'idéal ascétique de saint Basile," *Irénikon* 31 (1958), 289–92.

12 *Homilia dicta tempore famis et siccitatis*, 8 (PG 31:325). See S. Giet, *Les idées et l'action sociales de saint Basile* (Paris, 1941), pp. 113–14. In *Homilia in illud: Destruam horrea mea*, 2 (PG 31:265), Joseph's willingness to open the granaries for all (see Gen. 47:11–27) is presented as a model for the avaricious person to follow.

13 *Hom. in illud*, 7 (PG 31:276–77). Basil's ascetic fervor makes it difficult to distinguish at all times between what is merely a counsel and what a precept, an issue discussed by Paul Christophe, *L'usage chrétien du droit de propriété dans l'Ecriture et la tradition patristique*, Théologie, Pastorale et Spiritualité, Recherches et Synthèses 14 (Paris, 1964), pp. 116–27. Nevertheless, the question of *possessing* wealth yields answers which are advice to the laity, but the *use* of their wealth for the public good is a precept.

14 See canons 61 and 66 in *Ep.* 217 (ed. Courtonne, vol. 2, pp. 211–12). These offenses should be compared to money-lending, for which Basil legislated only that if the profits be given to the poor and the former moneylender reject his avarice, he can qualify for admission to the priesthood. See canon 14 in *Ep.* 188 (ed. Courtonne, vol. 2, p. 130).

15 *Hom. in div.*, 3 (PG 31:288). This passage in Luke is another of those criticisms of wealth which some early Christian commentators found necessary to interpret metaphorically (as was the case with Jesus' words to the rich youth); see G. Aicher, *Kamel und Nadelöhr*, Neutestamentliche Abhandlungen 1,5 (Münster, 1908).

16 *Hom. in div.*, 1 (PG 31:281). The ladder metaphor is used in section 5 of this homily (cols. 292–93). In the East, an imperial aristocracy began to accumulate vast riches only in the fourth century, and Basil responds to this beginning stage of acquisition. On the *nouveaux riches* in the East, see Jones, *The Later Roman Empire*, vol. 2, p. 1066.

17 *Hom. in div.*, 9 (PG 31:304).

18 *Hom. in div.*, 7 (PG 31:297–300). See also Eberhard F. Bruck, *Kirchenväter und soziales Erbrecht* (Berlin, 1956), pp. 6–7. For a parallel rejection of considerations for a patrimony, see Plutarch, *De cupiditate divitiarum*, 7 (*Moralia* 526Aff.) (ed.

G. N. Bernardakis in *Plutarchi Chaeronensis Moralia* [Leipzig, 1891], vol. 3, p. 362). On the relationship between this work and Christian literature, see Edward N. O'Neil, "De cupiditate divitiarum (*Moralia* 523C–528B)," in H. D. Betz, ed., *Plutarch's Ethical Writings and Early Christian Literature*, Studia ad Corpus Hellenisticum Novi Testamenti 4 (Leiden, 1978), pp. 289–362.

19 *Hom. in div.*, 8 (PG 31:300–01).

20 *Hom. in illud*, 4 (PG 31:268–69). In *Homilia 2 in Psalmum 14*, 1 (PG 29:268), Basil noted that the avaricious person (or more specifically, the usurer) hopes for others' poverty and misfortune like a peasant hopes for rain so his seeds will grow.

21 *Hom. in illud*, 7 (PG 31:276). Martin Hengel, *Eigentum und Reichtum in der frühen Kirche* (Stuttgart, 1973), pp. 10–11, argues that Basil uses an image here which Chrysippus had utilized to defend the right of private property. According to the Stoic, a seat in the theater belongs rightfully to whomever occupies it; for Basil, its use must reside in the public domain. However, Chrysippus notes that the seats in the theater belong to all in common. See the text in Cicero, *De finibus bonorum et malorum*, 3.20.67 (ed. J. N. Madvig [Copenhagen, 1876; repr. Hildesheim, 1963], pp. 458–60), and Manfred Wacht, "Privateigentum bei Cicero und Ambrosius," *JbAC* 25 (1982), 47–48.

22 *Hom. in illud.*, 1 and 3 (PG 31:261–64, 265). In much the same terms Cyprian had already made use of the *topos* that the natural elements (sunshine, rain, etc.) are for the common use of all humankind; see *De opere et eleemosynis*, 25 (ed. M. Simonetti, CCL 3A [Turnhout, 1976], p. 71).

23 *Hom. temp. fam.*, 8 (PG 31:325). Basil draws on images taken from nature to prove that sharing equally is the universal order of things: sheep and horses graze peacefully together with others of their own kind. One can, he says, further cite the humaneness of pagans who share all their food, or Jewish models of brotherly love as well.

24 *Hom. in div.*, 5 (PG 31:293); Augustinus Dirking, *S. Basilii Magni de divitiis et paupertate sententiae quam habeant rationem cum veterum philosophorum doctrina* (Münster, 1911), p. 64.

25 *Epistola canonica*, canon 6 (PG 45:232–33).

26 *Epistola canonica ad Letoium*, 1–2 (PG 45:225). For the senses' involvement in sin, see *Oratio 5 de oratione dominica* (PG 44:1185). On the function of love in Gregory's system of virtues, see Evangelos G. Konstantinou, *Die Tugendlehre Gregors von Nyssa im Verhältnis zu der Antik-Philosophischen und Jüdisch-Christlichen Tradition*, Das östliche Christentum, N.F. 17 (Würzburg, 1966), pp. 170–81. The senses' role in the origin of sin has been described by Walther Völker, *Gregor von Nyssa als Mystiker* (Wiesbaden, 1955), p. 87.

27 Gregory's catalogue of the sinful actions growing out of avarice is actually longer than these six items. In *Oratio 5 de beatitudinibus* (PG 44:1253; see also below, ch. 3, n. 67) he also includes lying, deceit, and war among the descendants of the vice. Basil had also noted in *Hom. in div.*, 7 (PG 31:297) that money was the cause of war.

28 *De Vita Moysis*, 2 (ed. H. Musurillo in *Gregorii Nysseni Opera*, 7,1 [Leiden, 1964], pp. 73–74).

29 *Oratio 4 in Ecclesiasten* (ed. J. McDonough and P. Alexander in *Gregorii Nysseni Opera*, 5 [Leiden, 1962], pp. 346–47). For avarice's preparatory function, see *De mortuis oratio* (ed. G. Heil in *Gregorii Nysseni Opera*, 9 [Leiden, 1967], p. 59).

30 *Orat. 5 de beat.* (PG 44:1260). See Plato, *Respublica*, 9 (590B) (ed. J. Burnet in *Platonis Opera*, vol. 4 [Oxford, 1954]); Terence Irwin, *Plato's Ethics* (Oxford, 1995), pp. 281–97. On Gregory's use of animal imagery for the passions, see Jean Daniélou, *Platonisme et théologie mystique*, Théologie 2 (Paris, 1944), pp. 73–79.

31 *Contra usurarios oratio* (ed. E. Gebhardt in *Gregorii Nysseni Opera*, 9 [Leiden, 1967], p. 205). For the opposition philanthropy – *filargyria*, see here pp. 196,10 and 198,12; R. P. Maloney, "The Teaching of the Fathers on Usury: An Historical Study on the Development of Christian Thinking," *VC* 27 (1973), 251–66.

32 *Contra usurarios oratio*, pp. 196,9 and 202,19; Jean Bernardi, *La prédication des pères cappadociens*, Publications de la Faculté des Lettres et Sciences Humaines de l'Université de Montpellier 30 (Marseilles, 1968), pp. 265–68.

33 On the date and references of the sermons, see Elena Cavalcanti, "I due discorsi *De pauperibus amandis* di Gregorio di Nissa," *Orientalia Christiana Periodica* 44 (1978), 170–80. Cf. Bernardi, *La prédication*, pp. 275–76.

34 *De beneficentia (De pauperibus amandis*, 1) (ed. A. Van Heck in *Gregorii Nysseni Opera*, 9 [Leiden, 1967], pp. 94–104). On Gregory's view of what portion of the patrimony should be given to the poor, see Bruck, *Kirchenväter*, p. 20. Gregory also contrasts (*Contra usurarios oratio*, p. 94, 17) true fasting to the useless fasting of Judas, which did nothing to change his avaricious habits. On the Platonic backgrounds of starving injustice, see A. Van Heck's commentary in *Gregorii Nysseni De pauperibus amandis orationes duo* (Leiden, 1964), pp. 57–58.

35 *Oratio 4 de oratione dominica* (PG 44:1169).

36 *Oratio catechetica magna*, 40 (PG 45:104). On the importance of baptism in Gregory's thought, see Völker, *Gregor von Nyssa*, pp. 96–99.

37 On Messalians, see A. Louth, "Messalianism and Pelagianism," in E. A. Livingstone, ed., *StP* 17,1 (Oxford, 1982), pp. 127–35; Antoine Guillaumont, "Messaliens," *Dictionnaire de Spiritualité ascétique et mystique*, vol. 10 (1980), cols. 1074–83; Guillaumont, "Liber Graduum," *ibid.*, vol. 9 (1976), cols. 749–54; Arthur Vööbus, *History of Asceticism in the Syrian Orient*, vol. 2, Corpus Scriptorum Christianorum Orientalium 197, Subsidia 17 (Louvain, 1960), pp. 127–39. On Basil's relationship to Messalianism, see Mary Ann Donovan, "The Spirit, Place of the Sanctified: Basil's *De Spiritu Sancto* and Messalianism," in E. A. Livingstone, ed., *StP* 17,3 (Oxford, 1982), pp. 1073–83.

38 *De virginitate*, 23.3 (ed. M. Aubineau, SC 119 [Paris, 1966], pp. 534–36). On the anti-Messalian nature of this passage, see the notes to pp. 536–40 of this edition. Reinhart Staats has shown that Gregory's *De instituto christiano* is a rewrite of Macarius/Symeon's work. See his edition of Makarios-Symeon, *Epistola Magna*, Abhandlungen der Akademie der Wissenschaften in Göttingen, Phil.-hist. Klasse, 3. Folge 134 (Göttingen, 1984), esp. pp. 28–33.

39 In *De virtute*, verses 469ff. (PG 37:714), Gregory notes that paradise flourished with plants, not with gold, amber, silver, and sparkling gems.

40 *Orationes*, 14.26 (PG 35:892). See Robert M. Grant, *Early Christianity and Society*

(New York, 1977), pp. 113–14; Hengel, *Eigentum und Reichtum*, p. 11; Christophe, *L'usage*, p. 131; O. Schilling, *Der kirchliche Eigentumsbegriff*, second ed. (Freiburg/Br., 1930), p. 46. The disintegration of a natural order due to a "justice" which favors the strong is an echo of Plato; see Francesco Trisoglio, "Reminiscenze e consonanze classiche nella XIV orazione di San Gregorio Nazianzeno," *Atti della Accademia delle Scienze di Torino, II: Classe di Scienze Morali, Storiche e Filologiche* 99 (Turin, 1965), p. 177.

41 *Orat.*, 14.25 (PG 35:889). Almsgiving as an imitation of God was a commonplace by the fourth century. For other authors who used the same argument, see W. Walsh and John P. Langan, "Patristic Social Consciousness – The Church and the Poor," in J. C. Haughey, ed., *The Faith that Does Justice: Examining the Sources for Social Change*, Woodstock Studies 2 (New York, 1977), pp. 126–27.

42 *Orat.*, 21.21 (ed. J. Mossay, SC 270 [Paris, 1980], p. 152).

43 When he resigned from the episcopacy of Constantinople in 381, Gregory remarked with bitter irony before 150 bishops that before taking office he had not known bishops were supposed to hunger for the goods of the poor in order to acquire superfluities for the church – see *Orat.*, 42.24 (PG 36:488). Writing later about his experience in Constantinople, he stated flatly that it was a disgrace to have been among the bishops there, who were "retailers of the faith" (κάπηλοι πίστεως) – see *De se ipso et de episcopis*, verses 152–53 (PG 37:1177). For his words on the avarice of the rich, see *Orat.*, 14.24 (PG 35:889). For the use of the fourteenth oration at Lyon in the sixteenth century, see Natalie Z. Davis, "Gregory Nazianzen in the Service of Humanist Social Reform," *Renaissance Quarterly* 20 (1967), 455–64.

44 PG 38:101–02. For further mentions of Midas and other figures from Antiquity in Gregory's works, see the Appendix. For Libanius' use of Midas as an example of a slave to the love of money, see below, p. 42 and n. 73. Cf. Joseph Dziech, "De Gregorio Nazianzeno Diatribae quae dicitur alumno," *Poznańskie Towarzystwo Przyjaciół Nauk. Prace Komisji Filologicznej* 3 (Poznań, 1927), pp. 78–80, nn. 85–90; J. R. Asmus, "Gregorius von Nazianz und sein Verhältnis zum Kynismus," *Theologische Studien und Kritiken* 67 (1894), 322. Grave-robbers are the subject of epigrams 31–94. Cf. Piotr Gruszka, "Die Stellungnahme der Kirchenväter Kappadoziens zu der Gier nach Gold, Silber und anderen Luxuswaren im täglichen Leben der Oberschichten des 4. Jahrhunderts," *Klio* 63,2 (1981), 663. By pointing to the Cynics and Stoics, one has not exhausted Gregory's debt to pagan philosophical schools; on his Platonism see Claudio Moreschini, "Il platonismo cristiano di Gregorio Nazianzeno," *Annali della scuola normale superiore di Pisa*, Classe di lettere e filosofia, serie 3, vol. 4,4 (1974), 1347–92.

45 On Gregory's medical knowledge, see Hermann J. Frings, *Medizin und Arzt bei den griechischen Kirchenvätern bis Chrysostomos*, Dissertation, Bonn (Bonn, 1959); Mary E. Keenan, "St. Gregory of Nazianzus and Early Byzantine Medicine," *Bulletin of the History of Medicine* 9 (1941), 8–30. For Gregory's relation to Cynic-Stoic diatribe, see Rosemary R. Ruether, *Gregory of Nazianzus* (Oxford, 1969), pp. 74, 80; Helen North, *Sophrosyne*, Cornell Studies in Classical Philology 35 (Ithaca, 1966), pp. 342–45; Bernhard Wyss, "Gregor von Nazianz, ein grie-

chisch-christlicher Denker des vierten Jahrhunderts," *Museum Helveticum* 6 (1949), esp. 196.

46 On using the fingers for usury, see *Adv. op. am.*, verse 117 (PG 37:865); on vomiting riches, verse 141 (col. 867 – see Job 20:15); on endless travels to satisfy one's avarice, verse 133 (col. 866); on joining day to night in worry, verse 114 (col. 865); on the toil of avarice, verses 55ff. (cols. 860–61); on the tyranny of the avaricious person, verse 48 (col. 860). For the backgrounds of avarice making itself felt in typical movements of the fingers, see the Appendix.

47 *Orat.*, 42.22 (PG 36:485).

48 *Orat.*, 4.72 (PG 35:596). For Horace's words on Democritus in a similar regard, see the Appendix. In oration 4, Gregory refers to the philosopher who threw his riches overboard as a different person (the footnotes to the text identify him as Zeno). In *De virt.*, verses 236–43 (PG 37:697), he speaks of him as Crates, though he is aware that some say it was another philosopher. Cicero, probably drawing on Diogenes Laertius, praises Aristippus for having thrown his money into the sea; see the Appendix.

49 *Orat.*, 43.60 (PG 36:573–76). Both J. Geffcken, *Kynika und Verwandtes* (Heidelberg, 1909), pp. 23–25, and Asmus, "Gregorius von Nazianz," pp. 315–16, discuss Gregory's citations of Crates, but represent it only as praise for the Cynic. In *Orat.*, 43.60, Gregory also refers to Diogenes' poverty and vainglory as a further way of emphasizing Basil's superiority to the philosophers, though he is more approving of the Cynic in *Epistolae*, 98 (PG 37:172), complaining that government officials who had attempted to fine Theotecnus would probably have tried to tax Diogenes' old cloak and staff as well. Basil himself urged Christians to act like sailors in a storm and throw their excess goods overboard (as alms) in *Quod rebus mundanis adhaerendum non sit*, 7 (PG 31:552).

50 *De vita sua*, verses 270–73 (ed. C. Jungck [Heidelberg, 1974], p. 66).

51 Gregory Presbyter, in his *Vita s. patris nostri Gregorii theologi*, praises Nazianzen's frugal life, even as a student in Athens. At one point (PG 35:256), he compares Gregory's lack of interest in possessions to that of Crates and Diogenes.

52 Gregory explicitly lays out the alternatives of poverty or almsgiving in *Orat.*, 14.18 (PG 35:880–81). For Basil's thoughts on those who give up the property they have enjoyed throughout life only when faced with their approaching death, see above, p. 28. On Gregory's testament, see F. Martroye, "Le testament de saint Grégoire de Nazianze," *Mémoires de la Société Nationale des Antiquaires de France* 76 (série 8, tome 6) (1924), 219–63. Gregory's father, also Bishop of Nazianzus, was married and had children and so felt unable to give his possessions to the poor (see Martroye, "Le testament," pp. 247–49).

53 Even this insistence could be built into the argument against the sin; see *Homilia 76 in Ioannem*, 3 (PG 59:413), where he addresses the congregation with: "And perhaps one of you will say, 'Every day you discourse on avarice.' If only I were able to speak about it every night, too!"

54 *Homilia 63 in Matthaeum*, 4 (PG 58:607); see Dolores Greeley, "St. John Chrysostom, Prophet of Social Justice," in E. A. Livingstone, ed., *StP* 17,3 (Oxford, 1982), pp. 1163–68. On almsgiving in Chrysostom's thought, see

Francis Leduc, "Péché et conversion chez saint Jean Chrysostome," *Proche-Orient Chrétien* 28 (1978), 45–51; Anastasia Sifoniou, "Les fondements juridiques de l'aumone et de la charité chez Jean Chrysostome," *Revue du droit canonique* 14 (1964), 241–69.

55 See *Quod non oporteat peccata fratrum evulgare*, 2 (PG 51:355–56); *In propheticum dictum illud: "Ego dominus . . ."*, 5 (PG 56:149). Cf. also Walsh and Langan, "Patristic Social Consciousness," pp. 128–29.

56 When Chrysostom wishes to stress the universality of avarice, he notes explicitly that both poor and rich can be greedy – see *Quod nemo laedatur nisi a seipso*, 6 (PG 52:467); *Homilia 18 in Epistolam 1 ad Timotheum, cap. 6*, 3 (PG 62:595). When he charges Christians not to pillage what is another's, he says he is speaking to the rich and the poor, for the poor seize things from those who are even poorer – see *Homilia 23 in Epistolam 1 ad Corinthios*, 6 (PG 61:197–98); *Homilia 10 in Epistolam 1 ad Thessalonicenses, cap. 5*, 4 (PG 62:460–61). In *Homilia 6 in Epistolam ad Philippenses, cap. 2*, 5 (PG 62:226) he says avarice does not consist in desiring a great quantity of money, but in desiring even a small amount. For poverty's value in cultivating virtue, see *De eleemosyna homilia*, 5 (PG 51:268) and Otto Plassmann, *Das Almosen bei Johannes Chrysostomus*, Dissertation, Bonn (Münster, 1960), p. 68.

57 *Hom. 77 in Ioan.*, 5 (PG 59:420).

58 *Homilia 66 in Genesim, cap. 48*, 4 (PG 54:571); *Hom. 34 in Ep. 1 ad Cor.*, 6 (PG 61:294–95).

59 *Hom. 23 in Matt.*, 9 (PG 57:319). He ultimately rejects the example of the businessman he has established for the sake of an argument, though not on the grounds of avaricious acquisition, but rather due to his failure to give alms. Cf. Christophe, *L'usage*, p. 141; and compare Brändle, *Matth. 25, 31–46*, pp. 91–92.

60 *Hom. 12 in Ep. 1 ad Tim., cap. 4* (PG 62:563).

61 Usury: *Hom. 38 in Matt.*, 4 (PG 57:433); *Hom. 56 in Matt.*, 5–6 (PG 58:557–58); *Hom. 13 in Ep. 1 ad Cor.*, 5 (PG 61:114); tax-collecting: *Homilia 2 de poenitentia*, 5 (PG 49:290); income during famines: *Hom. 39 in Ep. 1 ad Cor.*, 7–8 (PG 61:343–44; based on occurrences during a drought in Antioch); inheritance: *Hom. 13 in Ep. 1 ad Cor.*, 5 (PG 61:114). See also Plassmann, *Das Almosen*, p. 10. In *Hom. 34 in Ep. 1 ad Cor.*, 6 (PG 61:293), Chrysostom further mentions prostitution (male and female), witchcraft, and graverobbery as illicit means of gaining wealth. In *Hom. 85 in Matt.*, 3 (PG 58:761), Chrysostom rejects alms from illicitly acquired wealth on the grounds that Jesus (i.e., the poor) does not want to be nourished by avarice. Libanius treats the theme of avariciously desiring inheritances in his oration on greed where he describes an Egyptian who made his fortune by becoming the heir to a number of childless couples. Yet he always suffered because they never died soon enough. See Περὶ ἀπληστίας (Oration 6), 11 (ed. and trans. B. Schouler in Libanios, *Discours moraux*, Université Lyon II – U.E.R. des Sciences de l'Antiquité, Institut F. Courby, E. R. A. 60 [Paris, 1973], pp. 147–49). Chrysostom also identified Jews with avarice in a vicious anti-Jewish polemic: *Orationes contra Judaeos*, 1.7 (PG 48:853). For the backgrounds of his attitudes, see J. N. D. Kelly, *Golden Mouth: The Story of John Chrysostom*

(Ithaca, 1995), pp. 62–66; Wayne A. Meeks and Robert L. Wilken, *Jews and Christians in Antioch in the First Four Centuries of the Common Era*, Society for Biblical Literature: Sources for Biblical Study 13 (Missoula, Montana, 1978).

62 *Hom. 12 in Ep. 1 ad Tim.*, 4 (PG 62:563). Cf. Grant, *Early Christianity*, pp. 114–16, who describes the Platonic and Stoic backgrounds of Chrysostom's ideas here.

63 *Homilia de beato Philogonio*, 1 (PG 48:749). Epiphanes, according to Clement of Alexandria, had also used the opposition "mine–yours" to describe contemporary society's distance from the divine ideal. See *Stromata*, 3.2.7.3 (GCS 52 [15]:198); and above, ch. 1, p. 8.

64 *Homilia 11 in Acta Apostolorum*, 3 (PG 60:97). See Stanislas Giet, "La doctrine de l'appropriation des biens chez quelques-uns des pères," *Recherches de Science religieuse* 35 (1948), 74–75; Schilling, *Der kirchliche Eigentumsbegriff*, pp. 46–48.

65 See *In Isaiam*, 1.7 (PG 56:23).

66 Chrysostom frequently speaks of avarice as the cause of wars. See *Hom. 63 in Matt.*, 4 (PG 58:607); *Hom. 80 in Matt.*, 3 (PG 58:728); *Hom. 90 in Matt.*, 4 (PG 58:791); Rudolph Mehrlein, "De avaritia quid iudicaverit Ioannes Chrysostomus," Dissertation, University of Cologne, 1951, pp. 93–94. On the identification of avarice with robbery in Chrysostom's work, see Plassmann, *Das Almosen*, pp. 10 and 74. In *Hom. 17 in Ep. 1 ad Tim., cap. 6*, 3 (PG 62:595), Chrysostom remarks that if avarice were done away with, there would be no more wars and strife.

67 Chrysostom's use of Judas as an example of avarice is very frequent. For this and other scriptural figures which serve as examples of avarice in his works, see the Appendix.

68 *Hom. 28 in Matt.*, 5 (PG 57:356). On the cruelty of the avaricious sinner see also *Homila 19 in Epistolam ad Romanos*, 8 (PG 60:594).

69 On this characteristic of diatribe, see Geffcken, *Kynika*, p. 40; Paul Wendland, "Philo und die kynisch-stoische Diatribe," in P. Wendland and O. Kern, *Beiträge zur Geschichte der griechischen Philosophie und Religion* (Berlin, 1895), p. 3. Seneca turns to Avarice in *De beneficiis*, 7.10.1 (ed. and trans. F. Prechac, vol. 2 [Paros, 1927], p. 87); Persius uses this literary technique in *Saturae*, 5.132–42 (ed. W. V. Clausen [Oxford, 1959], pp. 22–23). Chrysostom explains his general understanding of personification in *Hom. 14 in Ep. ad Rom.*, 5 (PG 60:529–30). For parallels between Chrysostom's moral thinking and what one finds in diatribe, see Arnold Uleyn, "La doctrine morale de saint Jean Chrysostome dans le Commentaire sur saint Matthieu et ses affinites avec la diatribe," *Revue de l'Université d'Ottawa* 27 (1957), 5*-25*, 99*-140*.

70 *Hom. 90 in Matt.*, 4 (PG 58:791). One cannot overlook the view of sexuality involved in this passage. See also *Expositio in Psalmum 9*, 1 (PG 55:122), where Chrysostom describes the love of money as a love for a misshapen woman. Only when one is cured of it, can one recognize the deformity for what it is.

71 *Quod nemo laedatur*, 6 (PG 52:467), where he also terms avarice a lavish and public whore. Chrysostom uses the designation "tyrannos" in reference to the vice in *Expos. in Ps. 48*, 1 (PG 55:499); and "tyrannis" in *Hom. 21 in Matt.*, 1 (PG

57:294), etc. "Tyranny" is Chrysostom's regular designation for the rule of the passions over their victims. Cf. Mehrlein, "De avaritia," p. 28.

72 *Hom. 65 in Ioan.*, 3 (PG 59:364). For Chrysostom's use of the proverbial danger of avarice, see *Hom. 28 in Matt.*, 5 (PG 57:357).

73 *Orationes*, 25.22–25 (ed. Schouler, pp. 187–89). Chrysostom describes the greedy as slaves to their money or to avarice in (among others): *Hom. 21 in Matt.*, 1 (PG 57:294); *Homilia 4 in Epistolam ad Colossenses, cap. 1*, 4 (PG 62:331), where he says the Israelites were lovers of money during the exodus; *Hom. 7 in Ep. 1 ad Tim., cap. 2*, 3 (PG 62:538).

74 *Hom. 28 in Matt.*, 5 (PG 57:356). Chrysostom remarks that the avaricious sinner is fiercer even than what his demonic portrait demonstrates; in fact, the depth of his wickedness is so bottomless, Chrysostom says he prefers the company of ten thousand demons to one avaricious person.

75 *Hom. 74 in Ioan.*, 3 (PG 59:403).

76 *Hom. 13 in Ep. ad Rom.*, 10–11 (PG 60:521–24).

77 *Hom. 81 in Matt.*, 5 (PG 58:736–37). See Mehrlein, "De avaritia," p. 31.

78 *Hom. 83 in Matt.*, 3 (PG 58:749). See Sir. 20:4, 30:20. Chrysostom notes that lecherous and avaricious sinners are similar because both are slaves to their desire, in a state of anxiety, etc., in *Hom. 12 in Ep. ad Rom.*, 7 (PG 60:504).

79 See Theodoros Nikolaou, *Der Neid bei Johannes Chrysostomus*, Abhandlungen zur Philosophie, Psychologie und Pädagogik 56 (Bonn, 1969), esp. pp. 85–86; Francis Leduc, "Le thème de la vaine gloire chez saint Jean Chrysostome," *Proche-Orient Chrétien* 19 (1969), 3–32, esp. 6–8.

80 *Hom. 31 in Ep. ad Cor.*, 4 (PG 61:262–63).

81 *Hom. 20 in Gen., cap. 4*, 5 (PG 53:173).

82 *Hom. 87 in Ioan.*, 4 (PG 59:477).

83 *Hom. 20 in Matt.*, 2 (PG 57:288–89). In another homily he speaks explicitly of vainglory as the mother, root, and fount of avarice; see *Hom. 3 in Ioan.*, 6 (PG 59:45).

84 *Interpretatio in Isaiam, cap. 3*, 7 (PG 56:49). For vainglory's proverbial relationship to avarice, see *Adversus oppugnatores vitae monasticae*, 3.5 (PG 47:357).

85 Crates, Diogenes, and perhaps Aristippus are alluded to in *Hom. 35 in Ep. 1 ad Cor.*, 4 (PG 61:301–02). The connection of vainglory with almsgiving has been treated by Leduc, "Le thème," pp. 15–16.

3 ASCETIC TRANSFORMATIONS II: SOARING EAGLES OR SAFETY IN THE HERD — FROM ANCHORITIC TO CENOBITIC MONASTICISM

1 Peter Brown, *Power and Persuasion in Late Antiquity: Towards a Christian Empire*, The Curti Lectures, 1988 (Madison, 1992), p. 72.

2 For Evagrius' life, see the introduction to A. and C. Guillaumont, eds., *Evagre le Pontique, Traité Pratique, ou le Moine*, vol. 1, SC 170 (Paris, 1971), pp. 21–28. For the corpus of Evagrian works, see *Clavis Patrum Graecorum*, vol. 2, ed. M. Geerard (Turnhout, 1974), 2430–2482, pp. 78–97.

3 *Practicus*, 9 (ed. A. and C. Guillaumont, *Traité*, vol. 2, SC 171 [Paris, 1971],

p. 512). This chapter is in a section of the *Pract.* frequently referred to earlier as a separate work entitled *De octo vitiosis cogitationibus*. J. Muyldermans (in *Le Muséon* 42 [1929], see especially p. 86) demonstrated this section comprises chapters 6–14 of the *Pract.* On life in semi-anchoritic communities, see A. Guillaumont, *Traité*, SC 170:24–25.

4 *Antirrheticus*, 3.2 and 24 (ed. W. Frankenberg, *Euagrius Ponticus*, Abhandlungen der königlichen Gesellschaft der Wissenschaften zu Göttingen, Phil.-hist. Klasse, N.F. 13,2 [Berlin, 1912], pp. 494 and 496). I am indebted to Prof. Dr. R. Voigt for his help in translating this Syriac text.

5 *Tractatus ad Eulogium*, 11 (PG 79:1108).

6 See *De octo spiritibus malitiae*, 7 (PG 79:1152).

7 *Antirr.*, 3.25 (ed. Frankenberg, p. 496).

8 *Ibid.*, 3.34 (p. 498). The Egyptian anchoritic colonies soon acquired a reputation for their radical poverty. Jerome, *Epistulae*, 22.33.1–2 (ed. I. Hilberg, CSEL 54 [Vienna and Leipzig, 1910], pp. 195–96), reports that the community at Nitria had to assemble to decide what to do with 100 gold coins which a brother, recently deceased, had hoarded in his cell. Macarius, Pambo, and Isidore advised the monks to bury the money with its former possessor, repeating Peter's words to Simon (Acts 8:20): "May your money go with you to damnation."

9 *Antirr.*, 3.12 and 47 (ed. Frankenberg, pp. 494–96 and 500).

10 *De octo sp.*, 7 (PG 79:1152).

11 See *Antirr.*, 3.52 and 53 (ed. Frankenberg, p. 500) and especially *De diversis malignis cogitationibus*, 23 (PG 79:1225) for Evagrius' use of the biblical passage.

12 *De vitiis quae opposita sunt virtutibus*, 3 (PG 79:1141). In *Antirr.*, 3.29 (ed. Frankenberg, p. 498), avarice is seen as the force which drives a monk to work hard for the acquisition of material things to the virtual exclusion of all his monastic activities.

13 This stage is termed *praktike* in Evagrius' vocabulary and is defined in *Pract.*, 78 (SC 171:666). For Evagrius' teachings, see Simon Tugwell, "Evagrius and Macarius," in C. Jones *et al.*, eds., *The Study of Spirituality* (London, 1986), pp. 169–72; Siegfried Wenzel, *The Sin of Sloth: Acedia in Medieval Thought and Literature* (Chapel Hill, N.C., 1967), pp. 12–14; Hans Urs von Balthasar, "Die Hiera des Evagrius," *Zeitschrift für katholische Theologie* 63 (1939), esp. 95–102, 185–89; von Balthasar, "Metaphysik und Mystik des Evagrius Ponticus," *Zeitschrift für Aszese und Mystik* 14 (1939), 31–47; M. Viller, "Aux sources de la spiritualité de S. Maxime: Les œuvres d'Evagre le Pontique," *RAM* 11 (1930), esp. 161–82. Ἀπάθεια was not valued by all patristic authors; see W. Völker, *Praxis und Theoria bei Symeon dem Neuen Theologen: Ein Beitrag zur byzantinischen Mystik* (Wiesbaden, 1974), pp. 265–72; A. Dirking, "Die Bedeutung des Wortes Apathie beim heiligen Basilius dem Großen," *Theologische Quartalschrift* 134 (1954), 202–12; T. Rüther, *Die sittliche Forderung der Apatheia in den beiden ersten christlichen Jahrhunderten und bei Klemens von Alexandrien, Ein Beitrag zur Geschichte des christlichen Vollkommenheitsbegriffes*, Freiburger Theologische Studien 63 (Freiburg/Br., 1949); P. de Labriolle, "Apatheia," *RAC*, vol. 1 (1950), cols. 484–87; de Labriolle, "Apatheia," in *Mélanges de philologie, de littérature et*

d'histoire anciennes offerts à Alfred Ernout (Paris, 1940), pp. 215–23; G. Bardy, "Apatheia," *Dictionnaire de Spiritualité ascétique et mystique*, vol. 1 (1937), cols. 727–46.

14 Richard Newhauser, *The Treatise on Vices and Virtues in Latin and the Vernacular*, Typologie des sources du moyen âge occidental 68 (Turnhout, 1993).

15 *Pract.*, 18 and 99 (SC 171:546 and 710) should be consulted for Evagrius' concept of virtuous charity.

16 *De octo sp.*, 7 (PG 79:1152).

17 *De div. mal. cog.*, 23 (PG 79:1225) presents this idea quite clearly. See below, p. 54.

18 See especially *Antirr.*, 3.46 and 58 (ed. Frankenberg, pp. 500 and 502).

19 Consult *Rerum monachalium rationes*, 4 (PG 40:1256) and *Capita paraenetica*, 52 (PG 79:1253).

20 *De div. mal. cog.*, 22 (PG 79:1225).

21 *De viris inlustribus*, 11 (ed. E. C. Richardson, TU 14, 1 [Leipzig, 1896], p. 65). Irenée Hausherr identified Evagrius as the initiator of the octad on the basis of what he had found especially in the works of Origen: see "De doctrina spirituali Christianorum orientalium quaestiones et scripta, 3: L'origine de la théorie orientale des huit péchés capitaux," *Orientalia Christiana* 30,3 (1933), 164–75, repr. in Hausherr, *Etudes de spiritualité orientale*, Orientalia Christiana Analecta 183 (Rome, 1969), pp. 11–22. There is no evidence, however, that Evagrius found the motivation for eight categories in Origen's biblical exegesis. A. Guillaumont argues that the form of the octad was the original work of Evagrius (*Traité*, SC 170, see esp. pp. 82–83). If this is true, Gennadius' uncertainty on its origin is fairly surprising, and Cassian's silence (even considering the need for him to be cautious in the face of a suppression of Origenist tendencies in the East) is more so, for Cassian quoted Evagrius' works very often and yet consistently referred to the octad as the common teaching of Egyptian monasticism in general (*Conlationes*, 5.18 [ed. M. Petschenig, CSEL 13 (Vienna, 1886), p. 143]; *De institutis coenobiorum et de octo principalium vitiorum remediis libri 12*, praef. 7 [ed. M. Petschenig, CSEL 17 (Vienna, 1888), p. 6]). Had Evagrius been the first monk to use the octad, Cassian would have been in a position to know this. Others identify the Egyptian monks as the originators of the octad without limiting the question to Evagrius' activity alone: see A. Vögtle, "Woher stammt das Schema der Hauptsünden?" *Theologische Quartalschrift* 122 (1941), 217–37; Vögtle, "Achtlasterlehre," *RAC*, vol. 1 (1950), cols. 74–79 (a summary of his earlier article); Wenzel, *Sloth*, pp. 14–17. For further consideration of the sources of the octad, see Newhauser, *The Treatise*, pp. 101–04.

22 The Greek, Latin, and English equivalents in this system are as follows:

Γαστριμαργία	**G**ula	Gluttony
Πορνεία	**L**uxuria	Lust
Φιλαργυρία	**A**varitia	Avarice
Λύπη	**T**ristitia	Sadness
Ὀργή	**I**ra	Wrath

᾿Ακηδία	**A** cedia	Sloth
Κενοδοξία	**V** ana Gloria	Vainglory
῾Υπερηφανία	**S** uperbia	Pride

The mnemonic acronym used in the late Middle Ages, and taken from a system of seven sins, is SALIGIA. On this acronym (and others), see Morton Bloomfield, *The Seven Deadly Sins* ([East Lansing, Mich.], 1952; repr. 1967), esp. pp. 86–87; Arthur Watson, "Saligia," *Journal of the Warburg and Courtauld Institutes* 10 (1947), 148–50; Otto Zöckler, *Das Lehrstück von den sieben Hauptsünden*, in Zöckler, *Biblische und kirchenhistorische Studien* 3 (Munich, 1893), pp. 66–81.

23 Hausherr, "De doctrina spirituali," p. 172, though he is too strict in his understanding of this reflection. See also Rainer Jehl, "Die Geschichte des Lasterschemas und seiner Funktion. Von der Väterzeit bis zur karolingischen Erneuerung," *Franziskanische Studien* 64 (1982), 285, who attempts to relate the order of evil thoughts to the Platonic scheme of the parts of the soul; Newhauser, *The Treatise*, p. 104.

24 *Capita cognoscitiva*, 67 (ed. Muyldermans, p. 57).

25 *De div. mal. cog.*, 1, 24 (PG 79:1200–01, 1228) for Evagrius' use of the triad and its relationship to the temptations of Jesus. Evagrius gives the temptations in the order found in Luke, though Matthew's order (stones to bread, parapet, kingdoms of the world) was the one most frequently used by exegetes. A. Guillaumont, *Traité*, SC 170:90–92, accounts for the order of the eight *logismoi* by suggesting that the three thoughts corresponding to the three temptations formed the framework of the list and all the others were added around them. In Evagrius' works, however, the triad is found only in *De div. mal. cog.* If it were the basis for the octad, to which Evagrius referred frequently, one would expect it to appear more often than in a single work. For the history of patristic exegesis of the temptations of Jesus, see Giovanni Leonardi, "Le tentazioni de Gesú nella interpretazione patristica," *Studia Patavina* 15 (1968), 229–62; M. Steiner, *La tentation de Jésus dans l'interprétation patristique de Saint Justin à Origène*, Etudes Bibliques 54 (Paris, 1962); Klaus-Peter Köppen, *Die Auslegung der Versuchungsgeschichte unter besonderer Berücksichtigung der Alten Kirche: Ein Beitrag zur Geschichte der Schriftenauslegung*, Beiträge zur Geschichte der biblischen Exegese 4 (Tübingen, 1961). None of these works mention Evagrius.

26 Tertullian connected the temptations of the Israelites in the desert with those of Jesus, see *De baptismo*, 20.4 (ed. J. G. Ph. Borleffs, CCL 1 [Turnhout, 1954], pp. 294–95). For Origen's use of gluttony in his exegesis of the passage, see n. 29 below. This interpretation is seen often after the typological exegesis which connected Adam's fall to Jesus' victory over the devil became a commonplace of patristic commentary.

27 Clement of Alexandria, *Stromata*, 2.5.21.1ff. (ed. O. Stählin, fourth ed., ed. L. Früchtel, GCS 52 [15] [Clemens 2] [Berlin, 1985], p. 123); *Pseudo-Clementines, Homiliae*, 8.21.1–3 (ed. B. Rehm, GCS 42 [Berlin, 1953], pp. 129–30); see also Hippolytus Romanus' sermon 1.3 (in H. Achelis, *Die ältesten Quellen des orientalischen Kirchenrechtes. Erstes Buch: Die Canones Hippolyti* TU 6,4 [Leipzig,

1891], p. 281), mentioned by Köppen, *Die Auslegung*, p. 37, where *amor auri* probably refers to this temptation; Methodius Olympus, *De vita*, 7.4 (ed. G. Bonwetsch, GCS 27 [Leipzig, 1917], p. 215). For the *Pseudo-Clementines* see Berthold Altaner and Alfred Stuiber, *Patrologie*, ninth rev. ed. (Freiburg, 1980), pp. 134–35.

28 *Adversus haereses*, 5.21.2 (ed. A. Rousseau *et al.*, SC 153 [Paris, 1969], p. 270).

29 See *In Lucam homiliae*, 30 (ed. M. Rauer, second ed., GCS 49 (35) [Origenes 9] [Berlin, 1959], p. 172). For Origen's identification of the first temptation as *gastrimargia*, see *In Lucam fragmenta*, 96 (ed. M. Rauer, GCS 49 [35]:265). Lists of moral evils are common in Origen's works and one finds with some frequency a triad (though this is not generally a closed system) composed of lust, avarice, and vainglory. However, these three are not used as an interpretation of Jesus' temptations. See *In Librum Iudicum homiliae*, 2.5 (ed. W. A. Baehrens, GCS 30 [Origenes 7] [Leipzig, 1921], p. 479); *Commentarium in Canticum Canticorum*, prol. (ed. W. A. Baehrens, GCS 33 [Origenes 8] [Leipzig, 1925], p. 72). Origen is treated at great length by Steiner, *La tentation*, pp. 107–92.

30 Gregory Nazianzen, *Orationes*, 40.10 (PG 36:369–72), mentioned by G. Leonardi, "Le tentazioni," p. 248, but listed as "Gregorio Nisseno." Evagrius praised Gregory as the just man who had "planted" him; see the epilogue to *Pract.* (SC 171:712). For the further influence of this method of interpretation, found earliest in Gregory's work, see John Chrysostom, *Homilia 13 in Matthaeum*, 4 (PG 57:212) where the three temptations are understood as slavery to the stomach, action due to vainglory, and dependency on the madness of riches. For a similar triad, in a different context, see Gregory of Nyssa, above, ch. 2, pp. 30–31 and n. 26. In the West, see Ambrose, *Expositio Evangelii secundum Lucam*, 4.17 (ed. M. Adriaen, CCL 14 [Turnhout, 1957], p. 112).

31 Evagrius systematized Gregory's suggestive treatment of other topics as well, including the latter's tripartite anthropology. See Michael O'Laughlin, "The Anthropology of Evagrius Ponticus and its Sources," in C. Kannengiesser and W. L. Petersen, eds., *Origen of Alexandria: His World and His Legacy*, Christianity and Judaism in Antiquity 1 (Notre Dame, IN, 1988), pp. 357–73.

32 For some of the Greek authors who followed Evagrius' teaching on the triad, see A. Guillaumont, *Traité*, SC 170:90–91 n. 4.

33 Augustine's triad is *voluptas carnis, curiositas, superbia*. Its earliest appearance in his works is probably in *De Genesi contra Manichaeos*, 2.18.27 (PL 34:210; see also 2.26.40 [col. 217], 1.23.40 [col. 192]). In *De vera religione*, 38.70 (ed. K. Daur, CCL 32 [Turnhout, 1962], p. 233) he connected it to the three evils mentioned in 1John 2:16 ("desire of the flesh, desire of the eyes, and the pride of life") and to the three temptations of Jesus. Later, the triad was used in discussions of the fall of Adam, as was Evagrius' triad. On both of these groupings of three evil qualities, see Donald R. Howard, *The Three Temptations* (Princeton, 1966), pp. 44–56. Howard seems to attribute the gluttony – avarice – vainglory series to Gregory the Great, but his notes are filled with ample and helpful references to the further history of this triad in the Middle Ages. They can be supplemented by Brian O. Murdoch, *The Recapitulated Fall: A Comparative Study in Mediaeval Literature*,

Amsterdamer Publikationen zur Sprache und Literatur 11 (Amsterdam, 1974), pp. 41–44 nn. 41–43, 47.

34 See, for example, Bede, *In Lucae evangelium expositio*, 1.4.13 (ed. D. Hurst, CCL 120 [Turnhout, 1960], p. 98) where desire of the flesh is identified as *uxoris appetitus* and *gula*, desire of the eyes as *corporalium rerum curiositas quae est uana gloria*, and the pride of life as *avaritia*. In the later Middle Ages, see Innocentius III, *Sermo 13, Dominica prima in Quadragesima* (PL 217:371–72).

35 *Vita S. Antonii*, 5 and 30 (PG 26:845–48, 889). Some question Athanasius' authorship of this text; see Timothy D. Barnes, "Angel of Light or Mystic Initiate? The Problem of the *Life* of Anthony," *Journal of Theological Studies* n.s. 37 (1986), 352–68. See also the use of *philargyria* in the *Vita S. Syncleticae*, 72 (PG 28:1529).

36 *De octo vitiosis cogitationibus*, section περὶ φιλαργυρίας (PG 79:1452). The work is composed of material taken from Evagrius, Cassian, and Nilus. The material cited here is Nilus'.

37 *Historia Lausiaca*, 71 (ed. E. C. Butler, vol. 2, Texts and Studies 6,2 [Cambridge, 1904], pp. 167–68). See also *Hist. Laus.*, 10 (ed. Butler, vol. 2, pp. 29–31). Seeking financial support from the rich had been identified by Evagrius as a result of avarice – see R. Draguet, "L'Histoire Lausiaque', une œuvre écrite dans l'esprit d'Evagre," *Revue d'Histoire Ecclésiastique* 42 (1947), 37 (no. 287).

38 Initially, the sayings and narratives of this compilation were arranged in alphabetical order according to their speakers; later redactions organized this material under topical headings. See J.-C. Guy, *Recherches sur la tradition grecque des "Apophthegmata Patrum,"* Subsidia hagiographica 36 (Brussels, 1962).

39 Anthony, 20 (PG 65:81). A Latin version of this apophthegm can be found in a sixth-century translation of a lost Greek collection, in the chapter entitled *Contra philargyriam*: Pascasius of Dumium, *Apophthegmata Patrum*, 14.2 (ed. J. Geraldes Freire in *A Versão por Pascásio de Dume dos Apophthegmata Patrum* [Coimbra, 1971], vol. 1, p. 186). See also *Vitae patrum*, 5.6.1, 5.6.10, 3.68 (PL 73:888, 890, 772).

40 On the importance of retaining no money in the cell, see apophthegm 262 in the chapter on abandoning greed in the collection edited by F. Nau, "Histoires des solitaires égyptiens," *Revue de l'Orient Chrétien* 14 (1909), 368–69; and the Latin versions in Pascasius of Dumium, *Apoph. Pat.*, 14.4 (ed. Geraldes Freire, vol. 1, p. 187); *Vit. Pat.*, 5.6.22, 3.69 (PL 73:892–93, 772). See also *Vit. Pat.*, 5.6.21 (PL 73:892), mentioned in James Owen Hannay, *The Wisdom of the Desert* (n.p., 1904), pp. 163–64.

41 Apophthegm 392 in F. Nau, "Histoires des solitaires égyptiens," *Revue de l'Orient Chrétien* 18 (1913), 144. Latin versions are in Pascasius of Dumium, *Apoph. Pat.*, 14.6 (ed. Geraldes Freire, vol. 1, p. 188); *Vit. Pat.*, 5.6.5, 3.70 (PL 73:889, 772–73). In fact, of course, the monks read and produced many books; see Peter Brown, *The Body and Society* (New York, 1988), p. 252.

42 L.-Th. Lefort, "A propos d'un aphorisme d'Evagrius Ponticus," *Academie Royale de Belgique. Bulletin de la Classe des Lettres et des Sciences morales et politiques* 36 (Brussels, 1950), pp. 70–79. On the Pachomian influence, see C. de Clercq,

"L'influence de la règle de saint Pachôme en Occident," in *Mélanges d'histoire du moyen âge, dédiés à la mémoire de Louis Halphen* (Paris, 1951), pp. 169–76; H. Bacht, "L'importance de l'idéal monastique de saint Pachôme pour l'histoire du monachisme chrétien," *RAM* 26 (1950), 308–26. K. Heussi, *Der Ursprung des Mönchtums* (Tübingen, 1936), pp. 115–31, describes the success of the economic structure of the Pachomian institutions.

43 *Praecepta*, 81 (ed. A. Boon in *Pachomiana Latina*, Bibliothèque de la Revue d'Histoire Ecclésiastique 7 [Louvain, 1932], p. 37). The *Praecepta* were formulated originally in Coptic but are extant in complete form only in Jerome's rendering of a lost Greek translation. The image of avarice's war against ascetes is found in Pachomius' *Catechism Concerning a Vengeful Monk* (ed. and trans. L.-Th. Lefort in *Œuvres de S. Pachôme et de ses disciples*, Corpus Scriptorum Christianorum Orientalium 159–60, Scriptores Coptici 23–24 [Louvain, 1964–65]; here vol. 160 [24], p. 22); see also Armand Veilleux, "Le renoncement aux biens matériels dans le cénobitisme pachômien," *Collectanea Cisterciensia* 43 (1981), 58. Arguments for including precept 81 in the genuine works of Pachomius are reviewed by A. de Vogüé, "Les pièces latines du dossier pachômien: remarques sur quelques publications récentes," *Revue d'Histoire Ecclésiastique* 67 (1972), 49–51. While anchoritic monasticism did not find the motivation for *aktemosyne* in Jesus' poverty, Pachomius did – see P. Nagel, *Die Motivierung der Askese in der alten Kirche und der Ursprung des Mönchtums*, TU 95 (Berlin, 1966), pp. 18–19.

44 *Liber Orsiesii*, 27 (ed. A. Boon in *Pachomiana Latina*, pp. 127–28). On this work, see Heinrich Bacht, "Studien zum 'Liber Orsiesii'," *Historisches Jahrbuch* 77 (1958), 98–124, and especially 113–15 for the position of avarice in the *Liber*. On the function of the wall in Pachomian monasteries, see Henry Chadwick, "Pachomios and the Ideal of Sanctity," in S. Hackel, ed., *The Byzantine Saint. University of Birmingham Fourteenth Spring Symposium of Byzantine Studies*, Studies Supplementary to Sobornost 5 (London, 1981), p. 15 (repr. in Henry Chadwick, *History and Thought of the Early Church*, Variorum Collected Studies, CS 164 [London, 1982]).

45 *Regulae brevius tractatae*, 48 and 263 (PG 31:1116, 1261).

46 Homily 10.2.4 (ed. and trans. V. Desprez in Pseudo-Macaire, *Œuvres spirituelles, I: Homélies propres à la Collection III*, SC 275 [Paris, 1980], p. 158). The relationship between Macarius/Symeon and the Cappadocians, in particular Basil the Great, has been examined by Vincent Desprez, "Les relations entre le Pseudo-Macaire et Saint Basile," in J. Gribomont, ed., *Commandements du Seigneur et libération évangélique*, Studia Anselmiana 70 (Rome, 1977), pp. 208–21. See also Desprez's article "Le Pseudo-Macaire," pp. 175–89, in the same collection. For Macarius/Symeon's consideration of sin, consult Hermann Dörries, *Die Theologie des Makarios/Symeon*, Abhandlungen der Akademie der Wissenschaften in Göttingen, Phil.-hist. Klasse, 3. Folge 103 (Göttingen, 1978), esp. pp. 63–71.

47 On the beginnings of monasticism in the West, see Bernhard Lohse, *Askese und Mönchtum in der Antike und in der alten Kirche*, Religion und Kultur der alten Mittelmeerwelt in Parallelforschungen 1 (Munich and Vienna, 1969), pp. 214–26; Rudolf Lorenz, "Die Anfänge des abendländischen Mönchtums im 4. Jahrhun-

dert," *Zeitschrift für Kirchengeschichte* 77 (1966), 1–61; Friedrich Prinz, *Frühes Mönchtum im Frankenreich* (Munich and Vienna, 1965). J.-C. Guy, "Jean Cassien, historien du monachisme égyptien?" in F. L. Cross, ed., *StP* 8, TU 93 (Berlin, 1966), pp. 363–72, notes that Cassian's account of Egyptian monasticism is not without inaccuracies, but by putting ideas in the mouths of the desert fathers, he hoped to give weight to his teachings.

48 See Cassian's glowing words on Chrysostom in *De incarnatione domini contra Nestorum libri* 7, 7.30–31 (ed. M. Petschenig, CSEL 17 [Vienna, 1888], pp. 388–91). For Cassian's life and the problems involved in establishing a chronology of his activities, see Philip Rousseau, *Ascetics, Authority and the Church in the Age of Jerome and Cassian* (Oxford, 1978), pp. 169–76; Paul Christophe, *Cassien et Césaire*, Recherches et synthèses, Section de morale 2 (Gembloux and Paris, 1969), pp. 7–14; Owen Chadwick, *John Cassian*, second ed. (Cambridge, 1968), pp. 9–36; Hans-Oskar Weber, *Die Stellung des Johannes Cassianus zur ausserpachomianischen Mönchstradition*, Beiträge zur Geschichte des alten Mönchtums und des Benediktinerordens 24 (Münster, 1961), pp. 1–5.

49 On Cassian's sources and verbal parallels with Evagrius' work, see H.-O. Weber, *Die Stellung*; Jean-Claude Guy, *Jean Cassien: Vie et doctrine spirituelle*, Collection Théologie, Pastorale et Spiritualité, Recherches et synthèses 9 (Paris, 1961); S. Marsili, *Giovanni Cassiano ed Evagrio Pontico*, Studia Anselmiana 5 (Rome, 1936).

50 *Conl.*, 5.2 (CSEL 13:121); *Inst.*, 5.1 (CSEL 17:81).

51 *Conl.*, 5.6 (CSEL 13:124–26).

52 For the parallel passages in Cassian and Evagrius, see H.-O. Weber, *Die Stellung*, pp. 24–25.

53 *Conl.*, 5.3 (CSEL 13:121). Though envy is not part of the octad, Cassian remarks in *Inst.*, 7.5 (CSEL 17:131–32) that both *inuidia* and *filargyria* have no natural motivation. He speaks of envy in more particular terms in *Conl.*, 18.16 (CSEL 13:528–29) and *Inst.*, 5.21 (CSEL 17:99). See E. Pichery, "Les idées morales de Jean Cassien," *MSR* 14 (1957), 18–19.

54 Gregory Nazianzen, *Orat.*, 14.25–26 (PG 35:889–92); Chrysostom, *Hom. 15 in Matt.*, 11 (PG 57:237); Chrysostom, *Homilia 65 in Ioannem*, 3 (PG 59:364); Chrysostom, *Homilia 12 in Epistolam 1 ad Timotheum cap. 4*, 4 (PG 62:563–64). Chrysostom used the exact phrase (*para physin*) Evagrius employed in describing avarice's position "outside nature" in *Hom. 21 in Matt.*, 4 (PG 57:300); *Hom. 80 in Matt.*, 3 (PG 58:728).

55 *Conl.*, 5.8 (CSEL 13:128–29); *Inst.*, 7.1 (CSEL 17:130). Cf. also Jehl, "Die Geschichte," p. 293.

56 Among early Christian statements of the idea that the former age was free of avarice, see Cyprian, who refers specifically to the lack of greed in the apostolic community: *De ecclesiae catholicae unitate*, 26 (ed. M. Bevenot, CCL 3 [Turnhout, 1976], p. 267); *De lapsis*, 6 (ed. M. Bevenot, CCL 3 [Turnhout, 1976], p. 223). Lactantius, *Divinae institutiones*, 5.6.1–6 (ed. P. Monat, SC 204 [Paris, 1973], pp. 156–58) draws directly on the mythology of the Golden Age. See above, ch. 1, pp. 18–20.

57 *Conl.*, 5.3 (CSEL 13:121–22); the detailed discussion is found in *Conl.*, 5.4 and 7–9 (CSEL 13:122–24, 127–29).

58 *Conl.*, 5.8 (CSEL 13:129). See also *Inst.*, 7.21 (CSEL 17:144).

59 The close connection between avarice and wrath is mentioned explicitly in *Conl.*, 5.10 (CSEL 13:131). The two evils were related in patristic literature at least as early as Clement of Alexandria, *Protrepticus*, 3.42.9 (ed. O. Stählin, third ed., ed. U. Treu, GCS 12 [Clemens I] [Berlin, 1972], p. 32).

60 *Conl.*, 5.10 (CSEL 13:130).

61 Cassian further related the vices to already existing series which had become theologically important in one way or another. In *Conl.*, 5.6 (CSEL 13:124–27) he emphasized the correspondences between the sin triads, the temptations of Jesus, and the three stages of Adam's fall; in *Conl.*, 5.16–18 (CSEL 13:140–44) he connected the octad with the seven tribes which the Lord said were to be driven out of the land of Israel (Deut. 7:1–2); in *Conl.*, 24.15 (CSEL 13:691) he arranged seventeen vices among disturbances in the three Platonic parts of the soul.

62 The threefold division is given in *Conl.*, 5.11 (CSEL 13:133); *Inst.*, 7.14, 30, and 12.26 (CSEL 17:137–38, 148–49, and 224).

63 On the immediate success of Cassian's texts and their transmission through Lérins, Lyon, and elsewhere, see Prinz, *Frühes Mönchtum im Frankenreich*, pp. 68, 70 *et passim*.

64 *Conl.*, 5.16 (CSEL 13:142): "de filargyria [nascuntur] mendacium, fraudatio, furta, periuria, turpis lucri adpetitus, falsa testimonia, uiolentiae, inhumanitas ac rapacitas . . ."

65 Cassian cites Matthew's text in *Inst.*, 7.16 (CSEL 17:140). *Fraus* is found in Mark 10:19.

66 Along with Tit. 1:7, see also 1Tim. 3:8. The reference to *rapax* is from 1 Cor. 5:10.

67 Tertullian, *De idololatria*, 11.1 (ed. A. Reifferscheid and G. Wissowa, CCL 2 [Turnhout, 1954], p. 1110); *Vita S. Syncleticae*, 72 (PG 28:1529). Lactantius' list of evils which burst forth from greed includes deceptions and all types of fraud; see *Epitome divinarum institutionum*, 56(61).5(19) (ed. S. Brandt, CSEL 19 [Vienna, 1890], p. 739). Gregory of Nyssa included lying and deceit in his list of the descendants of the desire for more; see *Oratio 5 de beatitudinibus* (PG 44:1253). On Gregory of Nyssa's influence on Cassian, see A. Kemmer, "Gregorius Nyssenus estne inter fontes Joannis Cassiani numerandus?" *Orientalia Christiana Periodica* 21 (1955), 451–66.

68 *Homilia in divites*, 7 (PG 31:297).

69 For the *inhumanitas* of avarice, see Basil, *Homilia in illud: Destruam horrea mea*, 1 (PG 31:264); Gregory Nazianzen, *Orat.*, 14.25–26 (PG 35:889–92); Chrysostom, *Hom. 83 in Matt.*, 2 (PG 58:748). Chrysostom noted frequently that the avaricious were worse than animals and that avarice was an inhuman mistress; see Rudolph Mehrlein, "De avaritia quid iudicaverit Ioannes Chrysostomus," Dissertation, University of Cologne, 1951, pp. 14–15 and 108. On the *violentia* associated with avarice, see Ezek. 22:27; and in patristic literature besides the above, also Chrysostom, *Homilia 19 in Epistolam ad Romanos*, 8 (PG 60:594); Chrysostom, *Homilia 9 in Epistolam 1 ad Corinthios*, 4 (PG 61:80).

70 *Conl.*, 5.10 (CSEL 13:130). For Evagrius' own imagery, see above, p. 55; for Cassian's imagery, see the Appendix and *Inst.*, 7.21, 23–24 (CSEL 17:146–47, 147–48).

71 *Inst.*, 7.14, 30 (CSEL 17:137–38, 148).

72 *Antirr.*, 3.15 (ed. Frankenberg, p. 496). On Gehazi's connection with avarice, and more specifically with simony, see Hans-Jürgen Horn, "Giezie und Simonie," *JbAC* 8/9 (1965/66), 189–202; John A. Yunck, *The Lineage of Lady Meed*, University of Notre Dame, Publications in Mediaeval Studies 17 (Notre Dame, IN, 1963), pp. 25–26. Horn and Yunck do not refer to Evagrius.

73 Palladius, *Historia Lausiaca*, 17 (ed. Butler, vol. 2, pp. 43–47) further notes that John's greed was paid for with elephantiasis later in life. Jerome, *Vita S. Hilarionis Eremitae*, 18 (PL 23:36–37). Origen at least implies a link between Gehazi and the *philargyroi* in his commentary on 1 Cor (ed. C. Jenkins in "Origen on I Corinthians," *Journal of Theological Studies* 9 [1908], 364§24); see further in the Appendix.

74 Jerome, *Ep.*, 130.14 (CSEL 56 [Vienna and Leipzig, 1918], p. 194) and *Ep.*, 14.5.3 (CSEL 54:51). Both Clement of Alexandria, *Strom.*, 1.23.154.1 (GCS 52 [15]:96), and Origen, *Commentary on Matthew*, 15.15 (ed. E. Klostermann, GCS 40 [Origenes 10] [Leipzig, 1935], pp. 392–94) refer to the couple's lie, but without an explicit mention of avarice; see further in the Appendix.

75 There is mention of *pleonexia* (in some texts *pleonexia* and *philargyria*) in reference to Judas' thievery in the Acts of Thomas, but the somewhat oblique connection is not investigated further. See *Acta Thomae*, 84 (ed. M. Bonnet in *Acta Apostolorum Apocrypha* 2,2 [Leipzig, 1903; repr. Darmstadt, 1959], pp. 199–200). For Origen's understanding of Judas, see: *Contra Celsum*, 2.11 and 20 (ed. P. Koetschau, GCS 2 [Origenes 1] [Leipzig, 1899], pp. 139 and 151); *Commentary on Matthew*, 11.9 and 16.8 (GCS 40:49–50 and 489); *Commentariorum series*, 75, 78 and 117 (ed. E. Klostermann, GCS 38 [Origenes 11] [Leipzig, 1933], pp. 176, 186–87 and 244); *Commentary on John*, 32.19.241, 244 (ed. E. Preuschen, GCS 10 [Origenes 4] [Leipzig, 1903], p. 458). The text of *Contra Celsum*, 2.20 was also transmitted in the *Philocalia*, 23.13 (ed. E. Junod, SC 226 [Paris, 1976], p. 174), a collection of citations from Origen's works assembled by Basil the Great and Gregory Nazianzen. For other citations from early patristic literature connecting Judas with avarice, see R. B. Halas, *Judas Iscariot*, Catholic University of America Studies in Sacred Theology 96 (Washington, D.C., 1946), pp. 80–81. On Origen, see Samuel Laeuchli, "Origen's Interpretation of Judas Iscariot," *Church History* 22 (1953), 253–68.

76 Didymus the Blind, *Commentary on Job*, 4.5–9 (ed. and trans. A. Henrichs in *Didymos der Blinde, Kommentar zu Hiob (Tura-Papyrus)*, 1, Papyrologische Texte und Abhandlungen 1 [Bonn, 1968], pp. 32–34); Didymus the Blind, *Expositio in Psalmum 9* (PG 39:1200, 1204–05).

77 *Constitutiones asceticae*, 34 (PG 31:1424–48). See also among the genuine works of Basil, *Epistula* 53 (ed. and trans. Y. Courtonne in *Saint Basile, Lettres* [Paris, 1957], vol. 1, pp. 137–39), and in the early cenobitic tradition the *Bohairic Life of Pachomius*, 186 (trans. A. Veilleux in *Pachomian Koinonia*, 1, Cistercian

Studies Series 45 [Kalamazoo, Mich., 1980], p. 226). See further in the Appendix.

78 P. W. Harkins, "The Text Tradition of Chrysostom's Commentary on John," in F. L. Cross, ed., *StP* 7, TU 92 (Berlin, 1966), p. 219.

79 *Hom. 65 in Ioan.*, 3 (PG 59:363), reading μαθητοῦ <τοῦ> προφήτου.

80 On the difficulty of finding verbal parallels between Cassian and Chrysostom, see Rousseau, *Ascetics*, p. 171. The suggestive relationship between homily 65 on John and Cassian's understanding of avarice is even more striking when one notes that Chrysostom, too, emphasized here the punishments of the biblical examples of greediness and pointed out that *philargyria* is unnatural to humankind. Horn, "Giezie," p. 192 n. 23, lists some authors who refer to Gehazi either in connection with Judas or together with Ananias and Sapphira, but not all of them together. Horn does not mention Chrysostom.

81 *Inst.*, 5.23 (CSEL 17:145).

82 *Liber Orsiesii*, 31 (ed. Boon, p. 131).

83 *Inst.*, 7.17–18 (CSEL 17:140–43). In this way, the first Christian congregation actually became for Cassian a type of monastic movement. See Karl Suso Frank, "Vita apostolica als Lebensnorm in der alten Kirche," *Internationale Katholische Zeitschrift "Communio"* 8 (1979), 114–15; Lohse, *Askese*, p. 225.

84 On the more thoroughgoing rejection of individual possessions in the *coenobium*, see Heinrich Bacht, *Das Vermächtnis des Ursprungs*, Studien zur Theologie des geistlichen Lebens 5 (Würzburg, 1972), pp. 233–34. Cassian himself notes in *Conl.*, 19.9 (CSEL 13:543) that the anchorite will have difficulty especially achieving complete "ἀκτημοσύνη, id est contemptum ac priuationem materialium rerum."

85 Theodore, the leader of the Pachomian system of monasteries after Orsiesius' retirement, was already distressed because of the wealth of his *coenobia* and the threat to the monks' souls posed by their communal possessions. He sought advice on this matter from Orsiesius who could only respond that the possessions came from the Lord and He would reduce them if He felt it necessary. Theodore seems to have forced Orsiesius to formulate a policy of economic expansion. See the *Bohairic Life of Pachomius* (trans. A. Veilleux, pp. 244–47). On the problems associated with the wealth of the early monasteries in the East, see H. Chadwick, "Pachomios," pp. 21–22; D. Savramis, *Zur Soziologie des byzantinischen Mönchtums* (Leiden and Cologne, 1962), esp. pp. 45–52.

86 In *Inst.*, 4.39 and 43 (CSEL 17:75–76 and 77–78), Cassian has Pinufius say that a monk achieves a liberating charity first by renouncing the world, property, and family, and then by humility. See Adalbert de Vogüé, "Cassien, le Maître et Benoît," in J. Gribomont, ed., *Commandements du Seigneur et libération évangélique*, Studia Anselmiana 70 (Rome, 1977), p. 230.

87 *Inst.*, 7.9 (CSEL 17:134–35).

88 For Julien Leroy, "Les prefaces des écrits monastiques de Jean Cassien," *RAM* 42 (1966), 157–80, the anchoritic life remained for Cassian the true form of monasticism. In Claudio Leonardi's analysis, on the other hand, even the *Conlationes*, which has generally been taken as presenting anchoritic thought,

shows Cassian's growing dissatisfaction with this way of life ("Alle origini della cristianità medievale: Giovanni Cassiano e Salviano di Marsiglia," *Studi Medievali* 3, ser. 18,2 [1977], 491–608, esp. 508–13). Both Rousseau, *Ascetics*, pp. 177–82, and Peter Munz, "John Cassian," *Journal of Ecclesiastical History* 11 (1960), 1–22, emphasize Cassian's practical considerations in recommending the cenobitic life for the majority of men in spite of the theoretical excellence of the anchorites. Certainly much of what Cassian has to say concerning the social component of avarice could only have been important for cenobitic monks. Whether it was due to his practicality or not, his thinking on this vice shows that he was fully responsive to their need. On Cassian's systematization of the communal aspects of anchoritic life in the *Conlationes*, see Owen Chadwick, "Introduction," in John Cassian, *Conferences*, trans. C. Luibheid (New York, 1985), pp. 5ff.

89 *Inst.*, 7.10 (CSEL 17:135).

4 ASCETIC TRANSFORMATIONS III: THE LATIN WEST IN THE FOURTH AND FIFTH CENTURIES

1 See *De officiis ministrorum libri tres*, 1.30.149 (PL 16:72), where Ambrose suggests to his clergy that they give alms from their possessions rather than giving up everything altogether. Ambrose himself retained property which his brother administered. See below, p. 73, and F. Homes Dudden, *The Life and Times of St. Ambrose* (Oxford, 1935), vol. 1, p. 107. Ambrose's lack of concrete demands on the laity has been described by Ernst Dassmann, *Die Frömmigkeit des Kirchenvaters Ambrosius von Mailand*, Münsterische Beiträge zur Theologie 29 (Münster, 1965), p. 249. On Ambrose's debt to Basil, see Stanislas Giet, "La doctrine de l'appropriation des biens chez quelques-uns des pères," *Recherches de Science religieuse* 35 (1948), 66; Giet, "De saint Basile à saint Ambroise: la condemnation du pret à intérêt au IVe siècle," *Science Religieuse* [= *Recherches de Science religieuse* 32] (1944), 95–128; Homes Dudden, *Ambrose*, vol. 2, pp. 679–704. Ambrose came from the senatorial class and so had an even higher social station than the Cappadocians.

2 *De fuga saeculi*, 4.17 (ed. C. Schenkl, CSEL 32,2 [Vienna, 1897], p. 178).

3 Ambrose, *De off. min.*, 1.28.131–32 (PL 16:67) is a point by point reworking of Cicero, *De officiis libri tres*, 1.7.20–21 (ed. P. Fedeli [(Florence), 1965], pp. 34–35). See Manfred Wacht, "Privateigentum bei Cicero und Ambrosius," *JbAC* 25 (1982), 29–30; Louis J. Swift, "*Iustitia* and *Ius privatum*: Ambrose on Private Property," *American Journal of Philology* 100 (1979), 177–78; Baziel Maes, *La loi naturelle selon Ambroise de Milan*, Analecta Gregoriana 162 (Rome, 1967), p. 23; Paul Christophe, *L'usage chrétien du droit de proprieté dans l'Ecriture et la tradition patristique*, Théologie, Pastorale et Spiritualité, Recherches et synthèses 14 (Paris, 1964), pp. 169–70; Th. Deman, "Le 'De officiis' de saint Ambroise dans l'histoire de la théologie morale," *Revue des Sciences Philosophiques et Théologiques* 37 (1953), 409–24.

4 Compare Vincent R. Vasey, *The Social Ideas in the Works of St. Ambrose: A Study*

on De Nabuthe, Studia Ephemeridis "Augustinianum" 17 (Rome, 1982), pp. 105–42; and for reviews of the scholarship on this issue, see Wacht, "Privateigentum," pp. 51–52; Swift, *"Iustitia,"* pp. 179–80.

5 *De off.*, 1.7.24–8.25 (ed. Fedeli, pp. 36–37). Note especially the last sentence in 1.8.25: "Nec uero rei familiaris amplificatio nemini nocens uituperanda est, sed fugienda semper iniuria est." How far Cicero is from the thought of an equal distribution of goods in society can be seen in *De off.*, 2.21.73 (ed. Fedeli, p. 144) where he says that there could be no greater pest than this form of social equality.

6 *De off. min.*, 1.28.137 (PL 16:68).

7 *De Nabuthae*, 3.11 (ed. C. Schenkl, CSEL 32,2 [Vienna, 1897], p. 474). See also *Exameron*, 5.10.27–28 (ed. C. Schenkl, CSEL 32,1 [Vienna, 1897], p. 161). Basil's brief mention of Naboth occurs in *Homilia in divites*, 5 (PG 31:293). For further biblical figures used by Ambrose, see the Appendix. In *De off. min.*, 2.26.129–31 (PL 16:137–38), Ambrose notes that even at the revelation of the Decalogue it was considered necessary to curb this ancient vice; cf. also Wolf Steidle, "Beobachtungen zum Gedankengang im 2. Buch von Ambrosius, De officiis," *VC* 39 (1985), 285.

8 The implications of Ambrose's text should be compared to the explicit statement by his near contemporary, Zeno of Verona, in *Tractatus*, I 5 (I 9).3.10 (ed. B. Löfstedt, CCL 22 [Turnhout, 1971], p. 40).

9 *Expositio Evangelii secundum Lucam*, 7.124 (ed. M. Adriaen, CCL 14 [Turnhout, 1957], p. 256); *De off. min.*, 3.7.45 (PL 16:168); *Nab.*, 3.12 (CSEL 32,2:474). For the background in Basil's works, see above, ch. 2, n. 23.

10 *De off. min.*, 3.3.16–19 (PL 16:158–59). When dealing with *iustitia*, Cicero focuses in Stoic fashion on the rights of the individual within the framework of those of the community (one of the duties of justice enumerated in *De off.*, 1.7.20 [ed. Fedeli, p. 34] is to treat common property as common, but one's private possessions as one's own absolutely), but Ambrose revises the concept to make it more a matter of serving the needs of others, defining justice at one point as a disregard for one's own utility in order to maintain social equity (*De off. min.*, 1.24.115 – PL 16:62). See Swift, *"Iustitia,"* esp. pp. 181–82; Maes, *La loi naturelle*, pp. 134–38; Salvatore Calafato, *La proprietà privata in S. Ambrogio*, Scrinium Theologicum 6 (Turin, 1958); Dominikus Löpfe, *Die Tugendlehre des heiligen Ambrosius* (Sarnen, 1951), pp. 140–46; J. T. Muckle, "The De Officiis Ministrorum of Saint Ambrose," *Mediaeval Studies* 1 (1939), 78.

11 *Expositio Psalmi 118*, 8.22 (ed. M. Petschenig, CSEL 62 [Vienna, 1913], pp. 163–64).

12 Ambrose, *Epistolae*, 10.76, esp. sect. 19 (ed. M. Zelzer, CSEL 82,3 [Vienna, 1982], pp. 118–19). In *Sermo contra Auxentium de basilicis tradendis*, see sect. 17 (PL 16:1055). Cf. Reinhold Bohlen, "'Täglich wird ein Nabot niedergeschlagen.' Zur homiletischen Behandlung von 1 Kön 21 in Ambrosius' De Nabuthe," *Trierer Theologische Zeitschrift* 88 (1979), 228. Ambrose accepted private property as an institution despite his theoretical rejection of its origins; see Ernesto Frattini, "Proprietà e ricchezza nel pensiero di S. Ambrogio," *Rivista internazionale di filosofia del diritto* 39 (1962), 754–55; Jean Gaudemet, *L'Eglise dans l'Empire*

romain (IVe-Ve siècles), Histoire du Droit et des Institutions de l'Eglise en Occident 3 (Paris, 1958), p. 572; O. Schilling, *Der kirchliche Eigentumsbegriff*, second ed. (Freiburg/Br., 1930), pp. 48–49. Compare G. E. M. de Ste. Croix, "Early Christian Attitudes to Property and Slavery," in D. Baker, ed., *Church Society and Politics*, Studies in Church History 12 (Oxford, 1975), pp. 29–31 (and *The Class Struggle in the Ancient Greek World* [London, 1981], pp. 435–46), who finds Ambrose (along with Origen and Basil) a partial exception to the common Christian view of property ownership, though probably based only on the bishop's theoretical considerations of the Golden Age.

13 *De excessu fratris*, 1.55 (ed. O. Faller, CSEL 73 [Vienna, 1955], pp. 238–39). On the incident with Prosper, see Homes Dudden, *Ambrose*, vol. 1, pp. 178–79; Vasey, *The Social Ideas*, pp. 17–18. Compare Ambrose's understanding of thrift to what Lactantius had to say on the virtue (above, ch. 1, n. 80).

14 On the accumulation of wealth in the West, see A. H. M. Jones, "Ancient Empires and the Economy: Rome," repr. in the author's *The Roman Economy*, ed. P. A. Brunt (Oxford, 1974), pp. 135–37; Jones, *The Later Roman Empire, 284–602* (Oxford, 1964; repr. 1973), vol. 2, pp. 1045–46. For Ambrose's use of avarice as the retention of wealth, see *De bono mortis*, 2.4 (ed. C. Schenkl, CSEL 32,1 [Vienna, 1897], p. 705); *De Iacob et vita beata*, 2.5.23 (ed. C. Schenkl, CSEL 32,2 [Vienna, 1897], p. 45); and *Nab.*, 4.18 (CSEL 32,2:476–77), where he describes a miser he knew who would eat only one small loaf of bread a day while traveling to his country estate.

15 See the manuscript titles of Zeno's treatises I 5 (I 9) ("De avaritia"), I 14 (I 10) ("Tractatus de avaritia"), and I 21 (I 11) ("De avaritia"), CCL 22:38–42, 57–59, 68; Gaudentius, treatise 13 ("Contra avaritiam Iudae et pro pauperibus"), ed. A. Glueck, CSEL 68 (Vienna and Leipzig, 1936), pp. 114–24; Peter Chrysologus, sermon 29 ("De Matheo secundus <seu> de avaritia"), ed. A. Olivar, CCL 24 (Turnhout, 1975), pp. 167–72; Maximus, sermon 18 ("Sequentia de avaritia et de Anania"), ed. A. Mutzenbecher, CCL 23 (Turnhout, 1962), pp. 67–69; and the title ("De auaritia") supplied by Gennadius to Maximus' sermon 17 (CCL 23:63–65), to which Maximus himself may have referred as dealing primarily with avarice in *Serm.*, 30.2 (CCL 23:117). The titles have been transmitted in the best textual traditions of these sermons and treatises, either in codices roughly contemporary with the authors (Maximus, Chrysologus), or in the earliest manuscripts extant (Zeno, Gaudentius). The only other works from this same period which can also be understood as dealing with avarice as their central issue are Valerianus of Cimiez's *Homiliae*, 20 (PL 52:751–56) [for Valerianus, see *CPL* 1002–04], Salvian's *Ad ecclesiam* (see below, pp. 85–86), Augustine's sermon 177 (see below, n. 70), and the *Tractatus de divitiis* (see below, pp. 89–90). On the life and works of some of the northern Italian bishops, see Carlo Truzzi, *Zeno, Gaudenzio e Cromazio: Testi e contenuti della predicazione cristiana per le chiese di Verona, Brescia e Aquileia (360–410 ca.)*, Testi e Ricerche di Scienze Religiose 22 (Brescia, 1985). For their emphasis on avarice as the most important of the "social sins," see Luigi Padovese, *L'Originalità cristiana: Il pensiero etico-sociale di alcuni vescovi norditaliani del IV secolo*, Istituto Francescano di Spiritualità, Studi e

ricerche 8 (Rome, 1983). For their relationship to Ambrose, see Rita Lizzi, "Ambrose's Contemporaries and the Christianization of Northern Italy," *The Journal of Roman Studies* 80 (1990), 157–61.

16 Alexander Murray, *Reason and Society in the Middle Ages* (Oxford, 1978), p. 61; Murray, "Money and Robbers, 900–1100," *Journal of Medieval History* 4 (1978), 89–90; Lester K. Little, "Pride Goes before Avarice: Social Change and the Vices in Latin Christendom," *The American Historical Review* 76 (1971), 16, 20. See also the earlier judgments of Morton Bloomfield, *The Seven Deadly Sins* ([East Lansing, Mich.], 1952; repr. 1967), p. 95, and Johan Huizinga, *The Waning of the Middle Ages*, trans. F. Hopman (London, 1924; repr. New York, 1954), pp. 27–28.

17 1 Tim. 6:10: Zeno, *Tract.*, I 5 (I 9).1.4 (CCL 22:38); Gaudentius, *Tract.*, 18.17 (CSEL 68:157); Chrysologus, *Serm.*, 29.1 (CCL 24:168); Maximus, *Serm.*, 18.2 (CCL 23:67); Chromatius of Aquileia, *Sermones*, 12.7 (ed. R. Etaix and J. Lemarié, CCL 9A [Turnhout, 1974], p. 56). Cf. Ambrose, *De Helia et ieiunio*, 19.69 (ed. C. Schenkl, CSEL 32,2 [Vienna, 1897], p. 452); *Ep.*, 2.15 (PL 16:921). I have found absolutely no use of the biblical authority for placing pride at the head of a list of sins, Sir. 10:15, in the works of the northern Italian bishops. With the evidence supplied by these authors, one must look again at such evaluations of medieval psychology as that given by Murray, *Reason*, p. 77: "Pride had always been acknowledged as the root of sin."

18 *Tract.*, I 5 (I 9).1.2 (CCL 22:38); cf. also Padovese, *L'Originalità*, pp. 77–92. On the buried caches, see Lellia Cracco Ruggini, "Milano nella circolazione monetaria del tardo impero: esigenze politiche e risposte socioeconomiche," in G. Gorini, ed., *La zecca di Milano*, Atti del convegno internazionale di studio (Milano 9–14 maggio 1983) (Milan, 1984), esp. appendix III, pp. 55–58. For the actions of the *avari* see *Tract.*, I 5 (I 9).2.8 (CCL 22:39). The closest the bishops come to establishing a scheme of sins is Chromatius' reflection of the two-ways teaching in *Tract.*, 34.1 (CCL 9A:365). The bishops also relate avarice to other sins, though not in a systematic way: Gaudentius, *Tract.*, 13.19 (CSEL 68:119 – wrath and avarice), *Tract.*, 13.28–29 (CSEL 68:122 – lust and avarice); Chrysologus, *Serm.*, 116.4 (CCL 24A:705 – avarice, drunkenness, lust); Maximus, *Serm.*, 42.3 (CCL 23:170–71 – lust and avarice), *Serm.*, 37.5 (CCL 23:147 – the snake venom of avarice and the scorpion of lust [see Luke 10:19]).

19 On the social and economic crises of the period, see A. H. M. Jones, "Over-Taxation and the Decline of the Roman Empire," in his *The Roman Economy*, pp. 82–89; Jones, *The Later Roman Empire*, vol. 2, pp. 1025–68; Lellia Ruggini, *Economia e società nell' "Italia Annonaria,"* Fondazione Guglielmo Castelli 30 (Milan, 1961), pp. 56–84, who argues that while all northern Italian cities showed signs of stagnation and decay between 370 and 400, economic activity continued to flourish in large urban centers like Milan, Turin, and Verona; and see on both Jones and Ruggini, Peter Brown, "The Later Roman Empire," *Economic History Review* ("Essays in Bibliography and Criticism"), 56, second ser., 20 (1967), 327–43, repr. in the author's *Religion and Society in the Age of Saint Augustine* (London, 1972), pp. 46–73, esp. pp. 51–57, 70–71.

20 *Serm.*, 18.3 (CCL 23:68–69). Chrysologus, *Serm.*, 29.2 (CCL 24:168), speaks of

Joseph's bondage in Egypt (Gen. 37:28ff.) as slavery to the barbarians. Zeno speaks
of the merits of some Veronese in redeeming prisoners in *Tract.*, I 14 (I 10).5.8
(CCL 22:59). O. Maenchen-Helfen, "The Date of Maximus of Turin's *Sermo
XVIII*," *VC* 18 (1964), 114–15, has argued that Maximus' sermon was probably
delivered as a reaction to an edict, issued on Dec. 3, 408, which ordered that
people bought back from the barbarians had to repay the price of their redemption
or reimburse their redeemers with five years of labor. See also Pietro Bongiovanni,
S. Massimo vescovo di Torino e il suo pensiero teologico, Pontificium Athenaeum
Salesianum, Facultas Theologica, Theses ad Lauream 23 (Turin, 1952).

21 Cf. Christopher Chaffin, "Civic Values in Maximus of Turin and his Contemporaries," in *Forma Futuri. Studi in onore del cardinale Michele Pellegrino* (Turin,
1975), p. 1047.

22 Maximus, *Serm.*, 17.2 (CCL 23:64); Gaudentius, *Tract.*, 13.23 (CSEL 68:120);
Zeno, *Tract.*, I 5 (I 9).1.3 (CCL 22:38). On Maximus' literary qualities, see
Boniface Ramsey's introduction to his translation of *The Sermons of St. Maximus
of Turin*, Ancient Christian Writers 50 (New York and Mahwah, 1989), pp. 8–11.
On avarice among the social sins in Maximus' thought, see Padovese, *L'Origina-
lità*, pp. 223–34.

23 *Serm.*, 18.2 (CCL 23:68). The most immediate reaction to the invasions was to
flee with all one's possessions, and in *Serm.*, 82.2 (CCL 23:336) Maximus spoke of
such panic as amounting to the neglect of one's civic duties and as motivated by
avarice.

24 Compare *Serm.*, 17.2 (CCL 23:64) to Gregory of Nyssa's first sermon *De
pauperibus amandis*, for which see above, ch. 2, p. 32. Possible borrowing here
perhaps came from the East via Ambrose or Gaudentius, who was educated in
Greek and had traveled to Cappadocia and Jerusalem, but even these two
bishops' knowledge of Gregory of Nyssa's works is far from certain. See Francesco
Trisoglio, "Appunti per una ricerca delle fonti di S. Gaudenzio da Brescia,"
Rivista di Studi Classici 24 (1976), 50–125. For closer parallels to Basil's words on
avarice, compare Zeno's view of money as a fish hook, in *Tract.*, I 5 (I 9).4.12
(CCL 22:40), with Basil's imagery of the greedy man as a fish (see the Appendix);
for Zeno's proof that avarice is worthless because it cannot add a day to the life of
the *avarus* or heal sicknesses, in *Tract.*, I 5 (I 9).5.16 (CCL 22:41), compare Basil,
Hom. in div., 7 (PG 31:297).

25 *Tract.*, I 14 (I 10).1.1 (CCL 22:57); see also the wholly negative view of the usurer
in *Tract.*, I 5 (I 9).4.12 (CCL 22:40); Maximus, *Serm.*, 43.4 (CCL 23:176). On
usury, see Ruggini, *Economia e società*, pp. 190–202.

26 *Serm.*, 28.3–5 (CCL 24:163–65). See Joseph Frickel, "Die Zöllner, Vorbild der
Demut und wahrer Gottesverehrung," in E. Dassmann and K. S. Frank, eds.,
Pietas: Festschrift für Bernhard Kotting, JbAC, Ergänzungsband 8 (Münster, 1980),
pp. 369–80.

27 Note the presence of millenarian ideas: Ambrose, *Exp. Luc.*, 10.10 (CCL 14:348)
was convinced that the barbarian invasions signaled the approaching end of the
world (cf. Pierre Courcelle, *Histoire littéraire des grandes invasions germaniques*,
third ed. [Paris, 1964], p. 22).

28 *Serm.*, 31.4 (CCL 9A:141–42); Padovese, *L'Originalità*, pp. 169–73. For the harmonious state under the apostles, see Cyprian, *De ecclesiae catholicae unitate*, 25 (CCL 3:267); Maximus, *Serm.*, 18.1 (CCL 23:67), and *Serm.*, 17.1 (CCL 23:63) where it is referred to as a *ius fraternitatis*.

29 See *Serm.*, 18.1 (CCL 23:67). The same observation holds true for Gaudentius' words against Judas in *Tract.*, 13.13 (CSEL 68:118). For Maximus' views on penance, see Alan Fitzgerald, "The Relationship of Maximus of Turin to Rome and Milan," *Augustinianum* 27,3 (1987), esp. 475–86. On the persistence of paganism in Italy in the late fourth century, see Lizzi, "Ambrose's Contemporaries," pp. 161–64.

30 Domenico Devoti, "Massimo di Torino e il suo pubblico," *Augustinianum* 21 (1981), 155–56, many of whose observations on Maximus are equally valid for his contemporaries. On the general question of social relations between pagans and Christians at this time, see A. H. M. Jones, "The Social Background of the Struggle between Paganism and Christianity," in A. Momigliano, ed., *The Conflict Between Paganism and Christianity in the Fourth Century* (Oxford, 1963), pp. 17–37.

31 Cf. E. A. Thompson, "Christianity and the Northern Barbarians," in A. Momigliano, ed., *The Conflict Between Paganism and Christianity in the Fourth Century* (Oxford, 1963), pp. 56–78.

32 *Tract.*, 13.28 (CSEL 68:122); cf. also Padovese, *L'Originalità*, pp. 114–18. Zeno, *Tract.*, I 14 (I 10).2.4–3.6 (CCL 22:58), uses Ps. 113:12 ("The idols of the heathens are gold and silver"; see also Ps. 134:15) as his biblical authority when exhorting his congregation to give up the internal idolatry which is avarice, just as they loathe the actual worship of idols. See Devoti, "Massimo di Torino," pp. 160–63; Franz Joseph Dölger, "Christliche Grundbesitzer und heidnische Landarbeiter," in his *Antike und Christentum*, vol. 6 (Münster, 1950), pp. 305–09. In commenting on passages like this one, Lizzi, "Ambrose's Contemporaries," pp. 167–68, emphasizes that the church did not itself attempt to do away with paganism in rural areas, but delegated this task to landowners.

33 On the need for largess in alms, see for example, Gaudentius, *Tract.*, 13.20–21 (CSEL 68:119–20); Maximus, *Serm.*, 17.2–3, 56.3 (CCL 23:64–65, 225–26); Chromatius, *Serm.*, 12.7 (CCL 9A:56). See Boniface Ramsey, "Almsgiving in the Latin Church: The Late Fourth and Early Fifth Centuries," *Theological Studies* 43 (1982), esp. 230–33, 235–40; for Maximus in particular, see Luigi Padovese, "La dottrina sociale di Massimo da Torino," *Laurentianum* 22 (1981), 167–68; and for Gaudentius, John Matthews, *Western Aristocracies and Imperial Court AD 364–425* (Oxford, 1975; repr. 1990), pp. 185–86. On justice in the fight against avarice, see Zeno, *Tract.*, I 5 (I 9).1.1 (CCL 22:38); Maximus, *Serm.*, 17.3 (CCL 23:65).

34 For the phrase "[avaritia] fidem frangit," see Zeno, *Tract.* I 21 (I 11) (CCL 22:68); Chrysologus, *Serm.*, 29.1 (CCL 24:168). Maximus, *Serm.*, 18.2 (CCL 23:67), remarks, "qui pecuniam adpetit fidem perdit."

35 *Tract.*, 31.3.3 (CCL 9A:347). For the author's phrase *avaritia saeculi*, see also *Serm.*, 26.1 (CCL 9A:119).

36 *Serm.*, 29.3 (CCL 24:170). For these bishops' depiction of almsgiving as a type of pious usury, see Zeno, *Tract.*, I 14 (I 10).5.8 (CCL 22:59); Maximus, *Serm.*, 27.1 (CCL 23:105); cf. Ramsey, "Almsgiving," pp. 247–49. For Ambrose's and Maximus' disillusionment with the avarice of northern Italian officials, see Peter Brown, *Power and Persuasion in Late Antiquity: Towards a Christian Empire*, The Curti Lectures, 1988 (Madison, 1992), pp. 147–48.

37 See, for example, Ambrosiaster, *Commentarius in Epistulam ad Timotheum primam*, 6.10.2 (ed. H. J. Vogels, CSEL 81,3 [Vienna, 1969], p. 290); Quodvultdeus, *Liber Promissionum*, 1.39.56 (ed. R. Braun, CCL 60 [Turnhout, 1976], p. 65).

38 *Psychomachia*, praef.11–14 (ed. M. P. Cunningham, CCL 126 [Turnhout, 1966], p. 149). For a review of scholarship on typology in the poem, consult Macklin Smith, *Prudentius' Psychomachia: A Re-examination* (Princeton, N.J., 1976), pp. 25–26, and see his examination of typology, pp. 177–94. On the piety of Spanish Christianity in this period, see Matthews, *Western Aristocracies*, pp. 146–49.

39 On models which may have influenced Prudentius, see Ralph Hanna III, "The Sources and the Art of Prudentius' *Psychomachia*," *Classical Philology* 72 (1977), 108–15; Morton Bloomfield, "A Source of Prudentius' *Psychomachia*," *Speculum* 18 (1943), 87–90; for a review of literature, see Jennifer O'Reilly, *Studies in the Iconography of the Virtues and Vices in the Middle Ages* (New York and London, 1988), pp. 1–38.

40 Compare Hanna, "Sources," p. 113; and see Christian Gnilka, *Studien zur Psychomachie des Prudentius*, Klassisch-Philologische Studien 27 (Wiesbaden, 1963), p. 74.

41 *De Helia*, 19.69 (CSEL 32,2:452). Ambrose's arguments against avarice are directed to the rich, but he also says that poverty in itself is not a moral good – see *Exp. Luc.*, 5.53 (CCL 14:153).

42 *Avaritia* and *Discordia* both use disguise as a method of attack, though this is not a causal relationship. Half of *Luxuria's* weaponry against humankind consists of over-indulgence in wine; the connection between drunkenness and avarice can be noted in the similarity of their designations (*uini sitis et sitis auri*) in Prudentius' *Amartigenia*, 396 (ed. M. P. Cunningham, CCL 126 [Turnhout, 1966], p. 130). On narrative allegory in the *Psychomachia*, compare Kenneth R. Haworth, *Deified Virtues, Demonic Vices and Descriptive Allegory in Prudentius' Psychomachia* (Amsterdam, 1980).

43 *Studien*, pp. 69–70. For Avarice's *amplos . . . sinus* (verses 458–59), see Juvenal, *Saturae*, 1.87–88 (ed. A. E. Housman [Cambridge, 1956], p. 4).

44 *Peristefanon*, 2.241–44 (ed. M. P. Cunningham, CCL 126 [Turnhout, 1966], p. 265). For illuminations of Avarice's hand movements in the *Psychomachia*, see Richard Stettiner, *Die illustrierten Prudentiushandschriften*, 2 vols. (Berlin, 1895–1905), nos. 55 and 56.

45 For usurers counting up their interest on their fingers, see Ambrose, *De Tobia*, 7.25 (ed. M. Giacchero, Publicazioni dell' Istituto di Filologica Classica e Medioevale 19 [Genoa, 1965], p. 103) – and see further in the Appendix. That the

avari retract their hands instead of giving alms is asserted by Maximus, *Serm.*, 43.4 (CCL 23:176) – and see further in the Appendix. For Gregory Nazianzen, see above, ch. 2, p. 36 and n. 46.

46 In one of his two preserved homilies, Laurentius, Bishop of Novae (in what is today Bulgaria) in the early fifth century, remarked that the bodily senses catch humankind in sin: "Where avarice occurs, the right hand has been armed with poisoned fangs in order to strike, to overthrow, to snatch away what belongs to another" (*Homiliae*, 1 [PL 66:96]). See further in the Appendix.

47 Compare Smith, *Prudentius' Psychomachia*, p. 155. Perhaps the personifications mentioned in verses 629–30 should be considered additional subdivisions of avarice, but they, too, can be seen either as attributes of the avaricious sinner (Fear, Hardship) or as the concrete results of the vice (Violence, Crime, Fraud).

48 Many of the details Prudentius used to describe these figures were borrowed from Virgil. For studies of Prudentius' use of Virgil, consult the bibliography in Stephan A. Barney, *Allegories of History, Allegories of Love* (Hamden, Conn., 1979), pp. 80–81; and see Smith, *Prudentius' Psychomachia*, pp. 234–300.

49 On the mixture of personifications and human beings, compare Reinhart Herzog, *Die allegorische Dichtkunst des Prudentius*, Zetemata 42 (Munich, 1966), pp. 107–08.

50 Verses 562–63 (CCL 126:169).

51 Hans Robert Jauss, "Form und Auffassung der Allegorie in der Tradition der Psychomachia," in H. R. Jauss and D. Schaller, eds., *Medium Aevum Vivum: Festschrift für Walter Bulst* (Heidelberg, 1960), p. 186, argues that once a figure is named, there is no difference between its form and its meaning, but this presupposes that the concept which it personifies is static and a given for the audience.

52 It has been termed Prudentius' own invention to depict a vice disguised as a virtue. Besides its similarity with Allecto's change in Book 7 of Virgil's *Aeneidos*, this incident can also be compared to the Trojans disguising themselves in Danaan emblems in *Aeneidos*, 2.389–402 (ed. Mynors, p. 139). See Smith, *Prudentius' Psychomachia*, p. 292; Albertus Mahoney, *Vergil in the Works of Prudentius*, The Catholic University of America Patristic Studies 39 (Washington, D.C., 1934), p. 52; H. J. Thomson, "The *Psychomachia* of Pruden-tius," *The Classical Review* 44 (1930), 111. Cunningham's note to verse 553 (CCL 126:169) also draws attention to Prudentius' debt to Juvenal. Avarice's metamor-phosis has been examined as an "invention de Prudence" by Marc-René Jung, *Etudes sur le poème allégorique en France au moyen âge*, Romanica Helvetica 82 (Berne, 1971), p. 29. C. S. Lewis found the incident one of the few episodes of merit in the poem because it revealed "adequate recognition of the great fact of self-deception" (*The Allegory of Love* [London, 1936; repr. 1971], p. 71).

53 *Epistolae*, 167.6 (ed. A. Goldbacher, CSEL 44 [Vienna and Leipzig, 1904], pp. 593–94); Chrysostom, *Adversus oppugnatores vitae monasticae*, 3.7 (PG 47:359–60). Compare Lactantius' view of thrift (above, ch. 1, n. 80) to what is seen here. Augustine's rhetorical training is in evidence here; see the *Rhetorica ad Herennium*, 4.34.46 (ed. F. Marx in *M. Tulli Ciceronis scripta quae manserunt*

omnia 1, corr. ed. W. Trillitzsch [Leipzig, 1964], p. 159), which defines the type of allegory produced by contrast: "Ex contrario [permutatio] ducitur sic, ut si quis hominem prodigum et luxuriosum inludens parcum et diligentem apellet."

54 Cf. verses 570–71 (CCL 126:170). On the heuristic problem involved here, see John P. Hermann, "Some Varieties of Psychomachia in Old English – I," *American Benedictine Review* 34 (1983), 83.

55 Verses 609–12 (CCL 126:171). Not all scholars have recognized the ascetic implications of *Operatio*'s words; compare Laura Cotogni, "Sovrapposizione di visioni e di allegorie nella *Psychomachia* di Prudenzio," *Rendiconti della R. Accademia Nazionale dei Lincei*, Classe di scienze morali, storiche e filologiche 6,12 (Rome, 1936), p. 450.

56 *De gubernatione Dei*, 1.2.10 (ed. G. Lagarrigue, SC 220 [Paris, 1975], p. 110).

57 *Timothei ad ecclesiam libri quattuor*, 1.1.3 (ed. G. Lagarrigue, SC 176 [Paris, 1971], p. 140). See Gennadius' title for the *Ad ecclesiam* in *De viris inlustribus*, 68 (ed. E. C. Richardson, TU 14 [Leipzig, 1896], p. 84). On Salvian's reasons for publishing this work anonymously see Norbert Brox, "Quis ille auctor? Pseudonymität und Anonymität bei Salvian," *VC* 40 (1986), 55–65. Of the works written during this period outside northern Italy which use the criticism of avarice as a structural principle, two are by authors closely connected with the monastery at Lérins: Salvian and Valerianus of Cimiez. For Valerianus' connection with Lérins, see J. A. Fischer, "Valerian v. Cemele," *Lexikon für Theologie und Kirche*, second ed., vol. 10 (1965), cols. 603–04; Friedrich Prinz, *Frühes Mönchtum im Frankenreich* (Munich and Vienna, 1965), esp. p. 470. For Salvian's connection to Lérins, see Hubert Fischer, *Die Schrift des Salvian von Marseille "An die Kirche,"* Europäische Hochschulschriften 23,57 (Bern and Frankfurt/M., 1976), p. 14.

58 Claudio Leonardi, "Alle origini della christianità medievale: Giovanni Cassiano e Salviano di Marsiglia," *Studi Medievali* 3. ser. 18,2 (1977), 561–62.

59 *Ad eccl.*, 1.10.53 (SC 176:176). Cf. H. Fischer, *Die Schrift*, pp. 59–60, for Salvian's consideration of leaving all one's goods to the poor at the end of one's life as an *ultimum remedium*; and compare Eberhard F. Bruck, *Kirchenväter und soziales Erbrecht* (Berlin, 1956), p. 117.

60 *Ad eccl.*, 1.7.31–8.39 (SC 176:160–66). On the social implications of Salvian's thought, see A. G. Hamman, "L'actualité de Salvien de Marseille: Idées sociales et politiques," *Augustinianum* 17 (1977), esp. 388–90; Michele Pellegrino, *Salviano di Marsiglia*, Lateranum, N.S. 6,1–2 (Rome, 1940), pp. 168–70.

61 *Ad eccl.*, 2.10.47–11.51 (SC 176:220–22). Cf. C. Leonardi, "Alle origini," pp. 566–68; compare H. Fischer, *Die Schrift*, p. 57.

62 *Ad eccl.*, 2.3.12 (SC 176:194). Cf. Hamman, "L'actualité," pp. 390–93; C. Leonardi, "Alle origini," pp. 568–70.

63 *Dialogi*, 1.8.6 (ed. C. Halm, CSEL 1 [Vienna, 1866], p. 160). The man from Gaul was probably referring to Epistle 22, which is cited later on in the dialogue. In *Epistulae*, 22.33.1 (ed. I. Hilberg, CSEL 54 [Vienna and Leipzig, 1910], p. 195), Jerome stated his intention to write of avarice.

64 *Ep.*, 22.32.4 (CSEL 54:195). See David S. Wiesen, *St. Jerome as a Satirist*, Cornell

Studies in Classical Philology 24 (Ithaca, N.Y., 1964), pp. 65–112, for a more complete view of Jerome's criticism of the church. See also Paul Antin, "Saint Jérome et l'Argent," *La Vie Spirituelle* 79 (1948), 285–93.

65 *Ep.*, 52.6.1 (CSEL 54:425). See also *Ep.*, 69.9.1 (CSEL 54:696–97) and cf. Ignaz Seipel, *Die wirtschaftsethischen Lehren der Kirchenväter*, Leo-Gesellschaft, Theologische Studien 18 (Vienna, 1907; repr. Graz, 1972), pp. 142–43. For a brief presentation of imperial legislation which furthered the church's increase of wealth, see Franz Pototschnig, "Christliche Eigentumsordnung in rechtshistorischer Sicht," *Österreichisches Archiv für Kirchenrecht* 27 (1976), 288–91.

66 *Ep.*, 71.3.3 (CSEL 55:4). Jerome also referred to Crates in his *Commentariorum in Matthaeum libri 4*, 3.19 (ed. D. Hurst and M. Adriaen, CCL 77 [Turnhout, 1969], p. 172). On asceticism and the renunciation of wealth, see Jerome's translation of Theophilus' paschal letter of 404 and the material which it borrows from Basil (e.g. the comparison between the *avarus* and hell, etc.), in *Ep.*, 100.15.1–4 (CSEL 55:229–30). See also Philip Rousseau, *Ascetics, Authority and the Church in the Age of Jerome and Cassian* (Oxford, 1978), pp. 99–124.

67 *Ep.*, 130.14.1 (CSEL 56:193). Parsimony and frugality have their place, too, in Jerome's conception of vices and virtues, in particular in his arguments against the Pelagians. See the *Dialogus adversus Pelagianos*, 3.11 (PL 23:608) and cf. Paul Antin, "Les idées morales de S. Jérome," *MSR* 14 (1957), 143.

68 For Jerome's words on grace, see *Ep.*, 130.12.3 (CSEL 56:192). Cf. W. H. C. Frend, *Saints and Sinners in the Early Church* (London, 1985), pp. 118–40; J. N. D. Kelly, *Jerome* (London, 1975), pp. 312–13; and compare Wiesen, *Jerome*, pp. 35–36. On the similarities and differences between the two heretical sects, see A. Louth, "Messalianism and Pelagianism," in E. A. Livingstone, ed., *StP* 17,1 (Oxford, 1982), pp. 127–35.

69 See *De civitate Dei*, 12.8 (ed. B. Dombart and A. Kalb, CCL 48 [Turnhout, 1955], p. 362). On justice in Augustine's thought, see M. T. Clark, "Augustine on Justice," *Revue des Etudes Augustiniennes* 9 (1963), 87–94; F.-J. Thonnard, "Justice de Dieu et justice humaine selon saint Augustine," *Augustinus* 12 (1967), 387–402; Jeremy D. Adams, *The Populus of Augustine and Jerome* (New Haven and London, 1971), pp. 17–21 (but see the remarks by E. Fortin, "The Patristic Sense of Community," *Augustinian Studies* 4 [1973], esp. 191–92). On the social reflex of sin in general in Augustine's thinking, see Michael Seybold, *Sozialtheologische Aspekte der Sünde bei Augustinus*, Studien zur Geschichte der Moraltheologie 11 (Regensburg, 1963). My analysis deals for the most part with Augustine's mature thought on avarice. For the possible extent of the influence of Cicero's *Hortensius* on Augustine's thought on riches during his period at Cassiciacum, see Jean Doignon, "L'enseignement de l'*Hortensius* de Cicéron sur les richesses devant la conscience d'Augustin jusqu'aux *Confessions*," *L'Antiquité Classique* 51 (1982), 193–206; R. R. Russell, "Cicero's *Hortensius* and the Problem of Riches in Saint Augustine," in C. P. Mayer, ed., *Scientia Augustiniana, Festschrift Adolar Zumkeller zum 60. Geburtstag*, Cassiciacum 30 (Würzburg, 1975), pp. 12–19.

70 Compare Augustine, *Sermones*, 177.3 (ed. C. Lambot in *Sancti Aurelii Augustini*

sermones selecti duodeviginti, Stromata Patristica et Medievalia 1 [Utrecht and Brussels, 1950], p. 66 [=PL 38:955]) with his famous letter to Proba, *Ep.*, 130, esp. 6.12 (CSEL 44:53–54). As Peter Brown, *Augustine of Hippo: A Biography* (Berkeley and Los Angeles, 1967), p. 351, has written, Proba, the "heiress of a vast agricultural empire . . . was allowed to remain unchanged in the midst of such wealth." J. Mausbach, *Die Ethik des hl. Augustinus*, second ed. (Freiburg, 1929), vol. 1, pp. 289–91, argued simply that superfluity for Augustine was what served no purpose, was mere waste, or was what served avarice, without defining the terms in which waste could be measured or making note of what purpose Augustine had in mind. Ernst Troeltsch, *Augustin, die christliche Antike und das Mittelalter*, Historische Bibliothek 36 (Munich, 1915), p. 141, noted that Augustine's definition of "superfluous" included what was more than one needed for personal use, for the duties of one's class, or for inheritance. Sermon 177 was delivered at Carthage shortly before June 24, 397. A copy of it was in the library at Hippo under the title *De Avaritia*.

71 See *Enarratio in Psalmum 118, sermo 11*, 6 (ed. E. Dekkers and J. Fraipont, CCL 40 [Turnhout, 1956], p. 1699); *Confessiones*, 3.8.16 (ed. L. Verheijen, CCL 27 [Turnhout, 1981], p. 36). Augustine is referring to the principle of Roman civil law known as *pluris petitio*; see Max Kaser, *Das römische Zivilprozessrecht*, second ed., ed. K. Hackl, Handbuch der Altertumswissenschaft 10.3.4 (Munich, 1996), pp. 323–25. See also Chrysostom's use of a similar idea as a proverbial truth (above, ch. 2, p. 42 and n. 72).

72 *Enarr. in Ps. 51*, 14 (CCL 39:633). For the proverbial phrase, see also Horace, *Sermones*, 1.1.62 (ed. F. Klingner in *Q. Horati Flacci opera* [Leipzig, 1970], p. 163); Plutarch, *De cupiditate divitiarum*, 7 (*Moralia* 526C) (ed. G. N. Bernardakis in *Plutarchi Chaeronensis Moralia* 3 [Leipzig, 1891], p. 362). On the connections between *pauper* and *dives*, both as terms in Augustine's vocabulary and as interrelated social phenomena in fourth- and fifth-century North Africa, see Paola Vismara Chiappa, *Il tema della povertà nella predicazione di Sant'Agostino*, Università di Trieste, Facoltà di Scienze Politiche 5 (Milan, 1975), pp. 89–96 and the bibliography there. For Augustine's thinking on an exclusively monastic poverty, see Adolar Zumkeller, *Das Mönchtum des heiligen Augustinus*, secon. rev. ed., Cassiciacum 11 (Würzburg, 1968), pp. 179–89.

73 For Augustine's thinking on the legitimacy of property in particular, see Rebecca H. Weaver, "Wealth and Poverty in the Early Church," *Interpretation: A Journal of Bible and Theology* 41, 4 (1987), 378–80; D. J. Macqueen, "St. Augustine's Concept of Property Ownership," *Recherches Augustiniennes* 8 (1972), 187–229; Salvador Vicastillo, "La doctrina sobre los bienos terrenos en San Augustin (Enarrationes in Psalmos–Sermones)," *La Ciudad de Dios* 180 (1967), 86–115; G. J. M. Pearce, "Augustine's Theory of Property," in F. L. Cross, ed., *StP* 6, TU 81 (Berlin, 1962), pp. 496–500; Giet, "La doctrine," pp. 77–82. On the question of inheritances, see Bruck, *Kirchenväter und soziales Erbrecht*, pp. 84–88.

74 Speaking to the indigent, he noted that the apostles: "recognized that even poor men, though they had no money, were avaricious nonetheless. And so that you will know it is not money which is condemned in the rich, but avarice, listen to

what I say: you see the rich person standing next to you; perhaps he has money with him and no avarice, while you have no money and yet avarice. [Lazarus] was taken by angels to the bosom of Abraham. . . . Read the Scriptures and you will find that Abraham was rich. So that you will know that riches are not faulted, Abraham had a great deal of gold, silver, animals, servants; he was rich, and the poor person, Lazarus, was taken up in his bosom. . . . Is it not better for both to be rich for God and poor in greed?" (*Enarr. in Ps. 51*, 14 [CCL 39:634]). Cf. F. van der Meer, *Augustinus der Seelsorger*, third ed. (Cologne, 1958), p. 159. For Augustine's view of the avarice of ascetics, see Henry Chadwick, "The Ascetic Ideal in the History of the Church," in W. J. Sheils, ed., *Studies in Church History* 22 (Oxford, 1985), pp. 12–14 (repr. in Henry Chadwick, *Heresy and Orthodoxy in the Early Church*, Variorum Collected Studies, CS 342 [London, 1991]).

75 Text edited by C. P. Caspari, *Briefe, Abhandlungen und Predigten* (Christiania, 1890), pp. 25–67 (=PLS 1:1380–1418); textual emendations in Michael Winter-bottom, "Pelagiana," *Journal of Theological Studies*, N.S. 38,1 (1987), 108–16. On the author, see Robert F. Evans, *Pelagius: Inquiries and Reappraisals* (New York, 1968), p. 77; John Morris, "Pelagian Literature," *Journal of Theological Studies*, N.S. 16 (1965), esp. 25–40. Hilarius' characterization is found in Augustine's correspondence in *Ep.*, 156 (CSEL 44:448). Augustine's initial response to Hilarius is in *Ep.*, 157.4.23–39 (CSEL 44:472–86), and see his later summary of the work, which agrees essentially with Hilarius, in *De gestis Pelagii liber*, 11.23, 33.57 and 35.65 (PL 44:334, 353 and 357). The Synod of Jerusalem in July, 415 used this argument to condemn Pelagians; cf. Christophe, *L'usage*, p. 198.

76 Peter Brown, "Pelagius and his Supporters: Aims and Environment," *Journal of Theological Studies*, N.S. 19 (1968), 93–114; repr. in Brown, *Religion and Society*, pp. 183–207, esp. pp. 197 and 201. Cf. also J. N. L. Myres, "Pelagius and the End of Roman Rule in Britain," *Journal of Roman Studies* 50 (1960), 27–29. On the work's audience, see W. Liebeschuetz, "Pelagian Evidence on the Last Period of Roman Britain?" *Latomus* 26 (1967), 445.

77 *Tract. de div.*, 5.3 (PLS 1:1384). He then argues that it is even better to follow Luke 14:33 and renounce all one's goods. Compare this use of Jewish and Christian texts to Basil the Great, above, ch. 2, pp. 25–26. On this typical use of "sufficiency," compare Morris, "Pelagian Literature," p. 50.

78 See the author's justification for coupling a discussion of wealth with a consideration of the vice: "As if it were one thing to be an *avarus* and another again to want to have wealth! For whoever seeks wealth due to avarice also possesses avarice due to wealth (if the *avarus* possesses at all, that is, and is not rather possessed himself), and as long as wealth continues to exist, it will be preserved, as I might say, by its mother, avarice. For he is not an *avarus* who pays out liberally to the poor from that which he has; and he who has already undertaken to pay out his goods liberally will not begin to have a superfluity; and he who has no superfluity will also not be able to be rich henceforth, since someone is judged to be rich by his superfluous excess of possessing. Thus, when someone stops being an *avarus*, he also stops being rich" (*Tract. de div.*, 2 [PLS 1:1381]). For the sin triad, see sect. 1.2–4 (1380–81).

79 *Tract. de div.*, 12.2 (PLS 1:1401). For the author's consideration of wealth's origin, see sect. 7.3–5 (1388).

80 The *uti/frui* distinction is used in combating avarice in *Serm.*, 177.8 (ed. Lambot, p. 70 – PL 38:958). On the differentiation between "use" and "enjoyment" in Augustine's thought, see Georg Pfligersdorffer, "Zu den Grundlagen des augustinischen Begriffspaares 'uti-frui'," *Wiener Studien* N.F. 5, Bd. 84 (1971), 195–224, and Rudolf Lorenz, "Die Herkunft des augustinischen FRUI DEO," *Zeitschrift für Kirchengeschichte* 64 (1952/53), 34–60, 359–60. The correct orientation of the will was what Augustine understood as *caritas* in its widest sense; cf. John P. Langan, "Augustine on the Unity and the Interconnection of the Virtues," *Harvard Theological Review* 72, 1–2 (1979), esp. 91–95. To understand the social destination of private property involved the individual's moral distance to earthly wealth more than an actual renunciation of it. For Ambrose see *De Cain et Abel*, 1.5.21 (ed. C. Schenkl, CSEL 32,1 [Vienna, 1897], p. 358). For the frequent metaphorical sense of "poverty" in Ambrose's writings, see Michel Poirier, "'Christus pauper factus est' chez saint Ambroise," *Rivista di storia e letteratura religiosa* 15 (1979), 255; Seipel, *Die wirtschaftsethischen Lehren*, p. 66.

81 See *Serm.*, 11.2 (ed. G. Morin, PLS 2:678–79); *Serm.*, 50.3–6 (ed. C. Lambot, CCL 41 [Turnhout, 1961], pp. 625–28); cf. also *De uera religione*, 3.4 (ed. K.-D. Daur, CCL 32 [Turnhout, 1962], p. 190).

82 *Serm.*, 177.4 (ed. Lambot, p. 67 – PL 38:955); see also *Serm.*, 107.10 (PL 38:632); 261.5 (ed. Lambot, pp. 91–92 – PL 38:1205); *Enarr. in Ps. 118, sermo 11,* 6 (CCL 40:1699) where Augustine noted that the devil thought Job only praised God for the material advantages this could bring him. For Ambrose's influence on Augustine's use of Job, see J. R. Baskin, "Job as Moral Exemplar in Ambrose," *VC* 35 (1981), 222–31. In the material battle against avarice Augustine demanded that Christians give alms, though of course not so they themselves would become needy; see the excellent article by H. Rondet, "Richesse et pauvreté dans la prédication de saint Augustin," *RAM* 30 (1954), esp. 218–31, for this issue.

83 *De fide*, 5.5.57 (ed. O. Faller, CSEL 78 [Vienna, 1962], p. 239).

84 The Vulgate's *avaritia, avarus*, represents the Greek *pleonexia*, etc., in the following passages: Mark 7:22; Luke 12:15; Rom. 1:29; 1Cor. 5:10–11, 6:10; 2Cor. 9:5; Eph. 4:19, 5:3, 5:5; Col. 3:5; 1Thess. 2:5; 2Pet. 2:3, 2:14. *Cupiditas, cupidus* is used to render *philargyria*, etc., in 1Tim. 6:10 and 2Tim. 3:2. In one instance *avari* translates *philargyroi* (Luke 16:14) and in one instance (Sir. 14:9), here due to the Old Latin Version, one finds the opposite exception. For Jerome's original contribution to the Vulgate, and his revision of the Latin text of the New Testament, see E. F. Sutcliffe, "Jerome," in G. W. H. Lampe, ed., *The Cambridge History of the Bible*, vol. 2 (Cambridge, 1969), pp. 99–100.

85 *Commentariorum in epistolam ad Ephesios libri*, 2.4 (PL 26:537–38): "I said earlier that the action of all uncleanliness in avarice does not pertain to avarice in its simple signification but to sexual desire and lust. I should confirm this meaning with the evidence of another passage. . . . Observe carefully that when [Paul] rouses us to chastity and when he wants us to be content with our own wives alone, he says, 'No one should overreach his brother and ensnare him in an affair'

(1Thess. 4:6), that is, one should not abandon one's spouse and try to seduce another's wife. Where I have *et circumscribat in negotio fratrem suum*, one reads in the Greek text: καὶ πλεονεκτεῖν ἐν τῷ πράγματι τὸν ἀδελφὸν αὐτοῦ. But *pleonexia* is in Latin *avaritia*, which we can express in the present passage by changing the word's sense as follows: 'so that no one should overreach his brother and, as an *avarus*, deceive him in an affair'." See above, ch. 1, p. 7, for arguments against Jerome's reading of the passage.

86 *Commentariorum in Abacuc prophetam libri 2*, 1.2.9/11 (ed. M. Adriaen, CCL 76A [Turnhout, 1970], p. 605).

87   See Augustine, *Serm.*, 107.10 (PL 38:632).

88 *De Genesi ad litteram*, 11.15 (ed. J. Zycha, CSEL 28,1 [Vienna, 1894], p. 347); see also *Enarr. in Ps. 118, sermo 1*, 6 (CCL 40:1698–99). Augustine's harmonizing of the biblical authorities for assigning either pride or avarice the position of chief vice served as a model for the Scholastics – compare Heinrich Fichtenau, *Askese und Laster in der Anschauung des Mittelalters, II: Lasterkampf und Lasterlehre*, rev. and repr. in his *Beiträge zur Mediävistik* (Stuttgart, 1975), vol. 1, p. 85. The definition of "general avarice" is also to be found in *De libero arbitrio*, 3.17.48.166 (ed. W. M. Green, CCL 29 [Turnhout, 1970], pp. 303–04); *Enchiridion*, 13.45 (ed. E. Evans, CCL 46 [Turnhout, 1969], p. 74); Etienne Gilson, *Introduction à l'Etude de Saint Augustin*, Etude de Philosophie Médiévale 11 (Paris, 1949), p. 154, who termed it a "disposition of the soul which refuses to possess in common and to share, but wants rather to amass for itself and to take possession of things and appropriate them for itself as if they only existed for the satisfaction of a personal greed." Cf. also D. J. Macqueen, "*Contemptus Dei*: St. Augustine on the Disorder of Pride in Society and its Remedies," *Recherches Augustiniennes* 9 (1973), esp. 238–39.

89 *Enarr. in Ps. 118, sermo 11*, 6 (CCL 40:1699); see also *De moribus ecclesiae catholicae*, 19.35 (PL 32:1326). In *Enchiridion*, 45 (PL 40:254), Augustine noted that besides avarice, there were a number of other sins involved in the fall: pride, sacrilege, murder, spiritual fornication, and theft. For Satan's avarice, see *De Gen. ad litt.*, 11.15 (CSEL 28,1:347). On the interconnection between pride and avarice, see J. F. Procopé, "*Initium omnis peccati superbia*," in E. A. Livingstone, ed., *StP* 22 (Leuven, 1989), p. 319; Fichtenau, *Askese*, pp. 105–06; A. Solignac, "La condition de l'homme pécheur d'après saint Augustin," *Nouvelle Revue Théologique* 78 (1956), 370–72 (repr. in E. Ferguson, ed., *Doctrines of Human Nature, Sin, and Salvation in the Early Church*, SEC 10:112–14); compare J. Patout Burns, "Augustine on the Origin and Progress of Evil," in W. S. Babcock, ed., *The Ethics of St. Augustine*, Journal of Religious Ethics: Studies in Religious Ethics 3 (Atlanta, 1991), pp. 79–83.

90 See *Enarr. in Ps.* 38, 11 (CCL 38:412); *In Epistolam Joannis ad Parthos tractatus*, 10.4 (PL 35:2056).

91 *Serm.*, 107.10 (PL 38:632). The PL text must be emended by eliminating the question mark printed after *moriendi*.

92 See *Serm.*, 177.3–5 (ed. Lambot, pp. 66–67 – PL 38:954–56). In *Serm.*, 107.8 (PL 38:630), Augustine also remarked that even in adultery and idolatry there was

avarice, for on the one hand one's wife was not sufficient for him and on the other hand one's God was not. At this point one is close to Augustine's definition of sin *per se*. See Eugene F. Durkin, *The Theological Distinction of Sins in the Writings of St. Augustine*, Dissertationes ad Lauream 23 (Mundelein, IL, 1952), p. 12.

93 *Enarr. in Ps. 90, sermo 2*, 12 (CCL 39:1277). Compare Augustine's thinking to Lactantius' words on the usefulness of cupidity (above, ch. 1, p. 20).

94 *Enarr. in Ps. 90, sermo 1*, 8 (CCL 39:1260). The opposition between these "roots" is repeated in Prosper of Aquitaine's *Liber sententiarum*, 112 (ed. M. Gastaldo, CCL 68A [Turnhout, 1972], p. 282) and is applied to the *sancta et salutaris auaritia* which yearns for the possession of heaven by Paulinus of Nola, *Epistulae*, 34.8 (ed. W. v. Hartel, CSEL 29 [Vienna, 1894], p. 309).

95 Cf. Fichtenau, *Askese*, pp. 85–86.

5 SECULARIZING AVARICE AND CUPIDITY

1 The indebtedness of Caesarius' *Regula sanctarum virginum* to Cassian was examined by Maria C. McCarthy, *The Rule for Nuns of St. Caesarius of Arles*, The Catholic University of America, Studies in Mediaeval History, N.S. 16 (Washington, D.C., 1960), esp. pp. 99–106. For his debt to Cassian on matters of morality, see Paul Christophe, *Cassien et Césaire*, Recherches et Synthèses, Section de morale 2 (Gembloux and Paris, 1969), esp. pp. 67–68, who points out as well that Caesarius' common distinction of sins did not follow the octad but the normal division into *crimina capitalia* (including avarice) and *peccata minuta* (pp. 69–73). See also Henry G. J. Beck, *The Pastoral Care of Souls in South-East France During the Sixth Century*, Analecta Gregoriana 51 (Rome, 1950), pp. 187–222.

2 *Sermones*, 100A.8–11 (ed. G. Morin, CCL 103 [Turnhout, 1953], pp. 414–15). *Serm.*, 71.2 (CCL 103:301) has sections based on Maximus of Turin's *Serm.*, 17.2–3 and 18.2 (CCL 23:64–65, 67–68).

3 Caesarius, *Serm.*, 166.5 (CCL 104:681). Boethius, *Philosophiae consolatio*, 2.5.4 (ed. L. Bieler, CCL 94 [Turnhout, 1957], p. 26); cf. also Caesarius, *Serm.*, 81.1 (CCL 103:333) and 98.2 (CCL 103:401). Caesarius offers other oppositions to avarice as well: *misericordia* in *Serm.*, 6.4 (CCL 103:32); *elemosina* in *Serm.*, 18.1 (CCL 103:82).

4 Cassiodorus, *Expositio in Psalmum 118*, 36 (ed. M. Adriaen, CCL 98 [Turnhout, 1958], p. 1074). Martin of Braga, *Formula vitae honestae*, 8 (ed. C. W. Barlow in *Martini episcopi Bracarensis opera omnia*, Papers and Monographs of the American Academy in Rome 12 [New Haven, 1950], p. 249). Gregory the Great used a traditional and an innovative virtue as oppositions to avarice in the same work: continence in *Moralium in Iob libri 35*, 6.16.22 (ed. M. Adriaen, CCL 143 [Turnhout, 1979], p. 299); justice in *Mor.*, 9.25.38 (CCL 143:482–83).

5 *Pro repellenda iactantia*, 1 (ed. Barlow, p. 65). The order is changed to: 1 *inhumanitas*, 2 *rapacitas*, 3 *falsa testimonia*, 4 *violentiae*, 5 *periuria*, 6 *furta*, 7 *mendacium*, 8 *fraudatio* (in Cassian's *Conlationes*, 5.16 [ed. M. Petschenig, CSEL 13 (Vienna, 1886), p. 142] the order is 7, 8, 6, 5, *turpis lucri adpetitus*, 3, 4, 1, 2).

6 See A. Wilmart, "Les *Monita* de l'abbé Porcaire," *Revue bénédictine* 26 (1909),
479. Porcarius' student, Caesarius of Arles, used the same type of catalogue in his
Regula ad monachos (PL 67:1103); and the *Regula Magistri*, 5.3 (ed. A. de Vogüé,
SC 105 [Paris, 1964], p. 378) places *avaritia* in a series of thirty-three causes of evil
which the monk should cleanse himself of.

7 *Regula orientalis*, 25.6–7 (ed. A. de Vogüé, SC 298 [Paris, 1982], pp. 480–82). For
the possible date and location of this rule, see de Vogüé's introduction, SC
298:452–54. *Regula Benedicti*, 31.12 (ed. and trans. A. de Vogüé, SC 182 [Paris,
1972], p. 558).

8 *Reg. Ben.*, 57.4–8 (SC 182:624); *Reg. Mag.*, 85.1–7 (SC 106:346–48); cf. *Reg.
Mag.*, 87.24 (SC 106:358). On the stricture to sell at a price lower than the
common retail rate, see Karl Suso Frank, "Immer ein wenig billiger verkaufen
. . .," *Erbe und Auftrag* 53,4 (1977), 251–57. *Reg. Mag.*, 91.34 (SC 106:404) refers
to the vice when explaining that sons of aristocrats must give up all goods when
entering the monastery.

9 *Admonitio ad filium spiritualem*, cap. 9 (ed. P. Lehmann in *Die Admonitio
S. Basilii ad filium spiritualem*, Sitzungsberichte der Bayerischen Akademie der
Wissenschaften, Phil.-hist. Klasse Jg. 1955, Heft 7 [Munich, 1955], pp. 45–46). It
is likely that the text testifies to the reception of authentic treatises by Basil (and
the authority which his name carried). See *CPL* 1155a; Adalbert de Vogüé,
"Vestiges de l'*Admonitio ad filium spiritualem* du Pseudo-Basile dans la prédication de saint Eloi," *Revue bénédictine* 98 (1988), 18–20. For Benedict's dependence
on the *Admonitio*, see Eugène Manning, "L'*Admonitio S. Basilii ad filium
spiritualem* et la Règle de S. Benoît," *RAM* 42 (1966), 475–79.

10 *De vita contemplativa libri 3*, 3.4.1 (PL 59:479). As Pomerius himself says in 3.31.6
(PL 59:516–17), his entire work is based on Augustine.

11 *Serm.*, 48.7 (CCL 103:220).

12 For Gregory's biography, see Raoul Manselli, "Gregor der Große," *RAC*, vol. 12
(1983), cols. 930–40; Jeffrey Richards, *Consul of God: The Life and Times of
Gregory the Great* (London, 1980); Robert Gillet, "Saint Grégoire le Grand,"
Dictionnaire de Spiritualité, vol. 6 (1967), cols. 872–76; F. Homes Dudden,
Gregory the Great: His Place in History and Thought, 2 vols. (New York, 1905;
repr., 1967). Gregory's synthesis of the moral, practical, and pastoral has been
examined by Gillian R. Evans, *The Thought of Gregory the Great*, Cambridge
Studies in Medieval Life and Thought 4.2 (Cambridge, 1986); and J. Leclercq
et al., *La spiritualité du moyen âge*, Histoire de la spiritualité chrétienne 2
(Vienne, 1961), pp. 12–15.

13 *Mor.*, 31.45.87–90 (ed. M. Adriaen, CCL 143B [Turnhout, 1985], pp. 1610–12
[=PL 76:620–23]). For the smaller groupings of vices in Gregory's works, see
Leonhard Weber, *Hauptfragen der Moraltheologie Gregors des Grossen*, Paradosis 1
(Freiburg/CH, 1947), pp. 241–42; Paul Schulze, *Die Entwicklung der Hauptlaster-
und Haupttugendlehre von Gregor dem Großen bis Petrus Lombardus und ihr
Einfluß auf die frühdeutsche Literatur*, Dissertation Greifswald (Greifswald, 1914),
pp. 14–15.

14 *Registrum epistularum libri 14*, 12.6 (ed. D. Norberg, CCL 140A [Turnhout, 1982],

pp. 975–76). The letter is from January, 602. Cf. M. L. W. Laistner, *Thought and Letters in Western Europe, A.D. 500 to 900*, rev. ed. (Ithaca, N.Y., 1966), p. 106.

15 For Gregory's influence, see Morton Bloomfield, *The Seven Deadly Sins* ([East Lansing, Mich.], 1952; repr. 1967), *passim*; Jean Leclercq, *The Love of Learning and the Desire for God*, trans. C. Misrahi, second ed. (New York, 1974), pp. 32–34; and the following works by René Wasselynck: "La présence des Moralia de S. Grégoire le Grand dans les ouvrages de morale du XIIe siècle," *RTAM* 36 (1969), 31–45; "Présence de saint Grégoire le Grand dans les recueils canoniques (X^e–XIIe siècles)," *MSR* 22 (1965), 205–19; "L'influence de l'exégèse de S. Grégoire le Grand sur les Commentaires bibliques médiévaux (VIIe–XIIe s.)," *RTAM* 32 (1965), 157–204; "Les 'Moralia in Job' dans les ouvrages de morale du haut moyen âge latin," *RTAM* 31 (1964), 5–31; "Les compilations des Moralia in Job du VIIe au XIIe siècle," *RTAM* 29 (1962), 5–32; "L'influence des *Moralia in Job* de S. Grégoire le Grand sur la théologie morale entre le VIIe et le XIIe siècle," Dissertation Lille, 3 vols. (Lille, 1956); "La part des 'Moralia in Job' de S. Grégoire le Grand dans les 'Miscellanea' victorins," *MSR* 10 (1953), 287–94.

16 Cf. Robert Gillet, Introduction to Grégoire le Grand, *Morales sur Job, Livres 1 et 2*, second ed., SC 32bis (Paris, 1975), p. 90 (who says Gregory uses *filargyria* in his commentary on 1 Kings, though I have not been able to find the word there; the work presents other Greek *termini* for the vices: *desidia acediae* in *In Librum primum Regum expositionum libri 6*, 5.3 [ed. P. Verbraken, CCL 144 (Turnhout, 1963), p. 419] and cf. Siegfried Wenzel, *The Sin of Sloth: Acedia in Medieval Thought and Literature* [Chapel Hill, N.C., 1967], p. 24). On Gregory's knowledge and appreciation of Cassian's work, see Carole Straw, *Gregory the Great: Perfection in Imperfection*, Transformations of the Classical Heritage 14 (Berkeley, Los Angeles and London, 1988), esp. pp. 13, 61, 75, 132.

17 G. R. Evans, *The Thought of Gregory the Great*, pp. 22–23.

18 The heptad is: *inanis gloria, invidia, ira, tristitia, avaritia, ventris ingluvies, luxuria*. On the sources for Gregory's heptad, see Bloomfield, *Sins*, pp. 72–73; Gillet, Introduction, pp. 89–109; Otto Zöckler, *Das Lehrstück von den sieben Hauptsünden*, in Zöckler, *Biblische und kirchenhistorische Studien*, Heft 3 (Munich, 1893), pp. 42–49. The details of Gregory's revision of Cassian's octad have been presented by Bloomfield, *Sins*, p. 72; Otto Zöckler, *Die Tugendlehre des Christentums* (Gütersloh, 1904), pp. 109–10; Zöckler, *Das Lehrstück*, pp. 41–42. However, the *Epistula de octo uitiis ad Petrum papam* by Eutropius of Valencia (*c.* 580) may make reference to a heptad which its author rejects in favor of the Cassianic octad. See the edition of this text by M. C. Díaz y Díaz, in *Anecdota Wisigothica I*, Acta Salmanticensia, Filosofía y Letras 12,2 (Salamanca, 1958), p. 33 (cf. PL 80:14); Richard Newhauser, *The Treatise on Vices and Virtues in Latin and the Vernacular*, Typologie des sources du moyen âge occidental 68 (Turnhout, 1993), p. 184. On Eutropius, see also M. C. Díaz y Díaz, "La vie monastique d'après les écrivains wisigothiques (VIIe siècle)," in *Théologie de la vie monastique*, Théologie 49 (Paris, 1961), pp. 371–73 (repr. in Díaz y Díaz, *Vie chrétienne et culture dans l'Espagne du VIIe au Xe siècles*, Variorum Collected Studies, CS 377 [Aldershot, 1992]).

19 Cf. Robert Gillet, "Spiritualité et place du moine dans l'église selon saint Grégoire le Grand," in *Théologie de la vie monastique*, Théologie 49 (Lyon, 1961), pp. 338–43. Compare Rainer Jehl, "Die Geschichte des Lasterschemas und seiner Funktion. Von der Väterzeit bis zur karolingischen Erneuerung," *Franziskanische Studien* 64 (1982), 302. As Straw, *Gregory the Great*, pp. 10, 26, 217, points out, in Gregory's thought the suppression of desire only confounds reformation; the threat of individualism, on the other hand, is central to his thinking on the moral life of humanity.

20 *Mor.*, 31.45.89 (PL 76:621–22).

21 *Mor.*, 31.45.88 (PL 76:621). For the text of Cassian's enumeration of *filargyria*'s progeny, see above, ch. 3, n. 64.

22 *Homiliarum 40 in evangelia libri duo*, 1.16.2 (PL 76:1136). Cf. Lester K. Little, "Pride Goes before Avarice: Social Change and the Vices in Latin Christendom," *The American Historical Review* 76 (1971), 20; Donald R. Howard, *The Three Temptations* (Princeton, 1966), p. 45. *In Lib. Reg.*, 4.42 (CCL 144:317) implies a similar definition of the vice. In *Mor.*, 14.13.15 (CCL 143A:706) Gregory speaks of the action of sin *per se* on the mind in terms which amount to a digest of Augustine's *avaritia generalis*. In his comment on Job 18:10, Gregory notes that when the concupiscent mind seeks gain with sin and worldly prosperity with iniquity, it is as if it were attracted by the bait in a snare laid by the devil: "Dum itaque a concupiscente lucrum appetitur, quasi pedem mentis apprehendit decipula, quae non uidetur. Saepe ergo proponuntur animo cum culpa honores, diuitiae, salus et uita temporalis . . ." For a further indication of Gregory's debt to Augustine on the topic of avarice, see his remark in the *Regulae pastoralis liber*, 3.20 (PL 77:86), that someone who attempts to increase his riches is one who is *more avium captus* (cf. Augustine, *Serm.*, 107.8 [PL 38:631]). For other biblical figures to whom Gregory refers when writing of avarice, see the Appendix.

23 *Mor.*, 4.30.57 (CCL 143:201–02). On the stages in the development of all sins in Gregory's thought, see Ferruccio Gastaldelli, "Il meccanismo psicologico del peccato nei *Moralia in Job* di san Gregorio Magno," *Salesianum* 27 (1965), 563–605; Homes Dudden, *Gregory*, vol. 2, pp. 385–86. For the internal aspect of avarice and spiritual combat against all the sins, see Claude Dagens, *Saint Grégoire le Grand* (Paris, 1977), pp. 187–91.

24 *Libri de virtutibus s. Martini episcopi*, 1.29 (ed. B. Krusch, MGH Scriptores rerum Merovingicarum 1,2 [Hanover, 1885; repr., 1969], p. 152). Gregory probably completed the first book of this work by 575; see Henri Leclercq, "Grégoire de Tours," *Dictionnaire d'archéologie chrétienne et de liturgie*, vol. 6,2 (1925), cols. 1735–36. It is, thus, not impossible that Gregory the Great was influenced by Gregory of Tours' book on Martin, though there are no direct verbal parallels between the two on the topic of the *avarus*' self-delusion. Gregory the Great may also have derived material for his *Dialogi* from Gregory of Tours; see Adalbert de Vogüé, "Grégoire le Grand, lecteur de Grégoire de Tours?" *Analecta Bollandiana* 94 (1976), 225–33.

25 *Reg. past.*, 2.9 (PL 77:44). For Augustine's work, see above, ch. 4, n. 53. Gregory remarked on the vices' disguise of themselves as virtues elsewhere, as well – see

G. R. Evans, *The Thought of Gregory the Great*, pp. 72, 110–11. Gregory's words
to the pastor should be seen in the light of his warnings to the clergy against
simony: see *In Lib. Reg.*, 4.43–44 (CCL 144:317) and *Reg. ep.*, 9.219 and 11.38
(CCL 140A:782–90, 932–34).

26 *Reg. past.*, 3.20–21 (PL 77:83–89). The passages, and their specific use, are as
follows: for those who want to seize others' goods: Matt. 25:41, Hab. 2:6; who
want to enlarge their dwellings: Isa. 5:8; who want to increase their money: Qoh.
5:9; who hasten to become rich: Prov. 28:20; who ignore losses to increase their
wealth in this world: Prov. 20:21; who gain all they desire: Matt. 16:26; who must
learn to give without taking back through rapine as much as they give: Isa. 61:8,
Prov. 21:27; who offer to God what they take from the needy: Sir. 34:24; who
count out exactly the amount they give but not how much they seize from others:
Hag. 1:6; to instill the need for justice in giving to the needy: Matt. 6:1, Ps. 101:9,
Prov. 21:26; to show the miserly that they offend God: Ps. 48:8, Luke 3:9.

27 *Reg. past.*, 3.21 (PL 77:88). Usurpation within the church echoed that in secular
society, as Straw, *Gregory the Great*, pp. 82–83, notes. Gregory is the first to speak
of the "thorn of avarice"; see further in the Appendix.

28 For its use in Gregory's work, see *Reg. past.*, 1.11 (PL 77:26); *Mor.*, 14.53.65,
15.18.22, 20.10.21 (CCL 143A:739, 763, 1019); *Reg. ep.*, 9.219 (CCL 140A:783).
Compare John A. Yunck, *The Lineage of Lady Meed: The Development of
Mediaeval Venality Satire*, University of Notre Dame, Publications in Mediaeval
Studies 17 (Notre Dame, IN, 1963), p. 32.

29 Johan Huizinga, *The Waning of the Middle Ages*, trans. F. Hopman (London,
1924; repr. New York, 1954), pp. 27–28; Bloomfield, *Sins*, pp. 74–75; Heinrich
Fichtenau, *Askese und Laster in der Anschauung des Mittelalters, II: Lasterkampf
und Lasterlehre*, rev. and repr. in his *Beiträge zur Mediävistik* (Stuttgart, 1975),
vol. 1, pp. 86–87; Little, "Pride," esp. 34. For a brief critique of the simplified
sociological differentiation between avarice (as the sin of the middle class) and
pride (as the sin of the feudal nobility), see Rüdiger Schnell, *Zum Verhältnis von
hoch- und spätmittelalterlichen Literatur*, Philologische Studien und Quellen 92
(Berlin, 1978), pp. 80–82.

30 Isidore of Seville, *De differentiis rerum*, 40.161 (PL 83:96). On the importance of
this variant of the Gregorian heptad, see Wenzel, *Sloth*, pp. 28–29; Wenzel,
"'Acedia' 700–1200," *Traditio* 22 (1966), 75. For Gregory's influence on Isidore,
see Wasselynck, "Les 'Moralia in Job'," 6–11, and Zöckler, *Die Tugendlehre*,
pp. 119–21.

31 *Gulae concupiscentia, fornicatio* [from Cassian instead of Gregory's *luxuria*],
avaritia, invidia, tristitia, ira, inanis gloria, superbia.

32 *Quaestiones in Deuteronomium*, 16.3–4 (PL 83:366): *gastrimargia, fornicatio,
philargyria, ira, tristitia, accidia, cenodoxia, superbia. Allegoriae quaedam S.
Scripturae*, 164 (PL 83:120): *iracundia, avaritia, invidia, ventris ingluvies, inanis
gloria, fornicatio, superbia*. The list of nine vices in *Sententiarum libri*, 2.37.2 (PL
83:638 – *luxuria, odium, iracundia, timor, torpor zeli, tristitia, accidia, avaritia,
superbia*) is apparently not meant to be taken as a finalized scheme but only as a
less formal series of examples of the vices, for Isidore is thinking of Gregory's

heptad, referred to explicitly in *Sent.*, 2.37.8 (PL 83:639). A different list of eight "principalia vitia" can be found in the *Liber numerorum*, 9 (PL 83:189): *invidia, iracundia, tristitia, avaritia, ingluvies, luxuria, inanis gloria, superbia*. This work has been accepted as authentic by some (see *CPL* 1193), but was rejected from the Isidorian canon, pending further study, by Bernhard Bischoff, "Eine verschollene Einteilung der Wissenschaften," *Archives d'histoire doctrinale et littéraire du moyen âge* 25 (1958), 9–10 (repr. in Bischoff's *Mittelalterliche Studien* [Stuttgart, 1966], vol. 1, pp. 277–78); see also Robert E. McNally, "Isidorian Pseudepigrapha in the Early Middle Ages," in M. C. Díaz y Díaz, ed., *Isidoriana* (Leon, 1961), pp. 314–15.

33 *Isidori Hispalensis episcopi etymologiarum sive originum libri 20*, 8.11.95 (ed. W. M. Lindsay [Oxford, 1911], vol. 1).

34 Compare *Sent.*, 2.37.8 (PL 83:639) and 2.41.3–4 (PL 83:645–46). Cf. Little, "Pride," p. 19.

35 *Regula monachorum*, 3.2–3 (PL 83:871). Cf. Ph. Delhaye, "Les idées morales de saint Isidore de Séville," *RTAM* 26 (1959), 39.

36 In *De diff. rer.*, 39.157 (PL 83:95), Isidore presents *fortitudo* as the virtue which "pecuniam negligit, avaritiam fugit." In the same work, 40.170 (PL 83:98), he notes "avaritiam subjugat eleemosyna," and in *Sent.*, 2.37.2 (PL 83:638), he presents *largitas* as the opponent of avarice.

37 See Taio, *Sententiarum libri quinque*, 4.25 (PL 80:941–42) ([*c.* 650], which otherwise repeats Gregory the Great on matters concerning morality); *Commonitiuncula*, 12 (ed. A. E. Anspach in *S. Isidori Hispalensis episcopi Commonitiuncula ad sororem*, Scriptores Ecclesiastici Hispano-Latini Veteris et Medii Aevi 4 [Escorial, 1935], pp. 79–80) ([seventh century], formerly attributed to Jerome, Augustine, or Adalgerus; Anspach accepted the work as part of the Isidorian canon, but most other scholars have not followed him in this; see *CPL* 1219); *Liber de numeris*, 7.5 (see Robert E. McNally, *Der irische Liber de numeris*, Dissertation Munich [Munich, 1957], p. 112) (composed in the vicinity of Salzburg in the latter part of the eighth century). Cf. Jehl, "Die Geschichte," pp. 322–23.

38 Isidore, *Etym.*, 10.9 (ed. Lindsay, vol. 1). For the spread of Isidore's works and influence in the Middle Ages, see Jocelyn N. Hillgarth, "The Position of Isidorian Studies: A Critical Review of the Literature Since 1935," in M. C. Díaz y Díaz, ed., *Isidoriana* (Leon, 1961), pp. 60–69; and in the same collection Bernhard Bischoff, "Die europäische Verbreitung der Werke Isidors von Sevilla," pp. 317–44 (repr. in Bischoff's *Mittelalterliche Studien*, vol. 1, pp. 171–94); Berthold Altaner, "Der Stand der Isidorforschung. Ein kritischer Bericht über die seit 1910 erschienene Literatur," *Miscellanea Isidoriana* (Rome, 1936), pp. 28–31; and in this same collection A. E. Anspach, "Das Fortleben Isidors im VII. bis IX. Jahrhundert," pp. 323–56.

39 For *avaritia*, see above, p. 107 and n. 32. *Philargyria* is found in *Quaest. in Deut.*, 16.3 (PL 83:366) and *Reg. mon.*, 3.3 (PL 83:871).

40 *Sent.*, 2.41.5 (PL 83:646). For the place of *cupiditas* among the "biens indifférents," see Jacques Fontaine, *Isidore de Séville et la culture classique dans l'Espagne wisigothique* (Paris, 1959), vol. 2, pp. 700–02.

41 Isidore of Seville, *De differentiis verborum*, 2.4 (PL 83:9). See also the combination of *avaritia* and *cupido* in Horace, *Epistulae*, 1.1.33 (ed. F. Klingner [Leipzig, 1970], p. 241). These two species of avarice appear elsewhere in Isidore's work without specific designations – see *De diff. rer.*, 40.164 (PL 83:96); *Sent.*, 2.41.7 (PL 83:646) – where he stresses the *avarus'* fear of being without possessions. His emphasis on the desire to increase one's goods, on the one hand, and the fear of losing what one already possesses, on the other, was probably influenced by Gregory the Great, *Mor.*, 31.45.90 (PL 76:622).

42 For a list of Isidore's sources, and some of the medieval authors he influenced, see table 5 in Hans-Joachim Diesner, *Isidor von Sevilla und das westgotische Spanien*, Abhandlungen der Sächsischen Akademie der Wissenschaften zu Leipzig, Phil.-hist. Klasse 67,3 (Berlin, 1977), pp. 121–23. The *Admonitio* is not mentioned here.

43 Michel Mollat, *The Poor in the Middle Ages*, trans. A. Goldhammer (New Haven, 1986), p. 25.

44 Isidore, *Synonymorum . . . libri 2*, 1.8 (PL 83:829). For Isidore's concern with correcting the corruption of judges, see Hans-Joachim Diesner, *Isidor von Sevilla und seine Zeit*, Aufsätze und Vorträge zur Theologie und Religionswissenschaft 57 (Berlin, 1973), pp. 59–60; Yunck, *The Lineage*, p. 33.

45 See *Sent.*, 2.41.6 and 9 (PL 83:646–47). Cf. Delhaye, "Les idées morales," pp. 25–26. In *Syn.*, 2.93 (PL 83:866), Isidore argues that "divitiae nunquam sine peccato acquiruntur, divitiae nunquam sine peccato administrantur." The latter statement is taken from the monastic rejection of arguments, seen earliest in Clement of Alexandria's work, that avarice is avoided by the correct administration of money. Isidore's statements are aimed at those who desire to become wealthy, not at those who are already so; for the rich his theory of property depends on the same apology for wealth seen in Augustine. For Isidore's use of Augustine in this matter, see Diesner, *Isidor von Sevilla und das westgotische Spanien*, pp. 42–43. On Isidore's conception of the appropriate punishment for the *avari* (who burned with the fire of cupidity while alive) in the eternal flames of hell, see Sr. Patrick J. Mullins, *The Spiritual Life According to Saint Isidore of Seville*, The Catholic University of America, Studies in Medieval and Renaissance Latin Language and Literature 13 (Washington, D.C., 1940), p. 87.

46 I have treated the presence of avarice in penitential literature in "Towards modus in habendo: Transformations in the Idea of Avarice. The Early Penitentials through the Carolingian Reforms," *Zeitschrift der Savigny-Stiftung für Rechtsgeschichte* 106, Kanonistische Abteilung 75 (1989), 1–22. The best introduction to the penitential genre is Cyrille Vogel, *Les "libri paenitentiales,"* Typologie des sources du moyen âge occidental 27 (Turnhout, 1978), with a supplement to this volume by Allen J. Frantzen (Turnhout, 1985); see also Allen J. Frantzen, *The Literature of Penance in Anglo-Saxon England* (New Brunswick, N.J., 1983); G. Le Bras, "Pénitentiels," *Dictionnaire de théologie catholique*, vol. 12 (1933), cols. 1160–79. All three works contain ample bibliographies on the history of penance. For Isidore's concept of penance, see Delhaye, "Les idées morales," pp. 32–37.

47 Bede, *In Lucae evangelium expositio*, 1.4.13 (CCL 120:98–99). For further uses of

filargiria by Bede, see *In Marci evangelium expositio*, 3.10.23–24 (ed. D. Hurst, CCL 120, p. 561); *In Proverbia Salomonis libri 3*, 1.1.19 (ed. D. Hurst, CCL 120, p. 29). For Bede's knowledge of Cassian, see M. L. W. Laistner, "The Library of the Venerable Bede," in A. H. Thompson, ed., *Bede, His Life, Times and Writings* (Oxford, 1935), p. 251. See also the discussion of the penitential attributed to Egbert of York in Newhauser, "Towards modus," 12–14. For Bede's relationship with Egbert, see Dorothy Whitelock, "Bede and His Teachers and Friends," in G. Bonner, ed., *Famulus Christi* (London, 1976), p. 34.

48 *In Luc. evan. exp.*, 4.11.40 (CCL 120:241). For Bede's use of Gregory, see Paul Meyvaert, "Bede and Gregory the Great," *Jarrow Lecture* 7 (1964), repr. in his *Benedict, Gregory, Bede and Others* (London, 1977), no. 8, pp. 13–19. On the date of Bede's exposition of Luke, see W. F. Bolton, *A History of Anglo-Latin Literature, 597–1066* (Princeton, 1967), vol. 1, p. 112.

49 Bede's comments on *luxoria* and *avaritia* as the two daughters of the devil are found in *In Prov. Sal.*, 3.30.15–16 (CCL 119B:143–44), and note the use here of Juvenal, *Saturae*, 14.139 (ed. A. E. Housman [Cambridge, 1956], p. 128): "Crescit amor nummi quantum ipsa pecunia crescit." This verse became a standard ingredient in analyses of avarice later in the Middle Ages.

50 Not until the seventh century could Jerome's text be considered "on the way to winning domination" over the Old Latin text. See Raphael Loewe, "The Medieval History of the Latin Vulgate," in G. W. H. Lampe, ed., *The Cambridge History of the Bible*, vol. 2 (Cambridge, 1969), p. 110. For Jerome's reputation among the Carolingians, see Bernice M. Kaczynski, "Edition, Translation, and Exegesis: The Carolingians and the Bible," in R. E. Sullivan, ed., *"The Gentle Voices of Teachers": Aspects of Learning in the Carolingian Age* (Columbus, OH, 1995), pp. 171–72.

51 *De virginitate*, 2.2571–72 (ed. R. Ehwald, MGH Auctores antiquissimi 15 [Berlin, 1919; repr. 1961], p. 457). On the date of this work, see Bolton, *A History*, vol. 1, pp. 88–90.

52 *Prebiarum*, 25 (ed. R. E. McNally, CCL 108B [Turnhout, 1973], p. 163). For the date and provenance of the work, see McNally's preface, CCL 108B:155–59.

53 *Aenigmata Bonifatii, De virtutibus et vitiis, prologus.*11–15 (ed. Fr. Glorie, CCL 133 [Turnhout, 1968], p. 281). The subject of each riddle is identified in an acrostic in the opening hexameters of its section. The ten vices on the tree of death are the counterparts to the ten virtues on the tree of life.

54 *Aenigm. Bonif., De vitiis*, 3.22–24 (CCL 133:319).

55 Compare *Aenigm. Bonif., De vitiis*, 3.67 (CCL 133:323), in which *Cupiditas* describes how she would punish Paul: "Mordendo trepidi tremerent sub dentibus artus", with Defensor, *Liber scintillarum*, 25.12 (ed. H. M. Rochais, CCL 117 [Turnhout, 1957], p. 108): "[Avaritia] esurit semper et inops est, et, cum feralibus dentibus uniuersa regna mundi discerpserit . . ."

56 *Scarapsus*, 2.13 (ed. G. Jecker in *Die Heimat des hl. Pirmin*, Beiträge zur Geschichte des alten Mönchtums und des Benediktinerordens 13 [Münster, 1927], p. 44). Jecker felt this section was borrowed from a *Homilia sacra*, no longer extant in manuscript, printed in 1614 by G. Elmenhorst. However, the precise relationship of these texts seems unclear. Compare Arnold Angenendt,

Monachi Peregrini, Dissertation Münster (Munich, 1972), pp. 62–63. On the public of the *Scarapsus*, see Heinz Löwe, "Pirmin, Willibrod und Bonifatius. Ihre Bedeutung für die Missionsgeschichte ihrer Zeit," repr. in K. Schäferdiek, ed., *Die Kirche des früheren Mittelalters*, Kirchengeschichte als Missionsgeschichte 2,1 (Munich, 1978), p. 196.

57 *Scar.*, 2.27 (ed. Jecker, p. 61). On cupidity Pirminius cites the Tenth Commandment (Exod. 20:17, Deut. 5:21), Sir. 10:10, and 1Tim. 6:10. The biblical authorities are used in *Scar.*, 2.14 (ed. Jecker, p. 45). The AGLITAVS order witnessed first in Pirminius' treatise appears again in the early eleventh century in the vernacular in England; see below, Epilogue, p. 125 and n. 2.

58 Ambrosius Autpertus, *Conflictus*, 1 (ed. R. Weber, CCM 27B [Turnhout, 1979], p. 910). On the identification of the recipient of the work, see Weber's preface (CCM 27B:877–78). For Autpertus' *vita*, see Jacques Winandy, *Ambroise Autpert, moine et théologien* (Paris, 1953), pp. 13–30. The importance of the laity in Autpertus' thinking on avarice has been described by Claudio Leonardi, "Spiritualità di Ambrogio Autperto," *Studi Medievali* 3. ser. 9,1 (1968), 82.

59 Ambrosius Autpertus, *Oratio* [recension A], 2 (ed. R. Weber, CCM 27B [Turnhout, 1979], p. 936) and [recension B], 2 (CCM 27B:948). On the relationship between these two recensions, see Robert Weber, "La prière d'Ambroise Autpert contre les vices et son 'Conflictus vitiorum et virtutum'," *Revue bénédictine* 86 (1976), 109–15. Weber points out (pp. 114–15) that the sins which follow immediately after the seven chief vices in the *Conflictus* are generally drawn from Gregory's subdivisions of the heptad. Among those which follow *auaritia*, however, the pairs *furtum et fraus* and *fallacia atque mendacium* also use designations taken from Cassian, whose influence is apparent elsewhere in this work as well. In *Oratio* [B], 7 (CCM 27B:953) there is a suggestion that both pride and avarice have the chief rule among the seven vices, so that in this version of the work *superbia* has already lost some of its hegemony. The eleventh-century reworking of this text by Jean de Fécamp (ed. J. Leclercq, "La prière au sujet des vices et des vertus," in *Analecta Monastica* 2, Studia Anselmiana 31 [Rome, 1953], pp. 3–17) added nothing to Autpertus' discussion of avarice.

60 *Sermo Ambrosii Autperti presbyteri de cupiditate viris saecularibus utilis valde*, 1 (ed. R. Weber, CCM 27B [Turnhout, 1979], p. 963).

61 *Expositionis in Apocalypsin libri 10*, 2.2.6 (ed. R. Weber, CCM 27 [Turnhout, 1975], p. 107).

62 For the narrower sense of cupidity and avarice, see *Exp. in Apoc.*, 9.21.8 (CCM 27A:789); Cupidity's words in *Conflictus*, 16 (CCM 27B:920) – taken from Gregory, *Mor.*, 31.45.90 (PL 76:622); and the use of Ananias and Sapphira in *Exp. in Apoc.*, 1.1.5[b] (CCM 27:46). Compare Claudio Leonardi, "Spiritualità," pp. 80 and 84, for whom avarice is only one of the manifestations of cupidity. For the wider definition of the vice, see *Serm. de cup.*, 2 (CCM 27B:964). Autpertus notes further in this section that the two principal vices are combined by their implication in 1John 2:16. Autpertus also cites Gregory, *Hom. in ev.*, 1.16.2 (see above, p. 103 and n. 22), in *Exp. in Apoc.*, 2.2.10[b] (CCM 27:122). The two designations for the vice are equated as well in *Oratio* [B], 7 (CCM 27B:953).

63 *Serm. de cup.*, 1 (CCM 27B:963).

64 *Conflictus*, 16 (CCM 27B:921–22).

65 *Oratio* [A], 7 (CCM 27B:939); [B], 7 (CCM 27B:953).

66 *Serm. de cup.*, 14 (CCM 27B:977–79).

67 *Serm. de cup.*, 4 (CCM 27B:965). Princes and their administrators are the subject of sects. 6–8 (pp. 967–71). In sect. 9 (p. 971) he speaks more directly of a certain *huius saeculi opulentissimus princeps* whom he reprimanded on the matter of avarice only yesterday. This amount of specificity is unusual for sermons on avarice at the time; cf. Claudio Leonardi, "Spiritualità," p. 20.

68 *Serm. de cup.*, 6 (CCM 27B:967).

69 See Janet L. Nelson, "On the Limits of the Carolingian Renaissance," in D. Baker, ed., *Renaissance and Renewal in Christian History*, Studies in Church History 14 (Oxford, 1977), pp. 51–69.

70 For Charlemagne's monastic legislation, see Joseph Semmler, "Karl der Große und das fränkische Mönchtum," in *Karl der Große, Lebenswerk und Nachleben, 2: Das geistige Leben*, ed. B. Bischoff (Düsseldorf, 1965), esp. pp. 263–64.

71 *Libri Carolini sive Caroli Magni capitulare de imaginibus*, 2.30 (ed. H. Bastgen, MGH Leges 3, Concilia 2 Supplementum [Hanover and Leipzig, 1924], pp. 95–96). The list is: *gulae concupiscentia, fornicatio, invidia, ira, avaritia, tristitia, arrogantia* and *vana gloria*, and *superbia*. Cf. Jehl, "Die Geschichte," pp. 324–27. On the authorship of the *Libri Carolini*, and the history of debate on this issue, see Ann Freeman, "Theodulf of Orléans and the Psalm Citations of the 'Libri Carolini'," *Revue bénédictine* 97 (1987), 195–224.

72 For the date and function of the text, see Ann Freeman, "Carolingian Orthodoxy and the Fate of the Libri Carolini," *Viator* 16 (1985), 65–108.

73 *Capitula ecclesiastica*, 15 (ed. A. Boretius, MGH Leges 2, Capitularia Regum Francorum 1 [Hanover, 1883], p. 179). For the councils, see, e.g., *Concilium Cabillonense*, canon 32 (ed. A. Werminghoff, MGH Leges 3, Concilia 2,1 [Hanover and Leipzig, 1906], p. 279); *Concilium Remense*, canon 13 (MGH Leges 3, Concilia 2,1, p. 255); Newhauser, "Towards modus," 15.

74 Compare the following two texts by Paulinus of Aquileia, *Liber exhortationis*, 30 (PL 99:226) and Ps.-Basil, *Admonitio ad filium spiritualem*, 9 (ed. P. Lehmann, Sitzungsberichte der Bayerischen Akademie der Wissenschaften, Phil.-hist. Klasse, Jahrgang 1955, Heft 7 [Munich, 1955], p. 45):

Paulinus	Ps.-Basil
Cupidus enim vir animam suam	Cupidus etiam animam suam
venalem habet: si inveniet	venalem habet. Si invenerit
tempus ut concupiscat alicujus	tempus,
aurum aut argentum, seu vestes	
pulchras, vel etiam cujuslibet	
mulierem pulchram facie, pro	pro
nihilo perpetrat homicidium.	nihilo perpetrat homicidium.

See also above, p. 109. On Paulinus' use of the *Admonitio* and Pomerius' *De vita contemplativa*, see Franz Brunhölzl, *Geschichte der lateinischen Literatur des*

Mittelalters, 1 (Munich, 1975), p. 254; Hans Hubert Anton, *Fürstenspiegel und Herrscherethos in der Karolingerzeit*, Bonner Historische Forschungen 32 (Bonn, 1968), p. 83. In *De cavendis vitiis et virtutibus exercendis*, written by Hincmar, Archbishop of Reims, for Charles the Bald, nearly everything on the vice is taken from Gregory the Great's major monastic work, the *Moralia in Iob*, though there is also one short passage borrowed from Bede and a few others from Gregory's *Pastoral Rule*. Various dates have been proposed for the work, from 850 to 869. See Jean Devisse, *Hincmar: Archévêque de Reims 845–882*, Travaux d'histoire ethico-politique 29 (Geneva, 1976), vol. 2, p. 680. For Hincmar's use of the *Moralia*, see the table in Wasselynck, "Les 'Moralia in Job'," pp. 25–26, to which should be added the end of *De cav. vit.*, 2 (PL 125:881D-882B), where *avaritia* is compared to the ephah mentioned in Zech. 5:5–11 (lifted directly from *Mor.*, 14.53.64–65 [CCL 143A:737–39]). Compare Jehl, "Die Geschichte," p. 333, who attributes the passage to Hincmar. *De cav. vit.*, 2 (PL 125:873D) is taken from Bede, *In Prov. Sal.*, 3.30.15–16 (CCL 119B:143–44). The borrowings from the *Reg. past.* in Hincmar's *De cav. vit.*, 2 (PL 125:869C-870B) are noted in the PL text. For Hincmar's use of Salvian and his opposition to avarice, see Mollat, *The Poor in the Middle Ages*, p. 44.

75 *Liber de virtutibus et vitiis*, cap. 30 (ed. P. E. Szarmach in "The Latin Tradition of Alcuin's *Liber de Virtutibus et Vitiis*, cap. xxvii–xxxv, with Special Reference to Vercelli Homily xx," *Mediaevalia* 12 [1989], 31–32) (=PL 101:634). For the date of the text, see Luitpold Wallach, *Alcuin and Charlemagne: Studies in Carolingian History and Literature*, Cornell Studies in Classical Philology 32 (Ithaca, N.Y., 1959), p. 230. For Hrabanus' use of the text, see *De ecclesiastica disciplina libri 3*, 3 (PL 112:1245); for Jonas' work, see *De institutione laicali*, 3.6 (PL 106:245), and cf. Wasselynck, "Les 'Moralia in Job'," 20–21. For further borrowings, see Luitpold Wallach, "Alcuin on Vices and Virtues: A Manual for a Carolingian Soldier," *Harvard Theological Review* 48 (1955), 190–93. For Old English versions of part of this text, see R. Torkar, ed., *Eine altenglische Übersetzung von Alcuins "De virtutibus et vitiis," Kap. 20*, Münchener Universitäts-Schriften, Texte und Untersuchungen zur Englischen Philologie 7 (Munich, 1981), and the works listed by Paul E. Szarmach, "A Preliminary Handlist of Manuscripts Containing Alcuin's *Liber de virtutibus et vitiis*," *Manuscripta* 25,3 (1981), 133–34.

76 *De eccl. disc.*, 3 (PL 112:1245). See also the Old English translation of Alcuin's treatment of the Capital Vices in Vercelli Homily 20 where the three divisions are reduced to two and avarice is defined as the "swiðlic grædignes ægðer ge welan to hæbbenne ge to gehealdanne." See Szarmach, "The Latin Tradition," p. 31; P. E. Szarmach, ed., "Vercelli Homily XX," *Mediaeval Studies* 35 (1973), 11. Ps.-Hrabanus, *De vitiis et virtutibus et peccatorum satisfactione*, 3.51 (PL 112:1375) repeats Alcuin's threefold division, but only where he paraphrases Cassian's analysis of the vice. On the third book of this text by Ps.-Hrabanus, see below, pp. 123–24. For Cassian's influence on Alcuin's text, see Wallach, "Alcuin on Vices and Virtues," 188–89.

77 *Serm. de cup.*, 5 (CCM 27B:966); see also *Exp. in Apoc.*, 2.2.6 (CCM 27:107). For the use of *latrocinium* and *rapina* in the analysis of avarice in the penitentials, see

Poenitentiale Mediolanense, 3.3 (ed. O. Seebass, "Ein bisher noch nicht veröffent-lichtes Poenitential einer Bobbienser Handschrift der Ambrosiana," *Deutsche Zeitschrift für Kirchenrecht* 6 [1896–97], 32); Newhauser, "Towards modus," 10. For Paulinus' emphasis on murder as an essential part of the vice, see above, n. 74. For Isidore's mention of homicide, see *Sent.*, 2.41.5 (PL 83:646), quoted above, p. 109. As Wallach, "Alcuin on Virtues and Vices," p. 182, has demon-strated, Alcuin used the *Sententiae* directly. For the Cassianic and Gregorian progeny of the vice, see above, pp. 102–03.

78 *Libri Carolini*, 2.30 (MGH Leges 3, Concilia 2 Suppl.:95–96). Note also the opposition between avarice and *abstinentia*, in some manuscripts *largitas* and *contemptus mundi*, in chapter 34 (PL 101:637) of the *Lib. de virt.*

79 *Lib. de virt.*, 19 (PL 101:627–28). For Caesarius' sermon, see CCL 104:878–79 (and cf. Wallach, "Alcuin on Virtues and Vices," p. 184). Chapter 19 of Alcuin's work was taken over nearly verbatim in Hrabanus Maurus, *Homiliae*, 62 (PL 110:117D-118B).

80 Theodulf, *Fragmentum de vitiis capitalibus*, verse 266 (ed. E. Duemmler, MGH Poet 1,2 [Berlin, 1881], p. 451). For Prudentius, see above, ch. 4, n. 47; for Evagrius, see above, ch. 3, p. 53.

81 *Lib. de virt.*, 19 (PL 101:627–28).

82 *Liber de animae ratione*, 4 (PL 101:640); see Sibylle Mähl, *Quadriga Virtutum*, Beihefte zum Archiv für Kulturgeschichte 9 (Cologne and Vienna, 1969), pp. 121–23; but also Lactantius' similar discussion of the usefulness of desire referred to above, ch. 1, p. 20. Alcuin notes that "avarice disregards moderation" in *Lib. de virt.*, 19 (PL 101:628).

83 *Versus de patribus, regibus et sanctis Euboricensis ecclesiae*, verses 35–37 (ed. and trans. P. Godman in Alcuin, *The Bishops, Kings and Saints of York* [Oxford, 1982], p. 6). See *Epistolae*, 100 (ed. E. Duemmler, MGH Epistolae 4 [Berlin, 1895], p. 145). On the poem, see Donald A. Bullough, "Hagiography as Patriotism: Alcuin's 'York poem' and the Early Northumbrian 'vitae sanctorum'," in *Hagiographie, cultures et sociétés IVᵉ–XIIᵉ siècles*, Actes du Colloque organisé à Nanterre et à Paris (2–5 mai 1979) (Paris, 1981), pp. 339–59.

84 According to Otto Eberhardt, *Via Regia: Der Fürstenspiegel Smaragds von St. Mihiel und seine literarische Gattung*, Münstersche Mittelalter-Schriften 28 (Munich, 1977), pp. 195–263, the *Via regia* was composed *c.* 810 for Charle-magne. Fidel Rädle, *Studien zu Smaragd von Saint-Mihiel*, Medium Aevum, Philologische Studien 29 (Munich, 1974), pp. 62–68, argued for a date before 813 and for Louis the Pious as the addressee. Rädle essentially agrees with Anton, *Fürstenspiegel*, p. 166. Cf. also Joachim Scharf, "Studien zu Smaragdus und Jonas," *Deutsches Archiv für Erforschung des Mittelalters* 17 (1961), 333–51.

85 *Via regia*, 26 (PL 102:965).

86 *Ibid.* For the backgrounds of avarice's *ferales dentes*, see Defensor, *Lib. scint.*, 25.12 (CCL 117:108) and above, n. 55. On Smaragdus' discussion of the danger of avarice to the king and state, compare Eberhardt, *Via Regia*, pp. 603–04.

87 *Capitulare*, 10.59 (ed. C. de Clercq in *La législation religieuse franque de Clovis à Charlemagne*, Université de Louvain, Recueil de travaux publiés par les membres

des Conférences d'Histoire et de Philologie, 2ᵉ série 38 [Louvain and Paris, 1936], p. 343) [cf. PL 105:218]. The list of vices is: *gastrimargia, fornicatio, acedia sive tristitia, avaritia, vana gloria, invidia, ira, superbia.* On the dating of the capitularies, see Peter Brommer, "Die bischöfliche Gesetzgebung Theodulfs von Orléans," *Zeitschrift der Savigny-Stiftung für Rechtsgeschichte* 91, Kanonistische Abteilung 60 (1974), 23–24. On the use of these works, see Brommer's "Die Rezeption der bischöflichen Kapitularien Theodulfs von Orléans," *Zeitschrift der Savigny-Stiftung für Rechtsgeschichte* 92, Kanonistische Abteilung 61 (1975), esp. 145–46, 156–59. For the use of Theodulf's *Capitula* in Anglo-Saxon England, see H. Sauer, ed., *Theodulfi capitula in England*, Münchener Universitäts-Schriften, Texte und Untersuchungen zur Englischen Philologie 8 (Munich, 1978).

88 *De institutione clericorum*, 3.38 (ed. A. Knoepfler in *Rabani Mauri de institutione clericorum libri tres*, Veröffentlichungen aus dem Kirchenhistorischen Seminar München 5 [Munich, 1900], p. 275). On Hrabanus' theory of preaching, see Maria Rissel, *Rezeption antiker und patristischer Wissenschaft bei Hrabanus Maurus*, Lateinische Sprache und Literatur des Mittelalters 7 (Bern and Frankfurt/M., 1976), pp. 281–89. For Hrabanus' use of Gregory, see Wasselynck, "Les 'Moralia in Job'," 22–23; for his dependence on Augustine, see Bernhard Blumenkranz, "Raban Maur et saint Augustine: compilation ou adaptation? A propos du latin biblique," *Revue du Moyen Age Latin* 7 (1951), 97–110. The army of avarice and its opponents are as follows:

Avaritia	vs.	*Largitas*
proditio		fides non ficta
fraus		sinceritas
fallacia		veritas
periuria		non iurare
inquietudo		tranquillitas
violentiae		patientia
duritia		misericordia

89 On the date and addressee of this work, see Raymund Kottje, "Hrabanus Maurus," *Die deutsche Literatur des Mittelalters, Verfasserlexikon*, second rev. ed., vol. 4 (1983), cols. 178–79.

90 *De eccl. disc.*, 3 (PL 112:1245). See further in the Appendix.

91 *Commentariorum in Ecclesiasticum libri 10*, 3.2 (PL 109:827). For another view of the political context of *avaritia* by one of Hrabanus' pupils, see the poem on Theoderic's statue in Aachen written in 829 by Walahfrid Strabo. In *De imagine Tetrici*, verses 72–75 (ed. E. Duemmler, MGH Poet 2 [Berlin, 1884], p. 372), *Scintilla*, i.e. Walahfrid's *genius*, describes the vice's calamitous effect in history.

92 The work was attributed to Hrabanus in Colvener's edition of 1626 and printed there as part of *De vitiis et virtutibus et peccatorum satisfactione* (repr. in PL 112). On the date and place of origin of the text, see Franz Kerff, *Der Quadripartitus: Ein Handbuch der karolingischen Kirchenreform*, Quellen und Forschungen zum Recht im Mittelalter 1 (Sigmaringen, 1982), pp. 77–78. See also Kottje, "Hrabanus Maurus," col. 186; Kottje, *Die Bussbücher Halitgars von Cambrai und des*

Hrabanus Maurus, Beiträge zur Geschichte und Quellenkunde des Mittelalters 8 (Berlin and New York, 1980), p. 92 and n. 23.

93 *De vitiis*, 3.35 (PL 112:1366). Essential to Ps.-Hrabanus' proof of the similarity of Cassian's octad and Gregory's heptad is the equivalence of the former's *philargyria* and the latter's *avaritia*; see 3.2 (PL 112:1349). Ps.-Hrabanus provides unqualified evidence of the equivalence of the terms *avaritia, philargyria*, and *cupiditas*. All three occur in his chapter on the genesis of "*avaritia*, which in Greek is called *philargyria*," that traces the origin of "the insatiable fury, *avaritia*, which is also called *cupiditas*" (*De vitiis*, 3.34 [PL 112:1364]).

94 *Visio Wettini*, verses 500–01 (ed. E. Duemmler, MGH Poet 2 [Berlin, 1884], p. 320). Hrabanus, *De eccl. disc.*, 3 (PL 112:1244). On the *Visio*, see Brunhölzl, *Geschichte*, pp. 348–49; F. J. E. Raby, *A History of Christian-Latin Poetry*, second ed. (Oxford, 1953), pp. 183–84.

95 *Ep.*, 16 (MGH Epistolae 4:43). For Odo of Cluny, see Alexander Murray, *Reason and Society in the Middle Ages* (Oxford, 1978), p. 78.

EPILOGUE: FUTURE PERSPECTIVES

1 Rather of Verona uses the combination of *cupiditas* and *avaritia* as his regular designations for the vice in his sermons: *Sermo 2 de Quadragesima*, 8 (ed. P. L. D. Reid, CCM 46 [Turnhout, 1976], p. 67); *Sermo in Cena Domini*, 3 (CCM 46:99); *Sermo de octavis Paschae*, 5 (CCM 46:175). In *Contra philargyriam*, 3 (PL 145:533–34), Peter Damiani notes that the worst form of avarice is to both seek others' goods and retain one's own.

2 Burchard of Worms' influential *Decretorum libri*, 19.6, for example, repeats Gregory's list of vices as an octad and combines his sub-sins with material from the Evagrian/Cassianic tradition (PL 140:977); compare Morton Bloomfield, *The Seven Deadly Sins: An Introduction to the History of a Religious Concept* ([East Lansing, Mich.], 1952; repr. 1967), p. 98. For Pirminius' order of sins, see Wulfstan, *Homilies*, 10c (ed. D. Bethurum [Oxford, 1957], p. 203; and cf. her note, pp. 328–29) and 10b (p. 196 – the Latin version of the homily, closer to Pirminius, upon which 10c is based); and a work on confession which may depend on Wulfstan's homily (ed. H. Sauer in "Zwei spätaltenglische Beichtermahnungen aus Hs. Cotton Tiberius A.III.," *Anglia* 98 [1980], 27).

3 Rather of Verona, for example, speaks of the rich and merchants sinning by avarice and usury in *Praeloquiorum libri*, 1.17 and 1.5 (PL 136:178–84, 160). For Ælfric's justification of merchant activity, see his *Colloquy*, lines 149–66 (ed. G. N. Garmonsway, rev. ed., Exeter Medieval English Texts 12 [Exeter, 1978], pp. 33–34). For the influence of Augustine on this passage, see Eric Colledge, "An Allusion to Augustine in Ælfric's *Colloquy*," *Review of English Studies* N.S. 12 (1961), 180–81; and see the discussion in Earl R. Anderson, "Social Idealism in Ælfric's *Colloquy*," *ASE* 3 (1974), 154; Stanley B. Greenfield and Daniel G. Calder, *A New Critical History of Old English Literature* (New York and London, 1986), p. 87.

4 J. M. Wallace-Hadrill, *The Barbarian West 400–1000*, rev. ed. (Oxford, 1996),

p. 112. On coinage in the post-Carolingian period, see Peter Spufford, *Money and its Use in Medieval Europe* (Cambridge, 1988), pp. 74–86.

5 Mark R. Cohen, *Under Crescent and Cross: The Jews in the Middle Ages* (Princeton, 1994), pp. 79–80.

6 For the phrase "mercatores, id est, Judei et ceteri mercatores," see Markus Wenninger, "Juden und Christen als Geldgeber im hohen und späten Mittelalter," in A. Ebenbauer and K. Zatloukal, eds., *Die Juden in ihrer mittelalterlichen Umwelt* (Vienna, 1991), p. 282; Robert S. Lopez, *The Commercial Revolution of the Middle Ages 950–1350* (Englewood Cliffs, 1971), pp. 60–62.

7 Lester K. Little, *Religious Poverty and the Profit Economy in Medieval Europe* (London, 1978), pp. 19–41.

8 *Rodulfi Glabri Historiarum libri quinque*, 4.2 (ed. and trans. J. France [Oxford, 1989]), p. 172. *Filargiria* is, of course, the technical term for the vice inherited from Cassian which remained common in a monastic environment even when the understanding of the vice was indebted to Gregory the Great; compare Conrad Leyser, "Cities of the Plain: The Rhetoric of Sodomy in Peter Damian's 'Book of Gomorrah'," *Romanic Review* 86 (1995), 200 n. 48.

9 *De contemptu saeculi*, 6 (PL 145:256).

10 Besides the important study by John A. Yunck, *The Lineage of Lady Meed: The Development of Mediaeval Venality Satire*, The University of Notre Dame, Publications in Mediaeval Studies 17 (Notre Dame, IN, 1963), see for the later developments in reflections on avarice E. M. Katharina Brett, "Avarice and Largesse: A Study of the Theme in Moral-Satirical Poetry in Provençal, Latin and Old French, 1100–1300," Dissertation, University of Cambridge, 1986.

11 Egbert of Liège, *Fecunda ratis*, 1.1252 (ed. E. Voigt [Halle, 1889], p. 179). See Yunck, *The Lineage of Lady Meed*, p. 62.

12 Cf. Josef Benzinger, *Invectiva in Romam. Romkritik im Mittelalter vom 9. bis zum 12. Jahrhundert*, Historische Studien 404 (Lübeck and Hamburg, 1968), pp. 91–93.

13 For early developments in Romanesque sculpture in the Auvergne, see Priscilla Baumann, "The Deadliest Sin: Warnings against Avarice and Usury on Romanesque Capitals in Auvergne," *Church History* 59,1 (1990), 7–18; J. Martin-Bagnaudez, "Les représentations romans de l'avare: Etude iconographique," *Revue d'Histoire de la Spiritualité* 50 (1974), 397–432.

14 Gerhoh of Reichersberg, *De quarta vigilia noctis*, 11 (ed. E. Sackur, MGH Libelli de lite 3 [Hanover, 1897], pp. 509–10). See Henrietta Leyser, *Hermits and the New Monasticism: A Study of Religious Communities in Western Europe 1000–1150* (London, 1984), pp. 55–56; B. McGinn, ed., *Visions of the End* (New York, 1979), pp. 104–05; Peter Classen, *Gerhoch von Reichersberg: eine Biographie mit einem Anhang über die Quellen, ihre handschriftliche Überlieferung und ihre Chronologie* (Wiesbaden, 1960), pp. 292–98.

15 *Analecta Hymnica medii aevi*, ed. G. M. Dreves and C. Blume, vol. 45b (Leipzig, 1915; repr. New York, 1961), p. 74. See Dimitri Scheludko, "Klagen über den Verfall der Welt bei den Trobadors. Allegorische Darstellungen des Kampfes der Tugenden und der Laster," *Neuphilologische Mitteilungen* 44 (1943), 25.

16 Adso Dervensis, *De ortu et tempore Antichristi* (ed. D. Verhelst, CCM 45 [Turnhout, 1976], pp. 22–23, 26).

17 For Albuin's *Liber scintillarum collectus ab Albuino heremita*, addressed to Heribert, archbishop in Cologne; *Liber de virtutibus ad Arnaldum, Pariacensem canonicum* (the two works with the tract on the Antichrist); and *Liber Albuini*, see Adso Dervensis, *De ortu et tempore Antichristi necnon et tractatus, qui ab eo dependunt*, ed. D. Verhelst, CCM 45 (Turnhout, 1976), pp. 55–89.

18 Paris, Bibliothèque Nationale, MS. lat. 2780, fol. 69v: "Si itaque poteris omnia perficere, quae hic inueneris scripta, scio pro certo, quod secura uenies in die iudicii ante tribunal ihesu christi et defensa ab omnibus inimicis possidebis perpetuam coronam in coelis . . ."

19 Johannes Fried, "Endzeiterwartung um die Jahrtausendwende," *Deutsches Archiv für Erforschung des Mittelalters* 45 (1989), 439.

20 In Aquitaine at Saint-Martial, for example, Ademar of Chabannes worked on the *Psychomachia* and later copied Ps.-Nilus' *De octo vitiosis cogitationibus*. On Ademar, see Richard Landes, *Relics, Apocalypse, and the Deceits of History: Ademar of Chabannes, 989–1034* (Cambridge, MA, 1995).

21 Henri Maisonneuve, *La morale chrétienne d'après les conciles des Xe et XIe siècles*, Analecta mediaevalia Namurcensia 15 (Louvain and Lille, 1963), pp. 7–9, 31–32.

22 *Apologeticus* (PL 139:466A).

23 On the implications of simony for the laity, see Auguste Dumas in Emile Amann and Auguste Dumas, *L'Eglise au pouvoir des laiques (888–1057)*, Histoire de l'Eglise depuis les origines jusqu'à nos jours 7 (Paris, 1948), p. 473.

24 Vienne, Arch. Dépt., carton 3, no. 50: ". . . nostris temporibus crescente cupiditate videmus invadi, et seculi imminente fine, cum homines brevior vita perurgeat, atrocior cupiditas p<er>urget." I am grateful to Richard Landes for giving me access to this charter and to Georges Pon for the transcription I have used.

25 Lactantius, *Div. Inst.*, 7.15.7–8 (ed. S. Brandt, CSEL 19 [Vienna, 1890], pp. 631–32). See Bernard McGinn, *Apocalyptic Spirituality* (New York, 1979), pp. 57–58.

Bibliography

I PRIMARY SOURCES

1 Greek and Oriental (Hebrew, Syriac, Coptic)

Acta apostolorum apocrypha. Ed. R. A. Lipsius and M. Bonnet. 2 vols. Leipzig, 1891–1903.

Apophthegmata patrum. PG 65:72–440. Paris, 1858.

Ed. F. Nau. In: "Histoires des solitaires égyptiens." *Revue de l'Orient Chrétien* 12 (1907) 43–69, 171–89, 393–413; 13 (1908) 47–66, 266–97; 14 (1909) 357–79; 17 (1912) 204–11, 294–301; 18 (1913) 137–46.

Athanasius of Alexandria. *Opera omnia*. 4 vols. PG 25–28. Paris, 1884–87.

Barnabas. *Epistle*. Ed. and trans. P. Prigent and R. Kraft. SC 172. Paris, 1971.

Basil the Great. *Lettres*. Ed. and trans. Y. Courtonne. 3 vols. Paris, 1957–66.

Opera omnia. 4 vols. PG 29–32. Paris, 1885–88.

Basil the Great? *Admonitio ad filium spiritualem*. Ed. P. Lehmann. Sitzungsberichte der Bayerischen Akademie der Wissenschaften. Phil.-hist. Klasse. Jahrgang 1955, Heft 7. Munich, 1955.

Bion of Borysthenes. *A Collection of the Fragments with Introduction and Commentary*. Ed. J. F. Kindstrand. Acta Universitatis Upsaliensis. Studia Graeca Upsaliensia 11. Uppsala, 1976.

Chrysostom, John. *Opera omnia*. 18 vols. PG 47–64. Paris, 1862–63.

Clement of Alexandria. *Paedagogus*. Ed. O. Stählin. Third ed. Ed. U. Treu. GCS 12. Berlin, 1972. Pp. 87–292.

Protrepticus. Ed. O. Stählin. Third ed. Ed. U. Treu. GCS 12. Berlin, 1972. Pp. 1–86.

Quis dives salvetur? Ed. O. Stählin. GCS 17. Leipzig, 1909. Pp. 157–91.

Stromata, Books I-VI. Ed. O. Stählin. Fourth ed. Ed. L. Früchtel. GCS 52 [15]. Berlin, 1985. *Books VII-VIII*. Ed. O. Stählin. GCS 17. Leipzig, 1909. Pp. 1–102.

Clement of Rome. See *Patres apostolici*.

Pseudo-Clementines. Homiliae. Ed. B. Rehm. GCS 42. Berlin, 1953.

Didaché. Ed. and trans. W. Rordorf and A. Tuilier. SC 248. Paris, 1978.

The Didascalia Apostolorum in Syriac. Ed. and trans. A. Vööbus. 4 vols. Corpus Scriptorum Christianorum Orientalium 401–02, 407–08; Scriptores Syri 175–76, 179–80. Louvain, 1979.

Bibliography

Didymus the Blind. *Kommentar zu Hiob (Tura-Papyrus)*. Ed. and trans. A. Henrichs, U. Hagedorn, D. Hagedorn, and L. Koenen. Vol. 1–. Papyrologische Texte und Abhandlungen 1–. Bonn, 1968–.

Opera omnia. PG 39. Paris, 1863.

Evagrius Ponticus. *Antirrheticus*. Ed. W. Frankenberg. In: *Euagrius Ponticus*. Abhandlungen der königlichen Gesellschaft der Wissenschaften zu Göttingen. Phil.-hist. Klasse. N.F. 13,2. Berlin, 1912.

Capita cognoscitiva. Ed. J. Muyldermans. In: "Evagriana." *Le Muséon* 44 (1931) 51–57.

Capita paraenetica. PG 79:1249–61. Paris, 1865.

De diversis malignis cogitationibus. PG 79:1200–33. Paris, 1865. PG 40:1240–44. Paris, 1863.

De octo spiritibus malitiae. PG 79:1145–64. Paris, 1865.

De vitiis quae opposita sunt virtutibus. PG 79:1140–44. Paris, 1865.

Rerum monachalium rationes. PG 40:1252–64. Paris, 1863.

Tractatus ad Eulogium. PG 79:1093–1140. Paris, 1865.

Traité Pratique, ou le Moine. Ed. and trans. A. and C. Guillaumont. 2 vols. SC 170–71. Paris, 1971.

Gregory Nazianzen. *Discours*. Ed. J. Mossay. SC 270. Paris, 1980.

Opera omnia. 4 vols. PG 35–38. Paris, 1862–85.

De vita sua. Ed. and trans. C. Jungck. Heidelberg, 1974.

Gregory of Nyssa. *De pauperibus amandis orationes duo*. Ed. A. Van Heck. Leiden, 1964.

De virginitate. Ed. and trans. M. Aubineau. SC 119. Paris, 1966.

Opera. Vol. 1–. Berlin and Leiden, 1921–.

Opera omnia. 3 vols. PG 44–46. Paris, 1863.

Gregory Presbyter. *Vita s. patris nostri Gregorii theologi*. PG 35:244–304. Paris, 1885.

Hermas. *The Shepherd of Hermas*. Ed. M. Whittaker. GCS 48. Berlin, 1956.

Hippolytus Romanus. *Die Canones Hippolyti*. Ed. H. Achelis. TU 6,4. Leipzig, 1891.

Irenaeus of Lyon. *Adversus haereses*. Ed. and trans. A. Rousseau *et al.* 9 vols. SC 263–64, 293–94, 210–11, 100/1–2, 152–53. Paris, 1965–82.

Josephus, Flavius. *The Jewish War*. Ed. and trans. H. St.J. Thackeray. Cambridge, MA, 1927; repr. 1967.

Libanius. *Discours moraux*. Ed. and trans. B. Schouler. Université Lyon II – U.E.R. des Sciences de l'Antiquité. Institut F. Courby E.R.A. 60. Paris, 1973.

Lucian of Samosata. *Opera*. Ed. K. Jacobitz. 3 vols. Leipzig, 1881–1907.

Opera. Ed. M. D. Macleod. Vol. 1–. Oxford, 1972–.

Macarius/Symeon. *Epistola magna*. Ed. R. Staats. Abhandlungen der Akademie der Wissenschaften in Göttingen. Phil.-hist. Klasse. 3. Folge 134. Göttingen, 1984.

Homélies propres à la Collection III. Ed. and trans. V. Desprez. SC 275. Paris, 1980.

Methodius Olympus. *De vita*. Ed. G. Bonwetsch. GCS 27. Leipzig, 1917. Pp. 207–16.

Nilus. *Opera omnia*. PG 79. Paris, 1865.

Ps.-Nilus. *De octo vitiosis cogitationibus*. PG 79:1436–72. Paris, 1865.

Oracula Sibyllina. Ed. J. Geffcken. GCS 8. Leipzig, 1902.

Origen. *Commentaires inédits des psaumes*. Ed. R. Cadiou. Paris, 1936.

Bibliography

Homiliae in Jeremiam. Ed. P. Nautin. Trans. P. Husson and P. Nautin. 2 vols. SC 232, 238. Paris, 1976–77.

"Origen on I Corinthians." Ed. C. Jenkins. *Journal of Theological Studies* 9 (1908) 231–47, 353–72, 500–14.

Philocalie 21–27 sur le libre arbitre. Ed. and trans. E. Junod. SC 226. Paris, 1976.

Werke. 12 vols. GCS 2; 3; 6 (second ed.); 10; 22; 29; 30; 33; 38; 40; 41; 41, 2 (second ed.); 49 (second ed. of vol. 35). Leipzig and Berlin, 1899–1983.

Orsiesius. *Liber Orsiesii*. Ed. A. Boon. In: *Pachomiana Latina*. Bibliothèque de la Revue d'Histoire Ecclésiastique 7. Louvain, 1932. Pp. 109–47.

Pachomius. *Oeuvres de s. Pachôme et de ses disciples*. Ed. and trans. L.-Th. Lefort. Corpus Scriptorum Christianorum Orientalium 159–60, Scriptores Coptici 23–24. Louvain, 1964–65.

Praecepta. Trans. Jerome. Ed. A. Boon. In: *Pachomiana Latina*. Bibliothèque de la Revue d'Histoire Ecclésiastique 7. Louvain, 1932. Pp. 1–74.

The Bohairic Life of Pachomius. Trans. A. Veilleux. In: *Pachomian Koinonia* 1. Cistercian Studies Series 45. Kalamazoo, Mich., 1980. Pp. 23–295.

Palladius. *Historia Lausiaca*. Ed. E. C. Butler. 2 vols. Texts and Studies 6, 1–2. Cambridge, 1898–1904; repr. Hildesheim, 1967.

Patres apostolici. Ed. F. X. Funk. Second ed. 2 vols. Tübingen, 1901.

Philo of Alexandria. *Opera quae supersunt*. Ed. L. Cohn *et al*. 8 vols. Berlin, 1896–1930.

Plato. *Opera*. Ed. J. Burnet. 5 vols. Oxford, 1900–07; repr. 1950–54.

Plutarch. *Moralia*. Ed. G. N. Bernardakis. 7 vols. Leipzig, 1888–96.

Œuvres morales. Vol. 6. Ed. R. Flacelière. Paris, 1974.

Polycarp of Smyrna. *Epistulae ad Philippenses*. Ed. and trans. T. Camelot. Fourth ed. SC 10. Paris, 1969. Pp. 157–93.

Septuaginta. Id est Vetus Testamentum graece iuxta LXX interpretes. Ed. A. Rahlfs. Seventh ed. 2 vols. Stuttgart, 1935.

Sextus Pythagoreus? *The Sentences of Sextus*. Ed. H. Chadwick. Cambridge, 1959.

Talmud Bavli. Hebrew–English Edition of the Babylonian Talmud. Ed. I. Epstein, trans. M. Simon *et al*. 30 vols. London, 1990.

The Testaments of the Twelve Patriarchs. Ed. M. de Jonge. Pseudepigrapha Veteris Testamenti Graece 1,2. Leiden, 1978.

Theophilus. *Pascal Letter*. See Jerome.

Vita s. Syncleticae. PG 28:1485–1558. Paris, 1887.

2 Latin and Vernacular (Old English)

Abbo of Fleury. *Opera omnia*. PL 139. Paris, 1880.

Admonitio ad filium spiritualem. See Basil the Great.

Adso Dervensis. *De ortu et tempore Antichristi*. Ed. D. Verhelst. CCM 45. Turnhout, 1976. Pp. 1–30.

Ælfric. *Colloquy*. Ed. G. N. Garmonsway. Rev. ed. Exeter Medieval Texts 12. Exeter, 1978.

Homilies of Ælfric, A Supplementary Collection. Ed. J. C. Pope. 2 vols. EETS os 259–60. London, 1967–68.

Bibliography

Albuin. *Liber Albuini*. In: Paris, Bibliothèque Nationale, MS lat. 2780.

Alcuin. *Epistolae*. Ed. E. Duemmler. MGH Epistolae 4. Berlin, 1895. Pp. 1–481.

   Liber de virtutibus et vitiis, cap. 30. Ed. P. E. Szarmach. "The Latin Tradition of Alcuin's *Liber de Virtutibus et Vitiis*, cap. xxvii–xxxv, with Special Reference to Vercelli Homily xx," *Mediaevalia* 12 (1989) 13–41.

   Opera omnia. 2 vols. PL 100–01. Paris, 1851.

   Versus de patribus regibus et sanctis Euboricensis ecclesiae. Ed. and trans. P. Godman. In: *Alcuin: The Bishops, Kings and Saints of York*. Oxford, 1982.

Aldhelm of Malmesbury. *De virginitate*. Ed. R. Ehwald. MGH Auctores antiquissimi 15. Berlin, 1919. Pp. 211–471.

King Alfred, trans. *King Alfred's Old English Version of Boethius*. Ed. W. J. Sedgefield. Oxford, 1899; repr. Darmstadt, 1968.

   The Pastoral Care edited from British Museum MS. Cotton Otho B. ii. Ed. I. Carlson. Part 1. Acta Universitatis Stockholmiensis. Stockholm Studies in English 34. Stockholm, 1975. Part 2. Completed L.-G. Hallander. Acta Universitatis Stockholmiensis. Stockholm Studies in English 48. Stockholm, 1978.

Eine altenglische Übersetzung von Alcuins "De virtutibus et vitiis," Kap. 20. Ed. R. Torkar. Münchener Universitäts-Schriften. Texte und Untersuchungen zur Englischen Philologie 7. Munich, 1981.

Ambrose of Milan. *De Tobia*. Ed. M. Giacchero. Publicazioni dell' Istituto di Filologica Classica e Medioevale 19. Genoa, 1965.

   Opera. CCL 14–. Turnhout, 1957–.

   Opera. CSEL 32–. Vienna, 1897–.

   Opera omnia. 4 vols. PL 14–17. Paris, 1879–82.

Ambrosiaster. *Commentarius in epistulas Paulinas*. Ed. H. J. Vogels. CSEL 81,1–3. Vienna, 1966–69.

Ambrosius Autpertus. *Opera*. Ed. R. Weber. CCM 27–27B. Turnhout, 1975–79.

Analecta hymnica medii aevi. Ed. G. M. Dreves and C. Blume. 55 vols. Leipzig, 1886–1922; repr. New York, 1961.

Arnobius the Elder. *Aduersus nationes libri vii*. Ed. A. Reifferscheid. CSEL 4. Vienna, 1875.

Augustine of Hippo. *Opera*. CCL 27–. Turnhout, 1954–.

   Opera. CSEL 12–. Vienna, 1887–.

   Opera omnia. 16 vols. PL 32–47. Paris, 1865–1902.

   Sermones. Ed. G. Morin. PLS 2:657–708. Paris, 1960.

   Sermones selecti duodeviginti. Ed. C. Lambot. Stromata Patristica et Medievalia 1. Utrecht, Brussels, 1950.

Bede. *Opera*. CCL 118A–. Turnhout, 1955–.

Benedict of Nursia. *Regula*. Ed. and trans. A. de Vogüé. 7 vols. SC 181–86A. Paris, 1971–77.

Biblia sacra. Iuxta vulgatam versionem. Ed. R. Weber. 2 vols. Stuttgart, 1969.

The Blickling Homilies. Ed. R. Morris. 3 vols. EETS os 58, 63, 73. London, 1874–80.

Boethius. *Opera*. CCL 94–. Turnhout, 1957–.

Boniface. *Aenigmata Bonifatii*. Ed. Fr. Glorie. In: *Collectiones aenigmatum Merovingicae aetatis*, I. CCL 133. Turnhout, 1968. Pp. 273–343.

Bibliography

Burchard of Worms. *Opera omnia.* PL 140. Paris, 1880.

Caesarius of Arles. *Opera.* CCL 103–. Turnhout, 1953–.

Opera omnia. PL 67. Paris, 1865.

Regula sanctarum virginum. Ed. M. C. McCarthy. The Catholic University of America. Studies in Mediaeval History. N.S. 16. Washington, D.C., 1960.

De caritate et avaritia. Ed. E. Duemmler. MGH Poet 2. Berlin, 1884. Pp. 255–57.

Cassian, John. *Opera.* Ed. M. Petschenig. 2 vols. CSEL 13, 17. Vienna, 1886–88.

Cassiodorus. *Institutiones.* Ed. R. A. B. Mynors. Oxford, 1937; repr. 1963.

Opera. CCL 96–. Turnhout, 1958–.

Charlemagne. *Capitula ecclesiastica.* Ed. A. Boretius. MGH Leges 2, Capitularia Regum Francorum 1. Hanover, 1883. Pp. 178–79.

Charter of Saint-Hilaire in Poitiers. In Vienne, Arch. Dépt., carton 3, no. 50.

Chromatius of Aquileia. *Opera.* Ed. R. Etaix and J. Lemarié. 2 vols. CCL 9A, 9A Supplementum. Turnhout, 1974–77.

Cicero. *De finibus bonorum et malorum.* Ed. J. N. Madvig. Copenhagen, 1876; repr. Hildesheim, 1963.

De officiis libri tres. Ed. P. Fedeli. [Florence], 1965.

Ps.-Cicero. *Rhetorica ad Herennium.* Ed. F. Marx. In: *M. Tulli Ciceronis scripta quae manserunt omnia* 1. Corr. ed. W. Trillitzsch. Leipzig, 1964.

Commonitiuncula. Ed. A. E. Anspach. In: *S. Isidori Hispalensis episcopi Commonitiuncula ad sororem.* Scriptores Ecclesiastici Hispano-Latini Veteris et Medii Aevi 4. Escorial, 1935.

Concilia aevi Karolini. Ed. A. Werminghoff. MGH Leges 3, Concilia 2,1. Hanover, Leipzig, 1906.

Cyprian of Carthage. *Opera.* CCL 3–. Turnhout, 1972–.

Opera omnia. Ed. W. v. Hartel. CSEL 3,1–3. Vienna, 1868–71.

Defensor. *Liber scintillarum.* Ed. H. M. Rochais. CCL 117. Turnhout, 1957. Pp. vii–308.

Egbert of Liège. *Egberts von Lüttich Fecunda ratis zum ersten Mal herausgegeben, auf ihre Quellen zurückgeführt, und erklärt.* Ed. E. Voigt. Halle, 1889.

Eutropius (Bp. of Valencia). *Epistula de octo vitiis.* Ed. M. C. Díaz y Díaz. In *Analecta Wisigothica* I. Acta Salmanticensia, Filosofia y Letras 12,2. Salamanca, 1958. Pp. 27–35.

Gaudentius of Brescia. *Tractatus.* Ed. A. Glueck. CSEL 68. Vienna and Leipzig, 1936.

Gennadius of Marseilles. *De viris inlustribus.* Ed. E. C. Richardson. TU 14,1. Leipzig, 1896. Pp. 57–97.

Gerhoh of Reichersberg. *Libelli selecti.* Ed. E. Sackur. MGH Libelli de lite 3. Hanover, 1897. Pp. 131–525.

Glaber, Rodulfus. *Rodulfi Glabri Historiarum libri quinque.* Ed. and trans. J. France. Oxford, 1989.

Gregory the Great. *Opera.* CCL 140–. Turnhout, 1963–.

Opera omnia. 5 vols. PL 75–79. Paris, 1849–1903.

Gregory of Tours. *Liber de virtutibus s. Martini episcopi.* Ed. B. Krusch. MGH Scriptores rerum Merovingicarum 1,2. Hanover, 1885; repr. 1969. Pp. 134–211.

Hilary of Poitiers. *Opera*. CSEL 22–. Vienna, 1891–.

Hincmar of Reims. *Opera omnia*. PL 125, 126:9–648. Paris, 1852.

Horace. *Opera*. Ed. F. Klingner. Leipzig, 1970.

Hrabanus Maurus. *De institutione clericorum libri tres*. Ed. A. Knoepfler. Veröffent-lichungen aus dem Kirchenhistorischen Seminar München 5. Munich, 1900.
Opera omnia. 6 vols. PL 107–12. Paris, 1851–52.

Ps.-Hrabanus. *De vitiis et virtutibus et peccatorum satisfactione*. PL 112:1335–98. Paris, 1852.

Innocent III, Pope. *Opera omnia*. 4 vols. PL 214–17. Paris, 1889–91.

Isidore of Seville. *Etymologiarum sive originum libri 20*. Ed. W. M. Lindsay. 2 vols. Oxford, 1911.
Opera omnia. 4 vols. PL 81–84. Paris, 1850.

Isidore of Seville? *Liber numerorum*. PL 83:179–200. Paris, 1850.

Jean de Fécamp. *Oratio de vitiis et virtutibus*. Ed. J. Leclercq. In: "La prière au sujet des vices et des vertues." *Analecta monastica* 2. Studia Anselmiana 31. Rome, 1953. Pp. 3–17.

Jerome. *Opera*. CCL 72–. Turnhout, 1958–.
Opera. CSEL 54–. Vienna, 1910–.
Opera omnia. 9 vols. PL 22–30. Paris, 1845–89.

Jonas of Orléans. *De institutione laicali*. PL 106:121–278. Paris, 1851.
De institutione regia. Ed. J. Reviron. In: *Jonas d'Orléans et son "De institutione regia."* L'église et l'état au moyen âge 1. Paris, 1930.

Julianus Pomerius. *De vita contemplativa libri tres*. PL 59:415–520. Paris, 1862.

Juvenal. *Saturae*. Ed. A. E. Housman. Cambridge, 1956.

Lactantius. *Divinae institutiones, Book 5*. Ed. and trans. P. Monat. 2 vols. SC 204–05. Paris, 1973.
Opera omnia. Ed. S. Brandt *et al.* CSEL 19–. Vienna, 1890–.

Laurentius of Novae. *Scripta universa*. PL 66:87–124. Paris, 1866.

Libri Carolini sive Caroli Magni capitulare de imaginibus. Ed. H. Bastgen. MGH Leges 3. Concilia 2 Supplementum. Hanover and Leipzig, 1924.

Martin of Braga. *Opera omnia*. Ed. C. W. Barlow. Papers and Monographs of the American Academy in Rome 12. New Haven, 1950.

Maximus of Turin. *Sermones*. Ed. A. Mutzenbecher. CCL 23. Turnhout, 1962.

Odo of Cluny. *Opera omnia*. PL 133. Paris, 1881.

Orientius. *Carmina*. Ed. R. Ellis. In: *Poetae christiani minores I*. CSEL 16. Vienna, 1888. Pp. 191–261.

Othlo of St. Emmeram. *Opera omnia*. PL 146. Paris, 1884.

Ovid. *Metamorphoses*. Ed. W. S. Anderson. Second ed. Leipzig, 1982.

Pascasius of Dumium. *A Versão por Pascásio de Dume dos Apophthegmata Patrum*. Ed. J. Geraldes Freire. 2 vols. Coimbre, 1971.

Paulinus of Aquileia. *Opera omnia*. PL 99:17–684. Paris, 1851.

Paulinus of Nola. *Opera*. Ed. W. v. Hartel. 2 vols. CSEL 29–30. Vienna, 1894.

Persius. *Saturae*. Ed. W. V. Clausen. Oxford, 1959.

Peter Chrysologus. *Collectio sermonum*. Ed. A. Olivar. CCL 24–24B. Turnhout, 1975–82.

Bibliography

Peter Damiani. *Opera omnia.* PL 144–145. Paris, 1867.

Pirminius. *Scarapsus.* Ed. G. Jecker. In: *Die Heimat des hl. Pirmin.* Beiträge zur Geschichte des alten Mönchtums und des Benediktinerordens 13. Münster, 1927.

Poenitentiale Mediolanense. Ed. O. Seebass. In: "Ein bisher noch nicht veröffentlichtes Poenitential einer Bobbienser Handschrift der Ambrosiana." *Deutsche Zeitschrift für Kirchenrecht* 6 (1896–97) 24–50.

Poggii Florentini historia convivalis disceptative de avaritia. In: *Opera omnia.* Basel, 1538. Repr. in *Poggius Bracciolini. Opera omnia.* Ed. R. Fubini. Vol. 1. Turin, 1964.

Porcarius. *Monita.* Ed. A. Wilmart. In: "Les *Monita* de l'abbé Porcaire." *Revue bénédictine* 26 (1909) 475–80.

Prebiarum de multorium exemplaribus. Ed. R. E. McNally. In: *Scriptores Hiberniae minores* I. CCL 108B. Turnhout, 1973. Pp. 153–71.

Prosper of Aquitaine. *Opera.* CCL 68A–. Turnhout, 1972–.

Prudentius. *Carmina.* Ed. M. P. Cunningham. CCL 126. Turnhout, 1966.

Publilius Syrus. *Sententiae.* Ed. O. Friedrich. Berlin, 1880; repr. Hildesheim, 1964.

Quodvultdeus. *Opera tributa.* Ed. R. Braun. CCL 60. Turnhout, 1976.

Rather of Verona. *The Complete Works of Rather of Verona.* Trans. Peter L. D. Reid. Medieval and Renaissance Texts and Studies 76. Binghamton, N.Y., 1991.

 Opera minora. Ed. P. L. D. Reid. CCM 46. Turnhout, 1976.

 Opera omnia. PL 136. Paris, 1881.

Regula Magistri. Ed. A. de Vogüé. SC 105. Paris, 1964.

Regula orientalis. Ed. A. de Vogüé. SC 298. Paris, 1982.

Sacrorum conciliorum . . . collectio. Ed. J. M. Mansi. 31 vols. Venice, 1759–1798.

Sallust. *Catilinae coniuratio.* Ed. A. Kurfess. Third ed. Leipzig, 1968.

Salvian of Marseilles. *Œuvres.* Ed. and trans. G. Lagarrigue. 2 vols. SC 176, 220. Paris, 1971–75.

Seneca. *De beneficiis.* Ed. and trans. F. Préchac. 2 vols. Paris, 1927–61.

 Ad Lucilium epistulae morales. Ed. L. D. Reynolds. 2 vols. Oxford, 1965.

Smaragdus of St. Mihiel. *Opera omnia.* PL 102:9–976. Paris, 1865.

Sulpicius Severus. *Opera.* Ed. C. Halm. CSEL 1. Vienna, 1866.

Taio. *Sententiarum libri quinque.* PL 80:727–990. Paris, 1850.

Tertullian. *Opera.* 2 vols. CCL 1–2. Turnhout, 1954.

Theodulf of Orléans. *Capitulare.* Ed. C. de Clercq. In: *La législation religieuse franque de Clovis à Charlemagne.* Université de Louvain. Recueil de travaux publiés par les membres des Conférences d'Histoire et de Philologie. 2e serie 38. Louvain and Paris, 1936. Pp. 321–51.

 Carmina. Ed. E. Duemmler. MGH Poet 1,2. Berlin, 1881. Pp. 437–581.

Theodulfi capitula in England. Ed. H. Sauer. Münchener Universitäts-Schriften. Texte und Untersuchungen zur Englischen Philologie 8. Munich, 1978.

Tractatus de divitiis. Ed. C. P. Caspari. In: *Briefe, Abhandlungen und Predigten.* Christiana, 1890. Pp. 25–67.

PLS 1:1380–1418. Paris, 1958.

Bibliography

Twelfth-Century Homilies in MS. Bodley 343. Ed. A. O. Belfour. EETS os 137. London, 1909; repr. 1962.

Valerianus of Cimiez. *Scripta universa*. PL 52:681–836. Paris, 1894.

"Vercelli Homily XX." Ed. P. E. Szarmach. *Mediaeval Studies* 35 (1973) 1–25; 36 (1974) 493–94.

Virgil. *Opera*. Ed. R. A. B. Mynors. Oxford, 1969; repr. with correctlions 1972.

Vitae patrum. PL 73. Paris, 1879.

Walahfrid Strabo. *Carmina*. Ed. E. Duemmler. MGH Poet 2. Berlin, 1884. Pp. 259–423.

Wulfstan. *Homilies*. Ed. D. Bethurum. Oxford, 1957.

Zeno of Verona. *Tractatus*. Ed. B. Löfstedt. CCL 22. Turnhout, 1971.

"Zwei spätaltenglische Beichtermahnungen aus Hs. Cotton Tiberius A.III." Ed. H. Sauer. *Anglia* 98 (1980) 1–33.

II MODERN SCHOLARSHIP

Adams, Jeremy D. *The Populus of Augustine and Jerome*. New Haven and London, 1971.

Adinolfi, Marco. "Le frodi di 1 Tess. 4,6a e l'epiclerato." *Bibbia e Oriente* 18 (1976) 29–38.

Aicher, G. *Kamel und Nadelöhr*. Neutestamentliche Abhandlungen 1,5. Münster, 1908.

Altaner, Berthold. "Der Stand der Isidorforschung. Ein kritischer Bericht über die seit 1910 erschienene Literatur." In: *Miscellanea Isidoriana*. Rome, 1936. Pp. 1–32.

Altaner, Berthold and Alfred Stuiber. *Patrologie*. Ninth rev. ed. Freiburg, 1980.

Amann, Emile and Auguste Dumas. *L'Eglise au pouvoir des laiques (888–1057)*. Histoire de l'Eglise, depuis les origines jusqu'à nos jours 7. Paris, 1948.

Amand, David. *L'ascèse monastique de Saint Basile*. Maredsous, 1949.

Anderson, Earl R. "Social Idealism in Ælfric's *Colloquy*." *ASE* 3 (1974) 153–62.

Angenendt, Arnold. *Monachi Peregrini*. Dissertation Münster. Munich, 1972.

Anspach, A. E. "Das Fortleben Isidors im VII. bis IX. Jahrhundert." In: *Miscellanea Isidoriana*. Rome, 1936. Pp. 323–56.

Antin, Paul. "Les idées morales de S. Jérome." *MSR* 14 (1957) 135–50.

"Saint Jérome et l'Argent." *La Vie Spirituelle* 79 (1948) 285–93.

Anton, Hans Hubert. *Fürstenspiegel und Herrscherethos in der Karolingerzeit*. Bonner Historische Forschungen 32. Bonn, 1968.

Asmus, J. R. "Gregorius von Nazianz und sein Verhältnis zum Kynismus." *Theologische Studien und Kritiken* 67 (1894) 314–39.

Bacht, Heinrich. "L'importance de l'idéal monastique de saint Pachôme pour l'histoire du monachisme chrétien." *RAM* 26 (1950) 308–26.

"Studien zum 'Liber Orsiesii'." *Historisches Jahrbuch* 77 (1958) 98–124.

Das Vermächtnis des Ursprungs. Studien zur Theologie des geistlichen Lebens 5. Würzburg, 1972.

Baldwin, John W. *The Medieval Theories of the Just Price: Romanists, Canonists, and*

Bibliography

Theologians in the Twelfth and Thirteenth Centuries. Transactions of the American Philosophical Society, N.S. 49,4. Philadelphia, 1959.

Bardy, G. "Apatheia." *Dictionnaire de Spiritualité ascétique et mystique.* Vol. 1. 1937. Cols. 727–46.

Barnes, Timothy D. "Angel of Light or Mystic Initiate? The Problem of the *Life* of Anthony." *Journal of Theological Studies* N.S. 37 (1986) 352–68.

Athanasius and Constantius. Cambridge, MA and London, 1993.

"The Date of the Council of Gangra." *Journal of Theological Studies* N.S. 40 (1989) 121–24.

Barney, Stephan A. *Allegories of History, Allegories of Love.* Hamden, Conn., 1979.

Barsi, Balázs. "La péricope du jeune homme riche dans la litterature paleochretienne." Dissertation Strasbourg, 1982. 2 vols.

Baskin, J. R. "Job as Moral Exemplar in Ambrose." *VC* 35 (1981) 222–31.

Baumann, Priscilla. "The Deadliest Sin: Warnings against Avarice and Usury on Romanesque Capitals in Auvergne." *Church History* 59,1 (1990) 7–18.

Baumeister, Ansgar. *Die Ethik des Pastor Hermae.* Freiburger Theologische Studien 9. Freiburg/Br., 1912.

Beall, Todd. *Josephus' Description of the Essenes Illustrated by the Dead Sea Scrolls.* Society for New Testament Studies, Monograph series 58. Cambridge, 1988.

Beauvery, Robert. "Πλεονεκτεῖν in I Thess 4,6a." *Verbum Domini* 33 (1955) 78–85.

Beck, Henry G. J. *The Pastoral Care of Souls in South-East France During the Sixth Century.* Analecta Gregoriana 51. Rome, 1950.

Benzinger, Josef. *Invectiva in Romam. Romkritik im Mittelalter vom 9. bis zum 12. Jahrhundert.* Historische Studien 404. Lübeck and Hamburg, 1968.

Bernardi, Jean. *La prédication des pères cappadociens.* Publications de la Faculté des Lettres et Sciences Humaines de l'Université de Montpellier 30. Marseilles, 1968.

Berschin, Walter. *Griechisch-lateinisches Mittelalter.* Bern and Munich, 1980.

Bischoff, Bernhard. "Die europäische Verbreitung der Werke Isidors von Sevilla." In: M. C. Díaz y Díaz, ed. *Isidoriana.* Leon, 1961. Pp. 317–44. Repr. in Bernhard Bischoff. *Mittelalterliche Studien.* Stuttgart, 1966. Vol. 1, pp. 171–94.

"Eine verschollene Einteilung der Wissenschaften." *Archives d'histoire doctrinale et littéraire du moyen âge* 25 (1958) 5–20. Repr. in *ibid.* Vol. 1, pp. 273–88.

Bloomfield, Morton. *The Seven Deadly Sins: An Introduction to the History of a Religious Concept.* [East Lansing, Mich.], 1952; repr. 1967.

"A Source of Prudentius' *Psychomachia.*" *Speculum* 18 (1943) 87–90.

Blumenkranz, Bernhard. "Raban Maur et saint Augustine: compilation ou adaptation? A propos du latin biblique." *Revue du Moyen Age Latin* 7 (1951) 97–110.

Bogaert, Raymond. "Changeurs et banquiers chez les pères de l'église." *Ancient Society* 4 (1973) 239–70.

Bohlen, Reinhold. "'Täglich wird ein Nabot niedergeschlagen.' Zur homiletischen Behandlung von 1 Kön 21 in Ambrosius' De Nabuthe." *Trierer Theologische Zeitschrift* 88 (1979) 221–37.

Bolton, W. F. *A History of Anglo-Latin Literature: 597–1066.* Vol. 1. Princeton, 1967.

Bongiovanni, Pietro. *S. Massimo vescovo di Torino e il suo pensiero teologico.*

Pontificium Athenaeum Salesianum. Facultas Theologica. Theses ad Lauream 23. Turin, 1952.

Bori, Pier Cesare. *La chiesa primitiva*. Dipartimento di scienze religiose 2. Brescia, 1977.

Bornhäuser, Karl. *Der Christ und seine Habe nach dem Neuen Testament*. Beiträge zur Förderung christlicher Theologie 38,3. Gütersloh, 1936.

Brändle, Rudolf. *Matth. 25,31–46 im Werk des Johannes Chrysostomos*. Beiträge zur Geschichte der biblischen Exegese 22. Tübingen, 1979.

Brentano, Lujo. "Die wirtschaftlichen Lehren des christlichen Altertums." In *Der wirtschaftende Mensch in der Geschichte*. Leipzig, 1923. Pp. 87–101.

Brett, E. M. Katharina. "Avarice and Largesse. A Study of the Theme in Moral-Satirical Poetry in Provençal, Latin and Old French, 1100–1300." Dissertation, University of Cambridge, 1986.

Brommer, Peter. "Die bischöfliche Gesetzgebung Theodulfs von Orléans." *Zeitschrift der Savigny-Stiftung für Rechtsgeschichte* 91. Kanonistische Abteilung 60 (1974) 1–120.

"Die Rezeption der bischöflichen Kapitularien Theodulfs von Orléans." *Ibid.* 92. Kanonistische Abteilung 61 (1975) 113–60.

Brown, Peter. *Augustine of Hippo: A Biography*. Berkeley and Los Angeles, 1967.
The Body and Society. New York, 1988.

"The Later Roman Empire." *Economic History Review* "Essays in Bibliography and Criticism" 56, 2nd ser. 20 (1967) 327–43. Repr. in Peter Brown. *Religion and Society in the Age of Saint Augustine*. London, 1972. Pp. 46–73.

"Pelagius and his Supporters: Aims and Environment." *Journal of Theological Studies* N.S. 19 (1968) 93–114. Repr. in *ibid.* Pp. 183–207.

Power and Persuasion in Late Antiquity: Towards a Christian Empire. The Curti Lectures, 1988. Madison, 1992.

The Rise of Western Christendom: Triumph and Diversity AD 200–1000. Cambridge, MA and Oxford, 1996.

Brox, Norbert. "Quis ille auctor? Pseudonymität und Anonymität bei Salvian." *VC* 40 (1986) 55–65.

Bruck, Eberhard F. *Kirchenväter und soziales Erbrecht*. Berlin, 1956.

Brunhölzl, Franz. *Geschichte der lateinischen Literatur des Mittelalters*. Vol. 1. Munich, 1975.

Buchheit, Vinzenz. "Die Definition der Gerechtigkeit bei Laktanz und seinen Vorgängern." *VC* 33 (1979) 356–74.

"Goldene Zeit und Paradies auf Erden (Laktanz, inst. 5,5–8)." *Würzburger Jahrbücher für die Altertumswissenschaft* N.F. 4 (1978) 161–85, 5 (1979) 219–35.

Bullough, Donald A. "Hagiography as Patriotism: Alcuin's 'York poem' and the Early Northumbrian 'vitae sanctorum'." In: *Hagiographie, cultures et sociétés IVᵉ–XIIᵉ siècles*. Actes du Colloque organisé à Nanterre et à Paris (2–5 mai 1979). Paris, 1981. Pp. 339–59.

Burns, J. Patout. "Augustine on the Origin and Progress of Evil." In W. S. Babcock, ed. *The Ethics of St. Augustine*. Journal of Religious Ethics: Studies in Religious Ethics 3. Atlanta, 1991. Pp. 79–83.

Bibliography

Cadoux, Cecil J. *The Early Church and the World*. Edinburgh, 1925.

Calafato, Salvatore. *La proprietà privata in S. Ambrogio*. Scrinium Theologicum 6. Turin, 1958.

Capitaine, Wilhelm. *Die Moral des Clemens von Alexandrien*. Paderborn, 1903.

Capmany-Casamitjana, José. *"Miles Christi" en la Espiritualidad de San Cipriano*. Seminario Conciliar de Barcelona. Colectanea San Paciano, Serie Teológia 1. Barcelona, 1956.

Cavalcanti, Elena. "I due discorsi *De pauperibus amandis* di Gregorio di Nissa." *Orientalia Christiana Periodica* 44 (1978) 170–80.

Chadwick, Henry. "The Ascetic Ideal in the History of the Church." In W. J. Sheils, ed. *Studies in Church History* 22. Oxford, 1985. Pp. 1–23. Repr. in Henry Chadwick. *Heresy and Orthodoxy in the Early Church*. Variorum Collected Studies, CS 342. London, 1991.

Early Christian Thought and the Classical Tradition. Oxford, 1966.

"Pachomios and the Ideal of Sanctity." In S. Hackel, ed. *The Byzantine Saint. University of Birmingham Fourteenth Spring Symposium of Byzantine Studies*. Studies Supplementary to Sobornost 5. London, 1981. Pp. 11–24. Repr. in Henry Chadwick. *History and Thought of the Early Church*. Variorum Collected Studies, CS 164. London, 1982.

"The Role of the Christian Bishop in Ancient Society." *The Center for Hermeneutical Studies in Hellenistic and Modern Culture, Protocol of Colloquy 35*. Berkeley, 1980. Repr. in Henry Chadwick. *Heresy and Orthodoxy in the Early Church*. Variorum Collected Studies, CS 342. Aldershot, 1991.

Chadwick, Owen. *John Cassian*. Second ed. Cambridge, 1968.

"Introduction." In John Cassian. *Conferences*. Trans. C. Luibheid. New York, 1985. Pp. 1–36.

Chaffin, Christopher. "Civic Values in Maximus of Turin and his Contemporaries." In: *Forma Futuri: Studi in onore del Cardinale Michele Pellegrino*. Turin, 1975. Pp. 1041–53.

Christophe, Paul. *Cassien et Césaire*. Recherches et Synthèses, Section de morale 2. Gembloux and Paris, 1969.

L'usage chrétien du droit de propriété dans l'Ecriture et la tradition patristique. Théologie, Pastorale et Spiritualité, Recherches et synthèses 14. Paris, 1964.

Clark, M. T. "Augustine on Justice." *Revue des Etudes Augustiniennes* 9 (1963) 87–94.

Classen, Peter. *Gerhoch von Reichersberg: eine Biographie mit einem Anhang über die Quellen, ihre handschriftliche Überlieferung und ihre Chronologie*. Wiesbaden, 1960.

Cohen, Mark R. *Under Crescent and Cross: The Jews in the Middle Ages*. Princeton, 1994.

Colledge, Eric. "An Allusion to Augustine in Ælfric's *Colloquy*." *Review of English Studies* N.S. 12 (1961) 180–81.

Cotogni, Laura. "Sovrapposizione di visioni e di allegorie nella *Psychomachia* di Prudenzio." *Rendiconti della R. Accademia Nazionale dei Lincei*. Classe di scienze morali, storiche e filologiche 6,12. Rome, 1936.

Countryman, L. Wm. *The Rich Christian in the Church of the Early Empire:*

Contradictions and Accommodations. Texts and Studies in Religion 7. New York and Toronto, 1980.

Courcelle, Pierre. *Histoire littéraire des grandes invasions germaniques.* Third ed. Paris, 1964.

Dagens, Claude. *Saint Grégoire le Grand.* Paris, 1977.

Daniélou, Jean. *Platonisme et théologie mystique.* Théologie 2. Paris, 1944.

Dassmann, Ernst. *Die Frömmigkeit des Kirchenvaters Ambrosius von Mailand.* Münsterische Beiträge zur Theologie 29. Münster, 1965.

Davis, Natalie Z. "Gregory Nazianzen in the Service of Humanist Social Reform." *Renaissance Quarterly* 20 (1967) 455–64.

de Clercq, C. "L'influence de la règle de saint Pachôme en Occident." In: *Mélanges d'histoire du moyen âge, dédiés à la mémoire de Louis Halphen.* Paris, 1951. Pp. 169–76.

de Labriolle, P. "Apatheia." In: *Mélanges de philologie, de littérature et d'histoire anciennes offerts à Alfred Ernout.* Paris, 1940. Pp. 215–23.

"Apatheia." *RAC.* Vol. 1. 1950. Cols. 484–87.

de Ste. Croix, G. E. M. *The Class Struggle in the Ancient Greek World.* London, 1981.

"Early Christian Attitudes to Property and Slavery." In: D. Baker, ed. *Church Society and Politics.* Studies in Church History 12. Oxford, 1975. Pp. 1–38.

de Vogüé, Adalbert. "Cassien, le Maître et Benoît." In: J. Gribomont, ed. *Commandements du Seigneur et libération évangélique.* Studia Anselmiana 70. Rome, 1977. Pp. 223–39.

"Grégoire le Grand, lecteur de Grégoire de Tours?" *Analecta Bollandiana* 94 (1976) 225–33.

"Les pièces latines du dossier pachômien: remarques sur quelques publications récentes." *Revue d'Histoire Ecclésiastique* 67 (1972) 26–67.

"Vestiges de l'*Admonitio ad filium spiritualem* du Pseudo-Basile dans la prédication de saint Eloi." *Revue bénédictine* 98 (1988) 18–20.

Degenhardt, H.-J. *Lukas – Evangelist der Armen. Besitz und Besitzverzicht in den Lukanischen Schriften.* Stuttgart, 1965.

Deleani, Simone. *Christum sequi: Etude d'un thème dans l'œuvre de saint Cyprien.* Paris, 1979.

Delhaye, Ph. "Les idées morales de saint Isidore de Séville." *RTAM* 26 (1959) 17–49.

Delling, Gerhard. "Πλεονέκτης, πλεονεκτέω, πλεονεξία." *Theologisches Wörterbuch zum Neuen Testament.* Vol. 6. 1949. Cols. 266–74.

Deman, Th. "Le 'De officiis' de saint Ambroise dans l'histoire de la théologie morale." *Revue des Sciences Philosophiques et Théologiques* 37 (1953) 409–24.

Desprez, Vincent. "Le Pseudo-Macaire." In: J. Gribomont, ed. *Commandements du Seigneur et libération évangélique.* Studia Anselmiana 70. Rome, 1977. Pp. 175–89.

"Les relations entre le Pseudo-Macaire et Saint Basile." In: *ibid.* Pp. 208–21.

Devisse, Jean. *Hincmar: Archevêque de Reims 845–882.* Travaux d'histoire ethico-politique 29. 3 vols. Geneva, 1975–76.

Devoti, Domenico. "Massimo di Torino e il suo pubblico." *Augustinianum* 21 (1981) 153–67.

Díaz y Díaz, Manuel C. "La vie monastique d'après les écrivains wisigothiques (VIIe siècle)." In: *Théologie de la vie monastique.* Théologie 49. Paris, 1961. Pp. 371–73. Repr. in Díaz y Díaz. *Vie chrétienne et culture dans l'Espagne du VIIe au Xe siècles.* Variorum Collected Studies, CS 377. Aldershot, 1992.

Diesner, Hans-Joachim. *Isidor von Sevilla und seine Zeit.* Aufsätze und Vorträge zur Theologie und Religionswissenschaft 57. Berlin, 1973.

   Isidor von Sevilla und das westgotische Spanien. Abhandlungen der Sächsischen Akademie der Wissenschaften zu Leipzig. Phil.-hist. Klasse 67,3. Berlin, 1977.

Dihle, Albrecht. "Gerechtigkeit." *RAC.* Vol. 10. 1978. Cols. 233–360.

Dillon, John. "Plotinus, Philo and Origen on the Grades of Virtue." In: H.-D. Blume and F. Mann, eds. *Platonismus und Christentum. Festschrift für Heinrich Dörrie. JbAC* Ergänzungsband 10. Münster, 1983. Pp. 92–105.

Dirking, Augustinus. "Die Bedeutung des Wortes Apathie beim heiligen Basilius dem Großen." *Theologische Quartalschrift* 134 (1954) 202–12.

   S. Basilii Magni de divitiis et paupertate sententiae quam habeant rationem cum veterum philosophorum doctrina. Münster, 1911.

Dölger, Franz Joseph. "Christliche Grundbesitzer und heidnische Landarbeiter." In: Franz Joseph Dölger. *Antike und Christentum.* Münster, 1950. Vol. 6, pp. 297–320.

Dörries, Hermann. *Die Theologie des Makarios/Symeon.* Abhandlungen der Akademie der Wissenschaften in Göttingen. Phil.-hist. Klasse. 3. Folge 103. Göttingen, 1978.

Doignon, Jean. "L'enseignement de l'*Hortensius* de Cicéron sur les richesses devant la conscience d'Augustin jusqu'aux *Confessions.*" *L'Antiquité Classique* 51 (1982) 193–206.

Donovan, Mary Ann. "The Spirit, Place of the Sanctified: Basil's *De Spiritu Sancto* and Messalianism." In E. A. Livingstone, ed. *StP* 17,3. Oxford, 1982. Pp. 1073–83.

Draguet, R. "L''Histoire Lausiaque', une œuvre écrite dans l'esprit d'Evagre." *Revue d'Histoire Ecclésiastique* 41 (1946) 321–64, 42 (1947) 5–49.

Drexhage, Hans-Joachim. "Wirtschaft und Handel in den frühchristlichen Gemeinden (1.-3. Jh. n. Chr.)." *Römische Quartalschrift* 76 (1981) 1–72.

Durkin, Eugene F. *The Theological Distinction of Sins in the Writings of St. Augustine.* Dissertationes ad Lauream 23. Mundelein, IL, 1952.

Dziech, Joseph. "De Gregorio Nazianzeno Diatribae quae dicitur alumno." *Poznańskie Towarzystwo Przyjaciół Nauk. Prace Komisji Filologicznej* 3. Poznań, 1927. Pp. 26–266.

Eberhardt, Otto. *Via Regia: Der Fürstenspiegel Smaragds von St. Mihiel und seine literarische Gattung.* Münstersche Mittelalter-Schriften 28. Munich, 1977.

Eck, W. "Das Eindringen des Christentums in den Senatorenstand bis zu Konstantin d. Gr." *Chiron* 1 (1971) 381–406.

Evans, Gillian R. *The Thought of Gregory the Great.* Cambridge Studies in Medieval Life and Thought, 4.2. Cambridge, 1986.

Evans, Robert F. *Pelagius: Inquiries and Reappraisals.* New York, 1968.

Farner, Konrad. *Christentum und Eigentum bis Thomas von Aquin.* Mensch und Gesellschaft 12. Bern, 1947.

Bibliography

Festugière, A. J. *Antioche paienne et chrétienne.* Bibliothèque des Ecoles Francaises d'Athènes et de Rome 194. Paris, 1959.

Fichtenau, Heinrich. *Askese und Laster in der Anschauung des Mittelalters.* Vienna, 1948. Rev. and repr. in: Heinrich Fichtenau. *Beiträge zur Mediävistik.* Stuttgart, 1975. Vol. 1, pp. 24–107.

Living in the Tenth Century: Mentalities and Social Orders. Trans. P. Geary. Chicago and London, 1991.

Fischer, Hubert. *Die Schrift des Salvian von Marseilles "An die Kirche."* Europäische Hochschulschriften 23,57. Bern and Frankfurt/M., 1976.

Fischer, J. A. "Valerian v. Cemele." *Lexikon für Theologie und Kirche.* Second ed. Vol. 10. 1965. Cols. 603–04.

Fitzgerald, Alan. "The Relationship of Maximus of Turin to Rome and Milan." *Augustinianum* 27,3 (1987) 470–83.

Förster, Max. "Zur Liturgik der angelsächsischen Kirche." *Anglia* 66 (1942) 1–51.

Fontaine, Jacques. *Isidore de Seville et la culture classique dans l'Espagne wisigothique.* 2 vols. Paris, 1959.

Fortin, E. "The Patristic Sense of Community." *Augustinian Studies* 4 (1973) 179–97.

Frank, Karl Suso. "Habsucht." *RAC.* Vol. 13. 1984. Cols. 226–47.

"Immer ein wenig billiger verkaufen . . ." *Erbe und Auftrag* 53,4 (1977) 251–57.

"Vita apostolica als Lebensnorm in der alten Kirche." *Internationale Katholische Zeitschrift "Communio"* 8 (1979) 106–20.

Frantzen, Allen J. *The Literature of Penance in Anglo-Saxon England.* New Brunswick, N.J., 1983.

Frattini, Ernesto. "Proprietà e ricchezza nel pensiero di S. Ambrogio." *Rivista internazionale di filosofia del diritto* 39 (1962) 745–66.

Freeman, Ann. "Carolingian Orthodoxy and the Fate of the Libri Carolini." *Viator* 16 (1985) 65–108.

"Theodulf of Orléans and the Psalm Citations of the 'Libri Carolini'." *Revue bénédictine* 97 (1987) 195–224.

Frend, W. H. C. *Saints and Sinners in the Early Church.* London, 1985.

Frickel, Joseph. "Die Zöllner, Vorbild der Demut und wahrer Gottesverehrung." In: E. Dassmann and K. S. Frank, eds. *Pietas. Festschrift für Bernhard Kotting. JbAC,* Ergänzungsband 8. Münster, 1980. Pp. 369–80.

Fried, Johannes. "Endzeiterwartung um die Jahrtausendwende." *Deutsches Archiv für Erforschung des Mittelalters* 45 (1989) 381–473.

Frings, Hermann J. *Medizin und Arzt bei den griechischen Kirchenvätern bis Chrysostomos.* Dissertation Bonn. Bonn, 1959.

Gastaldelli, Ferruccio. "Il meccanismo psicologico del peccato nei *Moralia in Job* di san Gregorio Magno." *Salesianum* 27 (1965) 563–605.

Gatz, Bodo. *Weltalter, goldene Zeit und sinnverwandte Vorstellungen.* Spudasmata 16. Hildesheim, 1967.

Gaudemet, Jean. *L'Eglise dans l'Empire romain (IVᵉ–Vᵉ siècles).* Histoire du Droit et des Institutions de l'Eglise en Occident 3. Paris, 1958.

Georgi, Dieter. *Remembering the Poor.* Nashville, 1992.

Geffcken, J. *Kynika und Verwandtes.* Heidelberg, 1909.

Bibliography

Geldner, Johann. *Untersuchungen einiger altenglischer Krankheitsnamen.* Dissertation Würzburg. Braunschweig, 1906.

Giet, Stanislas. "La doctrine de l'appropriation des biens chez quelques-uns des pères." *Recherches de Science religieuse* 35 (1948) 55–91.

Les idées et l'action sociales de saint Basile. Paris, 1941.

"De saint Basile à saint Ambroise: la condemnation du prêt à intérêt au IVᵉ siècle." *Science Religieuse* [= *Recherches de Science religieuse* 32] (1944) 95–128.

Gillet, Robert. "Saint Grégoire le Grand." *Dictionnaire de Spiritualité.* Vol. 6. 1967. Cols. 872–76.

"Spiritualité et place du moine dans l'église selon saint Grégoire le Grand." In: *Théologie de la vie monastique.* Théologie 49. Lyon, 1961. Pp. 323–51.

Gilson, Etienne. *Introduction à l'Etude de Saint Augustin.* Etude de Philosophie Médiévale 11. Paris, 1949.

Gnilka, Christian. *Studien zur Psychomachie des Prudentius.* Klassisch-Philologische Studien 27. Wiesbaden, 1963.

"Usus Iustus. Ein Grundbegriff der Kirchenväter im Umgang mit der antiken Kultur." *Archiv für Begriffsgeschichte* 24 (1980) 34–76.

González, Justo. *Faith and Wealth.* San Francisco, 1990.

Grant, Robert M. "The Decalogue in Early Christianity." *Harvard Theological Review* 40,1 (1947) 1–17. Repr. in E. Ferguson, ed. *Christian Life: Ethics, Morality, and Discipline in the Early Church.* SEC 16:1–17.

Early Christianity and Society. New York, 1977.

Greeley, Dolores. "St. John Chrysostom, Prophet of Social Justice." In: E. A. Livingstone, ed. *StP* 17,3. Oxford, 1982. Pp. 1163–68.

Greenfield, Stanley B. and Daniel G. Calder. *A New Critical History of Old English Literature.* New York and London, 1986.

Greeven, Heinrich. *Das Hauptproblem der Sozialethik in der neueren Stoa und im Urchristentum.* Neutestamentliche Forschungen 3,4. Gütersloh, 1935.

Gribomont, Jean. "Eustathe de Sébaste." *Dictionnaire d'Histoire et de Géographie ecclésiastique.* Vol. 16. 1967. Cols. 26–33.

"Le renoncement au monde dans l'idéal ascétique de saint Basile." *Irénikon* 31 (1958) 282–307, 460–75.

Grubl, E. D. *Studien zu den angelsächsischen Elegien.* Marburg, 1948.

Gruszka, Piotr. "Die Stellungnahme der Kirchenväter Kappadoziens zu der Gier nach Gold, Silber und anderen Luxuswaren im täglichen Leben der Oberschichten des 4. Jahrhunderts." *Klio* 63,2 (1981) 661–68.

Guillaumont, Antoine. "Liber Graduum." *Dictionnaire de Spiritualité ascétique et mystique.* Vol. 9. 1976. Cols. 749–54.

"Messaliens." In: *ibid.* Vol. 10. 1980. Cols. 1074–83.

Guy, Jean-Claude. "Jean Cassien, historien du monachisme égyptien?" In: F. L. Cross, ed. *StP* 8. TU 93. Berlin, 1966. Pp. 363–72.

Jean Cassien. Vie et doctrine spirituelle. Théologie, Pastorale et Spiritualité. Recherches et synthèses 9. Paris, 1961.

Recherches sur la tradition grecque des "Apophthegmata Patrum." Subsidia hagiographica 36. Brussels, 1962.

Bibliography

Halas, R. B. *Judas Iscariot*. The Catholic University of America. Studies in Sacred Theology 96. Washington, D.C., 1946.

Hamman, A. G. "L'actualité de Salvien de Marseille: Idées sociales et politiques." *Augustinianum* 17 (1977) 381–93.

Hanna, Ralph III. "The Sources and the Art of Prudentius' *Psychomachia*." *Classical Philology* 72 (1977) 108–15.

Hannay, James Owen. *The Wisdom of the Desert*. N.p., 1904.

Hanson, R. P. C. *Allegory and Event*. London, 1959.

Harkins, P. W. "The Text Tradition of Chrysostom's Commentary on John." In: F. L. Cross, ed. *StP* 7. TU 92. Berlin, 1966. Pp. 210–20.

Hauschild, W.-D. "Christentum und Eigentum. Zum Problem eines altkirchlichen 'Sozialismus'." *Zeitschrift für Evangelische Ethik* 16 (1972) 34–49.

Hausherr, Irenée. "De doctrina spirituali Christianorum orientalium quaestiones et scripta, 3: L'origine de la théorie orientale des huit péchés capitaux." *Orientalia Christiana* 30,3 (1933) 164–75. Repr. in Irenée Hausherr. *Etudes de spiritualité orientale*. Orientalia Christiana Analecta 183. Rome, 1969. Pp. 11–22.

Haworth, Kenneth R. *Deified Virtues, Demonic Vices and Descriptive Allegory in Prudentius' Psychomachia*. Amsterdam, 1980.

Hengel, Martin. *Eigentum und Reichtum in der frühen Kirche*. Stuttgart, 1973.

Hermann, John P. "Some Varieties of Psychomachia in Old English." *American Benedictine Review* 34 (1983) 74–86, 188–222.

Herter, Hans. "Zur ersten Satire des Horaz." *Rheinisches Museum* N.F. 94 (1951) 1–42.

Herzog, Reinhart. *Die allegorische Dichtkunst des Prudentius*. Zetemata 42. Munich, 1966.

Heussi, K. *Der Ursprung des Mönchtums*. Tübingen, 1936.

Hillgarth, Jocelyn N. "Isidorean Studies, 1976–1985." *Studi medievali* 31,2 (1990) 925–73.

"The Position of Isidorian Studies: A Critical Review of the Literature Since 1935." In: M. C. Díaz y Díaz, ed. *Isidoriana*. Leon, 1961. Pp. 11–74.

Hinchliff, Peter. *Cyprian of Carthage and the Unity of the Christian Church*. London, 1974.

Homes Dudden, F. *Gregory the Great: His Place in History and Thought*. 2 vols. New York, 1905; repr. 1967.

The Life and Times of St. Ambrose. 2 vols. Oxford, 1935.

Horn, Hans-Jürgen. "Giezie und Simonie." *JbAC* 8/9 (1965/66) 189–202.

Howard, Donald R. *The Three Temptations*. Princeton, 1966.

Hudson, Winthrop S. "The Weber Thesis Reexamined." *Church History* 30 (1961) 88–99. Repr. *Church History* 57 (suppl.) (1988) 56–67.

Huizinga, Johan. *The Waning of the Middle Ages*. Trans. F. Hopman. London, 1924; repr. New York, 1954.

Irwin, Terence. *Plato's Ethics*. Oxford, 1995.

Jauss, Hans Robert. "Form und Auffassung der Allegorie in der Tradition der Psychomachia." In: H. R. Jauss and D. Schaller, eds. *Medium Aevum Vivum. Festschrift für Walter Bulst*. Heidelberg, 1960. Pp. 179–206.

Bibliography

Jehl, Rainer. "Die Geschichte des Lasterschemas und seiner Funktion: Von der Väterzeit bis zur karolingischen Erneuerung." *Franziskanische Studien* 64 (1982) 261–359.

Jones, A. H. M. "Ancient Empires and the Economy: Rome." In: *Third International Conference of Economic History, 1965.* Munich, 1970. Pp. 81–104. Repr. in A. H. M. Jones. *The Roman Economy.* Ed. P. A. Brunt. Oxford, 1974. Pp. 114–39.

The Later Roman Empire, 284–602. 2 vols. Oxford, 1964; repr. 1973.

"Over-Taxation and the Decline of the Roman Empire." *Antiquity* 33 (1959) 39–43. Repr. in A. H. M. Jones. *The Roman Economy.* Ed. P. A. Brunt. Oxford, 1974. Pp. 82–89.

"The Social Background of the Struggle between Paganism and Christianity." In: A. Momigliano, ed. *The Conflict Between Paganism and Christianity in the Fourth Century.* Oxford, 1963. Pp. 17–37.

Jung, Marc-René. *Etudes sur le poème allégorique en France au moyen âge.* Romanica Helvetica 82. Berne, 1971.

Kamlah, Ehrhard. *Die Form der katalogischen Paränese im Neuen Testament.* Wissenschaftliche Untersuchungen zum Neuen Testament 7. Tübingen, 1964.

Kaser, Max. *Das römische Zivilprozessrecht.* Second ed. Ed. K. Hackl. Handbuch der Altertumswissenschaft 10.3.4. Munich, 1996.

Kaczynski, Bernice M. "Edition, Translation, and Exegesis: The Carolingians and the Bible." In R. E. Sullivan, ed. *"The Gentle Voices of Teachers": Aspects of Learning in the Carolingian Age.* Columbus, OH, 1995. Pp. 171–85.

Keenan, Mary E. "St. Gregory of Nazianzus and Early Byzantine Medicine." *Bulletin of the History of Medicine* 9 (1941) 8–30.

Kehl, Alois and Henri-Irénée Marrou. "Geschichtsphilosophie." *RAC.* Vol. 10. 1978. Cols. 703–79.

Kellermann, D. "בצע." *Theologisches Wörterbuch zum Alten Testament.* Vol. 1. 1973. Cols. 731–36.

Kelly, J. N. D. *Golden Mouth: The Story of John Chrysostom – Ascetic, Preacher, Bishop.* Ithaca, N.Y., 1995.

Jerome. London, 1975.

Kemmer, A. "Gregorius Nyssenus estne inter fontes Joannis Cassiani numerandus?" *Orientalia Christiana Periodica* 21 (1955) 451–66.

Kerff, Franz. *Der Quadripartitus: Ein Handbuch der karolingischen Kirchenreform.* Quellen und Forschungen zum Recht im Mittelalter 1. Sigmaringen, 1982.

Klaar, Erich. "Πλεονεξία, -έκτης, -εκτεῖν." *Theologische Zeitschrift der Theologischen Fakultät der Universität Basel* 10 (1954) 395–97.

Koch, Robert. "Die Wertung des Besitzes im Lukasevangelium." *Biblica* 38 (1957) 151–69.

Köppen, Klaus-Peter. *Die Auslegung der Versuchungsgeschichte unter besonderer Berücksichtigung der Alten Kirche: Ein Beitrag zur Geschichte der Schriftenauslegung.* Beiträge zur Geschichte der biblischen Exegese 4. Tübingen, 1961.

Konstantinou, Evangelos G. *Die Tugendlehre Gregors von Nyssa im Verhältnis zu der*

Antik-Philosophischen und Jüdisch-Christlichen Tradition. Das östliche Christentum N.F. 17. Würzburg, 1966.

Kopecek, Thomas A. "The Social Class of the Cappadocian Fathers." *Church History* 42,4 (1973) 453–66.

"Social/Historical Studies in the Cappadocian Fathers." Dissertation Brown University, 1972.

Kottje, Raymund. *Die Bussbücher Halitgars von Cambrai und des Hrabanus Maurus*. Beiträge zur Geschichte und Quellenkunde des Mittelalters 8. Berlin and New York, 1980.

"Hrabanus Maurus." *Die deutsche Literatur des Mittelalters. Verfasserlexikon*. Second rev. ed. Vol. 4. 1983. Cols. 166–96.

Laeuchli, Samuel. "Origen's Interpretation of Judas Iscariot." *Church History* 22 (1953) 253–68.

Laistner, M. L. W. "The Library of the Venerable Bede." In: A. H. Thompson, ed. *Bede: His Life, Times and Writings*. Oxford, 1935. Pp. 237–66.

Thought and Letters in Western Europe, A.D. 500 to 900. Rev. ed. Ithaca, N.Y., 1966.

Landes, Richard. *Relics, Apocalypse, and the Deceits of History: Ademar of Chabannes, 989–1034*. Cambridge, MA, 1995.

Lane Fox, Robin. *Pagans and Christians*. New York, 1987.

Langan, John P. "Augustine on the Unity and the Interconnection of the Virtues." *Harvard Theological Review* 72,1–2 (1979) 81–95.

Larmann, Hans. *Christliche Wirtschaftsethik in der spätrömischen Antike*. Furche-Studien 13. Berlin, 1935.

Le Bras, G. "Pénitentiels." *Dictionnaire de théologie catholique*. Vol. 12. 1933. Cols. 1160–79.

Leclercq, Henri. "Grégoire de Tours." *Dictionnaire d'archéologie chrétienne et de liturgie*. Vol. 6,2. 1925. Cols. 1711–53.

Leclercq, Jean. *The Love of Learning and the Desire for God*. Trans. C. Misrahi. Second ed. New York, 1974.

Leclercq, Jean *et al. La spiritualité du moyen âge*. Histoire de la spiritualité chrétienne 2. Vienne, 1961.

Leduc, Francis. "Péché et conversion chez saint Jean Chrysostome." *Proche-Orient Chrétien* 26 (1976) 34–58; 27 (1977) 15–42; 28 (1978) 44–84.

"Le thème de la vaine gloire chez saint Jean Chrysostome." *Ibid*. 19 (1969) 3–32.

Lefort, L.-Th. "A propos d'un aphorisme d'Evagrius Ponticus." *Academie Royale de Belgique. Bulletin de la Classe des Lettres et des Sciences morales et politiques* 36. Brussels, 1950. Pp. 70–79.

Légasse, S. *L'appel du riche (Marc 10, 17–31 et parallèls)*. Paris, 1956.

Leonardi, Claudio. "Alle origini della cristianità medievale: Giovanni Cassiano e Salviano di Marsiglia." *Studi Medievali* 3. ser. 18,2 (1977) 491–608.

"Spiritualità di Ambrogio Autperto." *Ibid*. 3. ser. 9,1 (1968) 1–131.

Leonardi, Giovanni. "Le tentazioni de Gesú nella interpretazione patristica." *Studia Patavina* 15 (1968) 229–62.

Leroy, Julien. "Les préfaces des écrits monastiques de Jean Cassien." *RAM* 42 (1966) 157–80.

Lewis, C. S. *The Allegory of Love*. London, 1936; repr. 1971.

Leyser, Conrad. "Cities of the Plain: The Rhetoric of Sodomy in Peter Damian's "Book of Gomorrah." *Romanic Review* 86 (1995) 191–211.

Leyser, Henrietta. *Hermits and the New Monasticism: A Study of Religious Communities in Western Europe 1000–1150*. London, 1984.

Liébaert, Jacques. *Les enseignements moraux des pères apostoliques*. Recherches et synthèses. Section de morale 4. Gembloux, 1970.

Liebeschuetz, W. "Pelagian Evidence on the Last Period of Roman Britain?" *Latomus* 26 (1967) 436–47.

Lindberg, Carter. "Through a Glass Darkly: A History of the Church's Vision of the Poor and Poverty." *The Ecumenical Review* 33,1 (1981) 37–52.

Little, Lester K. "Pride Goes Before Avarice: Social Change and the Vices in Latin Christendom." *The American Historical Review* 76 (1971) 16–49.

Lizzi, Rita. "Ambrose's Contemporaries and the Christianization of Northern Italy." *The Journal of Roman Studies* 80 (1990) 156–73.

Löpfe, Dominikus. *Die Tugendlehre des heiligen Ambrosius*. Sarnen, 1951.

Löwe, Heinz. "Pirmin, Willibrod und Bonifatius. Ihre Bedeutung für die Missionsgeschichte ihrer Zeit." Repr. in: K. Schäferdiek, ed. *Die Kirche des frühen Mittelalters*. Kirchengeschichte als Missionsgeschichte 2,1. Munich, 1978. Pp. 192–226.

Loewe, Raphael. "The Medieval History of the Latin Vulgate." In: G. W. H. Lampe, ed. *The Cambridge History of the Bible*. Vol. 2. Cambridge, 1969. Pp. 102–54.

Lohse, Bernhard. *Askese und Mönchtum in der Antike und in der alten Kirche*. Religion und Kultur der alten Mittelmeerwelt in Parallelforschung 1. Munich and Vienna, 1969.

Lopez, Robert S. *The Commercial Revolution of the Middle Ages 950–1350*. Englewood Cliffs, 1971.

Lorenz, Rudolf. "Die Anfänge des abendländischen Mönchtums im 4. Jahrhundert." *Zeitschrift für Kirchengeschichte* 77 (1966) 1–61.

———. "Die Herkunft des augustinischen FRUI DEO." *Ibid.* 64 (1952/53) 34–60, 359–60.

Louth, A. "Messalianism and Pelagianism." In: E. A. Livingstone, ed. *StP* 17,1. Oxford, 1982. Pp. 127–35.

Lovejoy, Arthur O. and George Boas. *Primitivism and Related Ideas in Antiquity*. N.p., 1935; repr. New York, 1965.

Machielsen, John J. "Le problème du mal selon les pères apostoliques." *Eglise et Théologie* 12 (1981) 195–222.

Macqueen, D. J. "*Contemptus Dei*: St. Augustine on the Disorder of Pride in Society and its Remedies." *Recherches Augustiniennes* 9 (1973) 227–93.

———. "St. Augustine's Concept of Property Ownership." *Ibid.* 8 (1972) 187–229.

Mähl, Sibylle. *Quadriga Virtutum*. Beihefte zum Archiv für Kulturgeschichte 9. Cologne and Vienna, 1969.

Maenchen-Helfen, O. "The Date of Maximus of Turin's *Sermo XVIII*." *VC* 18 (1964) 114–15.

Maes, Baziel. *La loi naturelle selon Ambroise de Milan*. Analecta Gregoriana 162. Rome, 1967.

Mahoney, Albertus. *Vergil in the Works of Prudentius.* The Catholic University of America. Patristic Studies 39. Washington, D.C., 1934.

Maisonneuve, Henri. *La morale chrétienne d'aprés les conciles des Xe et XIe siècles.* Analecta mediaevalia Namurcensia 15. Louvain and Lille, 1963.

Maloney, R. P. "The Teaching of the Fathers on Usury: An Historical Study on the Development of Christian Thinking." *VC* 27 (1973) 251–66.

Manning, Eugéne. "L'*Admonitio S. Basilii ad filium spiritualem* et la Règle de S. Benoît." *RAM* 42 (1966) 475–79.

Manselli, Raoul. "Gregor der Große." *RAC.* Vol. 12. 1983. Cols. 930–51.

Marsili, S. *Giovanni Cassiano ed Evagrio Pontico.* Studia Anselmiana 5. Rome, 1936.

Martin-Bagnaudez, J. "Les représentations romans de l'avare: Etude iconographique." *Revue d'Histoire de la Spiritualité* 50 (1974) 397–432.

Martroye, F. "Le testament de saint Grégoire de Nazianze." *Mémoires de la Société Nationale des Antiquaires de France* 76 (série 8, tome 6) (1924) 219–63.

Matthews, John. *Western Aristocracies and Imperial Court AD 364–425.* Oxford, 1975; repr. 1990.

Mausbach, J. *Die Ethik des hl. Augustinus.* Second ed. 2 vols. Freiburg, 1929.

McCarthy, Maria C. *The Rule for Nuns of St. Caesarius of Arles.* The Catholic University of America. Studies in Mediaeval History. N.S. 16. Washington, D.C., 1960.

McGinn, Bernard. *Apocalyptic Spirituality.* New York, 1979.

McGinn, Bernard, ed. *Visions of the End.* New York, 1979.

McNally, Robert E. *Der irische Liber de numeris.* Dissertation Munich. Munich, 1957.

"Isidorian Pseudepigrapha in the Early Middle Ages." In: M. C. Díaz y Díaz, ed. *Isidoriana.* Leon, 1961. Pp. 305–16.

Mealand, David. "Philo of Alexandria's Attitude to Riches." *Zeitschrift für die neutestamentliche Wissenschaft* 69 (1978) 258–64.

Meeks, Wayne. *The First Urban Christians.* New Haven and London, 1983.
The Origins of Christian Morality. New Haven and London, 1993.

Meeks, Wayne A. and Robert L. Wilken. *Jews and Christians in Antioch in the First Four Centuries of the Common Era.* Society for Biblical Literature: Sources for Biblical Study 13. Missoula, Montana, 1978.

Mehrlein, Rudolph. "De avaritia quid iudicaverit Ioannes Chrysostomus." Dissertation Cologne, 1951.

Meyvaert, Paul. "Bede and Gregory the Great." *Jarrow Lecture* 7. 1964. Repr. in Paul Meyvaert. *Benedict, Gregory, Bede and Others.* London, 1977. No. 8.

Mollat, Michel. *The Poor in the Middle Ages.* Trans. A. Goldhammer. New Haven, 1986.

Moreschini, Claudio. "Il platonismo cristiano di Gregorio Nazianzeno." *Annali della scuola normale superiore di Pisa.* Classe di lettere e filosofia. Ser. 3, vol. 4,4. 1974. Pp. 1347–92.

Morris, John. "Pelagian Literature." *Journal of Theological Studies* N.S. 16 (1965) 26–60.

Moxnes, Halvor. *The Economy of the Kingdom: Social Conflict and Economic Relations in Luke's Gospel.* Philadelphia, 1988.

Muckle, J. T. "The De Officiis Ministrorum of Saint Ambrose." *Mediaeval Studies* 1 (1939) 63–80.

Mullins, Sr. Patrick J. *The Spiritual Life According to Saint Isidore of Seville*. The Catholic University of America. Studies in Medieval and Renaissance Latin Language and Literature 13. Washington, D.C., 1940.

Munz, Peter. "John Cassian." *Journal of Ecclesiastical History* 11 (1960) 1–22.

Murdoch, Brian O. *The Recapitulated Fall: A Comparative Study in Mediaeval Literature*. Amsterdamer Publikationen zur Sprache und Literatur 11. Amsterdam, 1974.

Murray, Alexander. "Money and Robbers, 900–1100." *Journal of Medieval History* 4 (1978) 55–94.

Reason and Society in the Middle Ages. Oxford, 1978.

Muyldermans, J. "La teneur du *Practicus* d'Evagrius le Pontique." *Le Muséon* 42 (1929) 74–89.

Myres, J. N. L. "Pelagius and the End of Roman Rule in Britain." *Journal of Roman Studies* 50 (1960) 21–36.

Nagel, P. *Die Motivierung der Askese in der alten Kirche und der Ursprung des Mönchtums*. TU 95. Berlin, 1966.

Nelson, Janet L. "On the Limits of the Carolingian Renaissance." In: D. Baker, ed. *Renaissance and Renewal in Christian History*. Studies in Church History 14. Oxford, 1977. Pp. 51–69.

Neusner, Jacob. *The Economics of the Mishnah*. Chicago, 1990.

Newhauser, Richard. "The Love of Money as Deadly Sin and Deadly Disease." In: J. O. Fichte *et al.*, eds. *Zusammenhänge, Einflüsse, Wirkungen*. Kongressakten zum ersten Symposium des Mediävistenverbandes in Tübingen, 1984. Berlin and New York, 1986. Pp. 315–326.

"Patristic Poggio? The Evidence of Győr, Egyházmegyei Könyvtár MS. I.4," *Rinascimento* 26 (1986) 231–39.

"Towards modus in habendo: Transformations in the Idea of Avarice. The Early Penitentials through the Carolingian Reforms." *Zeitschrift der Savigny-Stiftung für Rechtsgeschichte* 106, Kanonistische Abteilung 75 (1989) 1–22.

The Treatise on Vices and Virtues in Latin and the Vernacular. Typologie des sources du moyen âge occidental 68. Turnhout, 1993.

Nikolaou, Theodoros. *Der Neid bei Johannes Chrysostomus*. Abhandlungen zur Philosophie, Psychologie und Pädagogik 56. Bonn, 1969.

North, Helen. *Sophrosyne*. Cornell Studies in Classical Philology 35. Ithaca, N.Y., 1966.

Ogilvie, R. M. *The Library of Lactantius*. Oxford, 1978.

Ogilvy, J. D. A. *Books Known to the English*. Mediaeval Academy of America Publication 76. Cambridge, MA, 1967.

O'Laughlin, Michael. "The Anthropology of Evagrius Ponticus and its Sources." In C. Kannengiesser and W. L. Petersen, eds. *Origen of Alexandria: His World and His Legacy*. Christianity and Judaism in Antiquity 1. Notre Dame, IN, 1988. Pp. 357–73.

O'Neil, Edward N. "De cupiditate divitiarum (Moralia 523C-528B)." In: H. D. Betz, ed. *Plutarch's Ethical Writings and Early Christian Literature.* Studia ad Corpus Hellenisticum Novi Testamenti 4. Leiden, 1978. Pp. 289–362.

O'Reilly, Jennifer. *Studies in the Iconography of the Virtues and Vices in the Middle Ages.* New York and London, 1988.

Osiek, Carolyn. "Wealth and Poverty in the *Shepherd of Hermas.*" In: E. A. Livingstone, ed. *StP* 17,2. Oxford, 1982. Pp. 725–30.

Padovese, Luigi. "La dottrina sociale di Massimo da Torino." *Laurentianum* 22 (1981) 149–202.

L'Originalità cristiana: Il pensiero etico-sociale di alcuni vescovi norditaliani del IV secolo, Istituto Francescano di Spiritualità. Studi e ricerche 8. Rome, 1983.

Pearce, G. J. M. "Augustine's Theory of Property." In: F. L. Cross, ed. *StP* 6. TU 81. Berlin, 1962. Pp. 496–500.

Pellegrino, Michele. *Salviano di Marsiglia.* Lateranum N.S. 6,1–2. Rome, 1940.

Perels, Hans-Ulrich. "Besitzethik in den apokryphen Apostelgeschichten und in der zeitgenössischen christlichen Literatur." Dissertation, University of Heidelberg, 1976.

Pfligersdorffer, Georg. "Zu den Grundlagen des augustinischen Begriffspaares 'uti-frui'." *Wiener Studien* N.F. 5, Bd. 84 (1971) 195–224.

Pichery, E. "Les idées morales de Jean Cassien." *MSR* 14 (1957) 5–20.

Plassmann, Otto. *Das Almosen bei Johannes Chrysostomus.* Dissertation Bonn. Münster, 1960.

Pohlenz, Max. *Die Stoa.* Fourth ed. Göttingen, 1970.

Poirier, Michel. "'Christus pauper factus est' chez saint Ambroise." *Rivista di storia e letteratura religiosa* 15 (1979) 250–57.

Pototschnig, Franz. "Christliche Eigentumsordnung in rechtshistorischer Sicht." *Österreichisches Archiv für Kirchenrecht* 27 (1976) 276–309.

Prinz, Friedrich. *Frühes Mönchtum im Frankenreich.* Munich and Vienna, 1965.

Procopé, J. F. "*Initium omnis peccati superbia.*" In E. A. Livingstone, ed. *StP* 22. Leuven, 1989. Pp. 315–20.

Prunet, Olivier. *La morale de Clément d'Alexandrie et le Nouveau Testament.* Etudes d'histoire et de philosophie religieuses 61. Paris, 1966.

Raby, F. J. E. *A History of Christian-Latin Poetry.* Second ed. Oxford, 1953.

Rädle, Fidel. *Studien zu Smaragd von Saint-Mihiel.* Medium Aevum, Philologische Studien 29. Munich, 1974.

Rambaux, Claude. *Tertullien face aux morales des trois premiers siècles.* Paris, 1979.

Ramsey, Boniface. "Almsgiving in the Latin Church: The Late Fourth and Early Fifth Centuries." *Theological Studies* 43 (1982) 226–59.

Ramsey, Boniface, trans. *The Sermons of St. Maximus of Turin.* Ancient Christian Writers 50. New York and Mahwah, 1989.

Richards, Jeffrey. *Consul of God: The Life and Times of Gregory the Great.* London, 1980.

Rissel, Maria. *Rezeption antiker und patristischer Wissenschaft bei Hrabanus Maurus.* Lateinische Sprache und Literatur des Mittelalters 7. Bern and Frankfurt, 1976.

Ritter, A. M. "Christentum und Eigentum bei Klemens von Alexandrien auf dem

Hintergrund der frühchristlichen 'Armenfrömmigkeit' und der Ethik der kaiserzeitlichen Stoa." *Zeitschrift für Kirchengeschichte* 86 (1975) 1–25.

Rondet, H. "Richesse et pauvreté dans la prédication de saint Augustin." *RAM* 30 (1954) 193–231.

Rossano, P. "De conceptu πλεονεξία in Novo Testamento." *Verbum Domini* 32 (1954) 257–65.

Rousseau, Philip. *Ascetics, Authority and the Church in the Age of Jerome and Cassian.* Oxford, 1978.

Rowland, Christopher. "Apocalyptic, God and the World. Appearance and Reality: Early Christianity's Debt to the Jewish Apocalyptic Tradition." In J. Barclay and J. Sweet, eds. *Early Christian Thought in Its Jewish Context.* Cambridge, 1996. Pp. 238–49.

Rudolph, Kurt. *Die Gnosis.* Second ed. Göttingen, 1980.

Ruether, Rosemary R. *Gregory of Nazianzus.* Oxford, 1969.

Rüther, T. *Die sittliche Forderung der Apatheia in den beiden ersten christlichen Jahrhunderten und bei Klemens von Alexandrien. Ein Beitrag zur Geschichte des christlichen Vollkommenheitsbegriffes.* Freiburger Theologische Studien 63. Freiburg/Br., 1949.

Ruggini, Lellia Cracco. *Economia e società nell' "Italia Annonaria."* Fondazione Guglielmo Castelli 30. Milan, 1961.

——— "Milano nella circolazione monetaria del tardo impero: esigenze politiche e risposte socioeconomiche." In G. Gorini, ed. *La zecca di Milano.* Atti del convegno internazionale di studio (Milano 9–14 maggio 1983). Milan, 1984. Pp. 35–58.

Russell, R. R. "Cicero's *Hortensius* and the Problem of Riches in Saint Augustine." In C. P. Mayer, ed. *Scientia Augustiniana. Festschrift Adolar Zumkeller zum 60. Geburtstag.* Cassiciacum 30. Würzburg, 1975.

Savramis, D. *Zur Soziologie des byzantinischen Mönchtums.* Leiden and Cologne, 1962.

Scharf, Joachim. "Studien zu Smaragdus und Jonas." *Deutsches Archiv für Erforschung des Mittelalters* 17 (1961) 333–51.

Scheludko, Dimitri. "Klagen über den Verfall der Welt bei den Trobadors. Allegorische Darstellungen des Kampfes der Tugenden und der Laster." *NM* 44 (1943) 22–45.

Schilling, O. *Der kirchliche Eigentumsbegriff.* Second ed. Freiburg/Br., 1930.

Schnell, Rüdiger. *Zum Verhältnis von hoch- und spätmittelalterlichen Literatur.* Philologische Studien und Quellen 92. Berlin, 1978.

Schöllgen, Georg. *Ecclesia Sordida? Zur Frage der sozialen Schichtung frühchristlicher Gemeinden am Beispiel Karthagos zur Zeit Tertullians. JbAC* Ergänzungsband 12. Münster, 1984.

Schulze, Paul. *Die Entwicklung der Hauptlaster- und Haupttugendlehre von Gregor dem Großen bis Petrus Lombardus und ihr Einfluß auf die frühdeutsche Literatur.* Dissertation Greifswald. Greifswald, 1914.

Schwabl, Hans. "Weltalter." *Paulys Realencyclopädie der classischen Altertumswissenschaft.* Supplementband 15. 1978. Cols. 783–850.

Bibliography

Seipel, Ignaz. *Die wirtschaftsethischen Lehren der Kirchenväter.* Leo-Gesellschaft, Theologische Studien 18. Vienna, 1907; repr. Graz, 1972.

Semmler, Joseph. "Karl der Große und das fränkische Mönchtum." In: *Karl der Große, Lebenswerk und Nachleben, 2: Das geistige Leben.* Ed. B. Bischoff. Düsseldorf, 1965. Pp. 255–89.

Seybold, Michael. *Sozialtheologische Aspekte der Sünde bei Augustinus.* Studien zur Geschichte der Moraltheologie 11. Regensburg, 1963.

Sifoniou, Anastasia. "Les fondements juridiques de l'aumone et de la charité chez Jean Chrysostome." *Revue du droit canonique* 14 (1964) 241–69.

Smith, Macklin. *Prudentius' Psychomachia: A Reexamination.* Princeton, 1976.

Solignac, A. "La condition de l'homme pécheur d'après saint Augustin." *Nouvelle Revue Théologique* 78 (1956) 370–72. Repr. in E. Ferguson, ed. *Doctrines of Human Nature, Sin, and Salvation in the Early Church.* SEC 10:112–14.

Spanneut, Michel. *Le stoicisme des pères de l'église.* Patristica Sorbonensia 1. Paris, 1957.

Tertullien et les premiers moralistes africains. Paris, 1969.

Spufford, Peter. *Money and its Use in Medieval Europe.* Cambridge, 1988.

Staats, Reinhart. "Deposita pietatis – Die Alte Kirche und ihr Geld." *Zeitschrift für Theologie und Kirche* 76 (1979) 1–29.

Steidle, Wolf. "Beobachtungen zum Gedankengang im 2. Buch von Ambrosius, De officiis." *VC* 39 (1985) 280–95.

Steiner, M. *La tentation de Jésus dans l'interprétation patristique de Saint Justin à Origène.* Etudes Bibliques 54. Paris, 1962.

Stelzenberger, Johannes. "Adiaphora." *RAC.* Vol. 1. Stuttgart, 1950. Cols. 83–87.

Die Beziehungen der frühchristlichen Sittenlehre zur Ethik der Stoa. Munich, 1933.

Sternbach, Leo. "De Gnomologio Vaticano inedito." *Wiener Studien* 9 (1887) 175–206; 10 (1888) 1–49, 211–60.

Stettiner, Richard. *Die illustrierten Prudentiushandschriften.* 2 vols. Berlin, 1895–1905.

Straw, Carole. *Gregory the Great: Perfection in Imperfection.* Transformations of the Classical Heritage 14. Berkeley, Los Angeles and London, 1988.

Sutcliffe, E. F. "Jerome." In: G. W. H. Lampe, ed. *The Cambridge History of the Bible.* Vol. 2. Cambridge, 1969. Pp. 80–101.

Swift, Louis J. *Iustitia* and *Ius privatum*: Ambrose on Private Property." *American Journal of Philology* 100 (1979) 176–87.

"Lactantius and the Golden Age." *Ibid.* 89 (1968) 144–56.

Szarmach, Paul E. "A Preliminary Handlist of Manuscripts Containing Alcuin's *Liber de virtutibus et vitiis.*" *Manuscripta* 25,3 (1981) 131–40.

Teichtweier, Georg. *Die Sündenlehre des Origenes.* Studien zur Geschichte der katholischen Moraltheologie 7. Regensburg, 1958.

Tetzlaff, Gerhard. *Bezeichnungen für die sieben Todsünden in der altenglischen Prosa. Ein Beitrag zur Terminologie der altenglischen Kirchensprache.* Dissertation Berlin. Berlin, 1954.

Thompson, E. A. "Christianity and the Northern Barbarians." In: A. Momigliano, ed. *The Conflict Between Paganism and Christianity in the Fourth Century.* Oxford, 1963. Pp. 56–78.

Bibliography

Thomson, H. J. "The *Psychomachia* of Prudentius." *The Classical Review* 44 (1930) 109–12.

Thonnard, F.-J. "Justice de Dieu et justice humaine selon saint Augustine." *Augustinus* 12 (1967) 387–402.

Tillmann, Fritz. "Besitz und Eigentum bei Basilius dem Großen." In: M. Meinertz and A. Donders, eds. *Aus Ethik und Leben. Festschrift für Joseph Mausbach*. Münster, 1931. Pp. 33–42.

Tollinton, Richard. *Clement of Alexandria: A Study in Christian Liberalism*. London, 1914.

Trevijano, Raymundo. *En lucha contra las Potestades*. Rome, 1967.

Trigg, Joseph Wilson. *Origen*. Atlanta, 1983.

Trisoglio, Francesco. "Appunti per una ricerca delle fonti di S. Gaudenzio da Brescia." *Rivista di Studi Classici* 24 (1976) 50–125.

———. "Reminiscenze e consonanze classiche nella XIV orazione di San Gregorio Nazianzeno." *Atti della Accademia delle Scienze di Torino II: Classe di Scienze Morali, Storiche e Filologiche* 99. Turin, 1965. Pp. 129–204.

Troeltsch, Ernst. *Augustin, die christliche Antike und das Mittelalter*. Historische Bibliothek 36. Munich, 1915.

Truzzi, Carlo. *Zeno, Gaudenzio e Cromazio: Testi e contenuti della predicazione cristiana per le chiese di Verona, Brescia e Aquileia (360–410 ca.)*. Testi e Ricerche di Scienze Religiose 22. Brescia, 1985.

Tugwell, Simon. "Evagrius and Macarius." In C. Jones *et al.*, eds. *The Study of Spirituality*. London, 1986. Pp. 168–75.

Uleyn, Arnold. "La doctrine morale de saint Jean Chrysostome dans le Commentaire sur saint Matthieu et ses affinités avec la diatribe." *Revue de l'Université d'Ottawa* 27 (1957) 5*-25*, 99*-140*.

van der Meer, F. *Augustinus der Seelsorger*. Third ed. Cologne, 1958.

Vasey, Vincent R. *The Social Ideas in the Works of St. Ambrose: A Study on De Nabuthe*. Studia Ephemeridis "Augustinianum" 17. Rome, 1982. Pp. 105–42.

Veilleux, Armand. "Le renoncement aux biens matériels dans le cénobitisme pachômien." *Collectanea Cisterciensia* 43 (1981) 56–74.

Vicastillo, Salvador. "La doctrina sobre los bienos terrenos en San Augustin (Enarrationes in Psalmos–Sermones)." *La Ciudad de Dios* 180 (1967) 86–115.

Viller, M. "Aux sources de la spiritualité de S. Maxime. Les œuvres d'Evagre le Pontique." *RAM* 11 (1930) 156–84, 239–68, 331–36.

Vischer, Rüdiger. *Das einfache Leben*. Studienhefte zur Altertumswissenschaft 11. Göttingen, 1965.

Vismara Chiappa, Paola. *Il tema della povertà nella predicazione di Sant'Agostino*. Università di Trieste. Facoltà di Scienze Politiche 5. Milan, 1975.

Vögtle, A. "Achtlasterlehre." *RAC*. Vol. 1. 1950. Cols. 74–79.

———. *Die Tugend- und Lasterkataloge im Neuen Testament, exegetisch, religions- und formgeschichtlich untersucht*. Neutestamentliche Abhandlungen 16,4/5. Münster, 1936.

———. "Woher stammt das Schema der Hauptsünden?" *Theologische Quartalschrift* 122 (1941) 217–37.

Bibliography

Völker, Walter. *Gregor von Nyssa als Mystiker.* Wiesbaden, 1955.

Praxis und Theoria bei Symeon dem Neuen Theologen. Ein Beitrag zur byzantinischen Mystik. Wiesbaden, 1974.

Vööbus, Arthur. *History of Asceticism in the Syrian Orient.* 2 vols. Corpus Scriptorum Christianorum Orientalium 184, 197. Subsidia 14, 17. Louvain, 1958–60.

Vogel, Cyrille. *Les "libri paenitentiales."* Typologie des sources du moyen âge occidental 27. Turnhout, 1978. Supplement by Allen J. Frantzen. Turnhout, 1985.

Vogt, Hermann Josef. *Das Kirchenverständnis des Origenes.* Bonner Beiträge zur Kirchengeschichte 4. Cologne and Vienna, 1974.

von Balthasar, Hans Urs. "Die Hiera des Evagrius." *Zeitschrift für katholische Theologie* 63 (1939) 86–106, 181–206.

"Metaphysik und Mystik des Evagrius Ponticus." *Zeitschrift für Aszese und Mystik* 14 (1939) 31–47.

von Harnack, Adolf. *Die Mission und Ausbreitung des Christentums in den ersten drei Jahrhunderten.* Fourth ed. 2 vols. Leipzig, 1923–24.

Wacht, Manfred. "Gütergemeinschaft." *RAC.* Vol. 13. 1984. Cols. 1–59.

"Privateigentum bei Cicero und Ambrosius." *JbAC* 25 (1982) 28–64.

Wallace-Hadrill, J. M. *The Barbarian West 400–1000.* Rev. ed. Oxford, 1996.

Wallach, Luitpold. *Alcuin and Charlemagne: Studies in Carolingian History and Literature.* Cornell Studies in Classical Philology 32. Ithaca, N.Y., 1959.

"Alcuin on Vices and Virtues: A Manual for a Carolingian Soldier." *Harvard Theological Review* 48 (1955) 175–95.

Walsh, W. and John P. Langan. "Patristic Social Consciousness: the Church and the Poor." In: J. C. Haughey, ed. *The Faith that Does Justice: Examining the Sources for Social Change.* Woodstock Studies 2. New York, 1977. Pp. 113–51.

Wasselynck, René. "Les compilations des Moralia in Job du VIIe au XIIe siècle." *RTAM* 29 (1962) 5–32.

"L'influence de l'exégèse de S. Grégoire le Grand sur les Commentaires bibliques médiévaux (VIIe–XIIe s.)." *RTAM* 32 (1965) 157–204.

"L'influence de *Moralia in Job* de S. Grégoire le Grand sur la théologie morale entre le VIIe et le XIIe siècle." Dissertation Lille. 3 vols. Lille, 1956.

"Les 'Moralia in Job' dans les ouvrages de morale du haut moyen âge latin." *RTAM* 31 (1964) 5–31.

"La part des 'Moralia in Job' de S. Grégoire le Grand dans les 'Miscellanea' victorins." *MSR* 10 (1953) 287–94.

"La présence des Moralia de S. Grégoire le Grand dans les ouvrages de morale du XIIe siècle." *RTAM* 36 (1969) 31–45.

"Présence de saint Grégoire le Grand dans les recueils canoniques (X^e–XIIe siècles)." *MSR* 22 (1965) 205–19.

Watson, Arthur. "Saligia." *Journal of the Warburg and Courtauld Institutes* 10 (1947) 148–50.

Weaver, Rebecca H. "Wealth and Poverty in the Early Church." *Interpretation: A Journal of Bible and Theology* 41,4 (1987) 369–74.

Weber, Hans-Oskar. *Die Stellung des Johannes Cassianus zur ausserpachomianischen*

Bibliography

Mönchstradition. Beiträge zur Geschichte des alten Mönchtums und des Benediktinerordens 24. Münster, 1961.

Weber, Leonhard. *Hauptfragen der Moraltheologie Gregors des Grossen*. Paradosis 1. Freiburg/CH, 1947.

Weber, Robert. "La prière d'Ambroise Autpert contre les vices et son 'Conflictus vitiorum et virtutum'." *Revue bénédictine* 86 (1976) 109–15.

Wendland, Paul. "Philo und die kynisch-stoische Diatribe." In P. Wendland and O. Kern. *Beiträge zur Geschichte der griechischen Philosophie und Religion*. Berlin, 1895. Pp. 1–75.

Wenninger, Markus. "Juden und Christen als Geldgeber im hohen und späten Mittelalter." In A. Ebenbauer and K. Zatloukal, eds. *Die Juden in ihrer mittelalterlichen Umwelt*. Vienna, 1991. Pp. 281–99.

Wenzel, Siegfried. "'Acedia' 700–1200." *Traditio* 22 (1966) 73–102.

"The Seven Deadly Sins: Some Problems of Research." *Speculum* 43 (1968) 1–22.

The Sin of Sloth: Acedia in Medieval Thought and Literature. Chapel Hill, N.C., 1967.

Whitelock, Dorothy. "Bede and His Teachers and Friends." In: G. Bonner, ed. *Famulus Christi*. London, 1976. Pp. 19–39.

Wibbing, S. *Die Tugend- und Lasterkataloge im Neuen Testament*. Beihefte zur Zeitschrift für die Neutestamentliche Wissenschaft 25. Berlin, 1959.

Wiesen, David. *St. Jerome as a Satirist*. Cornell Studies in Classical Philology 24. Ithaca, N.Y., 1964.

Williamson, Ronald. *Jews in the Hellenistic World: Philo*. Cambridge Commentaries on Writings of the Jewish and Christian World 200 BC to AD 200 1, part 2. Cambridge, 1989.

Winandy, Jacques. *Ambroise Autpert, moine et théologien*. Paris, 1953.

Winterbottom, Michael. "Pelagiana." *Journal of Theological Studies*, N.S. 38,1 (1987) 108–16.

Winterstein, Alfred. *Die christliche Lehre vom Erdengut nach den Evangelien und apostolischen Schriften*. Mainz, 1898.

Wyss, Bernhard. "Gregor von Nazianz, ein griechisch-christlicher Denker des vierten Jahrhunderts." *Museum Helveticum* 6 (1949) 177–210.

Yunck, John A. *The Lineage of Lady Meed: The Development of Mediaeval Venality Satire*. The University of Notre Dame. Publications in Mediaeval Studies 17. Notre Dame, IN, 1963.

Zöckler, Otto. *Das Lehrstück von den sieben Hauptsünden*. In Otto Zöckler. *Biblische und kirchenhistorische Studien* 3. Munich, 1893.

Die Tugendlehre des Christentums. Gütersloh, 1904.

Zumkeller, Adolar. *Das Mönchtum des heiligen Augustinus*. Second rev. ed. Cassiciacum 11. Würzburg, 1968.

General index

abstinence, 50
adiaphoron, 39, 150n39
agape. See virtues: charity
akolasia. See avarice: and licentiousness
aktemosyne. See virtues: possessionlessness
Alemanni, 113
allegory, 1, 13, 79–84, 144n1, 181n42, 183n53
alms, 5, 9–12, 14–16, 21, 26–28, 33, 35, 37–42,
    45–46; 48, 50, 53, 72, 77, 82, 84, 90, 107,
    114–15, 117–19, 122, 146n15, 151n45,
    153n59, 160n41, 161n49, 52, 54, 162n59, 61,
    164n85, 175n1, 180n33, 181n36, 182n45,
    187n82
  not radical enough, 90
  redemptive value of, 153n63
anachoresis. See world: withdrawal from
angels, 1, 33, 186n74
Antichrist, 128–29, 204n17
Antiquity, 3, 17–18, 20, 23, 34, 41, 151n45,
    153n61, 65, 160n44
  Late Antiquity, xiii, 5, 8, 95–96, 112, 115, 120,
    123, 126
apatheia, 51, 55, 165n13
apocalypse, xiv, 9, 41, 127–31, 146n21
  Jewish, 2, 146n21
apophthegm, 58, 60, 169n38–41
apostasy, 1, 15, 154n69
apostolic community, 14, 16–17, 67, 77, 85,
    171n56
Arians, 72
asceticism, xiii, 4, 9–10, 12, 14, 21, 22–26,
    28–29, 31, 33–34, 37–38, 45, 47–49, 51,
    57–61, 64, 66–68, 70, 80, 85, 87–89, 91,
    115, 149n32, 156n9, 157n13, 183n55,
    184n66, 186n74
  and morality, 118
  extreme, 90
  secularization of, 73
aurea saecula. See Golden Age

aurea tempora. See Golden Age
autarkeia. See possessions: and self-sufficiency
avarice
  and licentiousness, 31, 81
  and society, xiv, 41, 45, 62, 72, 82, 89–90,
    116, 154n70
  deceitfulness of, 53
  definition of, xii–xiv, 8, 25, 70, 75, 84, 88, 91,
    95, 97–99, 128, 188n88, 192n22, 197n62
  designations for
    avaritia, vi, xii, xiv, 18–20, 74–75, 78,
      80–83, 86, 88, 92–98, 101–03, 106, 108,
      111, 115–16, 119–20, 122, 124–25, 127,
      147n24, 155n80, 82, 169n34, 177n15,
      180n35, 181n42, 185n70, 187n84, 188n85,
      191n18, 192n22, 193n31, 32, 194n36, 39,
      195n41, 198n71, 201n87–88, 91, 202n93, 1
    cupiditas, 17, 20, 92, 100, 107–08, 111–16,
      125, 147n24, 148n26, 154n70, 155n80, 82,
      187n84, 194n40, 196n55, 202n93,1,
      204n24
    filargyria, xi–xii, 61–68, 95, 97, 101, 103,
      125, 159n31, 171n53, 172n64, 191n16,
      192n21
    ἀπληστία, 56
    πλεονεξία (*pleonexia*), 3–4, 6–7, 25,
      30–31, 92, 147n25, 173n75, 187n84, 188n85
    φιλαργυρία (*philargyria*), xii, 3, 6, 24,
      31–32, 41–42, 48, 52–55, 57–58, 60, 66, 70,
      92, 108, 111, 120, 125, 169n35–36, 39,
      173n75, 174n80, 187n84, 193n32, 194n39,
      202n93,1
  dominance of, xiii, 74, 114–15, 124, 126, 131
  etymology, xi–xii, 7, 108, 127
  evil thought, 49, 55, 57–58, 60, 66–68
  foolishness of, 36, 115
  iconography of, 36, 81–82, 113, 127
  in / outside human nature, 20, 43, 62,
    71–72, 112, 171n54

Index of names

Index of names

CAMBRIDGE STUDIES IN MEDIEVAL LITERATURE